This book attempts to cover all parts of the subject, though giving most atten/ tion to the great cycles of mystery plays, since these have been best preserved. It deals with the medieval drama, not primarily as if its importance lay in its significance for the development of Elizabethan drama, but as something important and significant in itself and significant for the understanding of the medieval world. At the same time the influence of the medieval religious drama on drama of the Renaissance is not neglected. The book is not intended to supersede Sir Edmund Chambers's *The Medieval Stage* (1903) but to sup/ plement it in fields which Chambers did not cover; and the author hopes it will be found to be in the same sense a complement to *The Drama of the Medieval Church* by the late

Karl Young

ENGLISH
RELIGIOUS DRAMA
OF THE MIDDLE AGES

ENGLISH
RELIGIOUS DRAMA
OF THE MIDDLE AGES

BY

HARDIN CRAIG
VISITING PROFESSOR OF ENGLISH IN THE
UNIVERSITY OF MISSOURI

OXFORD
AT THE CLARENDON PRESS

Oxford University Press, Amen House, London E.C.4

GLASGOW NEW YORK TORONTO MELBOURNE WELLINGTON
BOMBAY CALCUTTA MADRAS KARACHI LAHORE DACCA
CAPE TOWN SALISBURY NAIROBI IBADAN ACCRA
KUALA LUMPUR HONG KONG

FIRST PUBLISHED 1955
REPRINTED LITHOGRAPHICALLY IN GREAT BRITAIN
AT THE UNIVERSITY PRESS, OXFORD
FROM CORRECTED SHEETS OF THE FIRST EDITION
1960, 1964

PREFACE

To two great books in the field of the religious drama of the
Middle Ages I am of course deeply indebted: Sir Edmund
Chambers's *The Mediaeval Stage* (Oxford, 1903) and the late
Professor Karl Young's *The Drama of the Medieval Church*
(Oxford, 1933). The Clarendon Press has kindly given me per-
mission to use numerous citations and quotations from these works.
For a number of documents and facts I am indebted to *Mysteries' End*
(New Haven, 1946) by Father Harold C. Gardiner, S.J. I have his
generous permission to reproduce them and also the permission of his
publishers, The Yale University Press. The Houghton Mifflin Com-
pany has permitted me to reproduce a drawing of the stage for *Mary
Magdalene* (Bodleian Digby MS. 133) by the late Dr. Joseph Quincy
Adams in his *Chief Pre-Shakespearean Dramas* (Boston, 1924). Mrs.
Lucy C. Brown has assisted me in preparing the original manuscript,
reading the proofs, and making the index, so that I wish to thank her.
Other smaller favours are acknowledged gratefully in text and notes.

It was unfortunate for me that Mrs. Grace Frank's *The Medieval
French Drama* (Oxford, 1954) appeared after my book was in process
of printing, so that I was able only to give a few references to it.
Nothing was further from my thoughts than to give any account of
the French medieval drama as such, which was in dramatic skill,
expansive range, secularity, and sophistication ages ahead of the contemporary English drama. And yet it is obvious that I could not fail
to take the French religious drama into consideration, since the English religious drama originated mainly in France and was from time
to time influenced by the French. I was compelled to proceed on the
basis of texts (not always readily accessible), scattered articles on special
subjects, and the works of older historians of whose theories I could
not always approve. There will therefore be found in my books a few
good-natured complaints about possible imperfections to be encountered in the scholarship of the French field. I was convinced that,
however brilliant and progressive the French religious drama seems
to be, it must nevertheless have travelled over the same road as the
religious drama of England; that is, from Latin to vernacular, simple

to complex, and religious to secular. Mrs. Frank's book has done much to set these matters right and has, besides, afforded excellent criticisms of French plays and important citations of special studies and scholarly works. Another important book that appeared too late for me to make use of it is *Bibliography of Medieval Drama* (Berkeley and Los Angeles, 1954) by Carl J. Stratman, C.S.V.

In listing mystery and miracle plays in the index conventional titles have been employed, and where it seemed necessary additional names have been supplied. Footnotes are ordinarily not indexed, and, to save space, casual references to history and literature when not immediately related to the religious drama have been omitted.

H. C.

Columbia, Missouri

17 January 1955

CONTENTS

Introduction

THE drama we are about to study began in the church and not in the theatre, in song and not in spoken dialogue, in worship and not in entertainment, and in Latin and not in English. To be sure, the machinery of theatres, stages, and actors somewhat as we know them came into existence as it was needed, and Latin was not, strictly speaking, a foreign language during the Middle Ages. It was the language of learned culture throughout the Christian world, that is, throughout most of Europe. It was not only the language of the church, the law, the government, and the schools, but, to a far greater degree than we realize, it was the language of commerce, travel, and ordinary affairs. Medieval Latin had an extensive and often ambitious literature of its own, and, above all, perhaps, Latin was the language of record. Between us and the earliest medieval drama there stands only the rather easily crossed barrier of ecclesiastical Latin, easily crossed because a large part of the Christian world still uses it in prayers, hymns, and liturgical formularies of all sorts in a state but little changed from that of the medieval church, and the rest of the Christian world rehearses the same story and expresses the same ideas and attitudes in vernacular languages. In spite of many differences, claims, and counter-claims, the vast system of Christian theology is still intact and in operation. Between the modern English reader and the later medieval religious drama there stand only certain late and rather disordered Middle English dialects.

This drama when it was in Latin and within the church cannot have been very different in essence from what it was after it left the church and adopted the vernacular. There were, so far as one can see, no new and revolutionary elements that came in with the change and no new motives. There were only the awkwardness and verbosity of modern language as compared to Latin and the intrusion of slight amounts of popular and secular materials. The Latin drama of the church is, moreover, fundamental to all other religious drama of the Middle Ages. There is another reason why it concerns us in our

attempt to understand the English medieval religious drama. Complete comprehension of a system that extends through time, or indeed
anything that constitutes an event as such, seems to arise only from
genetical knowledge. In order to understand almost anything we
need to know the beginning, the middle, and the end. To gain a
comprehension, as ample as may be, of the liturgical drama will
therefore be our first task.

The Latin drama of the medieval church or, as we say, the liturgical drama has been extensively studied by many scholars and has
been collected, edited, and analysed in excellent fashion by the late
Professor Karl Young.[1] His work is so complete and so intelligently
presented that one might think it done once for all, and it is. But it
was no part of Young's purpose to study the relation of the liturgical
drama to the English religious drama of which it formed a foundation
or to answer many rather puzzling questions that arise in the poorly
documented area of the transition of the drama from church to street,
from clergy to laity, and from Latin to vernacular. We must give
attention to this period, for in it seems to lie the secret of that variety in
unity that characterizes particularly the medieval religious drama in
its vernacular forms. In other words, we must know something about
cycle-building, the interrelation of cycles of plays, and the persistence
of individual plays.

The ready and almost customary approach to the medieval religious
drama is through the application to the mystery plays of the principles
of drama as an art form. This yields little satisfaction possibly because
it is often ignorantly done without realization of the purposes and
methods (or rather lack of method) of the religious drama. Such
commentators forget or do not know that in the mystery and miracle
plays we have to do, not with the free choice of subject, the liberty to
modify plots, and the deliberate search for dramatic effects that
characterize the modern drama and, to a less degree, the Elizabethan
drama, but with a communal, anonymous, traditional drama the
choice of whose subjects was predetermined (subjects that might
not have one jot or tittle added to them) and whose end and aim was
not dramatic but religious. It is well to remember that neither the
Middle Ages nor the Renaissance had been subject to literary opinion

[1] Karl Young, *The Drama of the Mediaeval Church* (2 v. Oxford, 1933).

looking to the exaltation of drama. Further, even when the point of view of the productive period is recognized and adopted, the critic must be prepared to allow for human nature when confronted, often more or less accidentally, with subjects and themes that possess, like the story of the sacrifice of Isaac, an inherent human interest. Of course medieval people were stirred by emotion, solemnized by danger, inspired by goodness and courage, convinced by reason, and moved by conscience, although these effects were in their drama produced more or less unconsciously. Medieval people preferred quite naturally things that were interesting to things that were dull, although some things were interesting to them that are dull to us and the other way about. Medieval writers did, however, in general exploit their better themes, and in so doing they no doubt taught themselves to be better playwrights. There was, indeed, an advantage in their situation that is not to be forgotten. Because of their strong faith, their earnest purpose, and their very lack of sophistication they did a more effective job in dramatizing their stories and their sermons than a modern man could do. Somewhere in the region of this simple naturalness lies the supremacy of the unknown authors and revisers of the mystery plays acted at York and Chester.

A number of other considerations of incidental but real importance need to be presented at the beginning of the study of the English medieval drama.

The first of these is the relation of the plays to the liturgy out of which they grew and from which they must at a later time have derived guidance and further sustenance. The liturgy of the church is closely related to the earliest medieval religious drama, is almost identical with it, and has therefore obvious interpretative value. So true is this that studies of the beginnings of the religious drama have been deluged with ritual.[1] It is not hard to see how this has come about. The service of the medieval church, and indeed of the modern Catholic church, was and is highly and, in some cases, almost completely symbolical. Each of the features of the story of man's fall and redemption and of God's plan and His mercy had its symbol or symbols that were combined, arranged, and interrelated in such a way as to appeal to the mind and heart of the sinner as well as the

---

[1] Young, op. cit. i. 1–197; with references.

man of God, and to do so immediately. The story as told is a religious
story varied, moving, impressive, and possessed of an almost inex-
haustible appeal. The symbolism of the service was of course religious
symbolism and so rich was it in human interest that in this region of
the emotions distinctions become difficult to draw. One would grant
that the liturgy had the interest and appeal of drama, but it was not
an exemplification of dramatic form. Before drama can be produced
there must be present in reasonable balance impersonation, dialogue,
and action. All three of these features are to be found in the service
of the church. They are there in such abundance that historians of the
drama have sometimes been confused by them. The word 'dramatic'
used in the sense of 'vivid', 'exciting', or 'interesting' has added to the
confusion. The origin of the religious drama must be thought of as a
special act of invention in which impersonation, action, and dialogue
happened to come together; it must not be thought of as something
that emerged of itself by natural process from a complex of vividness,
excitement, and human interest.

It is no doubt most desirable that the student of the religious drama
of the Middle Ages should know the Roman Mass and understand
not only its fundamental position in Christian worship but its
expansion into the service of the hours—Matins, Lauds, Prime,
Terce, Sext, Nones, Vespers, and Compline. But the benefit arising
from a knowledge of the service is primarily a spiritual one. A comprehension of Christian worship will enable a student of medieval
religious drama to perceive and appreciate the religious symbolism
on which the medieval religious drama rested throughout its career.
Indeed, the religious drama had no dramatic technique or dramatic
purpose, and no artistic self-consciousness. Its life-blood was religion,
and its success depended on its awakening and releasing a pent-up
body of religious knowledge and religious feeling. Therefore to carry
to the study of the medieval religious drama a body of criteria derived
from Aristotle, Horace, and their Renaissance followers, or of spe-
cialists in the technique of the modern drama or of drama in general
is to bring the wrong equipment. Writers of medieval religious drama
had no doubt their own ways (however simple) of presenting their religious themes effectively, but these techniques, originally merely
liturgical, have no connexion with the vast body of doctrine usually

referred to as 'the technique of the drama'. Few studies of the techniques of playwrights and actors of the medieval religious drama
have been made, except by persons who have not understood this
aspect of the task, and perhaps for lack of definite materials none
can be made, because we have here the strange case of a drama that
was not striving to be dramatic but to be religious, a drama whose
motive was worship and not amusement. The field, moreover, is
extremely varied.

The medieval religious drama is of such extent and complexity
that it is impossible to give more than a brief description of it or to
treat with adequacy more than a portion of it. For example, Young on
the basis of the work of Milchsack, Lange, Creizenach, Chambers,
and others and of his own extensive researches has presented us with
a brilliantly executed arrangement of all the known texts of Easter
dramatic offices, about 400 of them, from the St. Gall *Quem quaeritis*
trope to the great Easter plays from Klosterneuburg, Benediktbeuern,
and Tours.[1] Every possible form seems realized, but one must
remember in the evolutionary study of this great body of texts and
versions, and of other groupings of medieval religious plays similarly
presented, that there is no unified sequential development except in
the body of data regarded as a whole. Although every stage of theore-
tical completeness is to be found, this completeness was not achieved
by gradual development, in which each more advanced stage grew
out of an immediately preceding less advanced stage. Some of the
simplest forms seem to be of very late provenience, and some highly
developed forms are certainly very early. Probably some of the simpler
forms lived on in particular places for centuries unaffected by more
elaborate forms that were contemporary, or such simpler forms may
have been adopted at certain places at any intervening dates. Some
possibilities perhaps were never realized, some features or entire
episodes were no doubt borrowed or transmitted through special
channels, and many others must have been widely disseminated at
very early dates. The force that produced uniformity and completeness when it did produce them was not so much an evolutionary

[1] Young, op. cit. i. 293–450; Edmund K. Chambers, *The Mediaeval Stage* (2 v. Oxford, 1903), ii. 1–67; G. Milchsack, *Die Oster- und Passionsspiele* (Wolfenbüttel, 1880); C. Lange, *Die lateinischen Osterfeiern* (Munich, 1887) and other works; N. C. Brooks, *The Sepulchre of Christ in Art and Liturgy* (Urbana, 1921) and other works.

tendency from within as a directing influence from the top—the cursus of the liturgical year and continual contact with regularly repeated and always venerated religious services. Both borrowing and imitation must have played a constant part, but there was always the grand pattern of the liturgy making itself felt. The plays came into being and moved, if irregularly, towards completeness because of the telling through liturgy and accompanying drama of the same momentous story of man's fall and redemption. The perfect picture of an evolutionary process seen in the Easter plays may therefore be in some degree misleading. Although every stage and step is somewhere present, the completeness achieved is not unlike the meticulously perfect range of colours seen in the breeding of the fruit-fly: every possible colour is realized, but not by sequential transition from one shade to another.

In many places, perhaps in a majority of places where the services of the hours were performed, dramatic offices in Latin continued as regular parts of the services. Indeed, they are known to have been celebrated in England and elsewhere until the sixteenth century. Sometimes, moreover, single subjects connected with special feasts, such as the Conversion of St. Paul, the Purification of the Blessed Virgin Mary, and various saints' plays, were changed into the verna-cular and presented as local popular festivals. In such cases and those of the larger groups of plays when they emerged in the fourteenth century in the hands of the laity, the plays remained relatively simple and still religious.(The authors and revisers of this religious drama were seeking in ways that often seem crude to us to convert the world to Christ and to establish the belief of the faithful.) They were not en-gaged in the slow creation of an artistic drama, about which they knew nothing. Critics of the medieval religious drama have treated excrescences and aberrations as if such things, thought of as looking forward to the dramatic masterpieces of the Renaissance, were the end and purpose of centuries of dramatic activity. They have been interested in devils, raging tyrants, and clowns, in the shrewishness of Noah's wife, and in the sheep-stealing episode of the Towneley Second Shepherd's Play, and have sometimes been indifferent to the fact that the medieval religious drama existed for itself and for the discharge of a religious purpose and not as an early stage of secular drama. A hundred times we have been told that the medieval mind was so volatile that it could change in an instant from mere farce to reverent seriousness—as if this were not equally true of a later age—but, in any case, it need not be repeated here.

Another matter in which there has been much confusion, too, is that of authorship. In mystery plays the incongruity of versions begins at the beginning. Some versions are good and some bad, and writers on the subject of the mystery plays have been obsessed with the desire to find a special author for every play. The attempt has been singularly unfruitful and perhaps unintelligent. The beginnings of the religious drama were in the church service, were very simple, and of course anonymous. Once invented the plays had an existence of their own something like a popular ballad. The main component parts of the great cycles and the parts of these parts had many anonymous revisions and amplifications before the early fourteenth century when the Corpus Christi play was instituted in England. When the major groups, such as those belonging to Christmas and to Easter, were united, there may have been gaps to be filled, and there may have been at that time a considerable amount of anonymous new composition in order to complete the all-inclusive drama that extended from the Fall of Lucifer to the Judgement Day. These gaps might have been filled by borrowing or by imitation, but the new parts had already been invented long since in the liturgical drama, so that the themes and plots of such new parts were predetermined, and they were not, strictly speaking, original compositions. After that period and from time to time until the Corpus Christi play was abolished, there were rewritings of old plays, patchings of old plays, and additions of new plays and scenes usually not new in themselves but new to the cycles to which they were added. Such revisions were practically always anonymous.

Fortunately, even in wealthy places like York where money was abundant and trading companies numerous, small parts survived relatively unaltered and in something like their early simplicity, and this is an important clue to their method and course of change and development. New plays came into existence in response to the growth, very rapid in places like York, in the number of trading companies that wished to have a part in the great annual festival. Such new plays were usually the result of the expansion into a separate play of what had been a mere episode in some other play. New plays must also have come from related and appropriate biblical and apocryphal sources, although there are few cases that suggest much freedom of choice. What seem to be new subjects are apt to be found elsewhere in England or scattered widely over the continent of Europe. There was really very little place for what we think of as original authors. The choice of subjects of the Corpus Christi play and the contents of the individual plays that composed it were pretty definitely fixed by the Bible as it appeared in the cursus of the liturgical year. The subjects were treated there because they belonged authoritatively to the grand story of man's fall and redemption, and to find a passion or a resurrection play resting immediately say on the *Northern Passion* as its source is not necessarily to find the original source of that play even in the cycle in which it occurs, much less of these plays themselves. Every Easter play would have a play of the Resurrection and might have a play of the Passion. Such plays might have been rewritten by an anonymous writer who borrowed from a narrative source, or might have been created from a pattern. An answer to the problem of authorship is found in the fact that the material, which was more or less fixed by custom and authority, was common property. Some-times the number of performing guilds grew fewer, and in such cases there occurred the combination of two or more independent plays into one, although the grouping of many subjects into one play arises from a different reason. In the early history of the Corpus Christi play, when guilds were few and subjects many, the grouping together of many subjects into one pageant was inevitable. In some cycles this situation is apparent until the last.

Even many extensively revised plays kept at least in part their old simplicity, because they were found to be adequate, and the explana-tion is again to be found in symbolization. Symbols of the cradle in Bethlehem or of the cross on Calvary supplied their own background, and the stages on which the plays were acted with the primitive structures upon them were adequate because imaginative verisimili-tude came from the minds, beliefs, and pious feelings of the spectators. It might make the matter clearer to say that the pageant stage had no realism, and the absence of any attempt to be realistic on the part of the players and of any expectation on the part of the spectators of seeing the actual thing tended to put stress on action and event, for action and event were the bases of interest. The pageant stage was thus adequate for the purpose it sought to serve. The religious drama does not derive its importance from the belief that it led up to some, thing but from its presentation of medieval life, and that life it expresses extremely well.

When one considers the origin of the mystery plays within the medieval church, an origin without thought of dramatic or histrionic effect, and when one considers also how these plays passed into the hands of very simple medieval people—authors, players, managers, and all—one can see that their technique was inevitably naïve and firmly conventional. Their distances were symbolic distances, and their time was symbolic time. Noah had to build the ark in the midst of his taunting neighbours, had to get his live-stock and his recal, citrant wife on board, had to endure forty days and forty nights of rain, had to make a landing on Mount Ararat, and had to rear his famous sons all in a matter of minutes. The drama of the medieval people was anachronistic because it was symbolic and not realistic and because, like most Elizabethans also, its portrayers had not in the modern meaning an historical sense. This drama had no theory and aimed consciously at no dramatic effects, and, when it succeeded, its success came from the import of its message or from the moving quality of some particular story it had to tell.

The mystery plays were not much more backward in this matter than was the contemporary secular drama of the sixteenth century. Many conventions lived on into the age of Queen Elizabeth, for the technique of the mystery and miracle plays and of the main current of English popular drama consisted merely in telling a story on a stage by means of dialogue, impersonation, and action. Early Tudor plays have no definable technique unless they have imitated it from Latin comedy and tragedy. They have, even some of Shakespeare's, rotation speeches such as the mystery plays had, and, as for mono, logues, regular procedures in drama, they had no fixed function, and were, as in the mystery plays, frankly addressed to the audience. Prologues also come through in the same vague and untutored way. Perhaps the most striking of these inherited conventions was the unlocated scene. In mystery plays events relatively unconnected with place were played in the *platea,* and in the Tudor drama such events still continue to have and, in spite of the diligence of editors, still continue to need no particular place in which to happen. In the religious plays there also appeared from the beginning hymns and antiphons as service pieces, and they no doubt prepared the way for the free use of songs in Elizabethan drama. Actors on the pageants often pretended to be making long journeys over short distances, and the process did not make them ridiculous to the spectators. They lay down and pretended to sleep when the story demanded it. They neither had nor needed regular provision for entrances and exits, since usually all actors were, whether acting and speaking or not, on the stage all the time, and in the matter of visions, of which many were called for, substantial figures merely appeared and, since they were only symbols, were accepted without question as insubstantial. For some of these visions or assumptions the players employed windlasses, pretty crude affairs no doubt, and for the Assumption of the Blessed Virgin Mary the clouds used were made of white linen. An idea of the *mise en scène* of the mystery plays may be gained from selected records many of which are cited in this book.

As for Corpus Christi plays and other large dramatic pieces, they are not the result of the inspiration of an individual author who sat down and wrote a Corpus Christi play as the spirit moved him. They originated in the early fourteenth century mainly by the joining together in an all-inclusive cycle of a number of smaller pre-existent cycles and perhaps single plays. They were communal in the sense that they were instituted, performed, and managed by communities, and they grew by a sort of incremental amplification by anonymous writers from time to time. By the middle of the fifteenth century, when three of the greater English cycles were written down, this process had been going on for more than a century. The Corpus Christi plays were, moreover, no small or incidental things. To bring one into full form such as that of the cycles we possess required the support of a substantial municipality, and the learning and religious culture that went into the making of such cycles as the York and the Hegge plays were not present in more than a dozen places, if that many, in all England. Let us get rid of the idea that the Corpus Christi cycles were written, managed, and acted by ignorant peasants and townspeople of low class. Into them went the finest things that the English Middle Ages knew and felt.

The basis of a quiet and continued acceptance of a philosophy of life is hope and not comfort or gain. It may be the hope of an earthly paradise, but a heavenly paradise has certain advantages since it is not liable to be discredited by evil events and tendencies. It was the hope of an eternity of bliss for the faithful that supported and kept satisfied the people of the long and varied period we describe so summarily as the Middle Ages. But there was something else necessary to secure this lasting peace, and that too the people of the Middle Ages possessed. They were allowed to cling to and exploit actual present human life, although they were not allowed to put a premium on it. Human life must be considered as dross and dregs compared to life after death and must be renounced in favour of immortality. To renounce the present and all that goes with it is really to renounce self, and there is an instinct very strong in human nature to renounce self and escape its responsibilities. There was, no doubt, enough poverty, hardship, monotony, and danger to make it relatively easy for medieval people to lift their eyes to the hills and ignore the squalor of the valleys, but the men of the Middle Ages had a hope that pacified their impatience and reconciled them to the lot that it had pleased Almighty God to award to them. With this it must be remembered that the people of the Middle Ages, particularly rural and provincial people, had no patterns for an individual life. They did not dread it more than we do, for they did not know about it. That knowledge was of course not altogether absent, but it was not to come in a compelling flood until the dawn of the Renaissance. Meantime, the very thought of an aspiring individual life was submerged in a common union, and in union there is strength. No doubt medieval people found comfort in the absence of the worries and frustrations of a self-propelled individuality, and they did not know the sources of their peace and were not so anxious as are modern men to take refuge in a newly invented dominant ideology, because they had not been taught to strive as individuals. They did not seek to save the world, because they knew the world had already been saved.

There was also an essential liberty within their grand system of law. Men were allowed to satisfy their creative impulses, not in the building of cathedrals only, but also in the tasks of ordinary workmanship, and, since there was little repression of the creative instincts of the individual, there was little frustration. People must not be bored, and the church by providing almost endless ceremony, and the community by the activity of its guilds and orders, provided fields of action that compensated for the loss of an unwanted self. Communal action made the situation of the non-participant unendurable, and not to belong meant impotence. Within limits medieval men might pursue material gain and seek prosperity for themselves and their families, and they were not deprived of the honour that comes from skill in handicraft and leadership in the classes to which they belonged.

The social organization for the realization of a life of subordinated self was unsurpassed. The collective body was all-important, and man's eternity was provided for by the doctrines of the church. Men did not despise their lives as such. Indeed, they were eager to live, although they must believe that the life they were living was a mere propaedeutic of life as a whole. Possessions and comforts were minimized in their importance, for men are always ready to give them up in return for hope. In such a situation dreams and visions become potent instruments. It is treason to be practical in the presence of holiness and heavenly glory. It was not necessary to understand; it was necessary to believe, and uncertainties lost their power to disrupt. Combative and defensive instincts were not forgotten. Satan was never more important than in medieval life and religion, and there were Turks, pagans, and heretics to share his wicked eminence. Medieval life and religion were not without the stimulus that comes from unified and directed hate. So complete had uniformity become in the great community of the Middle Ages and so liberally on the whole did the system provide for the happiness of man on earth that many thinkers since have regarded the Middle Ages as the greatest social achievement of the world.

Medieval Christianity had great ability in organization, and our most enduring social institutions come from the time when it was dominant. In the study of the medieval religious drama in England one has to do, to be sure, with the 'waning' of the Middle Ages, a period of somewhat less than two centuries when the medieval church passed from the height of its power in the age of Abelard and St. Thomas Aquinas to a less effective and more corrupt state in the later fifteenth century. It follows that the farther back one goes toward the thirteenth century the purer and nobler in purpose is the medieval drama, but it is also true that in provincial England disruptive influences, whether theological or secular, were slow in their operation. From the point of view of religious discipline as it affected ordinary lives, fifteenth-century England, although possibly more ignorant and certainly less gifted than were thirteenth-century Europe and fourteenth-century England, adhered for the most part closely to the medieval system and lived contentedly within its bounds.

The struggles of the Christian religion were in a long-forgotten past. The Christian church was no longer a martyrs' church. The persecuting emperors—Nero, Domitian, Trajan, Maximian, Decius, Valerian, and Diocletian—were merely painted devils, and the compulsions of Constantine, Justinian, and their successors were heeded mainly against Wyclifites and Hussites. The heresies of the patristic age, although for want of something better still devoutly preached against, were relatively without significance. Nobody's salvation was threatened by Arianism, Nestorianism, Monophysitism, and Monothelitism. The teachings of the Fathers, eastern and western, had been digested into proper places. The fruits of Origen, Athanasius, Basil, the Gregories, and Chrysostom, as well as Ambrose, Jerome, and Augustine, had been gathered, selected, sorted, and put into manuals, and the works themselves were shelved away where they would cause neither harm nor good. The selections, it may be said, were well and judiciously chosen. The religious world was wound up like a clock, and one is forced to conclude that, if it had had more competent and attentive winders, it would not have run down when it did.

The organization of medieval religious life was so magnificent in its completeness that it has been an article of faith of innumerable men that the immediate power of God manifested itself in the church, its growth, and its institutions. We have to do with the church before the Council of Trent and are not concerned with the clarifications, adaptations, and regulations that have been carried into effect since the sixteenth century. The older church was undoubtedly more loosely organized than is the modern church, but it was nevertheless effective in its very variety and adaptability. It was a growth of the ages as well as an intelligent system. Like the Oxford of fifty years ago it operated with astonishingly few apparent rules and regulations. Oxford was an organized body that knew its own ways of doing things, although the statutes according to which it operated were deeply buried in the Registry. The medieval church had the necessary administrative features of an efficient corporate body, with division of functions among its hierarchy and deputation of power. We are not so much concerned with the directive—the Holy Father, the College of Cardinals, and the councils of the church—as with the all-important diocese, which seems to have had considerable independence. Parish priests and minor clergy were face to face with the popular dramatic activities we are about to consider. Monks and friars permeated the religious life of the Middle Ages and blended their functions with those of the secular clergy. They also lived in contact with ordinary people, and the complex presented is difficult to unravel. They had to do with charities, schooling, and the higher and more learned kinds of worship. Especially in their scholastic activities, monks and friars must have been an indispensable factor in the development of the medieval drama. Indeed, one does not know any other source from which the learned culture that went into the plays could have come. Since monastic orders continued to be proponents of learning, it must be that they supplied much of the knowledge and talent of the vast amplification that the Latin drama of the church underwent in the hands of the laity. We must not think because monks and friars were the targets of satirists that they failed as a whole to discharge their religious and social duties.

Obedience, as we shall see, was no doubt the characteristic feature of religious life in the Middle Ages, and the disorders of Holy Innocents' Day and rowdyism at plays and religious services were committed by ordinarily obedient people. Credulity and obedience go hand in hand, and the people of the Middle Ages were credulous to a degree we can hardly understand, and their masters were often as credulous as they; but their leaders enjoyed and had enjoyed for ages almost a monopoly of learning. There is no known way of securing enduring power equal to an alliance between government and learning, since from men of learning come the ideas on which both change and continuance are based. The dominance of the church had brought about an established order of uniformity that went so far indeed as to bring about a situation that has been puzzling to modern critics, namely, a state and practice of anonymity. There is nothing more unintelligible to the modernistic thinker than is anonymity, and anonymity was one of the first medieval practices discarded by the Renaissance. As we have seen, anonymity was mainly due to the supremacy of class and community. It may in part have arisen because medieval artists sometimes preferred having their names written in the book of life to the enjoyment of personal renown.

The medieval mind seems to have been controlled by hierarchical authority and maintained by faith and ceremony. To enlighten it, it had the Hebrew Bible, the New Testament, and their accretions and commentaries, and the story presented was so lifelike, so plausible, that, when it was selected and digested, it not only carried conviction but presented a form and order of man's life on earth greater in themselves than any others ever achieved. In the fourteenth and fifteenth centuries, in which the vernacular religious drama flourished in England, men confronted a Christianity that was the result of a gradual and perfect growth. Is it any wonder then that the ordinary man did not desire freedom from his bonds, did not know anything about individual liberty, and would not have known what to do with it if it had been thrust upon him?

The medieval religious drama existed primarily to give religious instruction, establish faith, and encourage piety. It did not exist as a free artistic enterprise as did the Elizabethan drama, the French classical drama, or drama in the modern world. Medieval religious drama has a right to be judged on its own intentions and its success in carrying them out. The best preparation for understanding and appreciating this drama is a knowledge of the Middle Ages. This in turn will bring with it an appreciation of the greatness resident in simple humanity and a respect for medieval Christianity. Let us not confine our interests to the decay of a noble form, whether that comes from the intrusion of farce and worldliness or from the verbose tendencies of a slowly awakening, although still ignorant, Renaissance.

To adopt or to inherit a doctrine of human life as a mere inconsiderable preliminary to endless living, however mitigated such a doctrine was, was to adopt a conservative philosophy with an appropriate conception of time. Time to the men of the Middle Ages was not irrecoverably dissipated here on earth. Its elapse was relatively futile, and there was slight reason to measure it in segments further than those provided by day and night. Time, so to speak, did not travel horizontally from one secular event to another.[1] Time developed here on earth and rose vertically into eternity, and the more completely merged with eternity mundane time became, the closer it came to permanence. It follows that earthly time was permanence incomplete and good as far as it went, being, as it was, in process of achievement and guided toward permanence by the forms inherent in being. Time with its brood of events was thus the ally of permanence, for its achievements, to some degree in man's control, furnished the materials out of which eternity was built. So far as ideas, methods, merits, forms, and styles existed, they were good, and the task of man on earth was to complete them and carry them to perfection. They were never exhausted and to be thrown away. Men did not start over again with something new, and that which the Middle Ages possessed they conserved with a view to its fulfilment. Thus life on earth was not to be condemned utterly, but used, for this life was but heavenly life defective and unfinished. To have rejected earthly things *per se* would have been an invitation to privation and evil. Indeed, the idea of evil as privation is indirectly the motive force of the age-long building operations, both material and institutional, of the people of the Middle Ages. This principle is illustrated in their architecture, their literature, and their social and religious systems, all of which are hierarchical in their conservatism and incremental in their procedure.

Moreover, in medieval philosophy heaven had its order of precedence, and so did earth. There was a shape or coherent scheme outlined in degrees of being, and each degree had its function and

[1] George Poulet in *The Hopkins Review*, Spring–Summer, 1953, pp. 7–25. For suggestions with reference to the medieval conception of time the author is indebted to an unpublished paper by Mr. Alan Stephens of the University of Missouri.

its virtue. In the proper discharge of its function each degree had its superiority. A stone, although inferior hierarchically to a flower, was superior to a flower in hardness, durability, and structural utility. Each order of being had its right to be judged generically, a peasant as a peasant and a king as a king. Each by divine plan operated in its own sphere. Hence men, as well as material objects, ideas, and angels, were defined in terms of the class to which they belonged. Men did not possess individuality so much as an identity that carried with it that strange equality that we so often mistake for democracy. We cannot imagine inferiority without disgrace, but in the Middle Ages each man had a soul to be saved and had the possibility of an angelic immortality. The men of the Middle Ages were truly a field full of folk. The criterion for recognition was sameness, each man's class being the essence of his existence. His name was in the logical sense an accident, often derived from his class or occupation, but he was free to operate within his class; whereas in the modern world men are recognized as individuals, may belong to any class, and difference is the criterion.

In this conservatism, resting as it did on a fixed ideal with a constant effort toward perfection, lies the story of the growth and development of the medieval religious drama. When and as often as the medieval drama lost this formative idea, it ceased to exist as such. The religious drama was thus in its relatively unimportant way a medieval institution like the church, the state, and the university. The institution and many similar medieval institutions came about through an adherence to a genuine conservatism sustained by obedience and the willing acceptance of subordination, qualities as natural to the medieval man as are independence, equality, and personal ambition to the modern man.

The habitual medieval procedure suggested above characterized the growth of all the cycles of mystery plays. They were built in the same fashion as buildings were built. Their changes were in some respects like new styles in architecture and, like them, seem more extraneous than they were. Outside influence was the exceptional and merely suggestive thing. We are able to understand the development and the meaning of the religious plays from their simple beginnings within the church by means of an absolute doctrine that

provided a complete account of the religious universe. Consequently
the drama might begin with a tiny incident and grow by the addition
of other tiny related incidents, but its beginning was a real beginning
and its additions were real fulfilments of a grand and predetermined
plan. The Latin *officia* were like the strong threads at the centre of a
great tapestry by which the whole fabric might be picked up and
moved. Extremely old elements might lie securely at the heart of the
medieval drama, for additions were fulfilments and, even when they
were secular, the liturgical centre maintained its power and its
significance.

   This incremental method appears throughout. It is seen, for
example, in a subject of some importance to us in this study, namely,
in poetic style. English poetry inherited from French and from Medieval Latin the tetrametric rhymed couplet and quatrain, and the *rime
couée*; also the Burns stanza, which W. P. Ker says[1] was invented
by William of Poitiers about the year 1100. These simple forms
contain or suggest most of the stanzaic effects achieved in Middle
English poetry. One may often see these primitive forms still intact
in the oldest parts of the fully developed cycles, and one may also see
that later and more complicated stanza forms were built up out of
these ancient elements. By preserving and using what they had the
poets invented the complicated stanzas of the later plays. This merely
illustrates a general practice. There were no doubt extraneous forms
and new inventions, but in general poets did not reject older forms in
favour of something new and different. They let these older forms
remain in the total fabric of their newer structures. One need not
suppose that in this matter poets were ignorantly following a medieval
tendency. On the contrary, they did what they did because they knew
their poetics so well, nor need one suppose that the later poets were
indifferent to or unappreciative of the simple symbolic parts of very
old plays that they chose to leave standing. These older parts were
perhaps their inspiration and served for their enlightenment, as they
still do for us. We must bear in mind that in this study we have to do
with the conservatism and the slow perfectionism of the Middle Ages.
It need not disturb us too much if we find that these efforts towards
perfection were often extremely ill-judged.

   [1] *Mediaeval English Literature* (Oxford, 1912), p. 114.

I

Origin of the Religious Drama
Plays of the Resurrection and the Passion

THE story of the origin of the religious drama of the Middle Ages is a very simple one, although it is often told as if it were a matter of great complexity. It happens that at a definite time and place there came together in an exercise of representative art the three factors that are the constituents of drama, namely, impersonation, action, and dialogue. The ecclesiastical persons responsible for this combination of elements were at first and for a long time entirely ignorant of the nature of what they had done, and it was perhaps 200 years before anybody realized that drama had again been invented, that the achievement attributed to the sixth-century B.C. Greek, Thespis, had been independently repeated. One says 'invented' because that is an appropriate word. Literary forms do not somehow arise out of a welter of circumstances and influences, approximations and imitations, but each literary form is a special discovery or invention. This brilliant and original idea or intuition literary historians, many of whom are unaware of its existence, owe to the late John Matthews Manly, whose statement of the principle, called 'Literary Forms and the New Theory of the Origin of Species', was published in 1907.[1]

A great deal of often interesting but to some degree irrelevant writing on the subject of the origin of the religious drama has grown out of an old-fashioned and now properly discredited idea that all sorts of related forms of public entertainment—monologues, masks, pantomimes, May games, *quêtes*, *débats*, and mere dialogues—are drama or the seeds or beginnings of drama, and of course that drama as an art form is incapable of exact definition. For example, writers on the subject of the services of the medieval church recognize, as we all do, that these services have been and are full of beauty, suspense, direct

---

[1] *Modern Philology*, iv (1906–7), 577–95.

and symbolic meaning, and pageantry. But they have failed to see that these things are not drama until they are cast into dramatic form, and it is a confusion of terms to describe them as 'dramatic' or, if one does so describe them, to fail to recognize that the word 'dramatic' as then used designates something as vivid, moving, exciting, or significant. But there is still in the popular mind and too often in the critical mind the idea that medieval religious drama somehow grew inevitably and naturally out of surroundings and practices that are closely connected with drama proper but are not the thing itself. Pantomime, mere dialogue, and the recitation of action might go on for a thousand years without ever developing into drama. The medieval religious drama came about more or less by happy accident in the fortuitous union of action, impersonation, and dialogue. No one of these may be absent, and impersonation, in spite of the late Professor Karl Young's commitment on the subject, is not the sole criterion of drama.[1] There are whole volumes dealing with church services, forms, and symbolisms, which things are important to know, significant, often beautiful, but they have only subsidiary connexions with the intention and growth of the medieval religious drama. Our drama of the modern world draws its materials and its spirit from the modern secular world; the medieval religious drama drew its materials and its spirit from the medieval church.

Dialogue is provided for in the liturgy in the greatest abundance, since, not only in antiphons and responses but in recitals of all sorts, singing was responsive—between a single leader and a chorus, between two parts of a divided chorus, or between any parts or groupings called for by the liturgy. There was of course also much symbolic action, gesture, and movement, and there were also present the elements of impersonation, inherent in vestments and in the allocation or assignment of parts or roles in the service. The participants in the service knew whose words were being spoken, and, although the speaker represented might change in a single celebrant from time to time, there was no bar to the imagination and no mystery connected with identifying the speaker. Elements of action and event were of course everywhere present in the whole cursus of the liturgical year and in the regular service of the Mass. There is, for

[1] Young, op. cit. i. 79–85.

example, the widely held opinion that the Mass itself is a symbolic representation of the life of Christ.[1] It will suffice to say that behind almost every liturgical event, whether common or proper, there was a ground of recorded fact.

The growth of the services of the liturgical year from traditional beginnings in the synagogue or in the immediate records of Christ's life and death is so vast a subject that one can only cite authorities.[2] The main divisions of the liturgical year were borrowed into the western church from Jerusalem and were there established. Since they concern us in the history of the religious drama and since they put their special marks on the plays after they came into existence, we need to take them into consideration. The liturgical year began with *Advent*, a season commencing with a Sunday that falls between 27 November and 3 December, which is the First Sunday in Advent, and there are three more Sundays. The end of Advent is the beginning of Christmastide. Advent is a season of fasting, prayer, and repent⁓ ance—a sort of spiritual inventory—as a preparation for the birth of the Saviour. Its chief importance for the religious drama is its pre⁓ sentation of the coming of Antichrist, a traditional incarnate devil, an opponent of God in the last days. From Advent came also the story of the Last Judgement and some other so⁓called eschatological themes.

Christmastide was the period of thirteen days from Christmas Eve until the Feast of the Epiphany on 6 January. The events com⁓ memorated dramatically in this season were the procession of the Messianic prophets (*Prophetae*), the Annunciation of the Blessed Virgin Mary with her Visit to Elizabeth, the Birth, the Visit of the Shepherds to the crib of Jesus (*Pastores*). There is no clear line be⁓ tween Christmas and Epiphany, so that Epiphany supplied the Visit

[1] Ibid. i. 81–85.

[2] Ibid. 85–102; F. Cabrol, *Les Origines liturgiques* (Paris, 1906), pp. 176 ff., and other works; L. Duchesne, *Christian Worship, its Origin and Evolution*. English translation by M. L. McClure (London, 1927), pp. 490 ff. *et passim*; W. H. Frere, *The Principles of Religious Cere⁓ monial* (London, 1906), pp. 103–60; E. DuMeril, *Origines latines du Théâtre moderne* (Paris, 1849, 1897), pp. 48–53 *et passim*. On the services of the liturgical year see Young, op. cit. i. 85–90; Cabrol, op. cit. pp. 174 ff.; Duchesne, loc. cit.; V. Staley, *The Liturgical Year* (London, 1907); P. L. P. Guéranger, *The Liturgical Year*. Translated from the French by L. Shepherd (8 v. London, 1869–1883; 4th ed., 15 v., Stanbrook Abbey, Worcester, 1895–1903).

of the Kings of the East (*Magi* or *Officium Stellae*) with the Slaughter of the Innocents and the Flight into Egypt which follow the representations of the Nativity without a break. In the season of Epiphany were commemorated also the Baptism of Jesus and the miracle of the marriage at Cana.

There were days after Epiphany, a period of variable length, followed by three Sundays immediately preceding Lent: *Dominica in Septuagesima*, *Dominica in Sexagesima*, and *Dominica in Quinquagesima*. This period has special importance to the drama, since at this time there appeared in the service of the year those stories from the Pentateuch of the Creation, the Creation and Fall of Man, Cain and Abel, Noah, Abraham, Isaac and Jacob, Joseph, and Moses—patriarchs and servants of God who had to await through the ages for salvation through the coming of the Messiah.

Lent, which extended from Ash Wednesday to Easter Eve, and the Easter season itself are rich and important, indeed primary, seasons for the origin of the religious drama. The Fifth Sunday in Lent is Passion Sunday, and is the first day of Passion Week. During that week the services trace Christ's ministry up to the Entry into Jerusalem. Palm Sunday commemorates the Entry, and Holy Week, which it opens, is devoted to the momentous events of the Passion itself. Thursday of Holy Week is Maundy Thursday, when there was celebrated the Last Supper. Good Friday of Holy Week was the day for the commemoration of the Crucifixion. The season after Easter embraced the fifty days from Easter Sunday until Pentecost. Easter Sunday may fall on any day from 22 March to 25 April, and Pentecost (Whitsunday), or the Descent of the Holy Spirit, on any day from 10 May to 13 June. Easter is devoted to the events of the Resurrection of Christ, and it was the discovery by the three Marys visiting the sepulchre and by the disciples that Christ had indeed arisen that constituted the first small beginning of the medieval religious drama, since that episode, as we shall see, assumed more or less by accident an actual dramatic form. Ten days before Pentecost occurs the Feast of the Ascension, and Pentecost itself commemorates the Coming of the Holy Ghost.

The services of the long period of the *Days after Pentecost* made, so far as one can see, few, if any, contributions of subjects to the medieval drama. Saints' plays may of course have originated during the Days after Pentecost, and, since it was the summer time, most acting of later plays took place then. The Sunday after Pentecost is Trinity Sunday, and the Thursday after Trinity Sunday is the Feast of Corpus Christi.

The services of the liturgical year were replete with event and with what might be called dramatic opportunity. Young points out various dramatic moments in connexion with processions and cere-monies, particularly the ceremony at doors and gates, usually at the dedication of churches.[1] In this service use is made of the last four verses of the 24th Psalm (A.V.):

Lift up your heads, O ye gates; and be ye lift up, ye everlasting doors; and the King of glory shall come in.

Who is this King of glory? The Lord strong and mighty, the Lord mighty in battle.

Lift up your heads, O ye gates; even lift them up, ye everlasting doors; and the King of glory shall come in.

Who is this King of glory? The Lord of Hosts, he is the King of glory.

Young cites also a service of Palm Sunday of Christ riding on an ass that long remained in European churches under the designation of *Palmesel*; also the service *Mandatum* (Maundy), a commemoration of Christ's washing of the disciples' feet; also services and customs con-nected with Holy Innocents' Day and the Feast of Fools. These he thinks were closely bordering on true drama, as indeed they were; but they did not achieve growth and development.

He finds an organizing element for Easter worship in the *Depositio* or Burial of the Cross and Host laid away on Good Friday in commemoration of the Burial of Christ, and the *Elevatio*, a symbolic representation of the Resurrection, on Easter Sunday. He regards these ceremonials as extra-liturgical, but thinks they had an organizing and prefatory influence on the play of the Resurrection. The *Visitatio*, the first actual drama, rose to co-ordinate position with the *Depositio* and the *Elevatio* as a fulfilment of these ceremonies. With the *Depositio* he connects the *Descensus Christi ad Inferos*, or the popular subject of the Harrowing of Hell. This story, based immediately on the apo-cryphal Gospel of Nicodemus, tells how in the interval between the

[1] Young, op. cit. i. 79–148, 149–79.

Crucifixion and the Resurrection, Christ descended into Hell, broke open the gates, released the imprisoned patriarchs, and bound Satan himself. This theme, widely circulated in the Middle Ages, seems to have assumed dramatic independence and, although in its dramatic form later than the *Quem quaeritis*, seems to owe nothing to the latter. Its original connexions were apparently with the *Depositio*, from which it was detached and carried over into the play of the Resurrection.

Historians of the religious drama of the Middle Ages have devoted much space to the relations between ancient and medieval drama and have usually concluded that there were no relations between them until the end of the medieval period, when, in some rare instances, the revived drama of Seneca, Plautus, and Terence broke in upon the medieval plays.[1] The Roman theatre as a place where comedies and tragedies were acted decayed before the fall of Rome. Farces and pantomimes took the place of true drama, and the *histrio* lost his dignity and social position; indeed, a stigma was placed on actors and acting. Even the words 'comedy' and 'tragedy' ceased to have dramatic reference, as everybody familiar with Dante and Chaucer knows. A comedy was a story in any form that turned out well, and a tragedy one that turned out badly. It is not an unimportant matter, since the medieval *mime* has been a subject of engrossing interest;[2] but it has only casual connexions with the rise of the religious drama.

All attempts to connect the stage and theatre of Byzantium with the origin and development of the western religious drama have amounted to little,[3] and the fact of there being no influence of Plautus and Terence, both well-known in the Middle Ages, upon the religious drama of the medieval church remains unaccounted for. One would like to bring into the connexion the dramas of Hrotsvitha, the

[1] Grace Frank, 'Introduction to a Study of the Mediaeval French Drama', *Essays and Studies in Honor of Carleton Brown* (New York, 1940), pp. 72–78; Young, op. cit. i. 1–12; Chambers, op. cit. i. 1–86; J. P. Jacobsen, *Essai sur les origines de la comédie en France au Moyen Âge* (Paris, 1910), pp. 1–66; W. Creizenach, *Geschichte des neueren Dramas* (2nd ed., 3 v. Halle, 1911–23), i. 1–40. W. Cloetta, *Beiträge zur Literaturgeschichte des Mittelalters und der Renaissance* (3 v. Munich, 1911–31), iii. 1015–56 *et passim*.

[2] P. S. Allen, *The Romanesque Lyric* (Chapel Hill, 1928), pp. 353 ff.; H. Reich, *Der Mimus* (Berlin, 1903), pp. 778 ff. *et passim*; Allardyce Nicoll, *Masks, Mimes and Miracles* (London, 1931), pp. 135 ff. *et passim*.

[3] Frank, op. cit. 64–65.

Benedictine nun of Gandersheim; also the so-called 'elegiac come-dies', including the *Geta* and the *Aulularia* of Vitalis of Blois, and the 'Horatian' comedies, but there seem to be no grounds for doing so. One need not, however, suppose complete ignorance on the part of medieval scholars of the fact that the dramas of the church were actually plays. A variety of names were bestowed on the religious plays of the Middle Ages: *officium, ordo, processio, ludus, repraesentatio, historia, similitudo, miraculum, misterium*—and some of these seem to suggest identification with the old established drama.[1]

More important for our purposes than the Roman Mass is the Canonical Office, for the service of the hours brought with it the narrative or action necessary to drama. This essential matter came in mainly in the form of readings or *lectiones*. Narrative matter was, however, widely distributed throughout the whole service and from the beginning. And it had not remained in the form of narrative only, but had impressed itself on its choral accompaniment. Choral pieces, referred to usually as antiphons, took over the substance of the matters with which they were associated and out of which they grew. Antiphons with accompanying responses and versicles carried a great deal of the primary teaching of the events and religious episodes out of which they had originated, events embodied in Scripture or lectionary, so that they provided a convenient outline of the lessons themselves. Therefore, when the composition of dramatic offices began, those who amplified them usually resorted not to Scripture but to the familiar choral parts of the service. Antiphons served to promote incremental growth of story or plot and usually supplied the language used in the expression of the new scene or theme.

To Matins there were three sequels called nocturns at which there were read daily not less than nine excerpts from sacred writings. There were also other occasions when *lectiones* were sung, but during the period when the religious drama was being created the nocturns in the service of Matins are of greatest importance. We need also to recall that these lessons or readings were systematic and extensive, although greatly reduced as time went on. They were so arranged, for example, as to recite throughout the year those parts of Holy Scripture that it was thought necessary for the religious to know in

[1] Ibid. 76–78.

order that they might learn how salvation might be achieved. They were carefully chosen and carefully reduced excerpts giving essential parts of Holy Writ. They were at hand, or rather in the memory, of choristers and ecclesiastics, so that in the amplification of plays already begun and in the invention of new plays the natural and common resort for materials was not to Scripture directly but to lessons (*lectiones*) and their accompanying antiphons that gave in conveniently condensed form the substance and sufficient particulars of the story to be turned into a dramatic office or a play.

BREVIARY

The service-books[1] ordinarily in use in the medieval church were two: (1) the Missal, a book that contained that which was said or sung at the Mass throughout the year, including the general features of all Masses, or common, and the special features of the occasion, or proper; also votive Masses and special prayers, and Masses for particular localities and occasions; and (2) the Breviary,[2] a large book containing the services of the canonical hours throughout the year. The Breviary was chiefly used in institutional services, and with it is our chief concern in the origin of the religious drama. The Breviary was divided into parts: *Temporale*, or Proper of the Seasons, containing the daily services in their assigned order in the cursus of the liturgical year, beginning with Advent and continuing through those parts of the Scripture that had to do with the fall of man and his salvation—services for all Sundays and ferial days with proper lessons, Gospels, antiphons, responses, versicles, and other formularies that were adapted to each occasion; also, of course, the Psalter, 150 psalms in the order fixed by tradition and institution. Also *Sanctorale*, or Proper of the Saints, with lessons, psalms, antiphons, and other formularies appropriate or common to the feasts of all the saints and proper to those who were honoured by special services. It will be noted that in the Breviary itself was embodied a book of saints of

---

[1] Young, op. cit. i, 20, 46–47; C. Wordsworth and H. Littlehales, *The Old Service Books of the English Church* (London, n.d.), pp. 170 ff.; F. Cabrol, *The Books of the Latin Liturgy* (London, 1932).

[2] S. Bäumer, *Geschichte des Breviers* (Freiburg, 1895); B. Batiffol, *L'Histoire du bréviaire romain* (Paris, 1893). English translation by A. M. Y. Bayley (London, 1912); F. Cabrol, 'Breviary', *Catholic Encyclopaedia*, with bibliography.

extensive proportions, since in its lessons it carried in convenient and familiar form subjects that might be used for miracle or saints' plays. Of course the *Sanctorale* carried with it also the 'common', or all the lessons, Gospels, antiphons, responsories, and versicles not reserved for use on special occasions or for the honour of particular saints. The complication of the Breviary, as well as its enormous scope, rendered necessary a *Calendarium*, which ordinarily accompanied it.

Each hour of the twenty-four had its particular service, but the hours followed the Roman division of the day into periods of three hours each: Prime (6 a.m.), Terce (9 a.m.), Sext (12 noon), Nones (3 p.m.), and Vespers (6 p.m.). Compline was a service held at nightfall. Vigils, or nights spent in prayer and devotion, were divided into two parts: Matins and Lauds. Matins was a long period in which there was time for lessons, study, and reflection, even, as we shall see, for those adornments and amplifications of the services that eventually became plays. Matins was divided into three nocturns or watches, for each of which there was a service. They were held at 9 p.m., midnight, and 3 a.m. The office of Lauds was traditionally to be recited at dawn.

An idea of the service of the hours may be gained from the following outline of a typical service of Matins:

A. Introduction—Versicle *Domine, labia mea aperies* (Ps. 50), and *Gloria Patri, Alleluia*

    Invitatorium *Venite, exultemus* (Ps. 94)
    Hymn

B. Nocturns—Nocturnus I:

    Antiphona–Psalmus; (nine psalms with antiphons)
    Lectio i–Responsorium; Lectio ii–Responsorium; Lectio iii–Responsorium
    (Lessons or readings of the First Nocturn are drawn from the Bible.)
    Nocturnus II
    Antiphona–Psalmus; (nine psalms with antiphons)
    Lectio iv–Responsorium; Lectio v–Responsorium; Lectio vi–Responsorium
    (Lessons of the Second Nocturn are drawn from homilies or from writings of
        the Fathers; on saints' days from legends or lives of the saints.)
    Nocturnus III:
    Antiphona–Psalmus; (nine psalms with antiphons)
    Lectio vii–Responsorium; Lectio viii–Responsorium; Lectio ix–Responsorium
    (The lessons of the Third Nocturn are drawn from homilies.)

C. Conclusion—*Te Deum Laudamus* (not used in Lent); collect of the day
    (Easter Matins consisted of one nocturn only; hence only one-third the usual
    number of psalms and lessons.)

It will be seen that the service consists of psalms (which are the
original or basic element) and canticles, antiphons, responsoria,
versicles (short chapters), hymns, *lectiones* (pericopes), collects
(prayers), and some other formularies. Out of the variety of these
elements came the invention of the Breviary (Latin *breviarium*, an
abridgement). Along with the growth of the attendant ritual in connexion with the recitation of the psalms in the earlier history of the
liturgy a more and more extensive library was needed for the full and
correct performance of the service: *Psalterium, Antiphonarium, Lectio-
narium* (selections from Scripture), *Passionarium* (acts of the martyrs),
Legendarium (lives of the saints), *Homilarium* (sermons on the Gospels),
Semilogus (sermons and writings of the Fathers), *Collectarium*, and
some others. The Breviary was a gradual combination of necessary
elements into one book, mainly wrought by the Order of St. Bene-
dict, from about the eighth century, but coming into its typical form
in the eleventh century. Pope Innocent III (1198–1216) extended
the use of the Breviary to the Franciscan friars, and its convenience in
that missionary group is evident. In the origin of the drama we have
to do mainly with the *lectiones* and their accompanying antiphons,
since they carry not only the vast commemoration of those matters
that underwent dramatization but also in convenient and familiar
form the particular matters used in the building of the earliest examples
of the religious drama. It is natural in the light of modern practice to
think that authors or amplifiers went to complete works—sermons,
lives, histories, chronicles, theological works, and the Vulgate Bible—
but it will be found that, although there may be occasional exceptions,
the substance of the earliest dramatic *ordines* are to be found close at
hand in the liturgy. In the older breviaries, such as those to be found
in the Vatican Library and elsewhere, *lectiones* or pericopes are very
much longer than they became in the later Roman breviaries, among
which there was, however, considerable variety in contents, and,
although the Bible and other theological and religious documents
were of course the sources of the Breviary, the *lectiones* plainly presented
an adequate selection of those parts of the Bible and other documents

that tell the story of man's fall and redemption and of exemplary lives of saints. The liturgy constituted a complete document, and from it, rather than from the Bible in its full form and from other relatively rare sources, were obviously drawn the materials from which were made dramatic offices and the great body of the earlier mystery and miracle plays. The liturgy of the church was always the guide and controlling force, and there was little or no free choice of subjects to be dramatized within the church or, for that matter, to any great degree after the plays became secular. The impelling force in the creation of the religious drama was religious and not artistic or theatrical, and such dramatic triumphs as the religious drama achieved were resident in the subjects treated or the results of the more or less accidental appearance of an author or redactor of genius. The list of dramatic subjects was a conventional one, since it consisted of those stories taken over from the Bible into the liturgy, and those only, that told a full and authorized story of the Fall and Redemption. Many moving or picturesque stories from the Bible were not included in the list and never became parts of the religious drama of the Middle Ages. The same principles apply, one may well believe, although the matter is less certain, to the earlier dramatization of the lives of the saints.

It is important therefore to see when in the liturgical year the significant readings were presented and in the case particularly of the *Temporale* what books of the Bible they were drawn from. No full use for dramatic purposes was made even of all those parts of the Scriptures that appeared in the liturgical year, but only such parts of the Bible as appeared in the *lectiones* were at any early time dramatized.

On the first of the four Sundays in Advent (or the four Sundays before Christmas), the lessons were drawn from the book of Isaiah and from the Epistles of St. Paul. Ferial or week days were important in Advent, which was the season of the vigils and offices of the dead, the Commendation of Souls, and other matters having to do with the life after death and the end of all things. The religious plays that grew out of Advent, so-called eschatological dramas, were three: *Sponsus*, or the Play of the Wise and the Foolish Virgins, *Antichristus*, and *Iudicium*.

As before said, Christmastide and Epiphany form together a period of thirteen days, which include the Vigil of the Nativity,

Christmas Day, the day of St. Stephen Proto-martyr (26 December), Holy Innocents' Day (28 December), the Feast of the Circumcision (1 January), and the Epiphany (6 January). The readings of the period were from St. Paul's Epistles, and the dramatic subjects treated were the *Prophetae*, the Annunciation, the Visit to Elizabeth, the Nativity, *Pastores*, the Magi (the Coming of the Kings), the Flight into Egypt, the Slaughter of the Innocents, the Presentation in the Temple, and one or two others.

On the first to the fifth Sundays after Epiphany the lessons (*Regula de Historiis inchoandis*) were from Genesis, Exodus, and Numbers with occasional extracts from other parts of the Pentateuch. In Holy Week, the week before Easter, the readings were from Jeremiah. At Easter and Paschal Time, they came from the Acts of the Apostles, the Apocalypse, Epistles of Sts. James, Peter, and John. On the Great Sabbath (Saturday before Easter Sunday) the Gospel accounts of the Passion were said or sung. In the Time after Pentecost (seventh Sunday after Easter) readings were from the books of Kings. In the month of August appeared Proverbs, Ecclesiastes, Wisdom of Solomon, Ecclesiasticus; in September, Job, Tobias, Esther; in October, Maccabees; in November, Ezekiel, Daniel, and the Minor Prophets.

The calendar of the *Sanctorale* was overcrowded, there was much local variation, and research on the sources and origins of saints' plays is much needed. Dates, besides those mentioned above, of frequent recurrence are: 25 January, the Conversion of St. Paul; 2 February, Purification of the Blessed Virgin Mary; 24 June, St. John Baptist; 29 June, Sts. Peter and Paul; 26 July, St. Anne's Day; 10 August, St. Laurence; 15 August, Assumption of the Blessed Virgin Mary; 25 November, St. Catherine; 6 December, St. Nicholas.

TROPES

The origin of the religious drama begins with tropes. If the services of the church had gone on in their normal course without interruption, there would never have been, however drama-like the services were, a religious drama. Tropes were additions to or amplifications of various passages in the authorized liturgy. They were attempts at beautification and were features of the Carolingian Renaissance in music and letters. These innovations were closely attached to the official liturgical texts, both prose and verse. They augmented it and interpreted it, but they did not change or seek to change the essential character of the parts affected. The term 'trope' is collective in its application and embraces sequences or proses, although there are slight differences between these terms. The accepted theory is that tropes began early in the eighth century with merely musical ampli-fications recorded in an imperfect system of musical notation called *neumae*. Tropes proper appeared in the ninth century and continued to be produced and widely used until the liturgy was purified and tropes (all but a few) were cast out by Pius V, who was Pope from 7 January 1566 to 1 May 1572. Tropes were so numerous that many books or collections of tropes were made. They were called *Troperia*.[1] Among the many tropes one of them had a special history and a very long one. It began in the very simplest form with the story of the visit of the Three Marys to the sepulchre of Christ and developed as time went on into a full drama of Christ's Resurrection including all important scenes of the Gospel account of that event, and at the same time brought about by analogy and imitation dramas dealing with many other parts of the services of the liturgical year. The trope in question is in a truly dramatic form and is spoken of as the *Quem quaeritis* trope. It happens to combine in its tiny compass the three necessary elements of dramatic form; that is, it has dialogue, impersonation, and action. In its earliest form it appears in a tenth-century manuscript from the Monastery of St. Gall in Switzerland. It was sung in connexion with the Mass of Easter and was an addition to that service.[2] It is as follows:

ITEM DE RESURRECTIONE DOMINI

Interrogatio:

> *Quem quaeritis in sepulchro, Christicolae?*

Responsio:

> *Iesum Nazarenum crucifixum, o caelicolae.*
> *Non est hic, surrexit sicut predixerat; ite, nuntiate quia surrexit de sepulchro.*

---

[1] Young, op. cit. i. 178–238; Chambers, op. cit. ii. 2 ff.; L. Gautier, *Histoire de la poésie liturgique au Moyen Âge: les Tropes* (Paris, 1886); W. H. Frere (ed.), *The Winchester Troper* (London, 1894), introduction; *Analecta Hymnica*, vii. 1–15; xvii. 5–42; xx. 5–7; liii. pp. v–xxx; liv. pp. v–xix.

[2] Young, op. cit. i. 201 ff.; Chambers, op. cit. ii. 2 ff.; L. Gautier, op. cit. 219–21.

Resurrexi

The trope serves as an introduction to the introit of the Mass, and the words in which it is composed come from Scripture, but from no one place, and are not in dialogue form in the original. The *interrogatio* is in the Gospel of St. Luke (xxiv. 5), and Young calls attention to no less than three antiphons and two responsories, all of the services of the Easter season, which supply the particular language out of which the trope is made. This situation in the building of dramatic offices is recurrent, since the makers of tropes continually used materials that were familiar and at hand in antiphons and responses.

Young describes, discusses, or refers to more than 400 texts of these Easter tropes and offices and accepts Lange's division into types.[1] Three stages are identified as, first, the dialogue between the Three Marys and the Angel; secondly, versions in which the apostles Peter and John visit the sepulchre in order to confirm the report of the Marys that Christ has risen; thirdly, the stage in which there appears the scene (known as *Hortulanus*) in which Christ himself as a speak-ing character converses with Mary Magdalen in the garden. Young declares that he undertakes 'not so much an exact demonstration of historical sequence as an orderly description of experiments and achievements'. With this understanding we may proceed, especially as he adds that most of the early additions to the *Quem quaeritis* trope are composed of antiphons and that, in spite of the extensive develop-ment undergone by the Easter drama at various places, 'many churches adopted or retained' the earliest type. Young is also fully aware[2] of incomplete dramatization in which, for example, liturgical passages still remain in the third person when the dialogue demands that they should be changed into the first or second person; or where, as in the case of the *Venite et Videte*, a speech is out of its proper narrative order and often so continued to be.

Young cites several versions of the *Quem quaeritis* differing but slightly from the St. Gall trope and notes a slight amplification in a tenth-century version from the monastery of St. Martialis at Limoges.

[1] Young, op. cit. i. 239–40; Chambers, op. cit. 9–40, 306–309.
[2] Ibid. 247–53.

This text has an additional prefatory verse that Young thinks might have been sung by the Angel at the tomb:

Psallite regi magno, deuicto mortis imperio!

this being followed by *Quem quaeritis in sepulchro, o Christicolae!* This trope is provided also with another sentence, which was addressed by the Three Marys to the choir:

Alleluia, resurrexit Dominus, hodie resurrexit leo fortis, Christus, filius Dei; Deo gratias, dicite eia!

After further examples of the *Quem quaeritis* in its simplest forms Young takes up the Visit to the Sepulchre in what he describes as its first stage. Among the versions cited is the familiar one from the *Regularis Concordia* of St. Ethelwold[1] prepared at Winchester between 965 and 975 for the guidance of Benedictine monasteries in England. It is one of the few examples of the *Quem quaeritis* ceremony preserved from England, although there must have been many that are now lost. The ceremony of the *Visitatio Sepulchri* had by this time grown very little, but the full rubrics given in the *Regularis Concordia* make it quite plain that the dramatic office is fully represented and understood. But for the very next stage one has to go to the continent of Europe. There is, however, nearer at hand a document that shows the trope grown into a dramatic office of considerable extent. It is treated fully by Young in its relation to the *Elevatio* and the *Depositio* and less fully by Chambers.[2] The service belongs to Sarum, and the manuscript, Bodleian S.C. 15846, was formerly the property of the Church of St. John the Evangelist in Dublin. The dramatic office shows a number of increments of growth beyond the original *Quem quaeritis*. It begins with a series of laments by the Three Marys. After the singing of these comes the *Quem quaeritis* proper; then an episode of the visit of the disciples Peter and John to the sepulchre; then a sequence *Victimae paschali laudes*, which Young shows to have been important

[1] Young, op. cit. i. 249–52, 581–3; Chambers, op. cit. ii. 14–21, 306–9; W. Logeman in *Anglia*, xiii (1891), 265–348; xv (1893), 20; extensive bibliography given by Chambers and by Young.

[2] Young, op. cit. i. 168–77, 347–50; Chambers, op. cit. ii. 32–33, 315–18 (App. R, in which is printed a text from MS. Bodl. 15846); J. M. Manly, *Specimens of the Pre-Shakespearean Drama* (2 v. Boston, 1897), pp. xxiii–xxvi; J. Q. Adams, *Chief Pre-Shakespearean Dramas* (Boston, 1924), pp. 11–14, where the play is provided with a translation into English.

in the development of the Resurrection play; then a dialogue between the Marys and the disciples; then a song of glorification by the choir, who no doubt are thought of as impersonating the disciples collectively; after that the *Te Deum* (ending of Matins) is sung, the Marys, the disciples, and the Angel withdraw, and the next regular service begins.

An important and characteristic addition to the *Quem quaeritis* is the Easter antiphon, *Et dicebant ad invicem: Quis revolvet nobis lapidem ab ostio monumenti?* used as a preface to the main trope. It is from Mark xvi. 3 and is found thus used in an early troper from Reichenau, tenth or eleventh century. An irregularity in the first stage of development, pointed out by Young, is a variation in the number of Marys and the number of angels. In a play from Toul[1] there is a rubric that says, *Tres vero cantores, qui et Marie dicuntur, vadant ad altarem Sancti Apri et accipiant vascula ibi posita,* about which Young says that this detour to a sidealtar by the Marys is possibly a first suggestion of their procurement of ointment with which to anoint the body of Christ. If so, it is the node from which grew the popular play of the ointmentseller, or *Unguentarius*. The introduction of this character illustrates the mind of the Middle Ages. In their literalness players and authors would wonder how, since the Marys were to anoint the body of Christ, they would get the ointment. Little by little this pressure of motivation caused the creation of a scene felt to be necessary and appropriate. When this supplier of ointment first makes his appearance, he is a mute figure. Later in a fourteenthcentury text from Prague he speaks, but does so briefly and reverently. In a still later Prague text he recommends his wares like a merchant and is on his way to becoming a comic character.

To the first stage of development (it would possibly suit the second stage better) is added a famous piece of liturgical poetry, the sequence *Victimae paschali laudes*, attributed to Wipo, chaplain to the emperors Conrad II and Henry III.[2] This sequence was most skilfully used in the more intimate construction and reconstruction of the drama in this early period, since it served to amplify and clarify the roles of the apostles Peter and John and to specialize the role of Mary

[1] Young, op. cit., pp. 259–68; 401–8.
[2] Ibid., pp. 273–88, 605 (bibliography); Chambers, op. cit. ii. 29–31.

Magdalen. It was, however, amplificatory in its function and was not, as sometimes thought, the origin of the Easter drama. An undated text from Narbonne shows kindred innovations in the introduction of laments sung by the Three Marys as they approach the tomb, and a text from Padua shows Mary Magdalen responding to the question *Dic nobis* from the *Victimae paschali*. It is apparent in some texts that two clerics, representing Peter and John, address this question to Mary Magdalen especially.[1] At any rate, it is natural that in this Easter service the minds of worshippers and celebrants should recall Christ's appearance to Mary Magdalen as recorded in St. John's Gospel; indeed, that this episode should be included in the play. *Hortulanus* is studied as a second stage. Several early plays do present this scene, but there is no reason to think that it was specially drama-tized from the Vulgate, since the substance of the scene was recorded in various antiphons and since the lessons were available in the liturgy. It is significant in the growth of the drama that the scene directs attention to a single known individual who was under emotional stress. In other words, the scene presents a histrionic development.

In this treatment of the third stage Young[2] insists that we have in the scene between Mary Magdalen and the Saviour in the garden a free adaptation of biblical narrative (John xx. 11–18), but for the reason cited above this seems unnecessary. The new scene seems of the same kind and composition as other additions, and the substance of the play was at hand in the liturgy. Besides, as Young himself shows, the appearance of such a scene was foreshadowed in other offices. There is also a considerable intermixture of phrases from other Gospels than the one cited as the chief source, and the language con-tinually recalls the antiphons and responses. The Fleury *Visitatio*, more-over, is preserved in the famous thirteenth-century Fleury Playbook that belonged to the Monastery of Saint-Benoît-sur-Loire. There had been a long period of experience in the making and developing of dramatic offices in that liturgical centre—poets enough and experi-ence enough to produce plays of very considerable artistic and lyrical

[1] John xx. 1–18.
[2] Young, op. cit. i. 369–450. For contents of MS. 201, Bibl. de la Ville, Orléans (known as the Fleury Playbook) see ibid., pp. 665–6.

merit—a thing to be expected. It does not presuppose a body of untrammelled playwrights working without ecclesiastical control and tradition.

Among the dozen or more texts of the *Visitatio* in the third stage and printed by Young is a document from a nunnery at Barking, near London, where it was prepared between 1363 and 1376 while Katherine of Sutton was abbess. It provides elaborate rubrics descrip- tive of the service and the first words of the speeches of the dialogue. Young notes that the parts of the Marys were in this case played by nuns, whose costumes the abbess provided. The contents of the play are typical, although, as Young points out, there are special liturgical features in the text—the laments of the women, the *Quem quaeritis* with one angel, a dialogue between Mary Magdalen and a second angel. Jesus, whom Mary Magdalen mistakes for the gardener, appears to her as in the *Hortulanus*. Jesus vanishes, but reappears, speaks to the Three Marys, and addresses them *Avete, nolite timere* (Matt. xxviii. 9–10). After that follow the dialogue between the Marys and the choir as the body of disciples and the one that begins *Dic nobis quid vidisti in via?*[1]

We come finally to four highly developed Latin Resurrection plays: one of the fourteenth century from the convent of Origny- Sainte-Benoîte and three of the thirteenth century, one from Kloster- neuburg, another in the *Carmina Burana* manuscript, and the third the famous Easter play from Tours. These are not, however, versions of the same play, since each has a separate history and its own special features. In this they are like the religious drama as a whole, whose variety is due to the varied history of individual plays and whose likeness is due to similarity in original sources and to the controlling influence of the liturgy. If we possessed a full series of Easter plays in Latin and in the vernacular, it would be possible to arrange the vernacular plays in groups and types by means of the special features of their Latin originals.

One of the earliest manifestations of the dramatizing habit is seen in the Journey to Emmaus, or the *Peregrini*, a play based on Luke xxiv. 13–35, which tells of the appearance of the risen Christ to Cleophas and conjecturally Luke on their way to Emmaus. The

[1] Ibid. i. 381–5. The *ordo* appears in Univ. Coll. Oxford MS. 169, pp. 121–4.

scriptural passage cited was used as the Gospel in the service of Monday after Easter Sunday and was thus readily available and contained in the liturgy itself. Again in the composition of this play use was made of associated antiphonal materials, so that there was still no occasion to resort to a full Vulgate text. The difference between the building of a drama out of a formal source and out of familiar parts of the service is important in its bearings on the nature of the liturgical drama. Versions of the play of the Travellers to Emmaus are found as early as the twelfth century, when methods would still have been relatively primitive. It is notable that in the most highly developed of these plays, those from Beauvais and Saint Benoît-sur-Loire, for example,[1] there appears a further incremental growth in that there appears at the end the scene in the upper chamber, as given in John xx. 25–28, that grew into the separate scene or play of the Incredulity of Thomas.

Finally, in the group of plays of the Easter season there is the play of the Ascension. Young[2] questions, perhaps unnecessarily, whether the play of the Ascension is of liturgical origin. The fourteenth-century text from Moosburg, which he prints, seems, however, to have been composed in the usual fashion and to have drawn its material from liturgy.

The preceding general sketch of the origin and development of the Easter play is based mainly on Young's authoritative account, which is in general most satisfactory;[3] but, since we wish to use it as a basis of a study of vernacular drama, it requires some further commentary. Particularly, we need to go over parts of the ground again in order to come to an understanding of the difficult problem of the origin of the Passion play.

Among the various versions of the *Visitatio Sepulchri*, or what Young calls the Third Stage, he cites as the most finished and original drama of Easter a text from the Monastery of Saint-Benoît-sur-Loire contained in the famous Fleury Playbook.[4] Another version of about the same degree of development from a thirteenth-century manuscript of Orléans in France is printed and translated by Adams.[5] This play

[1] Ibid., pp. 466–83.
[2] Ibid., pp. 483–9.   [3] Ibid., pp. 201–369.
[4] For publications and discussion see Young, op. cit. i. 393–7, 583, 665–6.
[5] Adams, op. cit., pp. 15–20.

or *ordo* of the Visit to the Sepulchre of the Three Marys is made up of three episodes or actions—the visit to the tomb by the Marys, the running to the sepulchre of the Apostles Peter and John in response to the announcement of the Marys that Christ has risen, and the appearance of Jesus to Mary Magdalen in the garden, the so-called *Hortulanus*. The Orléans version, like that in the Fleury Playbook, is fully provided with laments and lyrical passages, by way of adorn-ment, is accompanied by directions for the correct performance of the office, and ends with *Te Deum laudamus*, a circumstance that shows that the *ordo* is still a fully liturgical part of the service. It is perhaps unnecessary to speak of these offices as of the third, and presumably the final, stage of the development of the Easter play, since there are at least four other *ordines*, grouped by Young under the heading, 'The *Ludus Paschalis*', which, except for certain slight secular additions, do not differ from the Fleury and Orléans versions.[1] In other words, the distinction between the two groups is hardly valid. The secular additions are of course important and interesting, for they look for-ward to the secular drama, but they have not as yet affected the liturgical status of the *ordines*.

First of all, there is the introduction of the character of the ointment-seller or *unguentarius*, which with the aid of Young we have already examined. We shall also see the theme of the worldly life and con-version of Mary Magdalen appearing in the Benediktbeuern Passion play. Another feature of these more highly developed, yet still liturgical, plays is the appearance of the first antagonistic role, that of Pilate, the first villain in the religious drama. He appears with soldiers whom he sets to guard the tomb in order to prevent the disciples from removing Christ's body. Young[2] calls attention to the presence of this episode in merely descriptive form in a fifteenth-century text from Coutances. The soldiers there, as usually happens in later drama, are struck senseless, presumably by lightning, at the rising of Jesus. This episode of Pilate and the Setting of the Watch was widely dissemin-ated, indeed, became a regular part of the great cycles, and showed from the first in the speeches of Pilate a suggestion of secularity in the use of a sort of classical metre instead of the ordinary accentual kind. Another important addition with at least secular associations with the

---

[1] Young, op. cit. i. 411–50.   [2] Ibid., pp. 408–10.

Easter play is the famous Harrowing of Hell, of which something has already been said. It presented Christ's visit to Hell or to limbo, which adjoined Hell, in order to set free the patriarchs and the faithful who were awaiting impatiently the salvation of Christ. Young[1] states that the Klosterneuburg Easter play presents the first known actual dramatization of the Harrowing of Hell. The subject of Christ's descent into Hell, although closely connected with the events of the Resurrection and widely disseminated as a dialogue in the Middle Ages, did not, according to Young, make an early appearance in the Easter play. But the Harrowing of Hell is perhaps best accounted for not as an ordinary amplification of the Easter play but as a small independent drama that was intruded as a scene into that play. A scene of Christ's visit to Hades appears in the Klosterneuburg *Ludus Paschalis* immediately after the *Hortulanus*, and in some other plays at a different place. Being a new and, to some extent, extraneous event, it encountered uncertainty as to whereabouts in the course of the narrative it belonged. Indeed, this variation in position is observable in the fully developed vernacular cycles themselves. The story comes, as before said, from the apocryphal *Gospel of Nicodemus*, and according to it Christ is led by two angels to the gates of Hell. There he recites a portion of the twenty-third psalm (V.), familiar for its use in many ceremonies:[2] *Tollite portas, principes, vestras et elevamini portae eternales, et introibit rex gloriae.* Satan replies, *Quis est iste rex gloriae?* This exchange of speeches is repeated three times, then Christ breaks open the gates of Hell, and the spirits in prison greet him with a song of triumph: *Advenisti, desirabilis, quem expectabamus in tenebris, ut educeres hac nocte vinculatos de claustris.* It is noteworthy that in this scene there are the fundamental elements of drama, an actual participation in the action of an impersonated Christ, and evidence of independent origin.

There are, also as before noted, many minor differences among these fully developed Easter plays, and from that circumstance we may get an idea of that variety within a fixed pattern that remained a characteristic quality of the religious drama. All of these plays have

[1] Ibid., p. 430; also pp. 149–77, 561 (bibliography); Chambers, op. cit. i. 80–83; ii. 73–74; K. W. C. Schmidt, *Die Darstellung von Christi Höllenfahrt in den deutschen und den ihnen verwandten Spielen des Mittelalters* (Marburg, 1915).

[2] Chambers, op. cit. ii. 4–5, 20, 73–74; Young, op. cit. i. 149–77 *et passim*.

gone, with little or no interrelations, through the same course and career of development, and, although they greatly resemble one another, they have their differences. These differences, which were continued throughout the subsequent life of the religious drama, arose from local emphases and omissions. There might of course be borrowings and imitations, but in general the religious drama is not one unified stream with a main current, but a broad stream made up of many currents.

We have seen that a second dramatic *ordo*, developed in sequence to the *Visitatio Sepulchri*, deals with Christ's appearance to the disciples Cleophas and Luke on the road to Emmaus, the so-called *Peregrini*, and that to it was added the scene in the upper chamber in which Christ appeared to the whole group of the disciples, namely, the scene or play called the Incredulity of Thomas. The *Peregrini* was apparently developed early and was widely distributed. Young[1] prints a twelfth-century version from Sicily, a thirteenth-century text from Rouen, and a text from a fourteenth-century manuscript from Saintes in France that he considers the most primitive version of all. There was a *Peregrini* provided for in the Cathedral Statutes of Lich-field in the twelfth century,[2] but the only early version from England is that preserved in the player's part of Cleophas in *The Shrewsbury Fragments*.[3] This and two other players' parts that make up the manu-script seem to be the role of one actor who played the parts of the Third Shepherd in an *Officium Pastorum*, the Third Mary in a *Visitatio Sepulchri*, and of Cleophas in a *Peregrini*. There is no agreement among scholars as to the date of these fragments, but one would guess on general grounds that they belong to the early fourteenth century.

The subject that one might expect would be developed next after the *Peregrini* is that of the Ascension.[4] Ascension day was celebrated on the Thursday following the fifth Sunday after Easter, commem-orating the events recorded in the Book of Acts (i. 1–12). Possibly the dramatic office of Ascension day is very old. There is a widely disseminated trope belonging to the morning of Ascension day that

[1] Young, op. cit. i. 458–83.   [2] Chambers, op. cit. ii. 377.
[3] Young, op. cit. ii. App. B; Adams, op. cit., pp. 73–78.
[4] Young, op. cit. i. 483–9; Chambers, op. cit. ii. 11 *et passim*.

gives the gist of later Ascension plays. It is obviously imitative of the *Quem quaeritis* of the Easter service, as will be seen from the following text from *Analecta Hymnica*:[1]

Cantores   *Quem creditis super astra ascendisse, o Christicolae?*
Respondentes   *Iesum qui surrexit de sepulcro, o caelicolae.*
Cantores   *Iam ascendit, ut praedixit: Ascendo ad patrem meum et patrem vestrum, Deum meum et Deum vestrum, alleluia! Regna, terrae, gentes, linguae, decantate Domino. Quem adorant caeli cives in paterno solio, Eia!*
    Alleluia!   Omnes chorum intrabant.

There is also a dramatic office from Italy that shows some further development, and there were independent Ascension plays in English, Czech, and German. There seems no adequate reason for thinking that this trope of the Ascension did not develop into a dramatic office of the Ascension and later into a play, although Young prefers to regard the trope as merely a casual part of the service and to derive the play of the Ascension from the highly picturesque services of Ascension day, but in such an event the origin of the Ascension play would become a special case. Young quotes an elaborate service from a fourteenth-century *Ordinarium* from Moosburg, which, however, if one may argue backwards from the matured play, does not seem to be based on the original service behind the Ascension *ordo*. No doubt, if the inventors of these dramatic offices, practically all of whom are completely unknown, had had a free choice or had been endowed with our sense of dramatic opportunity, they would have dramatized these spectacular services; but there is no record of their having done so and no case where a Latin service play is known to have grown by deliberate choice of subject straight out of Scripture. Indeed, we know from many instances that the thing was not done in that way. There are early records of spectacular ceremonies at Pentecost that included the letting down of a dove and the filling of the church with incense to represent the descent of the Holy Spirit, but there are no early documents bearing on the dramatization of these services. We are without information, but, since the theme of Pentecost, the sending down of the Holy Spirit as a comforter, was needed for the completion of the Resurrection theme, one would think that

---

[1] Young, op. cit. i. 196 and note; Chambers, op. cit. ii. 11 and n.; *Analecta Hymnica*, xlix. 10; Frere, op. cit., p. 110 (text from British Museum MS. Cotton Caligula A. xiv).

such *ordines* might have originated in the usual way at a fairly early date.

Plays dealing with the Crucifixion certainly made their appearance at a late date in the history of the liturgical drama, and it has been suggested[1] that this lateness was due to a reluctance to represent dramatically the last occurrences of Christ's life, but such scruples would be modern and not medieval. The real explanation lies in the way in which the religious drama grew. There was from the beginning what might be called (in the logical sense) an accidental quality about the invention of new plays, and there was also at work a degree of con-servatism that kept the service of the church repeating year after year the forms already established. This is only to say that the motive force and the motivation of the religious drama were religious and not primarily artistic or dramatic. It happened that certain necessary subjects but relatively few in number received dramatic treatment and were from time to time amplified according to the pattern of the liturgy, and of course there was some pressure of motivation to make liturgical authors go outside their fixed series of subjects and dramatize other liturgical subjects. The element of dramatic interest probably did not enter to any great degree, and we may be certain that, the Middle Ages being what they were, medieval people were not deterred from drama-tizing such a subject as the Passion by any unwillingness to present sacred subjects. Indeed, the impulse would be quite the other way. They would, and later actually did, willingly stress this subject of the most moving, central horror. The play of the Passion simply was not invented until late.

If the play presenting the events of the crucifixion, ultimately the most popular and enduring of all the subjects treated in the mystery plays, came into existence in accordance with the same methods as did all other recorded examples, it would probably have happened in one of two ways: namely, either (1) as one or probably more scenes prefixed to an already fully developed Resurrection play, since there would have been a natural desire to provide earlier events in order to explain the happenings at the time of the Resurrection; or (2) as an independent *ordo* dealing with the events of Christ's ministry and with His death—the Ministry itself, the Betrayal, Capture, Trials,

[1] Young, op. cit. i. 492, 697–8 (bibliography).

Crucifixion, Death, and Burial. Of the two documents bearing on the question, to be presently described, one seems to look in the former direction and the other in the latter. By virtue of the amplifications preceding the Visit of the Three Marys to the Sepulchre of Christ, the Resurrection had come to contain Pilate's Setting of the Watch, soldiers stationed at the tomb to prevent the disciples from removing the body. In point of the sequence of time the Setting of the Watch belonged next after the Burial of Christ in the sepulchre provided by Joseph of Arimathea. Indeed, so far as indications derived from vernacular plays are concerned, the scene of the Burial may itself have developed from the Resurrection. There would, in any case, certainly be an urge to fill the gap still more adequately and to supply the events preceding the Burial. The want was eventually supplied, and the events added to fill the gap became in time far more popular and impressive than the older scenes of Christ's Resurrection and his appearances to his followers and disciples; the Passion was more engrossing dramatically than was the Resurrection.

There are two early plays of the Passion and one early fragment, a role-book of an actor in an early play that covered apparently both the Passion and the Resurrection. Of the two Passion plays in the Benediktbeuern manuscript printed by Young and a number of other editors,[1] the first is headed with the caption *Ludus breviter de Passione*, but it is really a prologue to a Resurrection play. It is mainly a mere mosaic of the Gospel accounts of the Passion, which, it will be remembered, were sung on four different days of Holy Week. It makes greatest use of the Gospel according to Matthew, but other gospel accounts appear. The passages from Scripture are put together in such a way as merely to tell the story, so much so that some historians of the liturgical drama have thought that we have to do with the work of an independent dramatist and not with one who was constructing an *ordo* for the sake of completeness and according to pattern. But it is unnecessary to resort to this explanation, since the *Ludus breviter de Passione* is plainly connected with a Resurrection

[1] Ibid., pp. 513–38; also 'Observations on the Origin of the Passion Play', *PMLA*, xxv (1910), 309–54; Chambers, op. cit. ii. 39–40, 75–76; W. Meyer, *Fragmenta Burana* (Berlin, 1901), pp. 64–76, 122–5; Creizenach, op. cit. i (1893), 84–87; N. C. Brooks, 'The Lamentations of Mary in the Frankfurt Group of Passion Plays', *Journal of English and Germanic Philology*, iii (1900–1), 415–30.

play by a rubric at the end stating that the play of the Resurrection will begin and quoting the first line of such a play. The little drama as we have it was apparently merely the first scene of a play of the Resurrection. The addition of simple quotations from Scripture or liturgy, usually of course of Scripture conveniently used in the liturgy, was the ordinary way of building up or amplifying the liturgical plays proper. This smaller play is plainly marked as a Passion play and contains in brief form the events needed to construct such a play. It presents the Last Supper, the Betrayal, the Accusation (Matt. xxvi. 61), the Trial before Pilate, the Condemnation, a lament of the Blessed Virgin Mary, and the Crucifixion and Death. Much of the action is presented merely by description in the rubrics, as are the preparation for the Last Supper, the flight of the disciples, the arrest of Jesus and his conveyance to the hall of Pilate, the piercing of Christ's side, and the burial in the tomb of Joseph of Arimathea.

The longer and fuller play of the Passion in the Benediktbeuern manuscript has no title, but is in contents an independent Passion play. It begins, according to the pattern of later vernacular Passion plays, with the Calling of Peter and Andrew and continues with the traditional subjects of the ministry of Christ, his Betrayal, Capture, Trials, Crucifixion, Death, and Burial. The play up to a certain point and beyond a certain point is made up, like the *Ludus breviter de Passione*, of simple Latin prose extracted from the Gospel story of the Passion sung or chanted during Holy Week, possibly an earlier feature of the service of the Great Sabbath. But, strange to say, in the middle of this prose account, there is a poetical part of a much more advanced stage of dramatization presenting the worldly life of Mary Magdalen, her repentance, and the Raising of Lazarus. At the point where the verse begins Mary Magdalen enters and, tempted by Satan, proceeds to buy cosmetics by the aid of which she hopes to ensnare her lover. She is presently, however, addressed by an angel and by her sister Martha and urged to repent of her sinful life. She does repent, renounces sinful pleasures, and proceeds to the house of Simon, where, to the displeasure of Judas, she uses the ointment to anoint the feet of Jesus (Luke vii. 37–38). Christ forgives her and cleanses her of her sins. The scene then shifts to Bethany, where her brother

Lazarus lies at death's door. Mary and Martha summon Jesus, Lazarus dies, and Jesus raises him from the dead. The verse in which the two special episodes, the Conversion of Mary Magdalen and the Raising of Lazarus, are written is partly in German, particularly the former scene, and the two scenes together may be recognized as constituting a highly developed dramatic office of the same general kind as that attributed to Hilarius and that from the Fleury Playbook, both to be considered later. This Benediktbeuern document gives rise to its own theory of the origin of the Passion play. Since the bare prose style with which the play begins is resumed after the Lazarus play, it looks as if a Passion play came into being by enlargement before and after the Magdalen–Lazarus office. That office was an independent work, and one would naturally think of it as much earlier than the prose parts before it and after it. The Benediktbeuern play would thus be not a mere prologue like the *Ludus breviter de Passione* but a separate dramatic office of the Passion. Of course any Passion play would be closely associated, perhaps actually united, with a play of the Resurrection.

Certain features of the vernacular religious drama confirm this opinion. The play of the Conversion of Mary Magdalen and the Raising of Lazarus, although it continued to enjoy an existence independent of the Passion play (and of course of the Corpus Christi play), was yet a regular part of that play. It is probable that this theory accounts for its double role and that the Magdalen–Lazarus play suggested or was used in the composition of an early Passion play. This theory does not preclude the possibility that some Passion plays may have followed some such pattern as that afforded by the *Ludus breviter de Passione* in its association with a Resurrection play.

Young regards the two dramatic offices referred to above, namely the *Versus de Resuscitatione Lazari* of the Fleury Playbook and the *Suscitatio Lazari* by Hilarius as liturgical, but hesitates whether to assign them to the Feast of St. Lazarus on 17 December or to the Easter season.[1] The latter dating seems the more probable in the light of the use of an *ordo* of the same sort in the composition of the Benediktbeuern Passion. At any rate the Magdalen–Lazarus play had a long history, and the marks of that history are still visible, as we shall

---

[1] Young, op. cit. ii. 199–219.

see, in the play of the *Repentance of Mary Magdalen* in the Digby manuscript.

The close association of the Passion with the Resurrection, a fact obvious in all vernacular cycles, is confirmed by a dramatic fragment from Sulmona in which a Passion and a Resurrection seem to be combined into one continuous play, and of course the name 'Passion Play' came to mean both a Passion play and a Resurrection play, although one usually finds both subjects mentioned. Young is not opposed to the idea that the scenes of the Conversion of Mary Magdalen and the Raising of Lazarus constituted an office independent of the Passion play, and the same suggestion is tentatively made by Meyer.[1] D'Ancona[2] records a Passion play as acted at Siena about the year 1200 and also a combined Passion and Resurrection as acted at Padua in 1243 or 1244. As to the fragmentary play mentioned above, it comes from Sulmona in Italy and is printed by Young,[3] who calls attention to the fact that the fragment is merely a player's part of the Fourth Soldier. It gives this part, some cues, the parts marked *Omnes*, and the stage directions. Since the part played by this soldier is limited in scope and stage appearance, the contents of the full play are not too clear. The part, so far as can be made out, indicates the presence of the Capture, the Trial before Pilate, the Scourging, and finally the Setting of the Watch, which last mentioned episode shows that the full play covered both the Passion and the Resurrection.

Creizenach, Julleville, Chambers, and practically all the earlier historians of the medieval religious drama have held that the liturgical drama proper never advanced beyond the depiction of the Resurrection and its attendant events and that the Passion play was of later and different origin, although the Benediktbeuern plays seem to destroy this limitation. These writers have fixed upon the *Planctus Mariae*, a group of lyrical and often beautiful poems in which the Blessed Virgin Mary expresses her grief at the Crucifixion of Jesus, as the origin and beginning of the play of the Passion. St. John was of course closely associated with the Blessed Virgin Mary, and some

---

[1] Meyer, op. cit., p. 65.

[2] A. D'Ancona, *Origini del teatro italiano* (2 v. Turin, 1891), i. 87–88, 90; Young, op. cit. i. 697–8.   [3] Op. cit. i. 701–8.

of the lyrical pieces took the form of dialogues between the Blessed Virgin Mary and St. John, she uttering her sorrow in the form of a *planctus* and he offering consolation. There is no doubt that such lyrical pieces appeared in Passion plays from the beginning. Even the *Ludus breviter de Passione* has at one point the rubric, *Maria planctum faciat quantum melius potest*. Although these *planctus* are always found in Passion plays and no doubt contributed much to the beauty of the plays, they are not in essence dramatic and are not the seed from which the Passion grew. This is also the conclusion of Young, who makes a careful and appreciative study of the *Planctus Mariae* and furnishes bibliographical references.[1] He is of the opinion that the *Planctus Mariae* may have been suggested to the ecclesiastical poets by the older laments of the Marys on their way to the tomb in the *Quem quaeritis* and reprints the beautiful *Planctus ante nescia*, the *Flete, fideles animae*, and a highly dramatic *planctus* beginning *Qui per viam pergitis*. Young prints also a description of an elaborate ceremony embodying *planctus* from a fifteenth-century manuscript of Regensburg and another even more elaborate from Cividale del Friuli, and argues that both the Regensburg and the Cividale ceremonies were truly dramatic, a contention that might be readily granted if there were in the ceremonies any definitely dramatic action, which there is not. He concludes, however, that the weight of evidence is in favour of a more conventional and traditional origin of the Passion play, that is, by the amplification of already existent offices by additions from Scripture or, as it seems to the author, of Scripture by way of liturgy. The question whether the makers and redactors of dramatic offices habitually went to the Bible for their materials or took it from those scriptural passages in ordinary use in the liturgy is not in itself of great importance, since the materials were the same, but to have resorted to Scripture, as a modern dramatist would do, would hardly be in line with the general practices of these unknown playwrights throughout the period of the creation of a drama within the medieval church.

[1] Ibid. i. 492–513.

II

Range and Extent of Liturgical Drama—The Christmas Cycle. The Plays of the Patriarchs, of Eschatology, and of the Saints. Other Plays

THERE was always present in the liturgical drama a tendency toward the expansion of individual units by the addition of particulars, so that the first simple, ceremonial offices, often tropes, came to represent more and more fully the stories they told. With this tendency and indistinguishable from it, was the invention of new scenes related to the original theme and in some sense demanded by it. Finally, as a part of the same search for completeness, there was the practice of combining separate dramatic offices into still larger units. This last tendency, to be treated later, may be described as cycle-building, an important feature in any study of the medieval religious drama. For example, there came into existence a cycle of plays connected with the story of the Nativity that may be said to have advanced rather far, indeed almost to completeness, before the Latin drama of the church became a secular drama in the hands of the laity.

The beginning, as we shall see, was a simple trope of the Christmas Mass imitative of the *Quem quaeritis* of Easter. To this in an expanded form was added a play of truly dramatic interest presenting the visit of the Magi as told in the Gospel of Matthew ii. 1–16. This story brought with it in due season the wicked plot of King Herod of Judea to destroy these wise men on their way home, its defeat, and the frustration and anger of Herod. The rage of the tyrant, recorded in Matthew ii. 16–18, led to his causing the male children of Judea under two years old to be destroyed (the Slaughter of the Innocents) and to the miraculous escape of the Holy Family (the Flight into Egypt). Egypt was a land of wonders, and there were traditional events that happened there at that time, such as the episode of the miraculous cherry-tree and the falling of the Egyptian idols on the appearance of Jesus. These happenings did not, so far as we know, appear in the liturgical drama, although there is, as we shall see, some provision for them in the Benediktbeuern Christmas play.

The Nativity cycle acquired also a great and rich prologue in a series of Messianic prophecies uttered by Old Testament prophets (*Processus Prophetarum*). In sequence to these prophecies there was an early-invented little scene of the Annunciation to the Blessed Virgin Mary and with it a visit to Elizabeth, mother of John the Baptist.[1] When these various scenes are arranged chronologically, as in the Benediktbeuern Christmas play, they form a series so connected that we may be sure we have an early, still liturgical form of the great continental cycles of the Nativity and also of those still used, although degenerated, popular Christmas plays of Spain, Spanish America, and certain parts of Europe. The Benediktbeuern Christmas play, which is somewhat confused and imperfect, shows nevertheless the union of a *Processus Prophetarum*, an Annunciation, a *Pastores* (with an appearance of the devil), an *Officium Stellae* (with a very dangerous Herod), a Slaughter of the Innocents, a Flight into Egypt, and the death of Herod (never an independent play). The Christmas play from Benediktbeuern is thus the farthest advance in cycle-building of the Latin drama, and, as we shall see, it is a pity that it is confused and incomplete.

PASTORES

An ingenious and obvious imitation of the Easter *Quem quaeritis* trope appeared as early as the eleventh century and became the original theme of the widely disseminated Christmas play of the Shepherds. The story was taken from the Gospel of St. Luke ii. 8-20 with slight additions from other Gospels. It was not highly dramatic, but was spectacular and, no doubt because of its presentation of simple and homely shepherds, had always great popular appeal. Young[2] prints an eleventh-century version from Limoges. Its imitation of the Easter *Quem quaeritis* is patent:

Quem quaeritis in praesepe, pastores, dicite?

[1] Luke i. 26-55. On the origin and development of the Christmas plays see Chambers, op. cit. ii. 41-59; Young, op. cit. ii. 1-196; Creizenach, op. cit. i (1893), 57-72 *et passim*; H. Anz, *Die lateinischen Magierspiele* (Leipzig, 1905).

[2] Op. cit. ii. 2-28.

Salvatorem Christum Dominum, infantem pannis involutum, secundum sermonem angelicum.

Adest hic parvulus cum Maria matre sua, de qua dudum vaticinando Isaias dixerat propheta: Ecce virgo concipiet et pariet filium; et nunc euntes dicite quia natus est.

Alleluia, alleluia! Iam vere scimus Christum natum in terris, de quo canite omnes cum propheta, dicentes:

Psalmus: *Puer natus est.*

It is not noted in this trope who it is that addresses the Shepherds, but from the apocryphal *Protoevangelium* of James it would have been understood that it was the midwives (*obstetrices*) at the crib who spoke. Like the original *Quem quaeritis*, this shepherds' trope arose in connexion with the Christmas Mass but was transferred to Matins, which transfer was no doubt the occasion of its growth and development. It came at the end of Matins and is said by Young to have formed an introduction to the First Mass of Christmas. This trope existed for a time in its simple form, but very early had prefixed to it an announcement of the Nativity to the Shepherds. This appears in a twelfth-century *Officium Pastorum* from Rouen:[1]

In Nativitate Domini, finito *Te Deum Laudamus*, pueri in uno loco ecclesiae baculis se sustentantes in similitudine Pastorum consistant; unus autem puer in excelso, amictu et alba indutus, in similitudine Angeli nativitatem Domini annuntiantis, hunc versum dicens:

Nolite timere, ecce enim evangelizo vobis gaudium magnum, quod erit omni populo, quia natus est vobis hodie Salvator mundi in civitate David, et hoc vobis signum: Invenietis infantem pannis involutum et positum in praesepio.

Sint item plures pueri dextra et sinistra parte similiter induti, qui, finita praefata antiphona, incipiant cantando:

Gloria in excelsis Deo, et in terra pax hominibus bonae voluntatis, alleluia, alleluia.

Hoc iterum finito, Pastores subsequentem antiphonam cantantes, ad locum in quo paratum fuit Praesepe accedant:

Transeamus usque Bethleem, et videamus hoc verbum quod factum est, quod fecit Dominus et ostendit nobis.

After this introduction the rest of the office merely repeats the original trope. The speeches *Nolite timere, Gloria in excelsis,* and *Transeamus usque Bethleem* are from Luke ii. 10–15, but were all in the liturgy. Enough versions of the *Officium Pastorum* are preserved, including two

[1] Ibid., pp. 12–13.

elaborate texts from Rouen, to show that the play of the Shepherds had an independent existence as the adoration of the shepherds, and yet it was destined to be subordinated to a play of the Epiphany. Young[1] gives some information about the connexion between the *Officium Pastorum* and those widely used plastic or constructural representations of the *praesepe* and rhe figures of the scene at the manger in Bethlehem, Rome, and many parts of Europe. The trope and the office that grew out of it are possibly to be associated with the ceremonies surrounding the manger in the Middle Ages, and one suspects that the use of the Messianic prophecy of Isaiah, which appears also in the *Prophetae*, suggested the second scene of the *Officium Pastorum*. At any rate, the preliminary scene of the shepherds in the fields tending their flocks when they hear a chorus of angels in the sky constitutes the charm of the famous little scene.

MAGI OR *STELLA*

The *Officium Pastorum* was, however, limited in scope, lacked dramatic events, and could not well undergo so extensive and immediate a growth as that which occurred in connexion with the Easter *Quem quaeritis*. It had, in the coming of the Magi celebrated at Epiphany (6 January), a powerful dramatic associate or sequence. The story of the coming of the Wise Men of the East is recorded in the Gospel of Matthew ii. 1–12, 16. By the fifth century the Magi had become oriental monarchs, were established as three in number, and were assigned various names of which Melchior, king of Tarsus; Caspar, king of Arabia; and Balthasar, king of Saba, were the most frequent designations. Tradition was assisted in the naming by a passage from the seventy-first psalm, v. 10: *Reges Tharsis et insulae munera offerent; reges Arabum et Saba dona adducent.* The offerings were gold, to signify royalty; frankincense, to signify godhead; and myrrh, to indicate the heritage of death. These Kings from their first appearance in the drama and always were costumed formally and magnificently and became favourite subjects of pictorial art; indeed, had their lives and deeds recorded in story and song. Antiphons and versicles in the liturgy of the Epiphany still give the gist of the medieval beliefs.

[1] Ibid., pp. 24–28.

A ceremony of the visit of the Kings probably made its first appearance in connexion with the *Oblatio* at Mass on Epiphany, the service
of which season was well supplied with formularies giving the
scriptural story of the Magi in abundant outline. A simple form from
the use of Limoges, early but undated,[1] has been often reproduced.
It is worth examining as the simplest form of this important play.
The pretentious quality of the Latin verse, although not composed
especially for this ceremony, is perhaps to be taken as an early example
of the practice of giving hexametric or other Latin verse forms to
foreign and royal personages:

Cantato offertorio, antequam eant ad offerendam, tres chorarii induti vestibus
sericis, habentes singuli coronam auream in capite suo, et cyphum deauratum, seu
aliud jocale pretiosum in manibus suis, ad instar trium Regum qui venerunt adorare
Dominum, ingrediuntur per portam majorem chori, incedentes cum gravitate, cantantes sequentem prosulam:

> *O quam dignis celebranda dies ista laudibus,*
> *In qua Christi genitura propalatur gentibus.*
> *Pax terrenis nunciatur, gloria caelestibus:*
> *Novi partus signum fulget orientis patrea.*
> *Currunt Reges orientis stella sibi praevia;*
> *Currunt Reges, et adorant Deum ad praesepia.*
> *Tres adorant Reges unum, triplex est oblatio.*

Primus dicit elevando cyphum:

> *Aurum primo.*

Deinde secundus dicit:

> *Thus secundo.*

Item tertius:

> *Myrrham dante tertio.*

Ordine praedicto primus dicit:

> *Aurum Regem.*

Secundus:

> *Thus caelestem.*

Tertius:

> *Mori notat unctio.*

Deinde existentes circa medium chori, unus eorum elevat manum ostendentem
Stellam pendentem in filo, quae antecedit eos, cantando altiori voce:

> *Hoc signum magni Regis.*

[1] Young, op. cit. ii. 34; Du Meril, op. cit., 151-3.

Tunc tres simul pergunt versus majus altare cantantes:

> *Eamus, inquiramus eum, et offeramus ei munera: aurum, thus, et myrrham.*

Et vadunt ad offerendam, relinquentes ibi sua jocalia. Post haec unus puer psallit retro majus altare, ad instar Angeli: alloquendo Reges cantat:

> *Nuncium vobis fero de supernis:*
> *Natus est Christus, Dominator orbis,*
> *in Bethleem Judae, sic enim propheta*
> *dixerat ante.*

Qua visione attoniti Reges et admirantes redeunt per portam quae ducit ad sacristiam cantando antiphonam:

> *In Bethleem natus est Rex caelorum.*

Young also prints a fully developed ceremony from Besançon providing for elaborate costumes in which a procession of the Three Kings, accompanied by attendants bearing gifts, advances to a pulpit, where the liturgical gospel is read, and then go to the main altar to tender their gifts, a case of complete impersonation within the service. This and the trope from Limoges are, Young says, the only cases in which the ceremony of the Kings is within the Mass of the Epiphany. He treats a fourteenth-century *ordo* from Rouen as a transitional ceremony, since there the Three Kings appear before the beginning of the Mass, although their offerings are still within the Mass.[1] The *ordo* is, however, in these cases relatively complete. Three of the superior clergy, dressed in copes and crowns as representing the Magi, meet before the main altar, each King accompanied by his servant bearing his official gift. They call one another's attention to the star, which they follow singing *Eamus ergo*, as a processional. There is a star-shaped cluster of lights over the altar of the Holy Cross. In Young's words: 'At this altar, upon which are the figures of the mother and child behind a curtain, the kings halt. Two clerics in dalmatics, one at each end of the altar, interrogate the visitors, and having heard their errand draw aside the curtain and disclose the child. The kings prostrate themselves in adoration, and present their gifts. Then both clergy and congregation bring additional offerings to the same altar. The kings now kneel in prayer, and presently fall asleep. Then a choir-boy, dressed in an alb to represent an angel, rouses them and warns them to return home by another route, lest

---

[1] Young, op. cit. ii. 37-58.

they give information which shall imperil the new-born child.' This office, though fully conceived, makes no mention of the encounter between the Three Kings on their way to Bethlehem with Herod, king of Judea, as recorded in Matthew ii. 3–8. It does, however, show at the end a consciousness of the situation and the danger.

This obviously dramatic addition had already made its appearance in an eleventh-century text from Nevers performed after the ninth responsory of Matins. In it the Kings go at once to Herod, who is completely informed of their errand. In an eleventh-century *ordo* from Compiègne Herod has scribes as his advisers. This version supplies much detail and carries the play to completeness by introducing the escape of the Three Kings and Herod's anger when their flight is reported to him. Much was to follow from the rage of Herod as regards further episodes and as regards Herod as a character in the religious drama.

The Latin play of the Magi, or *Officium Stellae*, in its more advanced form was widely known and performed and is well worthy of con-sideration in the growth of the religious drama.[1] There are varied, realistic, and highly developed treatments of the Herod theme and at the same time, of course, simpler Magi-plays on which the larger and more sensational treatments of Herod are based. There is a twelfth-century *Officium Stellae* from Sicily, which represents, Young thinks, the advanced Norman-French liturgical practices of that country. There is also a still more realistic and highly wrought version from Strassburg of about the year 1200. Young prints another *Officium Stellae*, perhaps from Rouen, which is notable in its dramatic ex-pression; also a quite marvellous twelfth-century *Ordo Stellae* from Bilsen in Belgium, a version from the Fleury Playbook, and, as a sort of culmination of tyrannical violence and craft, an eleventh-century *Officium Stellae* from Freising. These plays are all very early, and they reach a stage of dramatic manner and content that many other liturgical plays of relatively equal importance do not take on until long afterwards in their final forms.

In this one suspects the existence of a certain amount of inter-influence in the growth of the religious drama, particularly in certain plays that became famous. One sees also a principle that might be

[1] Ibid., pp. 59–101; Chambers, op. cit. ii. 42–52.

called an independence of chronology that characterizes religious drama as a whole. We are used to thinking that a document simple in form and contents is earlier than a complicated one, a thing that does not follow in the medieval drama. Quite primitive *ordines*, to be sure, may go back to the eleventh century, but possibly may have been composed at a much later date. The medieval world was in remoter regions rather static as regards communication and was varied in degree of artistic and cultural advancement. Many places seem to have been content to keep their older forms without change, whereas more progressive places, churches and ecclesiastical institutions in this case, might in the matter of dramatic development move centuries ahead of the general and accepted state. The dates of the manuscripts in which liturgical texts occur may or may not be significant. An early manuscript is indicative of an early play, but plays in their earliest forms, indeed mere tropes, might have been copied or might even have been in local use at any later dates. This would not be worth mentioning were it not that historians of the religious drama have often been misled by the dates of manuscripts.

The first combination of themes in the Christmas group is that between the *Pastores* and the *Stella*, and the point of junction is a fancied encounter between the Shepherds returning from their visit to the manger with the Three Kings as they approach. The two parties converse and proceed on their way. This feature appears in the twelfthcentury play from Sicily, the Strassburg play from about 1200, the twelfthcentury plays from Bilsen and Rouen, the thirteenthcentury play from SaintBenoîtsurLoire, and the eleventhcentury play from Freising. This union of the *Pastores* with the *Stella* was an expression of the tendency to combine scenes into larger wholes —a cycleforming tendency. In this case it may have occurred at various places independently, or it may have occurred at a certain place and the idea may have spread and caused such union elsewhere.

Meantime, in some places, another closely related scene, based on Matthew ii. 16–18, had made its appearance. This scene follows the *Stella* as a consequence of the anger of Herod over the escape of the Magi and is the earliest form of the widely known vernacular play, the Slaughter of the Innocents. Young has made careful studies of the origin of this play.[1] They are based mainly on a version of the scene attached to a thirteenth-century *Stella* from a Laon service-book. The *Stella* is in normal form, as is also the added scene of the Slaughter. Besides this case in which the play of the Innocents has already found its place in the larger play of Herod and the Kings, Young prints three other texts in which the Slaughter of the Innocents exists as a separate *ordo*. One of these is an eleventh- or twelfth-century text from the monastery of St. Martialis at Limoges; another, designated as *Ordo Rachelis*, from the Fleury Playbook; a third, also from the eleventh or twelfth century, from the cathedral of Freising. On the basis of these four examples, three independent and one attached to a *Stella*, Young concludes that the *Ordo Rachelis* arose as a separate office. In this he is certainly right, since such a separate *ordo* could hardly have come into existence at all if the scene had originated as a mere amplification of the Herod play.

The passages of Scripture upon which the play of the Innocents ultimately depends are deeply appealing. In the brief account of the assault upon the children, St. Matthew the Evangelist (ii. 16–18) is moved to quote a mystical passage from the Prophet Jeremiah that served to elevate the poetic tone of the whole:

> *Vox in Rama audita est, ploratus et ululatus multus: Rachel plorans filios suos, et noluit consolari, quia non sunt.*

The Gospel of Matthew in the same chapter, verses 13–23, gives the further account of the escape of the Holy Family and the occasion of their return to Nazareth on the death of Herod. These episodes were carried inevitably as the sequel to the Slaughter itself, and they, too, would have had great popular appeal. The Flight into Egypt underwent somewhat extensive traditional amplification at later times, but must have originated as a sequel to the spectacular Slaughter of the Innocents. The Latin plays enumerated are typical in their composition and have from the beginning an appropriate variety and beauty of style. The *ordo* is built from the Gospels, antiphons, sequences, and other parts of the liturgy mainly of Holy Innocents day on 28 December. As the *ordo* developed, it more and more employed verse in its expression. The following simple form from the *Officium Stellae* of Laon will illustrate. It begins with a procession of children carrying

[1] Young, op. cit. ii. 102–24; also the same author's *Ordo Rachelis* (Madison, 1919).

a lamb and singing *Ecce Agnus Dei.* Herod has given a sword to Archelaus and has cried out, *Indolis eximie, pueros fac ense perire*:

Interim Pueri, agnum portantes, intrant cantantes:

Ecce Agnus Dei, ecce qui tollit peccata mundi, alleluia.

Iterum et tertio veniunt Armati. Clamant Pueri dum occiduntur:

Quare non defendis sanguinem nostrum?

Angelus:

Adhuc sustinete modicum tempus, donec impleatur numerus fratrum vestrorum.

Venit Rachel, et exclamans cum fletu dicit:

> *O dulces innocentum acies!*
> *O pia lactantum pro Christo certamina!*
> *Parvorum trucidantur milia;*
> *membris ex teneris manant lactis flumina.*

Consolatrix:

Noli, virgo Rachel, noli, dulcissima mater,
Pro nece parvorum fletus reticere dolorum.

Rachel:

Gaudia non possunt, nam dulcia pignora non sunt,
Iudee florem, patrie lacrimando decorem.

Consolatrix:

Tu, que tristaris, exulta, que lacrimaris,
Namque tui nati vivunt super astra beati.

Rachel:

Heu! Heu!
Quomodo gaudebo dum mortua membra videbo?
Dum sic commota fuero per viscera tota
Me facient vere pueri sine fine dolere.

Consolatrix:

Supplico ne plores, que tanto sanguine flores
Ast oculos flentes, lacrimas quoque terge fluentes.

Rachel:

In dolorem est conversum quod habebam gaudium.

Consolatrix:

Quam beata sunt innocentum ab Herode cesa corpuscula!
Quam felices existunt matres, fuderunt que talia pignora!

Rachel:

Planctus matrum et Rachelis equa sunt suspiria
Nulla quidem consolatur magna pre tristitia.
Ey dolor est! Nolo consolari, quia non sunt.

Other versions of the play show additional details called for by the situation, more complete staging, and more and more ambitious poetry. A Flight into Egypt appears in the Fleury Playbook, and the characterization of Joseph, who was to play an important part in later plays, begins. All in all, the Slaughter of the Innocents rounds out and completes the Christmas series and helps to make of it, dramatically speaking, one of the most excellent of the larger units.

PROCESSUS PROPHETARUM

The play of the Messianic prophets is, as we shall see, most important in the history of the medieval religious drama. Moreover, its origin, which may be said to be liturgical, its growth, and its variety are well understood and most enlightening. The early development presents characteristically an even and gradual incremental growth. The lack of explanatory rubrics in the earliest forms of the *Prophetae* has caused some scholars to call in question its origin in and from the liturgy, but there seems little reason to do so, since the basic document, a sermon about to be described, was widely used as a lesson at Matins on Christmas day. Beginning with this homily, Marius Sepet in *Les Prophètes du Christ*[1] worked out a complete conjectural history of the rise and development of the prophet play. Although the Laon version was unknown to him, he put forward a theory that the *Prophetae* originated from this sermon used as a lesson and that the Old Testament plays arose as offshoots of the *Prophetae*. In the latter supposition he was certainly in large part wrong, but there seems no reason to question the validity of his work on the origin and growth of the play of the prophets.

Sepet began with the picturesque and rhetorical sermon attributed to St. Augustine but now known to have been composed by an unknown author as late as the sixth century. This sermon, in the form considered by Sepet, is found in a lectionary from Arles of the twelfth or thirteenth century and is called *Sermo contra Judaeos, Paganos et Arianos de Symbolo*. It was intended to convert unbelievers—Jews,

---

[1] M. Sepet, 'Les prophètes du Christ', *Bibliothèque de l'École des Chartres*, xxviii (1867), 1–27, 211–64; xxix (1868), 105–39, 261–93; xxxviii (1877), 397–443; also published separately in Paris in 1878; Young, op. cit. ii. 125–71; Chambers, op. cit. ii. 52–57; Hardin Craig, 'The Origin of the Old Testament Plays', *Modern Philology*, x (1912–13), 473–87.

Pagans, and Arians—to faith in Christ. It is the part directed toward the conversion of the Jews with which we have to do. The preacher declares that in Hebraic law it is written that the testimony of two witnesses is sufficient to establish the truth and says he will go farther than that and present many witnesses. He will call many witnesses from among the Jews themselves and will add also the testimony of pagans. He proceeds to call up one by one a series of Messianic prophets and to quote from their prophecies—Isaiah, Jeremiah, Daniel, Moses, David, and Habakkuk. He adds to them four witnesses from the New Testament: Simeon, Zacharias, Elizabeth, and John the Baptist, and three Pagans: Virgil, Nebuchadnezzar, and the Erythraean Sybil. Each testimony is composed of words and sentences traditionally thought to foretell the coming of Christ. The preacher, supposed to be St. Augustine, does the thing dramatically, although in reciting the prophecies he uses the word *inquit* as if he himself were the speaker and not the prophet. In the manuscript used by Sepet the names of the witnesses are some of them set in the margin like speech-headings in a play, and the testimonies themselves are encircled in red ink as if they were to be picked out from the text and recited separately. Young, who reprints the sermon, found a number of others, some in complete form and some in the form of *lectiones* to be used at Matins on Christmas day. Some of these are rubricated like the manuscript from Arles. He also reproduces a homily from the cathedral of Salerno, printed in 1594 but much older. This is almost certainly a further stage in the dramatization of the Pseudo-Augustinian sermon.[1] It shows the witnesses actually speaking and a Lector acting as mediator and commentator, his comments being, however, much shorter than those in the developed *Prophetae*. Young thus documents and further substantiates Sepet's theory.

The next version of the *ordo*, known to Sepet and long familiar, is a neat and simple *Prophetae* from the monastery of St. Martialis at Limoges. It is set to music and, although it has no stage directions, is a play closely modelled on the sermon. The speakers in the play and in the sermon are almost exactly the same, and the prophecies do not differ to any great extent. The next document, although it shows a considerable advance, may be said to follow a natural and gradual

[1] Young, op. cit. ii. 133–8.

development. It is a *Prophetae* of the thirteenth century from the cathedral of Laon in France, first published by U. Chevalier in 1897.[1]
It has a list of characters with brief descriptions of their costumes.
Isaiah, like other prophets, is bearded and clothed in a dalmatic,
Moses carries the Tables of the Laws, Daniel is a splendidly dressed
youth, Elizabeth is described as pregnant, and the Sibyl, crowned
with ivy, is said to be like an insane person. The play begins with
the hymn,

> Gloriosi
> et famosi
> regis festum
> celebrantes
> gaudeamus.

There are both *Appellatores* and Chorus. In contents the Laon
Prophetae agrees well with the Limoges play, but has one striking
peculiarity. At the end are two little plays: in one of them Simeon
receives the Child and utters a version of the *Nunc dimittis*; in the
other Balaam rides in on the ass, which he is urging on and goading
with his spurs. A boy concealed beneath the ass and impersonating
the speaking animal calls attention to the Angel standing in Balaam's
way. Both of these are mere bits and seemed to have been borrowed
from elsewhere and appended to the Laon play.

   The most famous and most highly developed of the Latin plays of
the prophets is from the cathedral of Rouen. This and the plays from
Limoges and Laon are reprinted by Young.[2] The Rouen play and
the Laon play resemble each other in general and in particular, but
the former is much more highly developed. The Rouen *Prophetae* has
twelve of the same prophetic witnesses as those appearing in the Laon
play, but it adds fourteen others and thus completes the roll of the
prophets, both major and minor. It shows in clear fashion the feature
to which Sepet attached so much importance, namely, two little
plays growing out of the *Prophetae* before one's eyes. The prophecy of
Nebuchadnezzar as recorded in Daniel iii. 24–25 was that three men
(Shadrach, Meshach, and Abednego) had been cast into the fiery
furnace, but that he had seen four, and the fourth was like unto the

---

[1] U. Chevalier, *Ordinaires de l'Église cathédrale de Laon* (Paris, 1897).
[2] Young, op. cit. ii. 138–71.

Son of God. In the Rouen version, there is a dramatization of this story with a specially constructed furnace into which the youths are thrust. There is also a fully developed Balaam play, but no special scene for Simeon. The following is the Balaam scene from the Laon *Prophetae:*

Apellatores:

> Dic, Balaam, ex Iudaica
> oriturum Dominum prosapia.

Balaam:

> Exibit de Iacob rutilans nova stella
> et confringet ducum agmina
> regionis Moab maxima potentia.

His veniat Angelus cum gladio. Balaam tangit Asinam, et illa non procedente, dicit iratus:

> Quid moraris, asina,
> obstinata bestia?
> Iam scindent calcaria
> costas et precordia.

Puer sub Asina respondet:

> Angelus cum gladio,
> quem adstare video,
> prohibet ne transeam;
> timeo ne peream.

There can be no doubt that the *Prophetae* of Laon, and particularly of Rouen, establish Sepet's thesis with reference to the Balaam play. Indeed, the situation he observed is still visible in the Prophet play of the Chester cycle. There was also certainly a play of Moses and the Tables of the Law that grew out of the *Prophetae*, and there may have been others. There seems, however, to be no play of Nebuchadnezzar in vernacular religious drama.

ANNUNCIATION

Another dramatic office that belonged regularly to the Christmas group and not primarily to that intended for the special honour of the Blessed Virgin Mary is the Annunciation. The subject was very popular in religious art, and the play was an essential feature of the Christmas cycle. The Feast of the Annunciation was assigned to

25 March and has always been celebrated on that date, but the liturgy that carries the story of the Annunciation belonged to Advent, indeed was widely scattered throughout the year. Certain churches, particularly those in Spain according to Young,[1] celebrated the feast on the Wednesday of Ember Days in December. There is, in any case, no reason to question the fact that the dramatic office as we have it was connected with the approaching Christmas season. The play became a regular part of the Christmas group and fitted into its proper place there, after the *Prophetae* and before the *Pastores*. The scene, which is very simple, may, however, in some places have had an independent existence. Young prints a well known version from Cividale in Italy. It is definitely liturgical and is made up of two main episodes: the announcement by the angel (understood to be Gabriel) to the Blessed Virgin Mary of her selection as the mother of the Saviour, and her visit to Elizabeth, who in her old age had conceived the child that was to be John the Baptist. These scenes remain characteristic of the theme in the vernacular drama. The vernacular plays have a scene of the suspicion and jealousy of Joseph, which, however, does not appear in the Latin forms. Young prints also a highly rubricated fourteenth-century office of the Annunciation from the cathedral at Padua in Italy. In cyclic combinations this subject followed immediately after the *Prophetae*.

THE PURIFICATION

There is no doubt also that the Purification of the Blessed Virgin Mary or, as it is sometimes called, the Presentation of the Infant Jesus in the Temple, was an original and customary addition to the service of Christmas rather than a special service honouring the Virgin. Indeed, it will be found that plays of the Blessed Virgin Mary are of two sorts, one in the main channel of liturgical drama and the other set apart in special honour of the Virgin. The event of the Purification, recorded in Luke ii. 22–38, is the ceremony in the Temple forty days after the birth of Jesus. The dramatic office no doubt was composed for the celebration of the Feast of the Purification of the Blessed Virgin Mary on 2 February, but was often detached from its own feast to become an addition to the play of the Nativity. Young[2] gives a

[1] Ibid., pp. 245–50.   [2] Ibid., pp. 250–5.

number of these *ordines* in slightly differing forms all built out of the liturgy of the feast: Simeon stands expectant of the coming of the Saviour; he receives a message from the Holy Spirit. Joseph and Mary bring their sacrifice, Simeon takes the Child in his arms and pronounces *Nunc dimittis, Domine, servum tuum in pace.* The Purification seems to have been played widely as an independent play, and its attachment to the main cycles was probably late and the exceptional rather than the regular thing. Most English cycles that have the Purification show some irregularity in connexion with it as to position or style.

OLD TESTAMENT PLAYS

The materials preserved of the Latin drama of the church, although much less abundant than one could wish, are nevertheless sufficient to indicate that the Old Testament plays originated in general in the same way we have seen exemplified in the plays derived from the New Testament; namely, by the composition from *lectiones* and accompanying parts of the liturgy of *ordines*, sometimes no doubt from tropes, dealing with subjects and events important in the plan of salvation and coming into existence at various seasons of the liturgical year. The period when instruction was given in the form of lessons or *lectiones* about the patriarchs, with whom we are immediately concerned, was the days after Epiphany. The Sundays were called *Dominicae in Septuagesima, in Sexagesima,* and *in Quinquagesima.* The same matter of instruction, i.e. from the Pentateuch, was carried over also into the succeeding period called *Quadragesima* or Lent. During this time lessons were drawn from Genesis and Exodus with certain small parts from Numbers and other books of the Pentateuch.

Three documents show us that four Old Testament subjects received treatment in the form of *ordines*. Two of them are considerable fragments, and, as usual, we owe to Young excellently edited texts from difficult manuscripts of these two fragments.[1] The first is *Ordo de Ysaac et Rebecca et Filiis eorum Recitandus.* It is a text from Vorau, Steiermark, Austria, and is dated by Young with some assurance as at the end of the twelfth century. The fragment dramatizes the story of Jacob and Esau as told in Genesis xxvii. 1–40, and the full form of the play may have covered all of the events recorded in that chapter.

[1] Ibid., pp. 258–76.

The play is elaborated by a careful presentation of allegories and types of Christ and is, as Young tells us, an example of the figurative or typological method of interpreting Scripture. It is provided with an elaborate *mise en scène* and shows very considerable dramatic and poetic skill.

The second of these fragments is *Ordo Joseph* from the thirteenth-century Laon manuscript that contains the Laon *Ordo Stellae*. The subject is the selling into Egypt of Joseph by his jealous brethren and his subsequent adventures and glories in that country.

There is finally in this series the famous Norman-French or Anglo-Norman *Jeu d'Adam*, which, although as early as the twelfth century, represents a much later stage in the development of the religious drama than do the Old Testament plays just described. It has, however, the form of an *ordo* or *officium* and is, in fact labelled *Ordo Representationis Adae*. The play, much admired for its dramatic skill, is written in French, but the rubrics, or stage directions, are in Latin, and the play is marked throughout by the use of *lectiones*, antiphons, and responsoria belonging to the service of Matins on *Septuagesima* Sunday. Mrs. Frank[1] makes clear the fact that the *Jeu d'Adam* was staged in the doorway of a church and suggests that the doorway was in close proximity to the choir of the church, which seems to have been in use in the playing of the play. Certainly the *Jeu d'Adam* was caught in the very act of leaving the church and had been developed, like other dramatic offices, within the church itself. Its liturgical features are unmistakable, and it helps us to form a conception of the origin of the Old Testament plays. The play consists of a long and elaborately staged play of Adam and Eve, a short play of Cain and Abel, and a rather perplexing prophet play about which something further will be said later.

There is a perfect parallel in subjects treated between the regular series of Old Testament plays and the lessons or *lectiones* from the Old Testament read or recited in the service of the days after Epiphany. This agreement is apparent even in the abridged service-books of the later period and is obvious in older lectionaries and breviaries. Matters pertaining to the Creation and the Creation and Fall of Man were read on *Septuagesima* Sunday and in the ferial services of that

[1] Grace Frank, 'Genesis and Staging of the Jeu d'Adam', *PMLA*, lix. (1944), 7-17.

week. All that pertains to Noah belongs to *Sexagesima* and its week, and Abraham and his immediate descendants occupy the Sunday and week of *Quinquagesima*. This matter of the patriarchs extends over into the Sundays and ferial days of *Quadragesima*. There one finds the stories of Joseph and of Moses. The major subjects treated are the following: Adam (The Fall of Lucifer is a later addition), Cain and Abel, Noah, Abraham and Isaac, Jacob, Joseph, and Moses (the Exodus). Of these seven subjects we have four that are known to be of liturgical origin, namely, Adam, Cain and Abel, Jacob, and Joseph. There are preserved, however, no Latin plays on Noah, Abraham and Isaac, and Moses and the Exodus, and yet these plays are *sine qua non* in Old Testament groups. Since these three plays are derived from the same sources and appear in their correct order, and since they still bear traces in the form of liturgical tags of such an origin, the most plausible conjecture is that they had their origin, like the others, from the liturgy, came into existence as more or less independent units, and were available for combination into Old Testament groups. As to rarer Old Testament subjects, the Death of Cain, Seth in Paradise, and Enoch, they need cause little perplexity, since there were liturgical sources at hand for them. Pericopes in lectionaries and breviaries varied considerably, and we do not know what may have been available at any particular place. For example, a reading presenting the Death of Cain, or the Lamech episode as recorded in Genesis iv. 18–24, is found in the Cologne breviary. We have to do in these matters, not with single inventions, but with various approximations to an established liturgical pattern.

The play of Daniel, which is preserved in two Latin versions, presents a special problem.[1] Daniel was not a patriarch and does not belong to that series. He was a prophet, and yet there is nothing to show that the Daniel play was an outgrowth of the *Processus Prophe-tarum*. If the play of Daniel did originate as a 'budding off' from the stem of the *Prophetae*, no trace of such an origin can be found. The book of Daniel was read in the service of November, and it remains to inquire whether it may not be an independent composition in connexion with the liturgy of the time of its origin.

The Daniel plays are *Ludus Danielis* from a twelfth-century

---

[1] Young, op. cit. ii. 276–306.

manuscript in the British Museum which comes from the cathedral school of the monastery of Beauvais. It shows literary skill and is soundly tied in with the liturgy. It is perhaps not significant that at the end of the play, which is a life of Daniel, the prophet should have uttered the prophecy associated with him in his role as a prophet. The other Daniel play is the *Historia de Daniel* in the manuscript of the famous wandering scholar Hilarius. This play is even more highly developed as a dramatic and poetic work than is the Beauvais *Daniel*, not quite so faithful to Scripture, but certainly liturgical, since at the end is a rubric that says, 'This being finished, if it is performed at Matins, let Darius begin *Te Deum laudamus*; but, if at Vespers, *Magnificat anima mea Dominum*.' Both plays are printed by Young with full details of all that is known about them. The Beauvais *Daniel* seems to have been played at Christmas, but it was not a play of the patriarchs, and was not gathered up with the plays of the Pentateuch into the group of Old Testament plays of the older tradition found in the vernacular cycles. It appears, to be sure, in *Le Mistère du Viel Testament*, but its inclusion there was after the traditional forms had lost their control. The subject of the play is not prophetic; it is biographical and heroic. The book of Daniel, with the twelve minor prophets, was read, in the form of *lectiones* or pericopes of course, in the month of November, and it may yet be possible to find a trope or simple *officium* out of which the play of Daniel grew, or it may be that the scholars at the monastery of Beauvais made their play in imitation of other liturgical *ordines*. From this view the *Daniel* would be regarded as a play independently written but for its own proper liturgical time.

The theory of the origin of the Old Testament plays in the medieval drama, long held and still widely current, is derived from Marius Sepet's dissertation, *Les Prophètes du Christ*.[1] As explained above, he there propounds the theory that the plays based on the Old Testament in the religious drama made their appearance as dramatic scenes in connexion with the various prophets of the *Processus Prophetarum*. As each character appeared, he told his story until one by one there arose the whole series of Old Testament plays from the Creation to the Nativity. Chambers and Creizenach both accept Sepet's doctrine.[2]

[1] Sepet, op. cit.; see above.
[2] Chambers, op. cit. ii. 52–59; Creizenach, op. cit. i (1893), 67–71.

But, as we have seen, the idea that the Old Testament plays, to use Chambers's expression, 'budded off from the stem of the *Prophetae*' is hardly adequate to account for all the phenomena. The Balaam play, the play of Moses and the Tables of the Law, and possibly others did so, and those Old Testament characters are prophets, but the theory of origination from the *Processus Prophetarum* does not apply to the patriarchs of the Pentateuch, those godly characters of the ancient world who, although true servants of God, had to wait in limbo for the salvation of Christ until the events of the Harrowing of Hell gave them admittance into heaven. We have tried to show a probability that these plays of the patriarchs originated in the period after Epiphany from the *lectiones* and accompanying ritual and that they were combined and perhaps amplified in the formation of cycles. Such a continuity is presupposed by the liturgical year itself, by the Gregorian *Liber Responsalis*,[1] and by works that express the theological concept that may be said to underlie medieval religious literature, as in the Old English *Genesis* with the other poems in the Junian manuscript, the sermons of Ælfric, and the *Cursor Mundi*.

Among Sepet's chief documents are the Rouen *Prophetae* and the *Ordo Representationis Adae*. With reference to the former he points out that the number of the prophets has been increased as compared to the Limoges *Prophetae*, and this is true also of the Laon *Prophetae*, which had not as yet been discovered. Such amplifications as those of the Rouen play and the Chester *De Mose et Rege Balaak et Balaam* no doubt appeared elsewhere, but in examining the prophet plays in their vernacular forms no evidence can be found that any basic list of Messianic prophets much more extended than the original was widely disseminated. The prophets common to the various English, French, and German prophet plays are apparently the original group: Isaiah, Jeremiah, Daniel, Moses, David, Habakkuk, Simeon, Zacharias, Elizabeth, and John the Baptist, together with Nebuchadnezzar, Virgil, and the Sibyl. This shows that a simple form of the *Prophetae* was disseminated over a wide area and that its variations were of an incidental character. In the Rouen play there are two cases of dramatic

---

[1] Migne, *P.L.* lxxviii. 725 *et seq.* See Adelina M. Jenney, 'A Further Word as to the Origin of the Old Testament Plays', *Modern Philology*, xii (1915–16), 59–64; Craig, 'The Origin of the Old Testament Plays', loc. cit., *passim*.

amplification. The second of these, and the one of less importance, as described above, is connected with the prophecy of Nebuchad/ nezzar. This episode appears nowhere in the regular cycles, and seems to have been merely sporadic, possibly suggested by a *lectio* from a sermon of Origen on the vigil of the Nativity at Matins.

When the prophet Balaam appears in the procession in the Rouen *Prophetae*, he is seated *super asinam*, and there is acted a little play of the speaking ass. This play, always associated in some fashion with a *Prophetae*, had apparently a wide currency. A Balaam scene appears in somewhat imperfect form in the Benediktbeuern Christmas play, in the Chester Whitsun plays, and in the French *Mistère du Viel Testament*. In the Chester cycle the Balaam scene is merely an episode, though the principal one, in the *Processus Prophetarum*, as it is in the Benediktbeuern play, and as it had been from the beginning. The Balaam play in the *Mistère du Viel Testament*, although appearing in that compilation, not as a whole of popular growth, is nevertheless the same Balaam play. It there appears as an episode in the life of Moses, and in the Chester cycle the scene follows that of Moses and the Tables of the Law, which play is probably also an offshoot of the *Prophetae* and therefore has a very different origin from the play of Moses and the Exodus, in which Moses is a patriarch and not a prophet. Sepet's theory seems to hold for the two plays of Balaam and of Moses and the Tables of the Law, but neither of them is a regular part of the Old Testament group based on the Pentateuch.

A further word needs to be said about the *Ordo Representationis Adae*, which is made up of a long and elaborate Adam play with full stage directions, a shorter Cain and Abel play in the same style, and an abridged prophet play ending with the part of Nebuchadnezzar. There is also in the manuscript a version of the Fifteen Signs of Judgement, material used in the composition of the prophecy of the Sibyl, as if collected for the purpose of carrying the prophet scene further. The Adam and the Cain and Abel, although traditional in contents, show deliberate literary composition, and the play as a whole may be an early and incomplete attempt at cycle/building. To make it conform to the general pattern would call for plays of Noah, Abraham and Isaac, Moses, and other patriarchs. Because of the presence of the *Prophetae*, the Adam has been regarded as a Christmas

play; but, since the play looks so strongly forward to the Passion and
Resurrection, it would seem to belong rather to the Easter season and
is possibly the beginning of a Passion play. Adam bewails his fate
and relies ultimately for salvation upon Christ. Adam and Eve,
Cain and Abel, and each successive prophet are dragged off in turn
to hell. This is not a theologically correct way in which to treat the
prophets. There are no other cases in which prophets are so disposed
of, although they sometimes appear with the patriarchs in hell
awaiting redemption. There are, however, other cases in which the
prophets are borrowed into the Easter series.[1] Such uses of the prophet
play are exceptional, since the normal and original function of the
prophets is to predict the Nativity. As against Sepet's theory of the
origin of the Adam and the Cain and Abel from the *Prophetae* with
which they are associated in the *Ordo Adae*, it is to be pointed out that
the traditional machinery of the prophet play, the introductory speech
of Augustine, does not precede the Adam play, but occurs in its
usual place at the beginning of the *Prophetae*. If the *Ordo Representationis Adae* is in the line of subsequent popular development at all, it is
as the forerunner of such a cycle as *La Nativité, la Passion et la Resurrection* of the Sainte-Geneviève manuscript to which in general structure
it seems to bear some resemblance.[2]

The greater number of popularly developed cycles had a somewhat
restricted list of subjects from the Old Testament, and usually
practically the same subjects, namely, the Fall of Lucifer, the Creation
with the Creation and Fall of Man, Cain and Abel, Noah, Abraham
and Isaac, and Moses and the Exodus. Mixed in with these themes
there appear less frequently a few other stories from the same source,
such as the Death of Adam, Seth in Paradise, the Death of Cain,
Abraham and Lot, and some others. The French *Mistère du Viel
Testament*, though in its main part originally a simple and conventional
play, has been over-developed through the exercise of a freedom
in the selection of subjects greater than was ever dreamed of in the
earlier centuries of the history of the religious drama. It has been filled
in almost solidly with stories from the Old Testament as far as that
of Solomon and the Queen of Sheba. The very idea of an Old

---

[1] Creizenach, op. cit. i (1893), 224 ff.
[2] L. Petit de Julleville, *Les Mystères* (2 v. Paris, 1880), ii. 379–94; Frank, op. cit. 9–10.

Testament cycle is a violation of the liturgical basis of the religious drama, since Old Testament subjects are merely beginnings. The plan of salvation caused the formation of cycles in fulfilment of a religious idea, and there was nothing about the natural activity of cycle-building so artificial as a division in terms of the Old Testament or the New. The different plays of *Le Mistère* show many traces of an original purpose to advance to the Redemption of Man but, as it now stands, it is an anomaly.

The matter can be best understood in terms of the two major groups of religious plays, the Christmas group and the Easter group. The elements in the composition of these groups were invented within the church and partly united into cycles in the liturgical stage. After the secularization of the plays the groups no doubt grew larger and more detailed, but they still maintained their integrity. The plays of the Nativity extended from the *Processus Prophetarum* to the Death of Herod, and the Easter group had to do with Man's Fall, the Passion of Christ, and His Resurrection. There was an irregularity about the placing of the first of these three elements, the story of man's fall from grace, in the Easter cycle. Sometimes the story of Adam's Fall and the manifestation of the hand of God in the history of the Chosen People stood out chronologically as the beginning of the cycle, sometimes it appeared in connexion with the Harrowing of Hell, and sometimes it did not appear at all. But the theological principles were always controlling. They had to be presupposed in any play of the Passion and the Resurrection.

In Germany the Passion plays developed into complete dramas of the Fall of Man, the Passion of Christ, and the Resurrection, with or without Old Testament plays dealing with the patriarchs. They were independent of the Nativity, which, however, usually existed as a separate cycle. The stages and peculiarities of this development can be seen by an examination of the plays preserved, although of course it is necessary to take into consideration special features and degrees of development as well as dates of preservation. In Germany, and certainly in France also, one finds logically complete plays that still go no further in essential themes than the simple Latin plays of the Passion and the Resurrection, with no regularly present Old Testament plays, no prophets, and no Nativity.

It throws some light on the matter to remember that such plays usually show an amplification of the role of the devil. At first he is merely the scriptural Satan; later he becomes Lucifer, and the story of his fall and his betrayal of man is introduced. In the Benedikt- beuern Passion play Satan appears as a mute character in connexion with the treason of Judas. This play of course contains no Harrowing of Hell scene, which must be the original entrance of Satan into the religious drama. The Kloster Muri fragments[1] contain a simple Harrowing of Hell scene in which Satan appears. There is also a similar appearance of Satan in an Innsbruck play of the Resurrection and in other plays of its type, such as the Frankfurt *Dirigierrolle*, the St. Gall Easter play, and others. In the Donaueschingen Passion play Satan appears in the Temptation of Jesus, the Remorse of Judas, Pilate's Wife's Dream, and the Harrowing of Hell. Disregarding certain developments of the part in the direction of *diablerie*, we may consider the Donaueschingen play as presenting the normal appear- ances of Satan in the more primitive plays. In another large group of German plays, such as the Redentin Passion play, the Frankfurt play, the Alsfeld play,[2] and the Tyrol plays,[3] there is an amplified story of the devil and his enmity to man. In this series of plays the stories of the Fall of Lucifer and of Man are frequently introduced in connexion with the prayers of Adam and the patriarchs for redemption from bondage, a feature seen also in some French plays.[4]

The point is that the Old Testament plays, in so far as they concern the patriarchs, are immediately connected with the Resurrection through the Harrowing of Hell and the function of the devil. There are, however, German Passion plays that show, like the Corpus Christi plays of England, a chronological arrangement. The Vienna Passion play,[5] which is one of the oldest Passion plays preserved, dating as it does from the early fourteenth century, begins with the presentation of the Fall of Lucifer and the Fall of Man. The Erlau

[1] R. Froning, *Das Drama des Mittelalters* (Stuttgart, 1891), pp. 228–44; Creizenach, op. cit. i. 114–15.
[2] F. J. Mone, *Schauspiele des Mittelalters* (2 v. Karlsruhe, 1846), i. 107–44, 375 ff., 562 ff.; Creizenach, op. cit. i (1893), 220 ff. *et passim*.
[3] J. E. Wackernell, *Altdeutsche Passionsspiele aus Tyrol* (Graz, 1897).
[4] Creizenach, op. cit. i (1893), 253 *et passim*; Julleville, op. cit. ii. 400 ff.
[5] Froning, op. cit., pp. 302–24; Creizenach, op. cit. i. 120–1 *et passim*.

Magdalen play[1] resembles the Vienna play in its arrangement. Creizenach[2] describes a Czech fragment, which turns out to be a borrowing from the Vienna Passion play. It also begins with the Fall of Lucifer. The Eger Passion play and the Künzelzau *Frohnleichnamspiel* put Old Testament subjects in their proper chronological position.[3] The Middle Frankish play from Mastricht seems also to be the fragment of a chronologically arranged cycle.

It is evident then that there are two main types of the larger cyclic plays—the one, familiar to us in the Corpus Christi plays, is chronologically arranged and complete in contents; the other, exemplified in German and French Passion plays, is not always chronologically arranged and is not complete, since it regularly has no Nativity plays and no *Prophetae*. As we have seen, however, Passion plays sometimes came close to the Corpus Christi type both in contents and to some degree in completeness and have, moreover, a logical completeness of their own, since they present as interdependent units the Fall and the Redemption of Man. Inasmuch as it is possible·to trace the development of the Passion play, even when entirely devoid of *Prophetae* and Nativity, it seems reasonable to believe that Old Testament plays belong logically to the Passion and Resurrection. It would be absurd to think that the Lucifer and Adam scenes of the German Passion plays originated from the *Prophetae*, with which they had no contact in their origin. Old Testament plays were demanded by the subject of the Passion plays. Man had sinned through Adam and his redemption was through Christ's sacrifice.

The series of Old Testament plays enumerated above stand, whenever they appear, as a single group with the same subjects in the same order. They had their proper significance in the story of man's fall and redemption and belonged to an established chronological and theological sequence. As they had come into existence as plays of the period after Epiphany in the growth of the religious drama, they were to some degree out of their chronological position. Sometimes, as in the Vienna Passion play, they found their proper place; sometimes, as in most Passion plays of the continent of Europe, they did not. In at least one case the Old Testament plays were placed in the largest

---

[1] Creizenach, op. cit. i (1893), 238–9 *et passim*.   [2] Ibid., pp. 351 ff.
[3] Ibid., pp. 227–9.

possible group in front of the Passion and the Resurrection. The case in point is the Cornish cycle, which was probably derived from similar plays in Brittany. It is made up of an *Origo Mundi* presenting the Fall of Lucifer and a series of Old Testament plays, a *Passio Domini* beginning with the Temptation and ending with the Burial, and a *Resurrectio Domini* extending from the Setting of the Watch to the Ascension. The Cornish drama thus presents a Passion play of cyclic formation. The pattern for such constructions was perfectly familiar. The chronological pattern furnished by the Bible itself had been embodied in the services of the liturgical year. There were epic or historical treatments hundreds of years old, such as the *Cursor Mundi*, the *Historia Scholastica* of Petrus Comestor, and many others, that presented chronologically all or some principal part of the total story. Such epic or historical accounts may have had some influence on the later forms of plays or may have suggested the cyclic arrange-ment, although the dramatic movement itself had an urge or impulse to form larger and larger groupings in chronological form.

One sees everywhere local differences but a generally similar growth and development, some places going far ahead and perhaps reaching some other places to influence them. The plays of England and Scotland, with many local variations no doubt, seem to have gone along with the general European movement. For example, the Cathedral Statutes of Bishop Hugh de Nonant (1188–98) show that at Lichfield a *Pastores* was to be acted at Christmas, and a *Quem quaeritis* and a *Peregrini* at Easter. At York the traditional statutes of York Cathedral provide for a *Pastores* and an *Ordo Stellae* at Christ-mas as late as about 1255. At Aberdeen the Christmas and the Easter groups were never united, and that was probably the case in Cornwall. The fact that so few documents concerning the Latin drama of the church have come down to us in England should not stand too much in our way when we consider the formation of the great English cycles. There is no reason to think that there was not plenty of material at hand from a flourishing liturgical drama in English churches and monastic institutions, but one has to go abroad for illustrations of what once existed in England. When the time of cycle-building came, the north of England and also to some degree the eastern and central parts adopted the Corpus Christi form, one of the most ambitious of all literary schemes, since it extended from the dawn of creation to the crack of doom. In the south of England, for example at London and at New Romney, the plays of the Nativity and the Passion seem to have remained apart.

PLAYS OF THE LAST JUDGEMENT

Advent, the season of the liturgical year including the four Sundays before Christmas, was devoted to matters of eschatology, that is, the theological doctrines of last or final things, such as death, immortality, and the Judgement. It was a period of prayer, preparation, and contemplation. The Scripture of first resort was the Gospel of St. Matthew, particularly chapters xxiv and xxv, the thirteenth chapter of St. Mark, and the prophecy of Ezekiel. The whole of Advent had long been given over to these contemplations, and the liturgy of the Advent season contains many *lectiones*, antiphons, and responses in connexion with which one or more dramatic offices might have been, and no doubt were, composed. Specifically we know that 2 Thessalonians, chapter ii, was read at Mass on Saturday in the fourth week of Advent. It furnishes the biblical source of the Antichrist play. We know also that the gospel source of the play of the Wise and the Foolish Virgins (Matt. xxv. 1–13) was read during the season of Advent as it was many times during the year and that it appears in the *Commune Virginis et Martyris*. It appears as the eighth lesson at Matins on All Saints' day (1 November). As to the *Judicium* proper, the source (Matt. xxv. 31–46) was a reading at the end of Advent, and the liturgy is full of allusions to it. This play, however, may not have had an independent origin but may have arisen as a second episode in an office of Antichrist.

The *Sponsus,* a play upon the theme of the Wise and Foolish Virgins, perhaps because of the wide dissemination of the subject, led an independent existence and was never embodied in the larger units or cycles. Its origin in a Latin *ordo,* in spite of much literary speculation, is not hard to see. There exists a very interesting version in which the story is presented in liturgical terms, but is ornamented and interpreted in very striking French verse, very dramatic and greatly admired. It is in an eleventh- or twelfth-century manuscript from the monastery of St. Martialis in Limoges. The play as a whole is incisive and rather stern, and the French verse with touching refrains brings out the pathos of the situations. Because of its literary interest the *Sponsus* from Limoges has had much critical interpretation devoted to it. This is summarized by Young, who gives us an excellent text of the play.[1] Young sees no connexion with the liturgy, but it is obvious that at its time it could have come into existence from no other source. As suggested by H. Morf,[2] the Latin lines carry the original play, and one has simply to ignore the amplifications in French in order to see that it began as a liturgical *ordo*. There is a play of the Wise and the Foolish Virgins from Eisenach, which is dated in 1322,[3] an *Oberhessisches Spiel von den zehn Jungfrauen* dated in 1428,[4] and there were no doubt others.

In the case of the *Antichristus* and the *Judicium* the problem of a liturgical origin becomes acute. The indications of an origin within the church and out of the service are not too numerous or too clear, but they seem sufficient to establish a probability that these plays, or this play, for they were probably originally one, arose in the usual and accepted manner of all other Latin religious dramas. We know that such plays as exist were known as plays of Advent and that the services of the season of Advent supplied the materials of which they were mainly composed as well as the background of religious thought and feeling that caused them to come into existence. The story of Antichrist was a widely distributed legend and belief of the medieval church. It rested primarily on 2 Thessalonians ii, which, however, was greatly reinforced from other more or less apocalyptic passages from Daniel and from the Gospels. The legend was definitely formed, was no doubt extremely familiar, and was available in many places. It has been widely held that a narrative source was used, and it is commonly stated that the *Libellus de Antichristo*[5] by Adso of Toul was the source of the *Antichristus*. This is no doubt true as regards amplified later versions, but it is hardly necessary to assume this as

---

[1] Young, op. cit. ii. 361–9.

[2] H. Morf, 'Das liturgische Drama von den fünf klugen und den fünf thörichten Jungfrauen', *Zeitschrift für romanische Philologie*, xxii (1898), 385–91.

[3] Creizenach, op. cit. i. 127–8.

[4] Ed. Max Rieger, *Germania*, x (1865), 311–37.

[5] Young, op. cit. ii. 496–500; Migne, *P.L.*, ci. 1291 *et seq.*; Creizenach, op. cit. i. 79–86 *et passim*.

regards the original *Antichristus* play. There is also a simpler narrative, *Liber de Antichristo*, thought to have been written in the early ninth century[1] that would have been adequate if one has to assume the use of a written source. If, on the other hand, we assume, as we properly may, that a dramatic office of Antichrist arose as a feature of Advent, we find the key to the mystery in an early vernacular play from Italy printed with little information or comment by D'Ancona.[2] It is a very simple version of an *Antichristus* and a *Judicium* written as one play and, whatever may be the date and the provenance, it is certainly a very primitive play. It is, however, sufficiently detailed to serve as an example of the original play of *Antichristus* and *Judicium* throughout Europe. It indicates that the two episodes of the plot, the Antichrist and the Last Judgement, were originally united into one play, although each of the scenes has its own claim to independent existence. The *Antichristus* was on a popular theme, and the *Judicium* was necessary to put all things to an end and thus form the closing subject in plays of the fullest possible scope. The two subjects are still united in the Lucerne play of the Bürgerbibliothek,[3] and that play of 1549 with its use of Ezekiel and other prophets, its *Antichristus* and its *Judicium*, furnishes in a more amplified form an exact parallel to the last three pageants in the Chester cycle.

The difficulty as to the origin of the Antichrist play has arisen because of the desire on the part of historians of the Latin religious drama to have the plays develop too fast and to find in the plays evidences of individual authorship and of that conscious dramatic skill that fulfils their aesthetic ideals. The usual thing was, however, slow, conventional, and imitative. There is no doubt, of course, that in a very few cases plays far ahead of their age in dramatic development made their appearance, but it is misleading to regard these bits of sporadic excellence as original and as always the basis of further developments.

There exists one of the most remarkable and, so to speak, precocious plays on the subject of Antichrist in the whole range of medieval drama, namely, *Ludus de Advento et Interitu Antichristi*, in the famous

---

[1] Migne, *P.L.*, xl. 1132. [2] D'Ancona, op. cit. i. 141–53.

[3] R. Brandstetter, 'Die Technik der Luzerner Heiligenspiele', *Archiv für das Studium der neueren Sprachen und Literaturen*, lxxv (1886), 384 ff.

Tegernsee manuscript formerly in the Staatsbibliothek in Munich. It is dated confidently in the twelfth century[1] and is a play of great literary skill and a high degree of dramatic development with a strong, though somewhat debated, political import. Chambers calls it a *Tendenzschrift*, as it certainly seems to be. It tells the Antichrist story as given by Adso and adds emblematic figures of *Gentilitas*, or heathen-dom; *Synagoga*, or Jewry; and *Ecclesia*, or Christianity, the last-mentioned being accompanied by *Misericordia* and *Justicia*. It has seven royal *sedes* with playing place or *platea* between, and so large is the cast and so extensive the action that Chambers suggests that the play must have taken up the whole nave of some great Church. Young thinks that the play is too extensive to have been acted in a church and must have been played out of doors. Many suggestions have been made as to the political import of the Tegernsee *Antichristus*,[2] and Young thinks that it must have been written about 1160 during the reign of the Emperor Frederick Barbarossa, when the emperor's relations with the king of France and with the pope were not friendly and when the Saracens were threatening the capture of Jerusalem. All of this, and much more about the play, is most interesting, but one must protest against regarding this highly developed play, written for a special purpose and with an unwonted display of literary skill and topical fitness, as the original form of the play of Antichrist as it appeared at later times and pretty much all over Europe. There are, besides the play from Lucerne, a fourteenth-century *Entkrist* from Munich,[3] a Frankfurt *Antichristspiel* of 1468-9,[4] an Antichrist episode in the *Künzelzauer Frohnleichnamspiel*,[5] the Chester Antichrist, and many others.[6]

The *Judicium* had an existence, starting probably in the fourteenth century,[7] independent of the *Antichristus*, when it was borrowed or imitated from the second and final episode of that play in order to make a fitting end to full-scope plays such as that of Corpus Christi.

---

[1] Young, op. cit. ii. 371–96.   [2] Chambers, op. cit. ii. 62–64.

[3] A. Keller, *Fastnachtspiele aus dem fünfzehnten Jahrhundert* (3 v. Stuttgart, 1853), Nr. 68, ii. 593–608; bibliography in Ehrismann, *Geschichte* (cited n. 6), pp. 582-4.

[4] Froning, op. cit. ii. 536–9.

[5] Ed. H. Werner, *Germania*, iv. 38 ff.

[6] Creizenach, op. cit. i, *passim*; G. Ehrismann, *Geschichte der deutschen Literatur bis zum Ausgang des Mittelalters* (Munich, 1935), T. 2.2.2, pp. 555-7.

[7] Creizenach, op. cit. i. 128, 244.

PLAYS IN HONOUR OF THE BLESSED VIRGIN MARY

We need, first of all, before we deal with them, an analysis of the plays in honour of the Blessed Virgin Mary and a discrimination between those plays belonging to the liturgical story of the Nativity, Passion, and Resurrection of Christ in which the Blessed Virgin Mary was merely an important and inevitable character, on the one hand, and those that arose at a later time in special honour of the Blessed Virgin Mary and her personal history as it appears in the New Testament Apocrypha, particularly the Gospel of the Nativity of Mary and the Gospel of Nicodemus, with perhaps certain later traditions from other sources. The two series of plays, those of the Nativity of Christ and those of the life of the Virgin, overlap and need to be distinguished the one from the other.

The typical play of the first group is the Annunciation, a liturgical subject widely scattered throughout the services of the liturgical year of which we have already given an account. We have also described the Purification of the Blessed Virgin Mary, sometimes called the Presentation of Christ in the Temple, a play that apparently arose from the liturgy of the feast of the Purification of the Blessed Virgin Mary on 21 November. This play was often merged with the plays of the Nativity and seems also to have been widely used as a separate play. Those dramatic appearances of the Blessed Virgin Mary in the action of the Passion and Resurrection seem never to have been detached from their historical positions, although the action of the Mother of Christ was extensively celebrated in the *Planctus Mariae*.

There are, besides these more strictly liturgical offices or scenes in plays, two other dramatic subjects, namely, the Presentation of the Blessed Virgin Mary in the Temple and the Assumption and Coronation of the Blessed Virgin Mary. The late Professor Karl Young made an important discovery that makes clear the original appearance of the plays of the first group in western churches.[1] A French nobleman and diplomat, Philippe de Mézières (1326 or 1327–1405), during his career as a diplomat in the Near East, became acquainted with a service in use in the Eastern Church of the Presentation of the Blessed Virgin Mary in the Temple. His piety caused

---

[1] Young, op. cit. ii. 225–45; Creizenach, op. cit. i. 226–8, 472–8.

him to introduce the service into the Western Church and about that introduction we have, thanks to Young, quite definite information. We have de Mézières' own transcript of the office containing a text of a dramatic performance and a letter of his concerning the reception of the new office in honour of the Blessed Virgin Mary in France and Italy. The letter is dated 21 November 1372, and we learn from it that, several years before, de Mézières had brought about in Venice a celebration of the feast, and with the approval of Pope Gregory XI it had been again celebrated at Avignon on 21 November 1372. The description of the feast as celebrated is most elaborate. There were twenty-two characters, the Blessed Virgin Mary being herself represented by a small girl accompanied by fourteen other small girls. It has, of course, Joachim and Anna, the parents of the Blessed Virgin Mary, and a most interesting supernatural group—the angel Gabriel, the archangels Raphael and Michael with nine other angels. It has *Ecclesia* and Synagoga, the fallen angel Lucifer; also two musicians. It is indeed a very fine work that very much needs a translation into English. The office is firmly attached to the Mass and is therefore liturgical. Further documents may yet be found, and there may be versions in a transitional or an early vernacular stage.

What we do have is evidence of a fully developed group of plays in honour of St. Anne, the mother of the Blessed Virgin Mary, and of course in honour of the Virgin herself.[1] Evidence of a cycle of plays performed in England on St. Anne's day (26 July) comes from two sources: a set of rather extensive records from Lincoln and a group of plays embodied in the so-called *Ludus Coventriae* or Hegge plays. That cycle has a set of banns (or prologue) used for advertising the plays. They are based on the plays when they were definitely to be acted on Corpus Christi day. At a date later than the banns there were inserted into the cycle a group of St. Anne's day plays in their proper chronological place in the original Corpus Christi play, but the banns were not altered. Therefore the banns show us by exclusion what plays are St. Anne's day plays. The first of these is a play called the Barrenness of Anna. It has a separate prologue. The second play, Mary in the Temple, also provided with a separate prologue, is the chief play of the group and is ultimately based on the office introduced

[1] Chambers, op. cit. ii. 118, 126-7; Creizenach, op. cit. i. 170, 207, 340; iii. 496-7.

into France and Italy in the fourteenth century by Philippe de Mézières. A play called Mary's Betrothal is partly from the Corpus Christi play and partly from the special matter pertaining to the Blessed Virgin Mary. This may also be true of a play called Joseph and the Midwives, but the play of the Trial of Joseph and Mary is almost certainly from the St. Anne's day play. It will be observed that the simple office of de Mézières has been expanded into several plays according to habit and practice in the handling of religious subjects. That is, to a central core there were usually added, sometimes by partition, subjects associated with the main theme. Mixed in with these St. Anne's day subjects are plays on the regular liturgical subjects, belonging to the Corpus Christi play, such as the Annuncia‑ tion, the Visit to Elizabeth, Joseph's Trouble about Mary, and part of Joseph and the Midwives, the Shepherds, and the Magi.

There was also a popular play in special honour of the Blessed Virgin Mary on the Assumption and Coronation of the Virgin. It is preserved as part of the York cycle and of the Hegge plays. Such a play once existed at Chester, but has been lost, and it has almost certainly been torn out of the Towneley manuscript. The Hegge plays (or *Ludus Coventriae*) show it in its finest form. The story comes from the apocryphal Gospel of Nicodemus. It narrates that when the time of her demise approached the Blessed Virgin Mary summoned to her death‑bed the disciples, who were abroad spreading the Gospel. They were conveyed thither in clouds. St. Thomas, who was in India, was brought in a special cloud. When her ascension occurred, doubting Thomas refused to believe the testimony of his own eyes; whereupon the Virgin let down her girdle for him to touch and thus be convinced. The play was often therefore called 'St. Thomas of India'.

There are few records of the services of the feast of the Assumption (15 August) in the earliest times. Young succeeded in finding only one. It is a description for liturgical purposes of the Assumption and is a sixteenth‑century *ordo* from Halle. It is printed by Young.[1] For some unaccountable reason the feast of the Assumption was an occasion for riotous behaviour, and against this the *ordo* gives warn‑ ing. The feast goes back to the eighth century when it received papal

[1] Loc. cit. ii. 255‑7.

sanction. One can only conclude that all early records have been lost, for the feast was widely celebrated and the play was well known, not only in England, but on the continent.

THE MIRACLE PLAY

The miracle play, as defined by the late John Matthews Manly in his important article 'Literary Forms and a New Theory of the Origin of Species', 'is the dramatization of a legend setting forth the life or the martyrdom or the miracles of a saint'. Miracle plays were widely distributed throughout Europe in the later Middle Ages, and no doubt great importance is to be attached to them in their influence on the development of the romantic drama in Tudor times. This point has been presented by Manly in his article 'The Miracle Play in Medieval England',[1] where he shows that miracle plays by their varied content supplied elements of human interest, romantic, spectacular, and dramatic. Only one complete miracle play, the *Croxton Sacrament Play*, has been preserved in English. It is possible that *Dux Moraud* is the fragment of a miracle play, and *The Pride of Life*, a morality, has miracle-play qualities; also certain mystery plays have in them elements of the saints' play. Considerable numbers have survived on the continent of Europe in French, German, Spanish, and Italian, and there is from France the extensive series known as *Miracles de Nostre Dame*. As usual one has to turn to the continent to get an idea of what once existed in England.[2] Our immediate concern is with the miracle play as it occurred in the service of the medieval church.

G. R. Coffman in *A New Theory of the Origin of the Miracle Play* contended that an account given by a monk of Bec in the early twelfth century points to the actual place and time of the invention of the miracle play. I quote his summary of the events: 'Some Cluniac monks at Crux, a subject monastery of St. Charitas in the Loire valley, on St. Nicholas's feast day ask permission of their prior to sing a new and popular history of that saint's life, but are denied the privilege by the prior because it is not the ecclesiastical chant, and because it is the facetious composition of secular clerks. As a

---

[1] J. M. Manly, in *Transactions of the Royal Society of Literature* (London, 1927), pp. 133–53.
[2] Creizenach, op. cit. i. 104–7, 128–9, 139–54, 157–8, 233–8, 279–81.

punishment to this prior, St. Nicholas appears to him on the night following his refusal and compels him to learn an antiphon used in his
feast day services, in one version O *Christi pietas*, and in the other O
Pastor Aeterne. When Gerard, the prior of St. Charitas, hears of this
miracle, he orders the history sung in all the subject monasteries.'
Coffman says further, 'I hold that the St. Nicholas *Miracle Plays*
originated in connexion with musical services, during the latter part
of the eleventh century as an unecclesiastical feature of his feast day
celebration, and that they are indebted to the medieval Latin hymn
for their form. The creative impulse characteristic of the medieval
renaissance found expression in some individual who applied the
dramatic method to a legend of this popular saint whose history had
already been set to music. The result is our first *Miracle Play*.' All the
plays arose, of course, out of an awakening of mind characterized as a
renaissance. Young[1] pointed out that, in saying that the history of
St. Nicholas had been set to music, Coffman had mistaken the
liturgical meaning of the word '*historia*'. *Historia* did not mean,
according to Young, story or legend, but meant the *cursus* or a
complete office or service of the day. It included antiphons, responses,
psalms, and hymns and did not necessarily or usually include narrative
elements contained in *lectiones*. The effect of Young's criticism was
to show that the *historia* or service prepared by the Cluniac monks at
Crux cannot be said to describe the origin of a play of St. Nicholas.
On the other hand, it does furnish an occasion on which there might
have arisen a miracle play of St. Nicholas. Therefore for Coffman's
particular statement of discovery Young substituted a general statement as follows, and there the matter stands: 'In so far, then, as we
can judge from the extant miracle plays, they rest not upon short and
summary references to the *vita* such as are found in liturgical embellishments, but directly upon the complete forms of the legends themselves.
The plays represent the incidents of the traditional narratives with
substantial fidelity, and they appear to have arisen through the application of the dramatic method to these stories.'[2] There is thus a distinction, but no great difference, between the views of Young and those

[1] G. R. Coffman, *A New Theory of the Origin of the Miracle Play*, a Chicago doctoral
thesis published at Menasha, Wisconsin, in 1914; Karl Young, 'Concerning the Origin of
the Miracle Play', *The Manly Anniversary Studies* (Chicago, 1923), pp. 254-68.
[2] Karl Young, *The Drama of the Medieval Church*, ii. 310.

of Coffman. Both believe that the miracle play of St. Nicholas was an independent composition by an individual author acting under the then established impulse of the dramatizing habit.

There is nothing improbable about this hypothesis, which has no proof one way or the other. There were plenty of minor amplifications and embellishments of the service on St. Nicholas's day, tropes galore, and *lectiones* that carried in themselves the legends ultimately used as sources for the St. Nicholas plays. One cannot say on the basis of the documents preserved that there may not have been a gradual growth of offices from tropes as in the case of many mystery-play subjects, amply illustrated in the Christmas and the Easter groups. Some of the St. Nicholas plays are simpler than others, and the question reduces itself to a matter of probability. Is it more probable that the St. Nicholas plays grew gradually in length after the patterns of the growth of other liturgical plays from simple tropes to complete plays and that the intervening steps have been lost, or that the dramatizing habit in the eleventh century had grown so strong that the plays were created by one or more large jumps from simple liturgical units? Two considerations may help us to make up our minds. The first of these is the fact that there was no early distinction between the service of the *Temporale* and the service of the *Sanctorale*. Honouring the saints was precisely as religious and as fundamental as the presentation of the *cursus* of the liturgical year that had to do with the fall of man, the birth of the Saviour, and man's redemption. The same practices and principles would hold. Secondly, the gap to be bridged, when looked at narrowly, i.e. that between the liturgical embellishments and the simplest plays, is not too wide to have been filled by lost intermediate offices. On the other hand, we must remember that the development of miracle offices was later than that of biblical offices and we may believe that, by the eleventh century, the develop-ment of the religious drama was in some places pretty far along; so that it is not beyond the range of possibility that full-length religious dramas may have been rather suddenly invented in order to fill in an occasion. One has a right to be dubious about this acknowledgement of what might be called free dramatic creation at that time, but there is a bare possibility of such individual authorship. So far we have no actual proof.

In the consideration of this rather extensively debated question of the origin of the miracle plays we are limited to the plays of St. Nicholas. If the lives, martyrdoms, and miracles of other saints were dramatized within the church, as they probably were, they have not come down to us. But there is no proof that there were not earlier saints' plays than those of St. Nicholas, and evidences of such drama-tizations may yet be found. Meantime, it is our duty to look at the St. Nicholas plays. As usual, Young provides us with full texts of all the plays preserved in Latin.[1] Adams[2] prints and translates into English texts of three out of four of them: *Ludus super Iconia Sancti Nicolai*, a twelfth-century play by Hilarius; *Tres Clerici*, a twelfth-century play from the Fleury Playbook; and *Adeodatus*, also of the twelfth century and also from the Fleury Playbook from the Abbey of Saint-Benoît-sur-Loire.

The first St. Nicholas play to which Young directs attention is *Tres Filiae*. Of this play there is an eleventh- or twelfth-century version from Hildesheim. It is in simple verse stanzas of four lines each with a *cauda*. The play is defective at the end, but there is enough of it to tell most of the story. A father, fallen from affluence into poverty, complains to his three daughters of his ill luck and asks their advice. The eldest daughter suggests that the daughters come to his assistance by earning their livings as prostitutes; she will lead the way. The father objects, not strenuously, and the second daughter warns against the damnation attending such a course of conduct. The third daughter turns to the Bible and cites the example of Job in the endur-ance of trouble. At this point, although there are no rubrics or stage directions, St. Nicholas throws a bag of money in at the window and hastens away. The father pursues him, learns who he is, and is ad-vised to give thanks to God. This is a very simple form of the legend. A much more theatrical form appears in a version of the thirteenth century from Fleury. In that play, when the eldest daughter makes her proposal, St. Nicholas throws money in at the window at once, a wooer immediately appears, marries the eldest daughter, and the money is used for her dowry. The father again complains of poverty to the two younger daughters. The second daughter argues against

[1] Ibid., pp. 307–60.
[2] Adams, op. cit., pp. 55–69.

prostitution as sinful, and St. Nicholas throws in more money. Another suitor appears and marries the second daughter, so that the money goes to pay her dowry. The father, again reduced to poverty, complains to his sole remaining daughter, who urges the will of God and the patience of Job. St. Nicholas throws in gold for the third time, a wooer promptly appears, and the third daughter is married to him. This time the father pursues St. Nicholas, learns who he is, and is advised to give thanks to God. We are not told what the father did after this; he may have had to go to work. The play is sufficiently rubricated and ends with *O Christi pietas*, an antiphon that connects it with the service of St. Nicholas's day. In these two versions of the same play there is evidence of growth.

The next play, *Tres Clerici*, is also from Hildesheim, and is also early and simple. The manuscript is dated in the eleventh or twelfth century. Three clerks arrive at an inn and ask for shelter. The host admits them and they go to bed. The host proposes to his wife that they murder the clerks for their money. She objects until she is told that nobody will know about it and then consents. They murder the clerks, apparently in pantomime. Just then St. Nicholas arrives in the guise of a poor wanderer and asks for hospitality in Christ's name. He is admitted, asks for fresh meat, which is denied him, and then accuses the host and his wife of murdering the clerks. He charges them to ask God's forgiveness. He prays with them that the murdered men be restored to life. They sing the antiphon *O Christi pietas*, and an angel announces that the clerks have been restored to life. Again, there is a much more highly developed version of this play from Fleury. It tells the same story but is much fuller of action and dialogue: the scholars talk about themselves and their needs before they reach the inn, the wife persuades her husband to admit them, in the night the innkeeper and his wife plot their murder and look at the travellers' purses. After the accusation of St. Nicholas the murderers recognize him as one of God's saints and beg for mercy. St. Nicholas prays with them, and the clerks are restored to life. The play is fully rubricated and ends with the singing of *Te Deum laudamus*. Young thinks there may have been connexions between Fleury and Hildesheim and that the plays were transferred from one place to the other. In that case, one would think that the plays originated at

Saint-Benoît-sur-Loire and were taken to Hildesheim in earlier and simpler forms. There is, besides these two versions, a fragment of *Tres Clerici* covering the end of the play. It represents a still more advanced stage of development. For example, St. Nicholas condemns the wife for her share in the murder and with God's help restores the murdered clerks to life. The fragment has more character in it, and Young thinks this fragment was also probably connected with the liturgy.

In the third place there is the *Ludus super Iconia Sancti Nicolai* by the wandering scholar Hilarius, which is much admired, not for itself, but because it is exceptional in literary quality. A pagan named Barbarus possesses an image of St. Nicholas. He leaves home and places his treasure in charge of the image. Robbers come and steal the treasure. Barbarus comes home, finds himself robbed, scolds the image and beats it. St. Nicholas hunts up the robbers and induces them by threats of exposure to return the treasure. Barbarus is much pleased and apologizes to the image. St. Nicholas appears and tells him to give his thanks to God. Thereupon Barbarus becomes a Christian. The play is excellently conceived and executed. It bears no obvious marks that would connect it with the liturgy but may well have been fitted into a proper place. It contains some French in the form of refrains. An interesting question is its relation to a play in the vernacular by Jean Bodel published from Arras that was certainly widely known.[1] In it the image possessed by the pagan is that of the heathen god Termagaunt. The action of the play is the same, but the beating of the image became a notorious feature. There was an actor hidden within the image of Termagaunt, and this actor made a most frightful outcry when the idol was beaten by the outraged pagan. This is the situation to which Hamlet refers in his advice to the Players when he says he would have such a fellow whipped for 'o'er-doing Termagaunt'. This *Ludus super Iconia Sancti Nicolai* is possibly the type-form of the play and may go back to an earlier time than Hilarius's play.

The fourth of the Latin St. Nicholas plays is *Adeodatus* or *Filius Getronis*. It comes from the Fleury Playbook and is dated in the twelfth century. There is only one version of it, and it need not concern us long. It is a romantic and ambitious play. A heathen

---

[1] Creizenach, op. cit. i. 137–42.

king, Marmorinus, orders his soldiers to conquer the world. In the city of Excoranda Getron and his wife, Euphrosina, parents of the saintly child Adeodatus, have taken him to a celebration of the feast of St. Nicholas in a church dedicated to that saint. Adeodatus is captured and led away by Marmorinus. This heathen is disposed to thank Apollo for his victories, but Adeodatus does not hesitate to set him right. Meantime, at Excoranda the mother of Adeodatus is praying St. Nicholas to restore to her her child. St. Nicholas answers her prayer and returns Adeodatus to his parents. The play is extremely elaborate in its dramaturgy, detailed and naturalistic, with many suggestions of an oriental source. Of course such a play must have been written under a relatively free exercise of dramatic choice and habit. It is nevertheless tied in with the liturgy in the service of St. Nicholas's day.

We need a history of the later developments and occurrences of the St. Nicholas play, and such a history to one familiar with German and French plays would be easy to write. There are few references to the play in England, where, however, it must have been of frequent occurrence, especially in schools and perhaps at Oxford and Cambridge. The companion piece, the play of St. Katherine, also associated with scholars and schools, was played in several places. Besides the record of the lost play of St. Katherine at Dunstable about the year 1100, there is an early play on the subject from Thuringia;[1] also a very early vernacular version of the widely disseminated play of St. Dorothea located by Creizenach in Upper Saxony or in northern Bohemia.[2] The subjects of other early miracle plays, besides those of St. Nicholas, St. Katherine, and St. Dorothea, were St. Agnes, St. George, and the Blessed Virgin Mary. Some of these must certainly have been liturgical, and it may be that a closer study of the earlier examples of vernacular plays would throw further light on the origin of the miracle play. A caveat should be entered against the frequent classification of *The Conversion of St. Paul* and *Mary Magdalene* from Digby MS. 133 as miracle plays, since both were originally mystery plays and of liturgical origin.

[1] Ibid., pp. 128–30.
[2] Ed. H. Schachner in *Zeitschrift für deutsche Philologie*, xxxv. 157–96.

III

Transitional Period

WE know that mystery plays had their origin in the medieval church and that they underwent very considerable development within the church. We know that liturgical plays or dramatic offices were in the hands of the clergy and that during a period of perhaps slightly more than 100 years, roughly from the beginning of the thirteenth to the beginning of the fourteenth century, the plays left the church and passed into the hands of the laity. How and why they did this we do not know with any great definiteness. They were liturgical and they became secular; this fact is obvious and needs no proof.[1] It has been conjectured very reasonably that the popularity of the plays and the consequent crowds of spectators that came to see them were too great to be accommodated within the sacred edifice and that, since the laity had been taken more and more into partnership with the clergy, the plays had become so secularized that they were no longer in any true sense ecclesiastical. Vernacular languages had crowded out the Latin, and the plays had, in response to popular demand, been made to include, not only non-liturgical Scripture, apocryphal narrative, and approved hagiography, but comic and sensational matter from mere folklore and from daily life.

But there are some qualifications that need to be applied to this view. It is certain that the plays were not expelled from the church. There had been a small number of reformers who had objected to drama in the church, and these reformers no doubt exerted influence at certain places and at certain times. But the transition from church to street, from Latin to vernacular, and from liturgy to secularity does not seem to have been offensive to the clergy. One has, in general, only accidental references and official records accidentally preserved

---

[1] Chambers, op. cit. ii. 68–105, with references; Creizenach, op. cit. i (1893), 108–61; Harold G. Gardiner, S.J., *Mysteries' End: An Investigation of the Last Days of the Medieval Religious Stage* (New Haven, 1946), pp. 1–19.

from which to learn about the religious dramas of the twelfth, thirteenth, and fourteenth centuries. For example, there is the well-known
case of a miracle play of St. Katherine acted in Dunstable in Bedfordshire before 1119.[1] Matthew Paris in his lives of the Abbots of St.
Albans recounts that Geoffrey, a Norman cleric who had come to
the Abbey of St. Albans to act as schoolmaster, arranged to have
played at Dunstable a *ludus de Sancta Katarina* (*quem miracula vulgariter
appellamus*). For use in this play Geoffrey borrowed from the Abbey
certain costumes (*capae chorales*) that unfortunately were burned while
they were in his possession. He was so smitten in his conscience by
this disaster that he renounced the worldly life, became a monk, and
was installed as Abbot of St. Albans in 1119. This record shows
the presence in England of a miracle play at a very early date. It is no
doubt significant that it was acted under the direction of a schoolmaster, for St. Katherine was a saint greatly honoured in schools.

Much information about the religious drama of this transitional
period can be derived from the attacks of various reformers on the
dramatic activities of clerics. It has been generally conceded, and
Father Gardiner has shown beyond question, that these attacks, as
well as the regulations promulgated by various councils, were
directed, not against mystery and miracle plays when acted with due
reverence and proper decorum, but against abuses and disorders that
made their appearance in connexion, we may believe, with the
performance of religious plays.[2] The best known case and the most
significant is that of Robert Grosseteste (d. 1253), English theologian,
Chancellor of the University of Oxford, and Bishop of Lincoln
(1235-53). In a letter to his archdeacons on the conduct of priests
(1244) he bids them bring to a complete end participation in miracles
and other plays (*Miracula etiam et ludos supra nominatos et scotales,
quod est in vestra potestate facili, omnino exterminetis*). The bishop's views
were certainly austere, but, when one considers his denunciation of
folk-plays and the Feast of Fools, one may conclude that it was the
association of miracles and mystery plays with these disorderly practices that moved him in his attack.[3] Certainly during Grosseteste's

[1] Matthew Paris, *Gesta Abbatum S. Albani*, ed. H. T. Riley (Rolls Series), i. 73; Chambers,
op. cit. ii. 64, 107, 366; Young, op. cit. ii. 541.
[2] Gardiner, op. cit., *passim*; Chambers, op. cit. ii. 98-103.
[3] Ibid. i. 39, 91, 321; ii. 100, with references.

time and long afterwards religious plays were being performed regularly in the cathedral at Lincoln. A more positive though less well-known prohibition of plays in churches comes from the Cathedral Registers of Hereford for the year 1348:[1]

> Whereas according to the word of the prophet, holiness becometh the house of the Lord, it is not convenient that anything should be done (*exerceri*) therein which is alien to true religion (*a cultu*). Since then in the plays that take place at times in churches there are ribaldry and obscenity which are ever forbidden by the Apostle, especially in the temple of the Lord which, as the Saviour says, should be called the house of prayer, and all other things tending to jesting by which the minds of the faithful, who ought to be intent on solemnities and devout prayers, are drawn towards inanities and deprived of devotion, to the wronging of God's Name and perilous example to those present (*assistencium et spectancium*); WE, being desirous, as we are bound to root out from our diocese such abuses, lest the honour of the Church should be stained by such turpitude, straitly bid you by virtue of holy obedience to study to prevent such inhibitions in L. church under threat of anathema, and to excommunicate transgressors or rebels, &c.

Another reformer of very serious character is Gerhoh of Reichersberg, German theologian who flourished in 1121 and 1161.[2] He reproves the monks of Augsburg because they neither sleep in quarters nor dine in the refectory unless there is some great entertainment, especially unless they can see represented Herod, the persecutor of Christ and the killer of the children, or other theatrical spectacles in the refectory, which at other times is empty. In a later work *De Investigatione Antichristi* Gerhoh devotes a whole chapter to the argument that in turning churches into theatres the clergy were doing the work of the very Antichrist whose story they were wont to act. The clergy, he charges, are given to avarice, there are women among the spectators, they see the wickedness of Antichrist and of Herod, they represent the crib of the Saviour, the wailing Infant, the lying-in of the Virgin, the flaming star of the Magi, the Slaughter of the Innocents, and the lament of Rachel—all feignedly and to the immense scandal of the church, which abhors theatrical spectacles in which men are shamelessly transformed into women, clerics into soldiers, and men into the likeness of demons. He refers to an *Elisaeus*, thought

---

[1] See *Extracts from the Cathedral Registers*, A.D. 1275-1535. Translated by Rev. E. L. Dew (Hereford, 1932), p. 66.

[2] Gerhohus, *Comm. in Ps. cxxxii*, Migne, *P.L.* cxciv. 890; Chambers, op. cit. ii. 98–99; Young, op. cit. ii. 524-5.

of as a lost play, although it is possibly only Elias, who appeared regularly in the play of *Antichristus*.

A milder tone and one expressive of what we may believe was the more general view[1] is found in Herrad of Landsberg, Abbess of Hohenberg in the twelfth century,[2] in her *Hortus Deliciarum*, where she complains that the old fathers of the church had instituted services at Epiphany and its octave in which one saw the star guiding the Magi to the crib of Jesus, the cruelty of Herod, the lying-in of the Blessed Virgin, the warning of the Magi by an angel, and other events connected with the Nativity. But nowadays these reverent services are destroyed by the license of youth and transformed into irreligion and extravagance. Priests are dressed as soldiers. In the church there is feasting and drinking, buffoonery, lewd jests, the clash of weapons, and the presence of shameless women. Rarely does such an assembly end without quarrelling. Again, in the *Manuel des Péchés* by the Anglo-Norman William of Waddington, the work on which is based Robert Mannyng's *Handlynge Synne* (1304), William distinguishes clearly between representations made reverently in the church and miracles played by foolish clerics.[3] Robert Mannyng's position is not quite clear, although it seems certain that he merely wishes to warn the clergy against public performances. He says,

> Hyt is forbode hym yn þe decre,
> Myracles for to make or se;
> For, myracles 3yf þou begynne,
> Hyt ys a gaderyng, a syght of synne.
> He may yn cherche, þurgh þys resun,
> Pley þe resurreccyun,—
> Þat ys to seye, how God ros,
> God and man yn my3t and los,—
> To make men be yn beleue gode
> Þat he ros with flesshe and blode;
> And he may pleye, withoutyn plyght,
> How God was bore yn 3ole nyght,

---

[1] See references and excerpts, Chambers, ibid.

[2] Chambers, op. cit. i. 318; ii. 98; Karl Pearson, *The Chances of Death and Other Studies in Evolution* (Cambridge, 1897), ii. 285-6.

[3] *Handlynge Synne*, ed. F. J. Furnivall, E.E.T.S. (1901, 1903), which reprints a large part of *Le Manuel des Péchés*; E. J. Arnould, *Le Manuel des Péchés: Études de littérature religieuse anglo-normande* (Paris, 1940), xiii.

> To make men to beleue stedfastly
> Þat he lyght yn þe vyrgyne Mary.
> 3if þou do hyt yn weyys or greuys,
> A syght of synne truly it semys.
> Seynt Ysodre, y take to wyttnes,
> For he hyt seyþ, þat soþe hyt es;
> Þus hyt seyþ, yn hys boke,
> Þey forsake þat þey toke—
> God and here crystendam—
> Þat make swyche pleyys to any man
> As myracles and bourdys,
> Or tournamentys of grete prys.
> Þese are pompes þou forsoke,
> Fyrst whan þou þy crystendam toke. (ll. 4637–62)

Dives and the Pauper,[1] a popular fifteenth-century book of religious instruction, is also quite clear in its endorsement of properly conducted *miracula*, although it denounces dancing and playing and other sins on holidays. Of *miracula* it says,

Miracles pleyes and daunces that ben done principaly for devocion honestye and myrthe, to teche men to love god the more and for no ribaudrye ne medleyd with ribawdry ne lesynges, ben leful, so that the people be nat therby lettyd from goddes servyce, no fro goddes worde hering and that ther be no erroure meddled in suche miracles and pleyes agenst the feith of holy churche, ne agenst gode lyvynge.

A different point of view, and one that would ultimately be fatal to medieval religious plays, is to be seen in a Wyclyfite document, *A Treatise of miraclis pleyinge*.[2] It sees sin, a violation of holiness, in the very act of dramatic presentation. It is sin, the preacher says, to make 'oure pleye and bourde of tho myraclis and werkis that God so ernestfully wrou3t to us. . . . myraclis pleyinge . . . makith to se veyne si3tis of degyse, aray of men and wymmen by yvil continuaunse, eyther styring othere to letcherie and of debatis.' This is outside of the general course of ecclesiastical teaching, is fairly late (*c.* 1500), and cannot have been influential except upon a few who were ready to adopt the moralistic view of the later sixteenth century. No doubt there was definite opposition to mystery and miracle plays from time to time in various places, such as a furious letter of the Dean of the

---

[1] Gardiner, op. cit., p. 14.
[2] *Reliquiae Antiquae*, ii. 42; Chambers, op. cit. ii. 102.

Faculty of Theology at Paris in 1445,[1] but, in general, clerical opposition is rare, and peaceful changes all over Europe indicate co-operation between clergy and laity.

The change of the religious drama from Latin into the various vernacular languages of Europe and from single plays and small groups of plays into more or less extensive cycles is a subject about which too little is known, and yet there are enough transitional plays preserved and enough widely scattered records of the performance of such plays now lost for us to be able to understand in general what happened and to fix on some of the motives that brought the changes about. We know that from the earliest times of the religious drama two tendencies were at work. One of these was a tendency towards amplification, and the other a tendency towards the combination of smaller units into larger ones. Both of these tendencies are characteristic of the medieval mind, a mind that was actuated by reason and dominated by logic, that dwelt on particulars and for its satisfaction demanded completeness. Whatever happened had a cause or arose out of a need, and the desire of the Middle Ages was to fit all details into their proper places according to large patterns. The greatest pattern of all was that of man's creation, fall, and redemption, and by far the greatest part of all medieval writing is devoted to the exploitation and fulfilment of this pattern.

The literature of chivalry has also a pattern, less well defined but potent in the same fashion. One is reminded of the interminable cycles of romance that present not only the ideals of courtesy, loyalty, and courage but the parentage, the costume, the accoutrements, the quests, the companions, the enemies, the daily routine of living, and the particulars of every adventure, brought in regardless of length or even pertinency and appropriateness. We have seen how the single slight episode of the visit of the Three Marys to the sepulchre of Christ was amplified into a complete drama of the Resurrection, an operation carried out, however, according to the pattern set down in the gospels with only a slight and varying element of free choice. As to combination or agglutination, it fits in with the particularizing tendency of the Middle Ages and was a natural result of amplification according to a vast theological pattern. It was an age of long and inclusive

[1] A. P. Rossiter, *English Drama from Early Times to the Elizabethans* (London, 1950), p. 59.

works. Chaucer was able to carry to completeness only about one-quarter of his large plan for the *Canterbury Tales*. *Acta Sanctorum* was a gigantic continuing work that took centuries to complete. *Cursor Mundi*, which is about 24,000 lines long, sought to do nothing less than record the whole story of man on earth from the creation to the time the epic was written.

No better illustration of a comprehensive plan can be found than the services of the liturgical year, which put into one framework all the duties of worship that it was incumbent on man to render to God and His saints day by day and hour by hour throughout the year—every prayer, every hymn, every symbolic act, every choral part, every event in the history of man's creation, fall and redemption, with the lives and martyrdoms of saints, popes, and confessors. There had been, of course, an original ecclesiastical and theological fixation of this *cursus* that need not concern us here, but the plan itself was a goal or ideal of achievement. Its vastness made it impossible of attainment, but its particularity put it within the range of many attempts. The tendency to inclusiveness readily accounts for the combination in the religious drama of single themes and small groups into cycles for which the services of the liturgical year afforded a complete and detailed outline. One has to remember, however, that there was a liberty under the law. Although the religious drama grew up under one system, it was not regimented. There was room for variety, and uniform completeness on the largest scale was only now and then and in favourable circumstances achieved. Since completeness was impossible, there was always a restricted, if not enforced, liberty in the choice of component parts and a very considerable liberty of emphasis operating under a constant influence of conservatism as demanded by the grand *cursus* of the divine services of the liturgical year. Every separate dramatic enterprise followed the general pattern, or certain parts of it, in its own way, which in the isolation of communities in the Middle Ages was usually the way in which it had begun. There are thus many kinds of medieval religious drama, each with its own local markings. Degrees of unity were varying, and completeness was a tendency and not a regulation.

The situation is very different from that to which we are accustomed in the consideration of secular literature. There was in the medieval religious drama no original single invention from which there were derived succeeding versions of one work. Since the authors were many and anonymous, the religious drama of the Middle Ages had all through its history a communal quality that prevents it from being arranged in one sequence with definitely ascertainable inter-connexions. The matter might be put in this way: the strictly liturgical drama was disseminated throughout Europe like so many seeds, and from these seeds there grew plants like the parent stock, but trimmed, set, and associated in different ways. Once established at dif-ferent places, the plays tended to stay where they were and undergo in communal fashion in each locale such modifications as circum-stances and desires might institute. The agents of the original dis-semination and of subsequent disseminations were no doubt varied. There must have been borrowings from one place to another. There must have been imitations of the plays of one town by another and, for all we know, independent invention within limits. Friars, travelling ecclesiastics, schoolmasters and their pupils, even wandering scholars must have played a part. Once rooted in the churches, the dramatic plant was subjected, as implied above, to a varied body of local and general influences, changing with the centuries. Wealth and poverty, local culture and progressiveness and their lack, and various kinds and degrees of motivation came into operation. In some places, not in all, a vernacular religious drama arose, but let it be remembered that it was a religious drama and was never essentially secular. Modern critics may not like the religious drama, but it is certainly erroneous to prize it for the things it was not and to think it important only when it ceases to be itself. Mystery and miracle plays were heterogeneous, communal things and anonymous. To be on the look-out for authors is to look at the religious plays from a wrong point of view. French historians of the religious drama seem, for example, to have worked backwards.[1] Since Petit de Julleville and the earlier historians of the French religious drama they seem to have given their attention to the latest redactors, such as Eustache Mer-cadé, Arnoul Greban, and Jean Michel, and to regard even early

[1] Julleville, op. cit., *passim*; G. Cohen, *Le Théâtre en France au moyen âge* (2 v. Paris, 1931), i. 46–68; Émile Roy, *Le Mystère de la Passion en France du xive au xvie siècle* (Dijon, 1903–4), pp. 243–355; A. Jeanroy, *Le Théâtre religieux en France du xie au xiiie siècle* (Paris, 1923), *passim*. But see Grace Frank, *The Medieval French Drama* (Oxford, 1954), *passim*.

communally created versions as somehow derivative from the work of well-known persons, in the age of individual authorship, who lived after the Renaissance had begun.

TRANSITIONAL FORMS

Results thus show that there was a general change from Latin to the vernacular and from the hands of the clergy within the church into the hands of the laity in the out of doors in towns and cities. The change was apparently a gradual and a voluntary one, and clergy and laity seem to have operated together in a series of communal projects. After all, the process went on for more than a century. Records and dramatic documents are not too numerous, and the interests of many historians of the religious drama have not been centred on growth but on social and dramatic aspects as seen by modern eyes. We have been asked to believe that the religious drama did not exist for itself but only that it might lead up to a more strictly dramatic drama that interests us more.

One notes at a very early time a disposition to introduce modern languages into Latin plays. A natural and no doubt valid reason for this would arise from the popularity of the Latin plays. There would be a strong desire to have the spectators, many of whom would not be able to understand Latin, know what was being said. In this desire there must be the real reason for the displacement of Latin by the vernacular languages, but at the very first the vernacular parts seem to be choral or explanatory rather than direct translation. This is true of the *Sponsus* or play of the Wise and the Foolish Virgins, since the Latin in that play carries the full story, and the French is merely ancillary. The same thing is true of the French introduced into the *Ludus super Iconia Sancti Nicolai* by Hilarius. It is, however, hardly true of the German language that appears in the Benedikt-beuern Passion play, in which certain parts having to do with the worldly life of St. Mary Magdalen show an obvious use of German for dramatic purposes. This, as we have seen, probably arose from a more or less complete popularization of the Mary Magdalen episode before it was embodied in the Benediktbeuern play. Chambers[1] calls attention to a fourteenth-century *Quem quaeritis* from the convent of

[1] Op. cit. ii. 89.

Origny-Sainte-Benoîte: here the whole play has been translated into French except certain original, familiar, and, we may believe, more or less sacred parts, such as the dialogue between the Marys and the angel and Christ's conversation with Mary Magdalen in the garden. This perhaps represents the commonest procedure. The Trier *Oster-spiel*, a simple play going no farther than the *Visitatio* and the *Hortu-lanus*, is in a somewhat similar state. Stage directions are in Latin, some of the commoner speeches are not translated, and in some instances the Latin passage and its translation stand side by side.[1] No doubt there were many variations in the manner in which the vernacular was substituted for the Latin. The general motive was probably translation, with, of course, a good deal of paraphrase. Chambers[2] illustrates this by the following passage from the Norman-French or Anglo-Norman *Ordo Adae*. The speech is that of the prophet Isaiah:

Egredietur virga de radice Jesse, et flos de radice ejus ascendet, et requiescet super eum spiritus domini.

This is paraphrased as follows:

Or vus dirrai merveilus diz:
Jesse sera de sa raiz.
Verge en istra, qui fera flor,
Qui ert digne de grant unor.
Saint esperit l'avra si clos,
Sor ceste flor iert sun repos.

An equally significant illustration with some additional features may be derived from the *Shrewsbury Fragments*.[3] These so-called fragments, as noted above, constitute a complete role, or part, of one actor, who in the *Pastores* played the part of the Third Shepherd; in the *Quem quaeritis* or Resurrection, the part of the Third Mary, and in the *Peregrini*, the part probably of Cleophas. Each role gives the speeches of the actor with his cues. The titles and rubrics are in Latin, as are those parts to be said or sung by more than one actor or by all the actors. A few of the speeches are still in Latin and in some cases

[1] Froning, op. cit., pp. 46–56; Creizenach, op. cit. i. 112–13.
[2] Chambers, op. cit. ii. 89–90.
[3] Adams, op. cit., pp. 73–78; Young, op. cit. ii. 514–23; *Non-Cycle Mystery Plays*, Osborn Waterhouse, E.E.T.S. (London, 1909), pp. xv–xxvi, 1–7.

are translated into English. The procedure is plain from the third and fourth speeches of the Third Mary in the *Quem quaeritis*:

> Heu! cur ligno fixus clavis
> Fuit doctor tam suavis?
> Heu! cur fuit ille natus
> Qui perfodit eius latus?

Translated into English this becomes:

> Allas! þat we suche bale should bide
> Þat sodayn sight so for to see,
> Þe best techer in world wide
>   With nayles be tacched to a tre!
> Allas! þat euer so schuld betyde,
>   Or þat so bold mon born schuld be
> For to assay oure Saueour side
> And open hit withoute pite!

The document illustrates, as well as it can be illustrated, the sort of thing that was going on between about the year 1200 and the end of the first quarter of the fourteenth century.

Considerable progress had been made towards the formation of cycles of mystery plays before the end of the liturgical period. One of the most striking of these is the Benediktbeuern Christmas play, of which some account has already been given.[1] It shows a *Prophetae* united with a full, or even amplified, series of scenes presenting the Nativity and the visit of the Magi, a combination already fully achieved in the Fleury *Stella* and in some other plays; and it carries on through the Flight into Egypt and the Death of Herod, having even traces of an Antichrist play at the end. The Benediktbeuern Passion, also a transitional play, shows that it was written to precede a play of the Resurrection, but we find no actual union of these two great elements until later, when it appears in the St. Gall Passion play and in one or two others of about the same date.[2] The *Ordo Adae*,[3]

---

[1] Young, op. cit. ii. 172–96 (with text); Chambers, op. cit. ii. 72 *et passim*; Creizenach, op. cit. i. 99. The play, which appears in Munich Staatsbibliothek MS. lat. 4660, saec. xiii, was first published under the editorship of J. A. Schmeller in *Carmina Burana* (Breslau, 1894), pp. 80–91.

[2] Creizenach, op. cit. i. 122–3 *et passim*.

[3] Chambers, op. cit. ii. 70–71; Frank, 'The Genesis and Staging of the Jeu d'Adam', loc. cit., *passim*; also *The Medieval French Drama*, loc. cit., pp. 76–84.

probably not complete and possibly not in the popular tradition, has scenes of Adam and Eve and of Cain and Abel, which are followed by an abbreviated *Prophetae*. The language, regarded as Anglo-Norman, is close to the liturgical source, and stage directions and quotations from the service are in Latin. The play, as noted above, was played beside the church, possibly partly inside and partly outside the church.

That the same sort of exodus from the church took place in England appears from an interesting early document referring to Beverley in Yorkshire. A passage in a thirteenth-century continuation of the *Vita* of St. John of Beverley[1] records a recent miracle done in the Beverley Minster (dated by Chambers about 1220), as follows:

It happened that at a certain time in summer a representation of the Lord's Resurrection was being performed between the buttresses on the north side of the Blessed St. John's Church, as is customary, in words and actions of players. There were gathered together a great multitude of people of both sexes drawn thither by a variety of motives, such as pleasure, or because of curiosity, or for the sake of a holy desire to awaken their devotion. When, however, on account of the density of the crowd there present, the desired view could not be achieved by many persons and especially those of short stature, numbers of them went into the church in order that they might pray, or look at the pictures, or, by some kind of recreation and solace, might escape the tedium of the day.

Some boys climbed into the triforium, or upper gallery along the aisle of the church. They did this in order that they might see through the windows the costumes and gestures of the actors and be able to listen more easily to the speeches of the players. They were driven out by a sexton, and one of them fell a long way down into the church, but the Blessed St. John of Beverley would not suffer his house to be stained with innocent blood. He accordingly wrought a miracle in the boy's behalf, so that he was not injured by his fall. This document reveals that early in the thirteenth century a play of the Resurrection at Beverley had gone out of the church into the churchyard, or was at least beside the church and on the outside. It was being played as a public spectacle by actors in costume.

[1] *Acta Sanctorum*, Maii, 189; A. F. Leach, 'Some Early Plays and Playgoers', *Furnivall Miscellany* (Oxford, 1901), pp. 206–8; Chambers, op. cit. ii. 338–9; Young (op. cit. ii. 539–40) gives a full text of the passage.

But these developments are as nothing compared with the reported contents of two plays staged in two European cities very distant from each other and at a very early time. The first of these is a play recorded as played about 1226 at Riga, a north-eastern Baltic city in what used to be Latvia, at the very limit of Christian civilization in Europe.[1] The other comes from Cividale in Friuli, a city in north-eastern Italy, and was played in 1298 and 1303. Neither play is preserved. It is reported of the former in *Gesta Livoniensis Episcopi* (1226?) that

> In the same summer there was a highly ornate play of the Prophets, such as Latins call a comedy, in the midst of Riga (*in media Riga*), in order that the unconverted (*gentilitas*) might learn the rudiments of the Christian faith even by ocular demonstration. The matter of this play and comedy was set forth diligently by an interpreter both to the neophytes and the pagans who were present. When, however, the army of Gideon fought with the Philistines, the pagans, fearing that they were going to be killed, began to run away, but were recalled gently (*caute*). . . . In the same play there were wars, such as those of David, Gideon, Herod. There was also the teaching of the Old and New Testaments.

This most surprising play shows little or no connexion with the liturgical drama as we know it, although the reference to the prophets and to the teaching of the Old and New Testaments is possibly to be taken as an indication that the Riga play was a dramatization of man's fall and redemption of an unexpectedly advanced degree of development.

The play recorded from Cividale[2] certainly belongs to the European tradition, and, coming as it does from the beginning of the fourteenth century, it may have been the earliest, or one of the earliest, complete cycles, and the pattern of the play may have passed with comparative rapidity from Italy to France and from France to England. It comes from *Cronaca Friuliana* by Giuliano da Cividale. The first entry is as follows:

> In the year of our Lord 1298 on the seventh day of May, namely, on the day of Pentecost and the two succeeding days, there was performed a representation of a play of Christ, that is, of the Passion, Resurrection, Ascension, Descent of the Holy Spirit, and the Coming of Christ to Judgement in the city courtyard of my Lord the Patriarch

[1] Creizenach, op. cit. i. 70–71; Chambers, op. cit. 70–71 and n.; Young, op. cit. ii. 542; *Gesta Alberti Livoniensis Episcopi*, ed. J. B. Gruber (Leipzig, 1740), p. 34.

[2] Young, op. cit. ii. 540–1. The dates and feasts in these entries are not consistent.

of Austria; this was done honourably and in praiseworthy fashion by the citizen clergy (*per Clerum civitatensem*).

The second entry is as follows:

In the year of our Lord 1303 there was performed by the Clergy, or by the lay chapter (*sive per Capitulum civitatense*), a play or rather plays as recorded below: in the first place, a play about the Creation of our first parents; next about the Annunciation to the Blessed Virgin; about the Nativity with many circumstances; and about the Passion and Resurrection; the Ascension and the Advent of the Holy Spirit; and about Antichrist and others; and finally about the Coming of Christ to the Judgement. And the aforesaid plays were performed solemnly in the courtyard of my Lord the Patriarch at the feast of Pentecost and the two days following, there being present the r. d. Ottobonus, Patriarch of the North, Master Jacobus q. D., bishop of the city of Ottonellum, and many other nobles of the fortified towns of Friuli, this being the fifteenth day of May.

This records a complete play of what subsequently became the Corpus Christi pattern. It was publicly performed before the highest ecclesiastical and civic dignitaries.

There are also other records of dramatic activities in the twelfth century, two of which, because they suggest plays on a large scale, should be mentioned. A record from Regensburg or Ratisbon,[1] a city of Lower Bavaria, is as follows:

In the year of our Lord 1194 there was celebrated in Ratisbon an *ordo* of the Creation of the Angels and the Fall of Lucifer and his followers, of the Creation and Fall of Man, and of the Prophets, this under Celestine III, Emperor Henry then reigning, always august, and Conradus ruling there the episcopate, on the seventh day of the Ides of February.

If 'prophets' is loosely used to denote patriarchs, or perhaps in any case, this Ratisbon play would be a very early example of an Old Testament play. It is especially interesting in its performance of a play of the Fall of Lucifer and the evil angels, a popular subject that appeared widely in the great fourteenth- and fifteenth-century cycles, but was not provided for in the *cursus* of the liturgical year and one that often shows by its style that it is an addition to the conventional cycles.

In London also there were extensive dramatic activities, although they are not particularized thus early. William Fitzstephen in his

[1] Creizenach, op. cit. i. 70; Young, op. cit. ii. 542; Chambers, op. cit. ii. 71–72; *Annales Ratisponenses*, ed. W. Wattenbach, *M.G.H.*, xvii. 590.

Life of St. Thomas Becket (*c.* 1170–80)[1] praises London for the religious nature of its plays:

> London has, instead of theatrical spectacles and stage plays, holy dramas, representations of miracles that holy confessors have wrought or the representations of the sufferings that the constancy of martyrs have illuminated.

York statutes of the thirteenth century (*c.* 1255) reveal something of the state of the religious drama at that centre:

> The treasurer shall provide stars with everything that pertains to them except *cirpos*, which the Bishop of the Boys or the fools [*futurorum* for *fatuorum*] shall provide, one on the natal night of the Lord for the Shepherds and two stars on the night of Epiphany if a presentation of the Three Kings is called for.

FINAL FORMS

The Benediktbeuern plays have already been described as possibly the farthest advanced groupings of biblical scenes that are still in Latin and almost certainly still liturgical and enacted within the church, but Germany furnishes also a number of interesting documents in an early vernacular stage. It has also a considerable body of plays in a variety of forms that tell us a good deal about the history and development of the religious drama. The patterns followed are not like those of France and England, but the manner of growth was apparently pretty much the same.[2] That is, there seems to have been an original core made up of one or sometimes a considerable number of traditional scenes from the liturgical drama that underwent, as time went on, various changes and amplifications but never lost its original features. There is evidence of some minor influences of play upon play and some similar groupings of plays in certain regions that suggest a common remote origin in those areas. But, for the most part, each German play seems to have retained its peculiarities and characteristic emphases. The result is that the religious drama presents in what it has retained a picture in vastly amplified form of the contents and variety of the drama of the medieval church. The German religious drama has a large number of single scenes or simple

---

[1] Chambers, op. cit. ii. 379–80, 399; Young, loc. cit., pp. 542–3.

[2] Creizenach, op. cit. i. 100–7, 210–19; Pearson, op. cit. ii. 246–406; Froning, op. cit.; F. J. Mone, *Altteutsche Schauspiele* (Leipzig, 1841), pp. 109–44.

combinations and a series of groupings of almost every conceivable form. One need not doubt that, if original dramatic offices had been preserved in sufficient numbers, almost every German vernacular play could be traced back to simple beginnings in the liturgical drama or to simple combinations made as the drama was outgrowing the church. It is necessary to say this because of the persistence of the modern and inapplicable idea that the medieval religious drama grew from one stem and had one order and course of develop/ ment.

There are simple plays from Trier and Wolfenbüttel.[1] The former, preserved in a manuscript of the fourteenth or fifteenth century, has been mentioned above as an example of the substitution of the vernacular for the Latin and as written in verse. It contains only a *Visitatio* and a *Hortulanus*. The Wolfenbüttel play, from a fifteenth/ century manuscript, shows growth to considerable proportions of the theme of the ointment/seller, a general characteristic of German plays. It reveals secular and religious growth in other respects also, since Pilate and the Setting of the Watch and the Harrowing of Hell are added to the original events of an Easter play. There are also two fragments, dated in the thirteenth century, of a manuscript originating at Kloster Muri in Switzerland,[2] and regarded by Creizenach as the oldest of German religious plays. It is possible from the small frag/ ments to tell only that the play had a lively scene of the ointment/ seller, that Pilate (already provided with a comic servant) played a boastful part, and that there was in the complete play a scene of the Harrowing of Hell. There are elaborate and early Easter plays, much admired by Creizenach,[3] from Innsbruck, Berlin, and Vienna. The Berlin play is a mere fragment devoted to the ointment/seller, but the Innsbruck play is well preserved.[4] It comes from a manuscript dated in 1391 and is said rather inconclusively to have political bearings. The play has an *Expositor ludi*. Pilate, a boastful tyrant described as 'ein König aus der Iudenland', sets his watch at the Sepulchre with every sort of buffoonery. This scene is followed by a merry Harrowing

---

[1] Creizenach, op. cit. i. 112–14; Froning, op. cit., pp. 15–16, 46–62.

[2] Creizenach, op. cit. i. 114–15; Froning, op. cit., pp. 225–44; ed. Bartsch, *Germania*, viii. 273 ff.

[3] Creizenach, op. cit. i. 115–21; Froning, op. cit., pp. 94–102 (selections), 302–24.

[4] Mone, *Altteutsche Schauspiele*, loc. cit.; Creizenach, op. cit. i. 116–20.

of Hell with an extensive group of the occupants of Hell drawn satirically from the occupations and pastimes of the world. The ointment-seller also appears accompanied by the omnipresent comic servant. The main popular interest of the play is no doubt already embodied in these secular additions but room is also found for reverent scenes of the Three Marys at the Sepulchre, Jesus and the incredulous Thomas, and a dialogue between Peter and John. Later and fuller German Easter plays, such as those from Redintin, Vienna, and Erlau,[1] need not concern us here, and yet it is already clear that the German medieval religious plays tended to grow by the develop-ment of comedy, and that such plays, as will be seen, differ in this important respect from the contemporary English religious plays.

Among the earlier German plays the Vienna Passion play is much the most significant for our purposes, since its general form was widely adopted in England.[2] It begins with the Fall of Lucifer followed by the Fall of Man, and the play, although imperfect, comprehends the three basal parts of Christian theology—the Fall, the Atonement, and the Resurrection. The manuscript dates from the early fourteenth century. Although it is chronologically arranged—Creation, Fall, and Redemption—it is nevertheless a Passion play and, as we shall see, does not have the historical completeness of the Corpus Christi play. The rebellion of Lucifer and the expulsion from Heaven of Lucifer and the wicked angels, which are not provided for in the Bible or the liturgy, are prologic features widely adopted in the medieval religious drama both, we may believe, for completeness and for the sake of the diablerie particularly characteristic of the German plays. In the Vienna Passion play the part of Satan is already greatly amplified and is provided with no less than two other devils. There is also provision for a well-developed temptation of Eve and fall of Adam, with a sorry lot of villains and cheats to be their companions in Hell. The next structural element is a Mary Magdalen play with the Resuscitation of Lazarus, which Creizenach rightly regards as like that in the Benediktbeuern Passion play. After this scene the play breaks off, but there is no doubt that the Vienna play is a Passion play. Some confirmation of this fact is to be found in a Czech

[1] Creizenach, loc. cit., pp. 238–41; Froning, op. cit., pp. 107–98.
[2] Creizenach, loc. cit., pp. 120–1 *et passim*.

Passion play borrowed from the Vienna play when the latter was in a simpler form.[1]

The most complete and typical of the early German plays of the Passion is the St. Gall Passion play.[2] According to Mone and Creizenach the play is not Swiss but German. No date has been determined, but the play is certainly very early. It follows the biblical stories closely, as do liturgical dramas, and this Creizenach strangely regards as the choice and style of an author rather than as an evidence of age and primitivity due to the closeness of the St. Gall play to one or more simple Latin originals. St. Augustine appears as prologue and expositor as in the Benediktbeuern Christmas play. There are prophets, but the number of them has been abridged no doubt from the use of the play by simple secular actors. The important thing is that the St. Gall Passion play presents the events of Christ's life from the Wedding at Cana through the Resurrection. Although rather bare in treatment, it is well stocked with action and event, some features of which are special, such as a scene of the Foot-washing, the Suicide of Judas, and the *Planctus* of the Virgin Mary. Pilate's Wife's Dream is there, as also the idea that Satan had changed sides and was really attempting to prevent Christ's sacrifice, which, he saw, would be contrary to his interests. There is also present the much-loved comic servant of the German plays, but, in general, the St. Gall Passion play is in its serious action a genuine Passion play. It is noteworthy that it has a good many Latin tags as if its translation from a Latin original were fairly recent.

Mone also prints from a St. Gall manuscript of the fourteenth century an extensive and interesting Christmas play[3] that is typical in its contents. It begins with a *Prophetae*, very simple and direct, in which each prophet introduces himself as he begins to speak—'Ich bin der alte Balaam', &c. It has a Betrothal of the Blessed Virgin Mary, an Annunciation, a *Pastores*, a Magi with the affair of Herod, a Presentation in the Temple, the Slaughter of the Innocents, the Flight

---

[1] The relation of the Czech play to the Vienna Passion play is studied by Hildegarde Wanous in an unpublished master's dissertation on file in the library of the University of Minnesota. Along with other Czech religious dramas, the play is translated into English in that work.

[2] Creizenach, op. cit. i. 122-3 *et passim*; Mone, *Schauspiele des Mittelalters*, i. 72 ff.

[3] Creizenach, op. cit., i. 123-4; Mone, ibid., pp. 143 ff.

into Egypt—all with more or less special amplifications. That the Christmas and the Easter groups came together early appears in a frag-mentary play dated by Creizenach in the middle of the thirteenth cen-tury, from Kloster Himmelgarten near Nordhausen.[1] The fragments indicate the presence in that Christmas play of a *Stella*, a Flight into Egypt, the Calling of Peter and Andrew, and the Wedding at Cana. Another early German vernacular religious drama is a play of the Wise and the Foolish Virgins in two manuscripts, one of 1428 from Hesse, and the other from Thuringia, which is, according to Creize-nach, perhaps a hundred years the older of the two.[2] Both seem to be normal developments of the original liturgical office.[3]

One gets an excellent idea of the medieval drama in Germany in its greater standard forms from some of the later plays. For example, a document of great interest is summarized by Creizenach.[4] It is called *Ordo sive Registrum* and is spoken of as the Frankfurt *Dirregierrolle*. It seems to be a sort of director's guide for the performance of an extensive religious drama, like a greatly expanded plot for the presenta-tion of an Elizabethan play, giving scenes, stage directions, names of characters, and first words of speakers. It is marked as the work of one Baldemar von Peterweil, who is mistakenly thought of as the author. The play belongs to the middle of the fourteenth century. It began with an elaborate *Prophetae*, St. Augustine acting as prologue and expositor. This is followed by a Temptation in the Wilderness, the Calling of Peter and Andrew, the Repentance of Mary Magdalen, the Raising of Lazarus; then the Passion, Death, and Burial. This was the action of the first day, which, it will be noticed, follows, after the first two episodes, the same order as the Benediktbeuern Passion play. The second day called for the Harrowing of Hell, the Setting of the Watch, the Ointment-seller, the *Visitatio* with scenes among the apostles, and the Incredulity of Thomas; finally an Ascension and, as an after-piece, the widely used disputation between Ecclesia and Synagoga. There is a long Passion play from Alsfeld (1501),

---

[1] Creizenach, loc. cit., pp. 124–5; play ed. E. Sievers, *Zeitschrift für deutsche Philologie*, xxi. 385–404.

[2] Creizenach, loc. cit., pp. 126–8.

[3] For early plays on Antichrist and the Last Judgement see ibid., *passim*; H. Jellinghaus, *Zeitschrift für deutsche Philologie*, xxiii. 426–38.

[4] Creizenach, loc. cit., pp. 219–21; text in Froning, loc. cit., pp. 325–74.

detailed in treatment and full of extraneous comedy, and a fully developed and rather more scriptural Passion play from Frankfurt;[1] also a Passion play from Heidelberg.[2] These three with some others establish a prevailing type of the western and southern German Passion play, which, in general, has no Old Testament plays, or at least does not begin with Old Testament plays, usually has no plays of the Nativity, and no plays of the Last Judgement. There are of course great individual differences among them. The Passion plays of the Tyrol seem to form a separate group and to be based originally on the Passion and Resurrection only.[3]

Something quite unlike these forms appears in a late fifteenth-century play from Eger in Czechoslovakia.[4] It resembles in general the fragmentary Vienna Passion play but has the fullest and most elaborate series of Old Testament plays to be found in the German field. This series begins with the Fall of Lucifer and ends with Solomon's Judgement, having even the rare scene of Lamech and the Death of Cain. The Eger manuscript has also a full set of Nativity plays, a Passion, a Resurrection, and an Ascension, and has the inclusiveness and range of a Corpus Christi play, although it is not so called. A play from Künzelzau (1479) achieves the completeness of the Corpus Christi play, extending as it does from the Fall of Lucifer to Doomsday. It is called 'ein Frohnleichnamspiel' or Corpus Christi play, and, with other continental plays so termed, would seem to indicate that the Corpus Christi play was a recognized form on the continent of Europe as well as in England and that its formal characteristic was the dramatization chronologically of the full story of the liturgical year. The Künzelzau play seems also to have had some connexion with the Corpus Christi Procession and was itself acted at stations along the way. This also appears to have been the case at Barcelona in Spain. A fragmentary Low German play, supposed by Creizenach to have been written by Arnold of Immessen, although, of course, Arnold was merely a redactor, covered in its complete form the whole of biblical history. Another Low German

---

[1] Froning, op. cit., pp. 375–534, 547–672.

[2] G. Milchsack, *Die Oster- und Passionsspiele* in Bibl. des litterarischen Vereins in Stuttgart, Bde. cl, clvi; Creizenach, op. cit. i. 222–3.

[3] Creizenach, op. cit. i. 225–6 *et passim*; Wackernell, loc. cit.

[4] Creizenach, loc. cit., pp. 223–4 *et passim*; Milchsack, loc. cit.

play found in a manuscript in the Royal Library at The Hague and dated at the end of the fourteenth century is also practically of full scope, and its simplicity and faithfulness to Scripture suggest that it is very ancient.[1] Creizenach,[2] however, regards the Corpus Christi play from an Innsbruck manuscript, dated in 1391, as the oldest Corpus Christi play of all.

Of plays outside the larger groups there were in Germany apparently considerable numbers. One of the most significant is an Assumption of the Blessed Virgin Mary from Innsbruck.[3] It is associated in the manuscript with two subjects that played a great part in the later medieval drama, namely, the Siege of Jerusalem and the Acts of the Apostles. Dramas on these subjects are to be found in other countries, and it may be that the Assumption was the starting-point for these two great plays. There are also various German saints' plays (St. George, St. Helena, St. Dorothea, Theophilus), and, most interesting of all, a play of Antichrist and the Last Judgement, the two subjects being still united. Such a play is mentioned in the records at various times in the fifteenth century, and from Lucerne in Switzerland comes a late play (1549) in the combined form.[4] We are not too much concerned with the various German Fastnachtspiele, some of which treat subjects also handled in the regular drama, but we should mention an Easter play from Redintin,[5] a vernacular play that remains reverent and in line with the liturgy. In those respects it is to be compared with the English play, *The Burial and Resurrection*, in Bodleian MS. e Museo, 160, f. 140. In Germany the Christmas plays continued in some places to lead a life independent of the great cycles and nearly always underwent amplifications characteristic of the German liking for comicality.

The development of the medieval religious drama in France is badly documented, and this is unfortunate for us since what happened

---

[1] Ibid., pp. 229–30; play edited by Julius Zacher, *Zeitschrift für deutsches Altertum*, ii. 302–50; play breaks off after Peter's denial.
[2] Innsbruck MS. 1391; Creizenach, loc. cit., p. 227; Mone, *Schauspiele*, loc. cit. i. 145 ff.
[3] Creizenach, loc. cit., p. 229.
[4] Ibid., pp. 232–3. See R. Brandstetter, loc. cit., lxxv. 383–418; K. Reuschel, *Die deutschen Weltgerichtsspiele des Mittelalters und der Reformationszeit* (Leipzig, 1906), pp. 207–320 *et passim*. On the German religious plays in general see Creizenach, op. cit. i. 89–99, 112–30, 219–29, *et passim*, and Ehrismann, op. cit., T. 2, 2, 2, pp. 570–3, with references.
[5] Creizenach, op. cit. i. 240–1 *et passim*.

in France in the formative stages is undoubtedly a key to what happened in England. Aside from the *Ordo Adae* and the fragmentary Tours *Resurrection*, there is almost nothing from the transitional period. The fifteenth century supplies mainly miracle plays, and there is a great abundance of them. There is from 1380 the story of the damage wrought by the discharge of a cannon in hell in what must have been the performance of a Passion play. Nevers in 1396 supplies plays of the Passion and of the Vengeance of Our Lord. There were Passion plays at St. Maur in 1398 and at Vienne in 1400. A brotherhood of the Passion was established in Paris in 1402. The Ste Geneviève manuscript, although not itself early, contains four mystery plays all of which are in rather simple, early forms: Nativity, *Stella*, Passion, and Resurrection.[1] There is some indication that these plays may have been acted together. The plays are relatively unsophisticated and are close enough to the Latin liturgical drama to indicate what must have happened in France as elsewhere, that is, that the religious drama grew by many revisions and accretions from simple beginnings to be found in the Latin liturgical plays. We should not let the strange failure of historians of the drama to understand a communal or rather incremental method of growth and their somewhat anachronistic belief in individual authorship blind us to this fact. The French religious drama of the Middle Ages must have passed over the same road as that of Germany and the rest of Europe. The first play in the Ste Geneviève manuscript begins with the Fall of Man and follows that with the scene of Seth and with prophets praying for deliverance from bondage. The play of the Magi is greatly amplified. Otherwise the plays are faithful enough to their sources. Besides the plays in this manuscript there is an immensely long (25,000 lines) play from Arras, which combines topics from Christmastide, Passiontide, and Easter. After that, one is confronted by the gigantic Passion play of Arnoul Greban than which there is nothing more elaborate in the medieval religious drama. It is odd that so good a historian as Creizenach[2] regards Greban, who merely told the same story in a traditional form and often in the same words, as an original

---

[1] Achille Jubinal, *Mystères inédits du quinzième siècle* (2 t. Paris, 1837), ii. 1–379; Creizenach, op. cit. i. 248–50.
[2] Creizenach, op. cit. i (1893), 251, 256, *et passim*.

author rather than as a skilful redactor. The surprise is increased when one finds the same historian attempting to derive the Passion play of Troyes, a traditional and composite work, from Greban's redaction of a similar work. Of course there are resemblances, some of them ancient and exceedingly close, between independent plays, such as the Passion of Troyes and that of Valenciennes, and the later and no doubt more artistic work of Arnoul Greban and Jean Michel. For lack of documents in the middle distance there is little enough to be learned about the development of the medieval religious drama in France, but certainly there is little to be gained by looking at it from the wrong end and by putting last things first. There are other French Passion plays, including great plays from Semur, Arras, and Angers, and various fragments.[1]

There are also many other medieval religious plays, besides plays of the Passion, recorded or preserved in France. An overgrown Nativity cycle comes from Rouen,[2] which draws extensively on medieval religious writers, such as Comestor and Nicholas de Lyra. There is also the famous *Le Mistère du Viel Testament*.[3] This is recognized by its editors as a composite work but is thought of as an independent, and presumably original, Old Testament cycle, and so, to be sure, it may be. Such a grouping may have originated by the joining together of separate plays from the period of Septuagesima and Sexagesima when *lectiones* were drawn from the Pentateuch, but the general pattern of man's fall and redemption calls for plays of Adam and the patriarchs as preliminary to the Passion and the Redemption. Indeed, the plays of the Old Testament have no theological significance in and for themselves. Such plays appear only in France and may have come into existence as separate units at a late time and as a matter of convenience. Since *Le Mistère du Viel Testament* looks constantly forward to the Redemption, one is inclined to believe that it came into existence by the mechanical cutting in two of a full play of the Corpus Christi type. Some confirmation of this view comes, as we shall see, from its relation to the Chester plays in England. *Le Mistère du Viel Testament* is most elaborate and contains many plays on Old Testa-

---

[1] See E. Picot, 'Fragments inédits de mystères de la Passion', *Romania*, xix. 263–82; Julleville, *Les Mystères*, ii. 226–627.

[2] Ed. Le Verdier (2 t. Rouen, 1885, 1886). See Creizenach, loc. cit., pp. 200, 207.

[3] Ed. Rothschild and Picot, Société des Anciens Textes Français (6 t. Paris, 1878–1891).

ment subjects not provided for in the general tradition. The question involved is whether *Le Mistère du Viel Testament* is a literary aggregation of Old Testament plays around an original and ancient Old Testament cycle or was arrived at by the partition of some lost cycle of the fullest scope.

There is a drama of Job in *Le Mistère* and also an independent play on that subject.[1] One would think of such a play as a relatively late invention, although the Book of Job was read in September during the services of the liturgical year, and the play of Job like others may have grown from ancient liturgical beginnings. Several independent dramas on Old Testament subjects lived on in France throughout the period of record, such as Abraham and Isaac, Daniel, Esther, Jonah, Susanna, Tobias. Creizenach thinks of such plays as having originated from the splitting up of the Old Testament cycle instead of being, as they probably are, originally liturgical plays that had led from the earliest times an independent existence, or perhaps, in some cases, relatively late compositions. Whether he thinks mistakenly of smaller ancient units, such as the Nativity and Mary Magdalen, as having come into existence by borrowing from larger groups and cycles is hard to determine.

French miracle plays are too abundant to be enumerated in this place, and, since plays about the lives and martyrdoms of saints are almost non-existent in England, we may omit them. The most striking feature is the great series of *Miracles de Nostre Dame.*[2]

Italy must of course have been among the leaders in the origination and development of the medieval religious drama, and progress there seems to have been very rapid. It is hard to tell from available accounts of religious drama just what happened in Italy.[3] The fact that some of the oldest pieces are already in the vernacular and that the lost Cividale play had achieved by the beginning of the fourteenth century such an extraordinary development suggests that Italy was far ahead of the rest of Europe. The religious drama there would also

---

[1] Creizenach, loc. cit., pp. 263–4.

[2] Ibid., pp. 143–54, 269 ff. *Miracles de Nostre Dame* were edited by G. Paris and U. Robert, Société des Anciens Textes (8 t. Paris, 1876–93); Julleville, op. cit. i. 115–86.

[3] A. D'Ancona, *Origini del Teatro italiano* (loc. cit.), and *Sacre Rappresentazioni dei secoli xiv, xv e xvi, raccolte e illustrate* (1872); Mario Apollonio, *Storia del teatro italiano* (3 v. Florence, 1943–6); Creizenach, op. cit. i. 299–304.

have suffered early from the encroachments of the Renaissance. D'Ancona[1] believes that much of the Italian religious drama took the form of dumb show, but the idea that it did so is improbable, and proof is lacking. There is no doubt, however, that in Italy the religious drama assumed unequalled spectacular qualities. Creize nach[2] argues on insufficient grounds that the great processions of Vicenza (1379), Milan (1336), Florence (1454), and elsewhere, some of which reveal the presence of the full scope of the Corpus Christi play, were not accompanied by acted drama. Texts and records of the medieval religious drama are not numerous, but such as exist, plays from Christmas and Easter for example, record a normal situation in Italy with, however, a development far advanced beyond the rest of Europe.

The medieval religious drama of Holland seems to have been of the German pattern, but with characteristic subjects and features of its own.[3] There was a region of normal development in Provence and another, apparently associated with it, in Spain.[4] Indeed, the early forms of the mystery plays seem to have appeared widely all over Europe. An area of special development not connected with the English plays is that of Brittany and Cornwall, where the language was Celtic. There are great Passion plays preserved from both regions that are manifestly of one general form and content. It is almost absurd to argue that such plays are derived from Arnoul Greban or Jean Michel.[5]

One of the interesting and important things to observe in a survey of the medieval religious drama of the continent of Europe is the wide distribution of the Corpus Christi play and its recognition as a special form.[6] We have noted its appearance in Italy. The Corpus Christi play as such can hardly have been instituted before the begin ning of the fourteenth century and, in view of the record of the lost Cividale play, its first institution may have been in Italy. There were plays of the Corpus Christi type in Spain, and there is a Corpus Christi play recorded as acted in Barcelona. Historians of drama tend to adopt an ill-supported theory of dumb show with reference to

---

[1] *Origini*, i. 92 *et passim*.
[3] Ibid., pp. 339–42.
[5] Ibid., pp. 343–5.

[2] Creizenach, loc. cit., pp. 301, 303, *et passim*.
[4] Ibid., pp. 346–9.
[6] Ibid., pp. 170–4, 227–9, *et passim*.

the Corpus Christi play, and the confusion is not unnatural, since there seems always to have been a Corpus Christi procession, in which pageants and characters from the play customarily appeared, as well as the play itself. Records of processions, which were only a part of the ceremony, have often been mistaken for the whole. Of course a Corpus Christi procession supplied with traditional biblical scenes presupposes a Corpus Christi play, and a procession would lose its meaning and its continuity from year to year without a Corpus Christi play with its component scenes and its responsible actors and managers. This becomes obvious from a study of the English Corpus Christi plays to be considered in later chapters of this book. For example, plays were forbidden to be acted in the Corpus Christi procession in Prague in 1366. Creizenach states[1] that a situation not unlike that in England prevailed in Zerbst and in Freiburg im Breisgau. There is a Corpus Christi play in a Provençal manuscript described as of 'the later Middle Ages',[2] which has, like the English cycles, an ending with the Last Judgement, and it must have been a Corpus Christi play of that form that established the English pattern. We can in this connexion be reasonably sure that a Corpus Christi play was translated into English to form the Chester cycle, and that the earlier part of that cycle was an earlier and simpler form of *Le Mistère du Viel Testament*.

English plays are left for later detailed consideration, and it will appear that they in their more limited field present among themselves the same aspect of variety, both in contents and arrangement, that has appeared in the foregoing sketch of the medieval religious drama on the European continent. They too had as a unifying principle the enormous scheme of Christian theology set up by the Church as the services of the liturgical year. We have seen that there were many different groupings with patterns within groups, that some single plays stood alone throughout their career, that the simplicity and relative bareness of the earlier plays was due to their closeness to the liturgy and not to a lack of inventiveness on the part of those who translated many of them from the Latin and perhaps gradually set

[1] Ibid., pp. 172, 189, 290.
[2] A. Thomas, 'Notice sur un recueil de mystères provençaux du quinzième siècle', *Annales du Midi*, ii. 385–418; *Mystères provençaux*, ed. A. Jeanroy et H. Teulie (Toulouse, 1893).

them up in the vernacular, and that, as we proceed farther and farther from the sources, extraneous elements intrude themselves more and more into the simple biblical or liturgical outlines—also, we may believe, gradually built up by one forgotten redactor after another. No names of authors or redactors appear except accidentally until the Middle Ages were over and the drama no longer medieval. From the point of view of the religious zeal that created these plays and kept them alive there is the story of one long progressive loss. One may prefer the volubility of a half-baked Renaissance to the sermonizing fullness of the fifteenth century when the Middle Ages were on the wane, but it is hard to see that either of these literary phases could be preferred to the innocent and reverent simplicity of the fourteenth and earlier centuries.

Comicality or buffoonery was an ancient intruder, and, as the German plays show, its intrusiveness and its banality increased as time went on. It is obvious that the Middle Ages did not feel the comic as a shock even when it was associated with the most sacred events. But the comic was not the only intruder. There was also a greater and greater introduction of legend, didactic religious matter, and ornamental padding. The French plays, for example, tend to be incredibly loquacious.

IV

Medieval Religious Drama in England
The Medieval Stage

FROM the very beginnings of the religious drama in the *Quem quaeritis* trope in the medieval church the conditions of performance dictated the convention of the multiple stage. That convention required that places actually close together should often be accepted by performers and spectators as far apart. In the *Quem quaeritis* there are two such places actually only the width of the chancel apart but imagined as at a distance from each other: the *sepulchrum Christi*, regularly and permanently placed on the north side of the chancel, and the stalls of the choir representing a place of assembly of the disciples in Jerusalem, which may have been on the other side of the chancel or wherever the architecture of the church had placed it. There is even in this early form a suggestion of pretended travel between places close together as if they were far apart. The following passage translated from the *Regularis Concordia* of St. Ethelwold will make this matter clear:[1]

While the third lection [at Matins] is being recited let four brothers costume themselves, of whom one shall be clothed in an alb, and as if for a purpose let him proceed to go secretly to the place of the sepulchre, and there let him sit quietly holding a palm in his hand. While the third responsion is being sung, let the remaining three advance, all indeed clad in copes, holding thuribles with incense in their hands, step by step (*pedetemptim*) in likeness of persons seeking something, to the place of the sepulchre. These things are, you see, done in imitation of the angel sitting at the monument and of the women coming with spices to anoint the body of Jesus. When therefore he who is sitting there shall see the three come near him, as it were wandering about and seeking something, let him begin in a modulated voice, but sweet, to sing, *Quem quaeritis*. This having been sung to the end, let the three respond in unison, *Ihesum Nazarenum*. The angel says to them, *Non est hic: surrexit sicut praedixerat. Ite nuntiate quia surrexit a mortuis*. At this voice of command let the three turn to the choir saying, *Alleluia: resurrexit dominus*. This having been said, let the one remaining at the tomb, as if calling them back, sing the anthem, *Venite et videte locum*: and while saying

[1] Chambers, op. cit. ii. 306–9; Young, op. cit. i. 249–52, 582–3.

these words let him arise, remove the veil, and show them the place now bare of the crucifix but yet containing the cloths in which the cross was wrapped. Having seen this, let them lay down the censers which they have used to cense the sepulchre, take up the cloths, extend them towards the choir to show that the Lord is risen and that he is not wrapped in them, and let them begin the antiphon, *Surrexit dominus de sepulchro,* and let the grave clothes be placed on the linen cloths of the altar. The antiphon finished, let the Prior, rejoicing in the triumph of our king because, death being conquered, he has achieved resurrection, begin the hymn *Te Deum laudamus.* When this has begun, let all the bells be struck.

A similar identification and fixation of various places for various actions accompany the growth of the Latin religious drama. The *Quem quaeritis* had its *sepulchrum* and its choir, the *Pastores* and the *Stella* had their *praesepe,* and in the *Pastores* there was a greater imagined distance, since the shepherds were tending their flocks in the fields when they heard the angels sing *Gloria in excelsis Deo,* and the angels themselves were somewhere aloft in the church; in the *Stella* there was not only a *praesepe* but a palace of Herod and some vaguely located action that took place on the open road. For the *Peregrini* a Fleury rubric provides 'a tabernacle in the likeness of the Castle of Emmaus'. These stations were called by various names, as *loca, domus,* and *sedes.* Chambers[1] speaks of the half-dozen such stations requisite for the play of the Raising of Lazarus and the Conversion of St. Paul. The Tegernsee *Antichristus,* a highly developed play, has not only a temple of the Lord, but seven regal thrones (*sedes regales*).

The Rouen *Prophetae* and, Chambers thinks, the *Antichristus* were played in church, as, there is no reason to doubt, were all the earlier plays. Following this idea that the first stations and actions were within the church, Chambers presents a most interesting interpretation of the verse prologue to the fragmentary Anglo-Norman play of the Resurrection. Following the description of the playing-places in that prologue to a Resurrection play, he locates these stations within the church or the chancel and provides a drawing of the result.[2] He quotes the Anglo-Norman Resurrection:

En ceste manere recitom	Tus les lius e les mansions:
La seinte resurrection.	Le crucifix primerement
Primerement apareillons	E puis apres le monument.

---

[1] Loc. cit., p. 79.
[2] Ibid., pp. 82–85; Pearson, op. cit. ii. 319–23; Mone, *Schauspiele des Mittelalters,* ii. 156.

Une jaiole i deit aver
Pur les prisons emprisoner.
Enfer seit mis de cele part,
E mansions de l'altre part,
E puis le ciel; et as estals
Primes Pilate od ces vassals.
Sis u set chivaliers aura.
Caïphas en l'altre serra;
Od lui seit la jeuerie,
Puis Joseph, cil d'Arimachie.
El quart liu seit danz Nichodemes.

Chescons i ad od sei les soens.
El quint les deciples Crist.
Les treis Maries saient el sist.
Si seit pourveu que l'om face
Galilee en mi la place;
Jemaus uncore i seit fait,
U Jhesu fut ai hostel trait;
E cum la gent est tute asise,
E la pes de tutez parz mise,
Dan Joseph, cil d'Arimachie,
Venge a Pilate, si lui die.

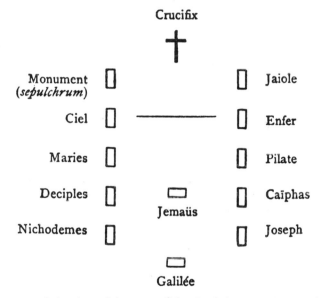

Conjectural drawing of the stage of the Anglo-Norman Resurrection.
From Chambers, *The Mediaeval Stage*, vol. ii, p. 82.

Chambers's comment is also enlightening:

The crucifix is where it would stand in the church, above the altar. The place of the monument corresponds to that most usual for the *sepulchrum* on the north side of the chancel. The positions of heaven and hell are those in the former case of the stairs up to the rood-loft, in the latter of the stairs down to the crypt; and what, in a church, should serve for hell and heaven but crypt and rood-loft? The Galilee answers to the porch at the west end of the church, which we know to have been so called; and the castle of Emmaus stands in the middle of the nave, just as it did in the Fleury *Peregrini*.

If this Anglo-Norman play was not acted in the church but out of doors, we may be sure that, in setting it up in the open, the producers followed the plan that had been gradually developed within the church itself and carried their indoor multiple stage into the open.

In confirmation of his theory Chambers goes farther and presents us with a reproduction of a sixteenth-century plan for the enactment of the Donaueschingen Passion play. It is the same in general form and order, but is more elaborate, since it is a stage for a Passion play as well as a Resurrection play:

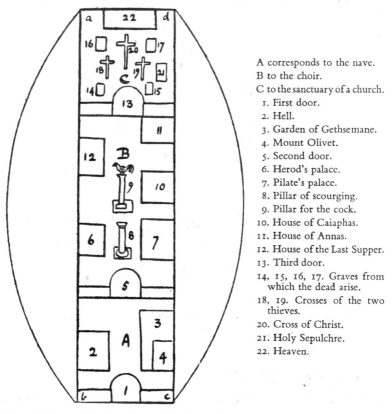

A corresponds to the nave.
B to the choir.
C to the sanctuary of a church.
1. First door.
2. Hell.
3. Garden of Gethsemane.
4. Mount Olivet.
5. Second door.
6. Herod's palace.
7. Pilate's palace.
8. Pillar of scourging.
9. Pillar for the cock.
10. House of Caiaphas.
11. House of Annas.
12. House of the Last Supper.
13. Third door.
14, 15, 16, 17. Graves from which the dead arise.
18, 19. Crosses of the two thieves.
20. Cross of Christ.
21. Holy Sepulchre.
22. Heaven.

Reproduction of the drawing of the stage of the Donaueschingen Passion play. From Chambers, *The Mediaeval Stage*, vol. ii, p. 84.

Let us now suppose that the plays have gone forth from the church into the community, as go forth they certainly did. How shall we provide opportunity for spectators in any considerable numbers to see the play with reasonable visibility? One way would be to act the play in a central area, normally circular, and to have the spectators look at it from every side. This device was probably the one resorted to most often in the staging of plays in fixed locations and was the basic form of the Tudor stage, although not many clear examples can be cited. J. Q. Adams in his *Chief Pre-Shakespearean Dramas*[1] publishes a reconstruction of a circular stage on which it seems most probable that the play *Mary Magdalene* from Digby MS. 133 was

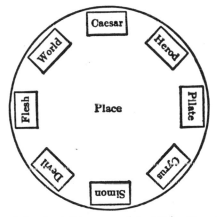

Conjectural drawing of the stage of the Digby *Mary Magdalene*.
From J. Q. Adams, *Chief Pre-Shakespearean Dramas*, p. 225.

performed. It will be observed that the drawing provides, not only for stations (*domus, sedes, loca*), as in the plays within the church, but also for a place, or *platea*, an open playing-place between or around the various stations. This *platea* goes back to the aisles and areas within the church, and looks forward to the Elizabethan drama. Where many scenes in that drama were actually located was a matter of no great importance to the author or the audience, since both were well acquainted with the use of a general playing-place, a general interstitial *platea*. Adams also reproduces an actual document, a drawing in the manuscript for the staging of *The Castle of Persever-ance*.[2] *The Conversion of St. Paul* was probably played on some such stage, although it may have been enacted on a platform out of doors:

[1] p. 225.
[2] p. 264. See also *The Macro Plays*, ed. F. J. Furnivall and Alfred W. Pollard, E.E.T.S. (London, 1904), frontispiece and p. 76.

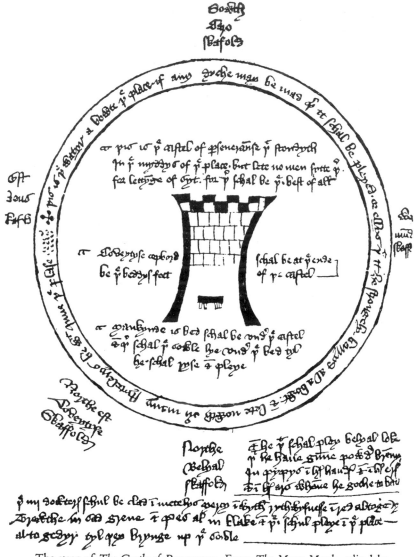

The stage of *The Castle of Perseverance*. From *The Macro Morals*, edited by
F. J. Furnivall for E.E.T.S.

Another way to solve this problem would be to arrange the stations
in an arc or a semicircle and let the audience watch the play from the
open side. This would give the audience a chance to be seated, and
it would be a most appropriate way in which to enact one of these

plays indoors, let us say, in a hall. There would be a platform at one end of the hall on which the stations might be placed, and the floor of the hall would be left for the occupancy of the audience. This solution, which is most important in the history of the modern stage, was arrived at we do not know how early. But we may say that whenever one of these composite dramas is being played indoors, we have a right to infer that the problem of the audience and the actors

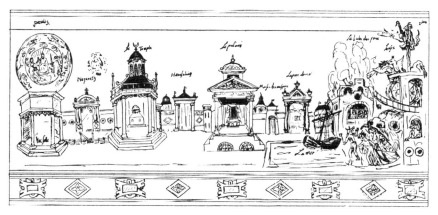

Drawing of the stage of the Valenciennes Passion play by Frank Eggers from the miniature in Bibl. Nat. MS. fr. 12536 (reproduced by Gustave Cohen, *Le Théâtre en France au Moyen Âge*, Paris, 1928, vol. i, pl. xl).

is probably being solved in some such way. Such stagings were used at a very early time, and, at any rate, would have suited well revivals of Terence and Plautus in the halls of schools and colleges, since in the classical plays there would be a series of successive unified scenes each in one place. There exists a most interesting picture of a composite stage in the famous manuscript of the *Mystère de la Passion*, played at Valenciennes in France in 1547. This manuscript is adorned with a series of brilliantly executed miniatures that are reproduced in heliogravure by Gustave Cohen in *Le Théâtre en France au Moyen Âge*.[1]

There is still another possibility, or maybe two, of solving the problem of the plays and the audience. In the first place, it is of course obvious that when composite plays were divided into separate scenes and played successively, or processionally, as in the Corpus Christi

[1] *Le Théâtre en France au Moyen Âge* (2 v. Paris, 1928), pls. xl–lx.

plays in England, the *loca* or *sedes* in the composite plays would have to be dispersed according to the needs of each individual scene or play. When that time came the particular settings or structures and arrangements needed for the playing of special episodes were loaded (or built) on large wagons and the plays carried out into various selected places in the streets and squares of cities and there enacted as units, so that the religious drama, having been gathered together into wholes made up of multiple parts, was again, in some places, re-distributed as single plays. This was not done with any special intent or regularity. One pageant or wagon might have several stations on it if more than one were needed, but we may be sure that each play always carried with it its bit of the *platea* for unlocated dramatic action. Indeed, in some plays actors, being dismounted from the pageant, made the street serve as a *platea* or playing-place, as in the famous case in the Coventry *Shearmen and Taylors' Pageant,* where occurs the quaint stage-direction: 'Here Erode ragis in the pagond and in the strete also.'[1]

The other possibility, which may have been followed at Wakefield and elsewhere, was to distribute pageants or stations round an open area, such as a public square in a town or city, and have the audience move from pageant to pageant as the play progressed. Whereas, when pageants were drawn from one selected open place, or station, to another, the audience would presumably remain at the same station and see each of the plays as they were successively played at that station.

One must of course understand that, when the units of a composite play were placed on pageants or movable stages in order to be drawn about a city and acted at various stations, it was not usual to pick up one solitary station (or *sedes* or *domus* or *locum* or *tabernaculum* or what not), since there were no units, except a few that were devoted to a single speech by a single speaker, that did not call for two or more *loca*. The movable stage on the pageant was therefore still a com-posite stage, still making use of the naïve convention of disregarding distances, although, of course, the convention of multiple location was greatly simplified. A good many, like the Presentation in the Temple (in its simple form), required only two; in that case the home of Joseph and Mary in Nazareth and the Temple in Jerusalem. In

[1] Adams, op. cit., p. 163; *Two Coventry Corpus Christi Plays,* loc. cit., p. 27.

others, especially when a number of themes were combined into one, there were a large number of different special places. *The Shearmen and Taylors' Pageant* of Coventry, for example, had about five localizations, although a good deal of the action is unlocated, that is, was performed in the *platea*. Guild plays were in fact usually played in small movable theatres constructed on the old principle. Some writers have been puzzled by this and have thought that the pageant vehicles must have been very large indeed, or that separate scaffolds were erected to serve as distant scenes. That was by no means necessary, since any distance, however small, might be received for any distance, however large.

There is indeed very little actual information about pageant vehicles. Two accounts are usually quoted, and one of them has unfortunately been taken as a norm. Dugdale in his *Antiquities of Warwickshire*[1] says that the Coventry pageants 'had theatres for the several scenes, very large and high, placed upon wheels, and drawn to all the eminent parts of the city, for the better advantage of the spectators'. He speaks of having known persons who had seen these plays.

The other account, which comes also from a date considerably later than the abolition of the plays at Chester, has been almost universally accepted, although manifestly it is wrong in many matters, or at best is applicable to pageants at Chester only, and is also too vague to be of much value. It is from *A Breviary, or Some few Collections of the City of Chester* in MS. Harl. 1944 written by David Rogers in 1609 on the basis of collections by his father, Robert Rogers, Archdeacon of Chester.[2] Archdeacon Rogers died in 1595 and would certainly have seen the Chester plays performed unless his manifest prejudice against them caused him to abstain. After recording the tradition of the origin of the plays at Chester and after giving a brief account of the playing, the dates, the stations in some parts of the city, and of the banns, he says,

These pagiantes or cariage was a highe place made like a howse with ij rowmes, beinge open on ye tope; the lower rowme they apparelled & dressed them selues; and in the higher rowme they played.

[1] See William Dugdale, *Antiquities of Warwickshire*, 2nd ed. revised by William Thomas (London, 1730), i. 183.

[2] First printed by Rupert Morris, *Chester in Plantagenet and Tudor Reigns*, available in *The Digby Mysteries*, ed. F. J. Furnivall, E.E.T.S. (London, 1882), pp. xviii–xxix; also in *The Trial and Flagellation with Other Studies in the Chester Cycle*, loc. cit., pp. 121–69 *et passim*.

But the actors in these plays did not dress themselves at the theatre or change their clothes. They came already clothed and played through several performances in one part and, as far as we know, did not change costumes at all. What misled Rogers was that by his time theatres had tiring houses or tiring rooms, and actors made changes in costume and sometimes doubled in their parts. He continues,

> And they stoode upon 6 wheeles. And when they had done with one carriage in one place, they wheeled the same from one streete to another: first from ye Abbeye gate to ye pentise, then to the watergate streete, then to the bridge streete, throughe the lanes, and so to the estgate streete. And thus they came from one streete to an other keapinge a direct order in euery streete; for before ye firste cariage was gone, ye seconde came, and so the thirde, and so orderly till ye laste was donne, all in order, without any stayeinge in any place; for, worde beinge broughte how euery place was neere done, they came, and made no place to tarye, till ye last was played.

This interesting document has been quoted in book after book as the way in which Corpus Christi plays were played, and it is, roughly speaking, the way in which many of them were played. But some Corpus Christi plays were not processional or, if they had once been carried about the city in regular rotation as the Chester plays were, they had ceased after a time to be so presented and had adopted a fixed location. As to the pageant vehicle itself, Rogers's description does not provide a workable stage for any known play and is not even generally correct, although it has been widely accepted as a true description.

A truer picture can be pieced together from an Inventory of Particulars appertaining to the Company of Grocers at Norwich.[1] We there have the following items:

> A Pageant, yt is to saye, a Howse of Waynskott paynted and buylded on a Carte wt fowre whelys.
> A square topp to sett over ye sayde Howse.
> A Gryffon, gylte, wt a fane to sett on ye sayde toppe.
> A bygger Iron fane to sett on ye ende of ye Pageante.
> iiij^{xx}iij small Fanes belongyng to ye same Pageante.
> A Rybbe colleryd Red.
> A cote & hosen wt a bagg & capp for dolor, steyned.
> 2 cotes & a payre hosen for Eve, stayned.
> A cote & hosen for Adam, Steyned.

[1] See Chambers, op. cit. ii. 388.

A cote wt hosen & tayle for ye serpente, steyned, wt a wt heare.
A cote of yellow buckram wt ye Grocers' arms for ye Pendon bearer.
An Angell's Cote & over hoses of Apis Skynns.
3 paynted clothes to hang abowte ye Pageant.
A face & heare for ye Father.
2 hearys for Adam & Eve.
4 head stallis of brode Inkle wth knopps and tassells.
6 Horsse Clothes, stayned, wt knopps & tassells.

This pageant is obviously a platform on wheels covered with a detachable ornamental roof probably held up by posts. It is open on all sides, but when our first parents were naked and unashamed the three painted cloths were hung round about the pageant at an appropriate height as in the *Ordo Adae*.[1] The truth of the matter is, pageants must have varied very greatly from one to another according to the demands of the scenes that were to be represented. In cases where heaven was part of the scene there was a demand for height, as also where there were hills or high buildings, such as temples. Some of them must have required very considerable differences of level within the one pageant, and these were matters affecting their structure. The whole matter has been confused because there could be no general description of a pageant except to say that it was a house-like structure built on four or six wheels.

The whole problem of the staging of medieval plays becomes somewhat clearer from a description of the early stage given by Joseph Strutt in his *Manners and Customs*.[2] His description is usually misunderstood, and nobody can tell where he got it, but it is really not hard to understand provided one realizes that Strutt is describing, not the wheeled pageants of certain northern English cities, but a great stage somewhat like the stage for the Passion play of Valenciennes, such as must have been in use in London and the south of England where mystery plays were acted on fixed multiple stages like those in customary use on the continent of Europe. He says,

In the early dawn of literature and when the sacred mysteries were the only theatrical performances, what is now called the stage did then consist of three several platforms, or stages raised one above another; on the uppermost sat the *pater cælestis*, surrounded

---

[1] For the play with the records just quoted see Adams, op. cit., pp. 88–93; also *The Non-Cycle Mystery Plays*, loc. cit., pp. xxvi–xxxv, 8–18.
[2] Edition of 1776, vol. iii, p. 130.

with his angels: on the second appeared the saints and glorified men; and the last and lowest was occupied by mere men, who had not yet passed from this transitory life to the regions of eternity. On the one side of this lowest platform was the resemblance of a dark pitchy cavern, from which issued appearance of fire and flames; and when it was necessary, the audience were treated with hideous yellings and noises, as imitative of the howlings and cries of the wretched souls tormented by the relentless daemons. From this yawning cave the devils themselves constantly ascended, to delight and to instruct the spectators; to delight, because they were usually the greatest jesters and buffoons that then appeared; and to instruct, for that they treated the wretched mortals who were delivered to them with the utmost cruelty, warning thereby all men care⁄ fully to avoid the falling into the clutches of such hardened remorseless spirits. But in the more improved state of the theatre, and when regular plays were introduced, all this mummery was abolished, and the whole cavern and the devils, together with the highest platform before mentioned, entirely taken away, two platforms only then remaining; and these continued a considerable time in use, the upper stage serving them for chambers, or any elevated situations.

This general account, possibly based to some extent on pictures, reveals the confusions of later generations as to how the mystery plays were staged. There is of course in Strutt's account an element of general conformity to inevitable conditions of staging. The Eliza⁄ bethan stage had a balcony or an elevated structure that served for scenes and speakers raised above the general level, such as castle walls and upper windows. Most of its business was carried out on a stage of normal elevation for the representation of affairs of street and house. Some plays, such as *Doctor Faustus*, must have been provided with an entrance to Hell corresponding to the ancient Hell⁄Mouth, and many of them called for trap⁄doors to lower regions. There are, indeed, no other ways by which differences in height can be represented. Strutt seems to think that all ancient stages were constructed with three, or rather four, permanent levels and that these levels were, like the stories of a house, one on top of another, a thing which is absurd. The picture of the stage of the Passion play from Valenciennes shows that, although differing in height, the structures were side by side. There must have been plenty of such composite stages in England, particu⁄ larly in southern England where the Passion play and not the Corpus Christi play was the prevailing type. As to the level he provides for 'saints and glorified men' intermediate between high heaven and streets and floors, he may have had in mind the thrones of princes and other dignitaries who on the stage he knew were seated above the common herd and yet not so high as God and the angels. If a particular play in the Corpus Christi cycle called for the appearance of Divinity, and by no means all of them did, we may be sure that an elevated station, as much as might be, was provided for in the construction of the pageant.

CORPUS CHRISTI PLAYS

The Feast of Corpus Christi is celebrated on the Thursday after Trinity Sunday, in honour of the Holy Eucharist. The origin of the feast is attributed to St. Juliana, a Belgian nun who was born in 1193 and died in 1258. As a result of a lifelong devotion to the cause of instituting a special feast in honour of the Body of the Lord she brought the matter before various great church dignitaries in her own country and finally before Pope Urban IV, who sanctioned her proposal. Robert de Thorete, then bishop of Liége, was about to cause through his synod the celebration of such a feast in 1247, but he died before it was carried through. There were other unsuccessful attempts, but the feast was promulgated by Pope Urban IV, confirmed by Pope Clement V, and ordered to be adopted at the council of Vienne in 1311. An office for the new feast, always praised for its great beauty, was composed at the pope's request by St. Thomas Aquinas, and indulgences of forty to one hundred days were provided for those who participated. None of the papal bulls called for a procession on the feast day in the fourteenth century, and yet a procession became its leading characteristic as a festival. Schaff-Herzog states that Pope John XXII (1316–34) instituted the procession, but apparently processions had already been used in the celebration of the feast. After the council of Vienne the feast spread with great rapidity. It was celebrated at Cologne in 1306, at Worms in 1315, at Strassburg in 1316, at Canterbury in 1318, at Ipswich in 1325, at London in 1347, and at Coventry in 1348. These are recorded instances of early adoption, but there were certainly many others.

The Corpus Christi procession was normally made up of a body of ecclesiastics, religious organizations, and ordinary worshippers who followed the Host from one location to another, usually from a starting-point, through a town or city by way of various churches and holy places, and back to the point of departure. This was always the essence of the Corpus Christi procession, but in some places there were added to the group actors and groups of actors from a full-scope religious drama, one that extended from the morning of creation to the day of final judgement. Why this was done in the first place is hard to see, but it is a matter of great interest. One can only advance what seems to be a probable conjecture. The liturgy of Corpus Christi day, although a noble exposition of the idea of the Atonement most broadly conceived, has nothing in it that would suggest an ocular and corporeal representation of the whole story of man's fall and redemption. There is no doubt, of course, that the presentation was appropriate, and that fact may have caused the plays to be added to the Corpus Christi procession. But, even so, the institution of the Corpus Christi play bears the marks of an invention. Such plays were not set up everywhere, and the casual spread from place to place throughout Europe would seem to be the following of an attractive ecclesiastical fashion. There was performed at Cividale in 1298 and 1303 a play of the prevailing form, and the device of adding such plays to the procession must have been first used in some city, possibly in Italy, and must have spread thence irregularly throughout the rest of Europe.

The Corpus Christi festival, and with it its procession, made its way very quickly over England, one might say over Great Britain and Ireland. The decree of Pope John XXII ordered not only the celebration of the feast of Corpus Christi in its proper liturgical form but also an attendant procession, this being symbolic of the procession of the Ark of the Covenant in the Jewish religion. Sprott said that the feast of Corpus Christi was a confirmed institution by 1318, and he was right. The festival was declared a principal feast of Canterbury in 1317, and there is mention of special services appointed for the festival.[1] There is also a significant entry in *Historia Monasterii Sancti Petri Gloucestriae*,[2] which says (1318), *Nota de festivitate Corporis Christi. Anno Domini Millesimo trecentesimo decimo octavo incoepit festivitas de Corpore Christi generaliter celebrari per totam ecclesiam anglicanam.* In considering the processional feature of the Corpus Christi festival, it is important to note that, although a procession was required, a wide

[1] Hist. MSS. Comm., Eighth Report, vii. 321.
[2] Rolls Series. *Chronicles and Memorials of Great Britain and Ireland during the Middle Ages,* ii. 44.

latitude was allowed to each diocese or parish as to the kind, extent, and manner of the procession. The fact that in large parts of England and to a less degree in other places the people hit upon the connexion of that procession with the mystery plays, already widely distributed and highly developed, must be regarded as a more or less accidental thing and a happy accident. A Council at Paris in 1323 speaks of the procession in this way: 'As to the solemn procession made on the Thursday's feast, when the Holy Sacrament is carried, seeing that it appears to have been introduced in these our times, by a sort of inspiration, we prescribe nothing at present and leave all concerning it to the devotion of the clergy and the people.'[1] To this invitation to freedom of invention we owe, not only the above-mentioned associa- tion of religious plays with the Corpus Christi procession, but probably the invention of the Corpus Christi plays as a special dramatic form.

At Ipswich the Merchants' Guild was reconstituted as a Guild of Corpus Christi in 1325, and its constitution provides for a procession on Corpus Christi day.[2] At London the fraternity of Skinners held a procession once every year on Corpus Christi day in the afternoon; this guild dates from 1327, and it is natural to conclude that the procession was part of its original institution.[3] The Tailors' Guild of Lincoln, founded in 1328, had a procession of the brethren and sisters on the feast of Corpus Christi, about which procession we may conclude the same thing. Similarly there are records of processions on Corpus Christi day at Coventry in 1348, at Leicester in 1349–50, and at Beverley at some time between 1330 and 1350.[4]

The earlier part of the fourteenth century, after 1311, would there- fore be the most probable time for the possible invention of the Corpus Christi play, and certainly the establishment of the Corpus Christi play in England would be after about 1318, if it arose, as it most certainly did, in connexion with the observance of the feast of Corpus

[1] P. L. P. Guéranger, *The Liturgical Year.* Translated from the French by L. Shepherd (London, 1867), vii, part 1, pp. 287 ff.
[2] Hist. MSS. Comm., Eighth Report, ix, 1, 245.
[3] John Stow, *A Survey of London,* ed. C. L. Kingsford (2 v. London, 1908), i. 230–1.
[4] Toulmin Smith, *English Gilds: Original Ordinances of More than a Hundred Gilds,* E.E.T.S. (London, 1870), pp. 182, 232; W. Kelly, *Notices Illustrative of the Drama, and Other Popular Amusements . . . of Leicester* (1865), p. 36; A. F. Leach, *Report on the Manuscripts of the Corpora- tion of Beverley,* Hist. MSS. Comm. 1900, p. ix.

Christi. The earliest and most outstanding case is that of Chester, where, according to a reliable tradition, plays were acted and a cycle established in 1327–8. To this tradition we shall give attention later. The earliest actual record of a Corpus Christi play comes from Beverley in Yorkshire in 1377. There also in 1390 they are spoken of as *antiqua consuetudo*. The next comes from York in 1378, where in 1394 the pageants are ordered to play at places *antiquitus assignatis*. The first mention of the Corpus Christi play at Coventry is in 1392. No others of the fourteenth century are known, but there are plenty in the fifteenth.[1] We may fairly take a Cambridge reference of about 1350 as bridging the long gap between the 1328 tradition as to the establishment of the Chester plays and the earliest Beverley record in 1377. It concerns a certain William de Lenne and his wife who joined the guild of Corpus Christi in Cambridge and at that time spent a mark 'in ludo filiorum Israelis'. In this case we should probably understand the *ludum filiorum Israelis* as being a play of the Slaughter of the Innocents, and therefore an ordinary part of a Corpus Christi cycle, especially since the play of the Sons of Jacob, which Creizenach takes this to mean, is otherwise unknown in England. The play of the Slaughter of the Innocents is, moreover, several times called 'The Children of Israel'.[2] At Beverley a lost play is so called; so also, apparently, is a pageant in the Dublin procession, although in the Norwich list the 'Children of Israel' refers to Moses and his host in the Pharaoh play. At any rate, the Cambridge reference probably indicates that there was a Corpus Christi play in Cambridge by about 1350. On *a priori* grounds—date, dramatic interest, and the necessity of providing a procession—the Chester tradition is credible. There is a paucity of records during the fourteenth century, which was a great century in England but was poor at book-keeping. This scarcity of records may possibly indicate that the plays in the middle of that century had not yet emerged from parochial or ecclesiastical control, for of course church records have suffered greater destruction than have municipal records. If this is true, the plays would more and more become affairs of municipal

---

[1] Chambers, op. cit. ii. App. W; *Two Coventry Corpus Christi Plays*, loc. cit., *passim*.

[2] Chambers, op. cit. ii. 344, quoting Masters, *History of Corpus Christi College, Cambridge* (edn. 1753), i. 5.

importance during the fourteenth century and would be noted in the regulations and accounts of towns and cities.

There is no evidence that the plays in England had been combined into all-inclusive cycles before the early part of the fourteenth century. Such combination had almost certainly been made on the continent, although we have only the one conspicuous case at Cividale in Italy in 1298 and 1303. The scanty English records of the thirteenth century point to a condition in which the plays were still in their original groups—Christmas and Easter. The Cathedral Statutes of Bishop Hugh de Nonant (1188–98) of Lichfield provide *Pastores* (and no doubt *Stella*) at Christmas and the Resurrection and the *Peregrini* at Easter.[1] We have already considered the thirteenth-century continuation of the life of St. John of Beverley that records a miracle performed in the Minster about 1220 while a crowd of spectators was watching the performance of a play of Christ's Resurrection in the churchyard beside the Minster.[2] The denunciations of plays by Grosseteste (1244) and other ecclesiastics of the century point to a close connexion between the plays and the church, and they may suggest one reason why the plays did leave the church. These denunciations grew less frequent and more specific after the plays became clearly secular.[3] The statutes of York Cathedral provide for *Pastores* and *Stella* about 1255, as we have seen, and there were, no doubt, Resurrection plays at York also at the same period. The so-called *Shrewsbury Fragments* are certainly a case in point. It is, of course, believed on linguistic and metrical grounds that many of the plays go back to the thirteenth century, and there is no reason why they should not. The body of the plays, those on traditional liturgical subjects, were not first composed in England at the time of the establishment of the feast of Corpus Christi: they had for the most part been in existence in England long before 1318. There is no stage of the early development that is not somehow represented in Great Britain by records if not texts. What happened was that the plays were gathered together from the traditional periods of Christmas and Easter and, no doubt, from other parts of the year, arranged in chronological sequence, and played all

[1] C. Wordsworth, *Statutes of Lincoln Cathedral* (Cambridge, 1892), ii. 15, 23.
[2] Rolls Series, *Historians of the Church of York*, i. 328; see above, p. 99.
[3] H. S. Symmes, *Les Débuts de la critique dramatique en Angleterre* (Paris, 1903), 6–12.

together at a new and better time of year. No doubt in many places new plays had to be written or borrowed to fill gaps in cycles and to fill out complete cycles, but at least some part of the substance was there already, and the various towns and cities apparently did not give up the plays they had on hand in favour of new ones. This is borne out by the special features that every cycle shows. To set up their cycles the playmakers must have needed a pattern, and we know of only one, Cividale, at the beginning of the fourteenth century. Again, if the Chester tradition is to be believed, as it should be, it will be seen that it provided a very early cycle pattern in England itself. There are several faint indications that the Chester cycle served as a model for other cycles. The best of these is the spread of the Doomsday play. That it did not carry with it its original first part, the Antichrist, is not significant, since it was the Doomsday play, and not the Antichrist, that was needed to end a cycle. In general, however, what seems to have been done after the establishment of the feast of Corpus Christi in northern England was to transfer to Corpus Christi day and to arrange in extensive cyclic form plays of already considerable cyclic development.

The establishment of the Corpus Christi cycles was a special thing, and there are some evidences that it was done formally and intelligently. An indication, for example, of this special establishment is certainly to be found in the subjects played by the various guilds in the cities. The way they fit together seems to point to deliberate assignment. The bakers at Beverley, Chester, and York played the Last Supper, probably because it seemed appropriate to someone for them to supply bread. The cooks of Beverley and Chester played the Harrowing of Hell, because, we may suppose, they could handle fire. The watermen at Beverley and Chester and the shipwrights of York and Newcastle-upon-Tyne for obvious reasons played Noah's Ark, and so on. There is often some connexion between the trade and the subject of the play, but there is another reason, also conventional, that seems to have operated in the matter of the assignment or choice of a play. It is pretty obvious from the records of Coventry and Beverley and other places that a trade guild often played a play having to do with its patron saint. These facts indicate that there was a time in the history of guild plays when there was a freedom to choose, or a reason to be assigned, a desirable or appropriate subject for the performance of which the guild might be held responsible in the annual presentation of the cycle of plays. This can hardly be the result of choice in pre-cyclic times, although that possibility is not to be ruled out in every case. There are belated instances of secularization at Leicester in 1477, where there was a debate about putting a Passion play into the hands of the crafts, and at Norwich in 1527, where the plays were shifted from St. Luke's Guild to all the guilds.[1]

We may believe, then, that the Corpus Christi play was set up, probably on the model of an inclusive dramatic form invented on the Continent, about the end of the first quarter of the fourteenth century at some place probably in the north of England, and spread thence to other places in the island. The play was recognized as a dramatic species in cosmic form; it had one principal geographical location in England; it was almost uniformly connected with trade guilds or crafts; it was completely established during the fourteenth century, so that by the end of that century the play had become an ancient custom, although there are evidences that the original parts of the play were as yet uncombined in the thirteenth century. There is also the evidence that the establishment of the Corpus Christi play was a conscious and deliberate community act.

Why should such an establishment have been suggested by the festival of Corpus Christi? There is, as has been said above, nothing deliberately prescriptive of the great cosmic theme of man's fall and redemption in the bull of Pope Urban IV, in the order of the Council of Vienne, or in the confirmation of the decree in the Canon Law; but there is something implicit to that end in the service of Corpus Christi day itself, and it is easy to see it. The service of Corpus Christi is theologically and ritualistically a consummation of the entire plan of salvation, and the grand cycle of religious themes from the Fall of Adam to the Ascension of the Saviour and the Passion-play theme as developed at Easter were an objectivization of the same grand theme. It epitomized schematically and sometimes imperfectly, but nevertheless adequately, the service of the liturgical year. Indeed, the plays as well as the service of the day may be said to portray the entire plan of salvation, culminating in Christ's sacrifice and always

[1] Chambers, op. cit. ii. 376–7, 386–9.

conscious of the types of Christ among the patriarchs. The service also presents in what were originally liturgical terms the subject of prophecy and the circumstances of its fulfilment in the birth of Jesus. It is the same great and familiar story of the fall and redemption of man as that which we have in epics, sermons, commentaries, and histories all through the Middle Ages. The Corpus Christi play tells this story in its completest possible form, and the Passion play may be said to be adequate for the heart of the story and to be often more highly particularized as well as longer than the Corpus Christi play ever became.

Since there was such latitude given to local powers in the determination of what the required procession should consist of, and since some of the plays of the full type are themselves in a certain sense processional, it has been suggested that the Corpus Christi plays began as dumbshow pageants in the procession and developed gradually from dumb show into drama as the procession moved along, or had added to them materials from the already secularized and pretty fully developed liturgical plays. But the plays were already entirely too long and too mature dramatically to have been recited by actors as pageants moved along a street. This theory of the development of mystery plays from pantomime was advanced by Charles Davidson,[1] one of the earlier modern students of the subject, and it has met with much favour among the greatest authorities on the religious drama[2] notwithstanding the fact that most of the historians present clear and for the most part convincing accounts of a very different origin for the mystery plays. It is possibly an ineradicable heresy. On the face of it, it misinterprets or mistakes the nature and purpose of the Corpus Christi procession. This was a religious ceremony performed at command, was a very much commoner thing than were the plays, and was independent of them. The dramatic figures of the Corpus Christi procession could have come only from the plays. The plays could not have come from the figures in the procession, because the plays were in existence long before the procession was instituted. There may have been cases in which the plays had ceased to be performed and the

[1] *Studies in the English Mystery Plays*; Yale Dissertation, 1892.

[2] Creizenach, op. cit. i (1893), 169 ff.; Chambers, op. cit. ii. 173 *et passim*; Petit de Julleville, *Les Mystères*, ii. 186–216; M. Lyle Spencer, *Corpus Christi Pageants in England* (New York, 1911), pp. 61 ff.

dramatic scenes and characters continued to appear in the procession, although such a thing would be rare and difficult to maintain; but, for the most part, the erroneous opinion and theory have come into existence because there happened to be in certain cases extant records of the Corpus Christi procession and no available records of the plays that accompanied them. The state of the case is illustrated by the substitution of the *Credo* play for the Corpus Christi play at York in 1535 and 1568 and of the *Pater Noster* play for it in 1558, without apparently affecting the Corpus Christi procession in either case.[1] An entry in the Corporation Register of Lincoln, 31 December 1521, indicates a similar independence on the part of the St. Anne's day procession at Lincoln: 'Every alderman to make a gown for the Kings in the pageant on St. Anne's day, and the Pater Noster play to be played this year.' The sacrament was carried in the St. Anne's day procession, which seems to have been essentially a Corpus Christi procession, although held on St. Anne's day. A Corpus Christi procession was a march of ecclesiastics and laity, usually the whole body of citizens, through the streets of the city; it was part of a religious service and usually required a return to the place of setting out. The citizens marched by crafts and in livery, and, since they were themselves both the spectators and actors of the plays, it is difficult to see how the plays could ever have been acted as part of the procession while it was on the move. It is doubtful, particularly in the early days of the procession, whether the acting of plays would ever have been suitable or acceptable, even if it were possible to act plays as the procession went along. The drawing of pageant wagons in the procession, perhaps with actors in costume on them, would have been appropriate enough and no doubt feasible. If these movable stages were constructed at the time of the establishment of Corpus Christi plays at various places, if the plays were matters of absorbing interest, if the plays were relatively short and time was plentiful, the procession may have stopped at various convenient places on its way to indulge in the acting of the plays, but that would have been as nearly proces- sional as the mystery plays ever were, although there is evidence that the actors in the plays were in the Corpus Christi procession in

---

[1] R. Davies, *Extracts from the Municipal Records of the City of York during the Reigns of Edward IV, Edward V, and Richard III* (London, 1843), pp. 256–8.

character. Spencer[1] finds some evidence that the plays were once actual parts of the Corpus Christi procession in the fact that at York the laity, including the guilds, marched behind the Host, whereas in many places the clergy held that position and the laity preceded, the idea being that, if the guilds were last in the procession, they might take their time in the acting of the growing plays. There might be something in this, but in general the records show separate times for the two events.

A good deal has been made of a record of 1558 from Draguignan in France[2] of a mimetic performance:

> Le dit jeu jora avec la procession comme auparadvant et le plus d'istoeres et plus brieves que puront estre seront et se dira tout en cheminant sans que personne du jeu s'areste pour eviter prolixité et confusion tant de ladite prosession que jeu, et que les estrangiers le voient aisement.

The interpretation of this is doubtful, but, at any rate, there is no record that suggests anything like it in connexion with the origin of the Corpus Christi plays and their association with the Corpus Christi procession in England. Various late descriptions, or lists, of actors from Corpus Christi pageants and of the pageants themselves in the Corpus Christi procession have been taken as indications of dumb show, but such things are merely continuations of the old custom of putting actors and pageant wagons in the procession. It is taken for granted, but without proper warrant, that the plays at Dundee, Dublin, and Hereford were already defunct at the time the descriptions of Corpus Christi processions with figures and floats from Corpus Christi plays were recorded.[3] Sometimes these processions are described by modern writers as 'mimetic'. There is no evidence, and it is most unlikely. These records do indicate that there once had been and probably still were Corpus Christi plays played at these places. Corpus Christi pageants did not always appear in Corpus Christi processions. The records of their appearances are late, and they betray themselves often by introducing figures from other local dramatic performances. For example, St. Katherine with three tormentors appears in the Hereford procession. The narrow and crooked streets of

[1] Op. cit., pp. 69–70.   [2] Julleville, *Les Mystères*, ii. 209.
[3] A. Maxwell, *Old Dundee* (Dundee, 1891), p. 562; Spencer, op. cit., pp. 71–73; Chambers, op. cit. ii. 362–6, 368–9.

medieval English towns would have made acting plays as the procession moved along a very impractical thing for both players and spectators.

Also a series of *pageants tableaux* on so extensive a scale, so orderly, and so highly developed dramatically as a Corpus Christi play, could hardly have come into existence at all until after the community involved had been educated by considerable familiarity with the plays. We should never have arrived at the uniform, definite result we have—Corpus Christi cycles with their general similarities, their local differences, and their constant dependence upon their liturgical predecessors—if a beginning had been made from any possible set of ideally constructed *pageants tableaux*. In other words, the particular set of subjects treated in the Corpus Christi plays are there, not because they were chosen to suit the idea of Corpus Christi, or because they were dramatically attractive in themselves, but because they were the liturgical themes and events handed down for centuries and thus ready to be combined into cycles on the occasion of the establishment of the feast of Corpus Christi (with its procession) in the early fourteenth century. Even the ceremony at Beverley of 1355, which was concerned with the celebration of the feast of the Purification, and has been cited as an example of a mimetic pageant,[1] was not necessarily in dumb show. The regular play on this subject must have had an independent existence for a long time. Such a scene appears in various cycles, but has no fixed place in the sequence, as if it were in every case originally outside the parent group of Nativity plays and had been added to them for the sake of completeness.

If one reduces a Corpus Christi cycle, say the Chester Whitsun plays, to its lowest terms, so to speak, and omits from it every play that might by any chance be a later addition, or the result of develop-ment during the history of the cycle as a whole, as well as all more or less useless homiletic materials, comicalities, and excrescences, we have yet a drama of very considerable extent, perhaps one-third to one-half the whole as it now stands; therefore a drama that would require for its presentation, even at a very limited number of stations, a considerable amount of time. The Chester cycle would demand the treatment of the following subjects: Fall of Lucifer, Creation, Fall of

---

[1] Spencer, op. cit., pp. 70 ff.; Smith, *English Gilds*, loc. cit., pp. 149–50.

Man, Cain and Abel, Noah, Abraham and Isaac, *Processus Pro-phetarum* (with episodes), Nativity (with a good deal of special material), *Pastores, Stella,* Slaughter of the Innocents with Flight into Egypt, Temptation, Lazarus (with the story of Mary and Martha), Woman Taken in Adultery (?), Entry into Jerusalem, Conspiracy, Last Supper, Capture, Trial, Crucifixion, Death and Burial, Harrowing of Hell, Setting of the Watch before the Tomb, Resurrection, *Hortulanus, Peregrini,* Doubting Thomas, Ascension, Pentecost, Antichrist (with Ezekiel), Doomsday. No matter how briefly these topics were treated in the beginning of the cycle, the outline itself is so extensive that it would have required a number of hours to present the play. If we grant, for the purpose of getting the plays on the road, that the individual plays started out with the Corpus Christi procession— bearing in mind, however, that there is no evidence for it—and stopped at various places to act these scenes one after another, it follows from the amount of time required, even from the first, that the Host, the clergy, the mayor, and the city fathers would have had to spend a long time on the road, almost certainly too long and too inconvenient. We must remember also that there were some places where, for all we know, the Corpus Christi plays were just as ancient as any, where the pageants were not drawn about the streets, but were acted on fixed stages. We may conclude, in any case, that the Corpus Christi play did not originate in dumb show, but by the union of pre-existent plays and groups of plays into vast cyclic combinations, extensive in scope, conventional in contents, long familiar to the people, and, for the most part, of native growth.

It is now pretty generally agreed that the English religious plays grew from liturgical origins on English soil and were not, in general, translated from the French.[1] This refers only to the Corpus Christi plays and the plays of their time, since of course there can be no doubt that England at one time or another borrowed the whole religious drama from France and other parts of the continent. It may be that, in some instances, the English had only patterns of continental dramas on which to work, but the probabilities are that in the earliest times they usually resorted to translation. France was far ahead of

---

[1] Chambers, op. cit. ii. 108, 146–7; Creizenach, op. cit. i. 181 ff., *passim*; Davidson, op. cit., p. 171 *et passim*; F. E. Schelling, *The Elizabethan Drama* (2 v. Boston, 1908), i. 12 ff.

England in the extent and development of the religious drama, and there is almost no religious play preserved or recorded in England that is not also to be found in France or in French records. This is a main reason why it is so disappointing that French plays and the records of French plays have been so poorly collected and studied. The evidence, mainly internal, that exists seems to indicate that the Corpus Christi play is made up with some exceptions from plays already existent in England.

The older view, which is not altogether wrong, believed in special authorship and foreign originals.[1] It was based on the well-known and entirely credible Chester tradition pointing to the year 1327-8 as the year of translation from the French and to Ranulf Higden as the translator.[2] Translation from the French of the English Corpus Christi plays is now rejected except for the Chester plays, in which the parallel with *Le Mistère du Viel Testament* and other French plays is obvious.[3] It is likely that both plays go back at least in part to a somewhat extensively combined Latin play, such as is represented by the corrupt and imperfect Benediktbeuern Christmas play, which is of the same original composition as the Chester cycle and the French Old Testament plays.[4] There are other cases of close approximation, such as the elaborate plays at Lincoln presenting the infancy and the Coronation of the Blessed Virgin Mary and in *Ludus Coventriae*. There is also a long list of titles of lost English plays that either exist in French or are recorded as having been performed in France. The matter of the translation of English plays from the French cannot be easily disposed of, and further light may be shed on the question when

[1] Thomas Warton, *History of English Poetry, from the Twelfth to the Close of the Sixteenth Century*. Ed. W. C. Hazlitt (4 v. London, 1871), i. 248; W. Hone, *Ancient Mysteries Described* (London, 1823), pp. 201 ff.; B. ten Brink, *History of English Literature* (3 v. London, 1893-6), II. i. 237 *et passim*; A. W. Ward, *A History of English Dramatic Literature to the Death of Queen Anne* (3 v. London, 1899), i. 9 ff., 76 ff.

[2] See particularly Chambers, op. cit. ii. 348 ff., where so much has been done to render intelligible the confused traditions of the origin of the Chester plays. See also Arthur Brown, 'A Tradition of the Chester Plays', *London Mediaeval Studies*, vol. ii, pt. 1 (1951), pp. 68-72. On Higden see below, pp. 168-70.

[3] H. Ungemacht, *Die Quellen der fünf ersten Chester Plays*. Münchener Beiträge, H. 11 (1890); S. B. Hemingway, *English Nativity Plays* (New York, 1909), pp. xxiv ff. To the parallels pointed out by these writers should be added the very significant one of the Balaam play in *Le Mistère*, which follows, as in the Chester plays, immediately after the scene of Moses and the Tables of the Law.

[4] Craig, 'Origin of the Old Testament Plays', loc. cit., pp. 486-7.

or if French documents become more available. England and Scotland had the same liturgical inheritance as had France, Germany,
and Italy, and there was a unity in medieval Europe, so that it is not
so much a matter of borrowing and translating as it is a matter of a
general spread of custom and practice throughout a great ecclesiastical
and social area. England and Scotland, when they had once established plays, were no doubt more tenacious than was France in
holding on to what they had and as apt to vary their plays according
to local demands and conditions as was France itself. The English
plays, as preserved, are surprisingly national, or rather local, in their
characteristics. The *Shrewsbury Fragments* show that the plays passed
on English soil from Latin to English by the usual method of repeating and amplifying Latin texts in the vernacular, examples of which
are to be found in the religious drama of all countries.[1]

Another matter that is now becoming clear is that the Corpus
Christi play, as we know it in the four full cycles, the fragments of
lost cycles, and the records, flourished in a comparatively restricted
area and was an independent dramatic form with its own definite
characteristics. Corpus Christi plays seem to have belonged mainly
to the north and east of England. There were plays of the Corpus
Christi type at Newcastle-upon-Tyne, Kendal, Preston, York, Beverley, Wakefield, Chester, Lincoln, Louth, Norwich, Ipswich, Worcester, and Coventry, and, more doubtfully, at about as many more
places. They appeared also in Ireland at Dublin and at several places
in Scotland. But Corpus Christi plays are by no means the only
great plays on biblical subjects in England. In fact these great cyclic
plays on biblical subjects, as well as other dramatic activities, were
much more varied than the histories of the religious drama in England
have indicated. These histories are based on the records of Corpus
Christi plays, which happen to be many times more numerous and
extensive than are the records of other plays, such as, for example, the
great Passion plays of the south of England.

'Corpus Christi play' is used dozens of times, and used discriminatingly, to denote the type of play we have in hand. John Heywood
in *The Four PP* (831) says: 'Oft in the play of Corpus Christi / He
had played the deuyll at Couentre.' In *The C Mery Talys* (lvi) one

---

[1] Chambers, op. cit. ii. 69 ff.; Creizenach, op. cit. i (1893), 108 ff.

finds 'Yf you beleue not me, then for a more suerte and suffycient auctoryte, go your waye to Couentre, and there ye shal se them all playd in Corpus Christi playe.' Fifteenth-century craft ordinaries from Newcastle-upon-Tyne[1] record 'Whensoever the generall plaies of Newcastle, antiently called the Corpus Christi plays, shall be plaied', &c. There are many such uses. The following from Weever's *Ancient Funerall Monuments* is most significant:[2]

This *Marlow* was Lord Maior in the yeare 1409, in whose Maioraltie there was a play at Skinners Hall, which lasted eight days (saith *Stow*) to heare which, most of the greatest Estates of England were present. The subject of the play was the Sacred Scriptures, from the creation of the world: They call this *Corpus Christi* Play in my country, which I haue seene acted at Preston, and Lancaster, and last of all at Kendall, in the beginning of the raigne of King *Iames*: for which the Townesmen were sore troubled: and vpon good reasons the play finally supprest, not onely there, but in all other Townes of the Kingdome.

Weever was born in Lancashire in 1576. He wrote about 1631, and he seems to recognize that the Corpus Christi play was a northern rather than a southern institution. So definite was the term that even when, as at some places, the play was no longer acted at Corpus Christi, it was still referred to as a Corpus Christi play. At Chester, where the plays were transferred at an early date to Whitsuntide, the Bakers' Charter of 1462 speaks of 'the play and light of Corpus Christi'; the Saddlers' Charter of 1471 has the same thing in Latin: *paginae luminis et ludi Corporis Christi*. These references may or may not be later than the transfer of the plays to Whitsuntide, but references of the sixteenth century make it clear that the Chester plays were always known by their old name. The 'White Book' (about 1544) speaks of 'pagyns in the play of Corpus Xpi.'.[3] From Norwich, where likewise the plays were at Whitsuntide, comes the jocular reference by J. Whetley in a letter to Sir John Paston[4] in speaking of Lord Suffolk and telling how 'ther was never no man that playd Herod in Corpus Christy play better and more agreable to hys pageaunt than he dud'. Finally, there is a record from Lincoln at the

---

[1] Chambers, op. cit. ii. 385.
[2] Ibid., p. 373; folio edition (1631), p. 405.
[3] Ibid., pp. 352-3.
[4] *Paston Letters*, 1422-1509, ed. J. Gairdner (2nd ed., 4 v. London, 1900), ii. 127, 433-6.

time of the Marian reaction. The corporation Register under date of 6 July 1554 contains this entry:

> Agreed at a Secret Council that St. Anne's guild with Corpus Christi play shall be brought forth and played this year, and that every craft shall bring forth their pageants as it has been accustomed, and all occupations shall be contributory as shall be assessed.[1]

On the other hand, where the cyclic plays were of another kind, they seem to have been called by other names. At New Romney in Kent there was a Resurrection play performed in 1456[2] and a 'play of the Interlude of our Lord's Passion' in 1463. It was a stationary play of considerable scope, and the circumstances of its representation lead one to conclude that it was of the type familiar in the Passion plays of the continent. There was much dramatic activity in that part of England, and the free interchange of performances among towns suggests that these towns must have had stationary stages and not the pageants of the Corpus Christi cycles. At Aberdeen, where the Passion group and the Nativity group were not united, the Passion, which was performed at Corpus Christi, was called 'the Haliblude play'. Similarly, at Leicester there is mention in the Hall Book of the Corporation in 1477 of a 'Passion Play'. There is no ground for connecting this play with Corpus Christi, although, unfortunately, details that might define it more closely are lacking. There is also the striking example of the Cornish *Creation, Passion,* and *Resurrection,* which is not a Corpus Christi play.[3] Finally, there are a few small pieces of evidence to show that the plays of London were of the same form as the Cornish plays; they were certainly not Corpus Christi plays. I refer to the record in the Issue Roll of the Exchequer for Easter to Michaelmas, 1391, of a payment to 'the Clerkes of the Parish Churches and to divers other clerkes of the City of London', as a gift from the king, 'on account of the play of the Passion of our Lord and the Creation of the World by them performed at Skinner Well, after the Feast of Bartholomew last past'. The entry of 1391 in

---

[1] Chambers, op. cit. ii. 379.

[2] Ibid., pp. 385–6; W. A. Scott-Robertson, 'The Passion Play and Interludes at New Romney', *Archaeologia Cantiana,* xiii. 216 ff.; Hist. MSS. Comm., v. 533.

[3] Chambers, op. cit. ii. 127, 433–5; E. Norris, *The Ancient Cornish Drama,* with translation into English (2 v. Oxford, 1859); *The Creation of the World,* ed. Whitley Stokes (London, Philological Society, 1859).

Malvern's continuation of Higden's *Polychronicon*, with which Chambers connects this payment, says merely: 'Item xviij° die Iulii clerici Londonienses fecerunt ludum satis curiosum apud Skinneres-well per dies quatuor duraturum, in quo tam vetus quam novum testamentum oculariter ludendo monstrabant.' There is also a refer-ence in Machin to a 'stage play at the Grey freers of the Passyon of Cryst' in 1557 during the reign of Queen Mary.[1] There were, then, at least two types of cyclic plays dealing with subjects from the Bible, and the Corpus Christi play was a different kind of play from the Passion play.

Besides these major forms, almost every known kind of religious play and stage of development seem to have been represented in England, and many very interesting plays have been lost or destroyed. Smaller towns and communities presented a variety of forms of the religious drama, for single plays did not disappear with the establish-ment of the greater cycles. Nearly all saints' plays have been lost as well as special plays at great towns, like the Pater Noster play at York, Beverley, and Lincoln, and the Creed play at York. There must have been plays dealing with the miracles of the Blessed Virgin Mary, but of such plays there are only a few doubtful traces. There were Resurrection plays at Bath (?), Kingston-on-Thames, Leconfield in Yorkshire, Leicester, Morebath in Devonshire, Magdalen College, Oxford, and possibly also at Reading, which last, however, may have been part of a full cycle. Nativity plays were acted separately from Resurrection plays at Aberdeen, at Leconfield, and at Leicester, as was often done on the continent. There was possibly also a Christ-mas play of some kind at Lincoln. It is referred to in the *computi* of the Cathedral chapter in 1406, 1452, and 1531[2] usually in this form: 'In serothecis emptis pro Maria et Angelo et Prophetis ex consuetudine in Aurora Natalis Dñi hoc anno.' With this one would associate another rather blind reference found also by C. Wordsworth.[3] In 1421 tithes to the amount of 8s. 8d. were assigned to Thomas Cham-berleyn for getting up a spectacle or pageant ('cujusdam excellentis

---

[1] Chambers, op. cit., gives a summary of all that is known about medieval religious plays in London.

[2] Wordsworth, *Lincoln Cathedral Statutes*, loc. cit., vol. ii, p. lv.

[3] *Notes on Mediaeval Services in England, with an Index of Lincoln Ceremonies* (London, 1898), p. 126; Chambers, op. cit. ii. 377-8.

visus') called *Rubum quem viderat* at Christmas. This was evidently a
little play of Moses and the Burning Bush or Moses and the Tables
of the Law such as would have been part of a *Prophetae* and such as
actually appears in the Chester cycle. Chambers in *The Mediaeval
Stage*, Appendix W, from which much of the foregoing material
has been drawn, gives references that indicate a variety of forms of the
religious drama in England and Scotland.[1] *The Digby Plays* offer
also a case in point, since the Digby manuscript presents four plays
of considerable length and interest none of which belonged to a
Corpus Christi cycle. *The Massacre of the Innocents* in that manuscript
is a part of an elaborate Nativity cycle, and the *Burial and Resurrection*

---

[1] For reference to plays, processions, and religious dramatic activities additional or supple-
tary to those given in Chambers, op. cit., App. W, see: M. Pierson, 'The Relation of the
Corpus Christi Procession to the Corpus Christi Plays', *Trans. Wisconsin Academy of Sciences,
Arts, and Letters*, xviii, pt. 1 (1915), 110–65. (Contains, with bibliography and references,
records of religious dramatic activity (some of which is not in Chambers' list) at Aberdeen,
Beverley, Bungay, Bury St. Edmunds, Canterbury, Chester, Coventry, Dublin, Hereford,
Ipswich, King's Lynn, Lincoln, London, Newcastle, Norwich, Salisbury, Shrewsbury, and
York; also Bath, Cambridge, Durham, Great Yarmouth, Leicester, Little Walsingham,
Reading, Kendal, Louth, and Preston.) L. Blair, 'A Note on the Relation of the Corpus
Christi Procession to the Corpus Christi Play', *Modern Language Notes*, lv (1940), 83–95.
Supplementary to Miss Pierson's study and based largely on churchwardens' accounts, with
references, it presents records from Reading (St. Lawrence's); Ashburton; Dunmow, Essex;
Walden (Notre Dame); Bristol (Christ Church, St. Ewen's, St. John's, St. Mary-le-Port,
St. Nicholas's); Canterbury (St. Dunstan's); Dover (St. Mary's); Sandwich (St. Mary's);
London (St. Andrew Hubbard, St. Margaret Pattens, St. Margaret's, Southwark, St. Mar-
garet's, Westminster, St. Martin's-in-the-Fields, St. Mary Outwich, St. Mary at Hill, St. Mary
Magdalene, Milk Street, St. Mary Woolnoth, St. Matthew's, Friday Street, St. Michael's, Corn-
hill, St. Olave, Southwark, St. Peter Cheap); Oxford (St. Michael's); Thame (Church of
the Virgin Mary); Ludlow; Bath (St. Michael's); Glastonbury (St. John's); Pilton (St. John
Baptist); Yeovil; Bungay (St. Mary's); Salisbury (St. Edmund's, St. Thomas's); Worcester
(Priory). W. vander Graaf, 'Miracles and Mysteries of S.E. Yorkshire', *Englische Studien*,
xxvi (1906), 228–30; *The Resurrection of Our Lord*, Malone Society Reprints, 1912 (1913);
M. H. Dodds, 'The Northern Stage', *Archaeologia Aeliana*, N.S. xi (1914), 36, 47 (Durham.
See R. Welford, *History of Newcastle and Gateshead in the Sixteenth Century*, 2 v. London,
1885, pp. 370, 413, 424); *A Calendar of the Records of the Borough of Doncaster* (4 v. London,
1899–1903), ii. 73; IV. xxi. 36–37, 83, and *Court Rolls of Doncaster, etc.* 27, 39,
88; *A Calendar of the Manuscripts of the Dean and Chapter of Wells*, Hist. MSS. Comm.
(from 1394 *passim*); A. J. Mill, *Mediaeval Plays in Scotland* (Edinburgh, 1927), *passim*; W. A.
Mepham, 'Village Plays at Dunmow and Heybridge in Essex', *Notes and Queries*, 19–20
May 1934 and 11 August 1934; 'Canterbury Text', *The Times*, 28 December 1937; V. Shull,
'Clerical Drama in Lincoln Cathedral, 1318–1561', *PMLA*, lii (1937), 946–66; W. O.
Hassall, 'Plays at Clerkenwell', *Modern Language Review*, xxxiii (1938), 564–7; Yorkshire
Archaeological Society, Record Series, lxxiv. 20–21 (Wakefield); H. C. Gardiner, op. cit.,
pp. 122–4; R. H. Robbins, 'An English Mystery Play Fragment ante 1300', *Modern Language
Notes*, lxv (1950), 30–35.

from Bodleian MS. e Museo 160 is apparently an independent Resurrection play.

Corpus Christi plays were characterized, in the first place, by completeness of cyclical content. They extended in their range from Creation to Doomsday, and they included plays of the Nativity as well as of the Passion and the Resurrection. They all seem to have been acted by craft guilds, with local differences as at Norwich, and to have been, to a greater or less degree, under municipal control, but there is very little actual evidence to connect the plays in their origins with the Corpus Christi procession, as is usually done.

The records of Corpus Christi plays are rather plentiful, most from Coventry and Beverley, but many from Norwich, Chester, York, and other places. In so far as the problems of control and expense were similar in various towns, and they were of course often similar, it is possible to work out certain general characteristics. Most of the records have to do with the regulation of the plays, and that is a somewhat dis-appointing subject. It may be that, as a general thing, religious guilds looked after the procession, and trade guilds looked after the plays, although the clergy did in some places participate in the plays—e.g. at Bungay, Beverley and Salisbury. There was possibly religious super-vision at Norwich and Lincoln, and this may represent the continua-tion of an earlier stage prevailing throughout most of the fourteenth century, when the clergy were gradually relaxing an earlier power to the municipality. In the York records and also in the records from Beverley there is a good deal about the order of the procession, and in many places there were regulations, and even penalties imposed, to compel guilds to take their share of responsibility for the plays and to pay their proper shares of expenses. Nothing will show this better perhaps than a selection of orders and regulations:

These men above writen wer acordid & agreed on munday next befor palme sunday. Anno H [VI] xxxj. [1453.] That Thom's Colclow skynner ffro this day forth shull have the Rewle of *the* pajaunt unto the end of xij yers next folowing he for to find *the* pleyers and all *that* longeth *th*erto all *the* seide time save *the* keper of the craft shall let bring forth *the* pajant and find Clothys *that* gon abowte *the* pajant and find Russhes *th*erto and every wytson-weke who *that* be kepers of *the* crafte shall dyne with Colclow & every master ley down iiijd and Colclow shall have yerely ffor his labor xlvjs viijd & he to bring in to *the* master on sonday next after corps xpi day *the* originall & ffech his vij nobullez and Colclow must bring at *the* later end of *the* timez all *the* garments *that* longen to *the* pajant as good as *they* wer delyvered to hym.—Coventry records.

This shows the appointment and the responsibilities of a pageant-master and also his pay, the care of gear or property belonging to the guild, and the return and deposit of the 'original', the authorized text of the play. Here it is of a single play, and that represents the situation at Coventry, although at York and perhaps at other places there was in the custody of the city government a general register of all the plays of all the companies.

The following, also from Coventry, gives a typical list of expenses incurred by the Weavers' company in the putting on of their pageant annually. The year is 1563:

In primis for ij rehersys	ijs
Item payd for the dryving of the pagente	vd
Item paid to Simeon	iijs iiijd
Item paid to Josephe	ijs iiijd
Item paid to Jesus	xxd
Item paid to Mary	xxd
Item paid to Anne	xxd
Item paid to Symeons clarke	xxd
Item paid to the ij angells	viijd
Item paid to the chylde	iiijd
Item paid for russhes, packthryd and nayls	iiijd
Item paid to James Hewete for his rygoles	xxd
Item paid for synging	xvjd
Item paide for gloves	ijs ijd
Item paid for meate in the bocherye	xs ixd
Item paid for bread and ale	vijs viijd
summe	xliiijs iijd

Such lists are fairly numerous, but so far, except in some measure for the work of M. Lyle Spencer, they have been presented only that they might be regarded as 'quaint'. They may be worth at least a careful study for what they might yield in the way of light thrown on staging and on the plays acted. It would, however, hardly be worth the trouble unless they were studied as particular items dealing with particular plays at particular places. Local variations were entirely too great for general study to be more than misleading. One more record, also from Coventry, has a peculiar interest, particularly because of its date. As late as 1587 the weavers of Coventry went

to the expense of tearing down their old pageant house in Mill Lane
and of building a new one, although at that time the pageants at
Coventry were actually in process of immediate decay. What could
have caused the weavers so far to mistake the trend of the times?

Item in prymis payd at takinge doune of the house and the tilles, for hieryng of a rope and caryinge the leade to the store house, & for drynk to the worke-men that same day	ijs xd
Item payd to carpenters for ther wages	iiijli iiiis iijd
Item payd to the masones for ther wages	viijs iiijd
Item payd to the tilers for tiling and dauhing	xvijs viijd
Item payd for stone and for carying of stone	xijs
Item payd for sand and claye	vs ijd
Item payd for lyme and for heare, to make mortar	ixs viijd
Tiles 9s. 6d., timber 30s. 8d., spars and stoods xis. viijd.	
Item payd for a hundred & halfe of bryckes	ijs ijd
Item payd at the rearyng of the house and on the nyght befor	
summe is	xjli xvijs xd

A good many entries have to do with agreements between crafts for
the playing of one play and their respective duties and obligations in
the matter of costs. There are also entries that indicate that certain
plays once acted as one play were divided between two crafts, the
introduction of new plays into the cycle, and the loss or omission of
plays that had once been acted. Many are merely attempts to make
various companies meet their financial responsibilities.

A matter of real importance in the study of the mystery plays is
that of playbooks and revisions. There seem to have been two sorts
of books in common use, but perhaps this was not a universal custom.
There was at York, in the hands of municipal authorities, a register
containing all the plays of the cycle, and there were single plays in the
hands of individual guilds. The plays of York are typical of this
situation, and many of the ideas in common circulation are based on
conditions at York generalized for all plays. York was a great ecclesiastical centre, the seat of an archbishop, and at York there was,
relatively speaking, careful supervision of plays. The consequence is
that the York cycle is at once the greatest and most religious of cycles,
but even at York there were certainly playbooks abroad in the possession of crafts. Either registers or individual plays might be referred to
as 'originals'. At Coventry I found no record that indicated that

there was such a thing as a register of all the plays, but every evidence that the guilds had copies of their own plays and that they provided freely for the revision of such plays. There are five manuscripts of all the Chester plays, but it is at least questionable whether there was ever a formal register of all plays. Certainly the plays at Chester were, as at other places, subject to individual revision by the crafts that played them, and there seems to be no evidence of the revision of all the plays at one time and as one effort. Indeed, each play seems to have its own textual history. In the *Shearmen and Taylors' Pageant* of Coventry it is still possible to see an unobliterated juncture between the Nativity scenes originally belonging to the shearmen and the Three Kings of Cologne scenes presumably originally belonging to the tailors. Pageants were subject, most of them, to rewriting, to merging with another play, and to division into two or more parts, each of which constituted a new and separate play.

An interesting aspect of the mystery plays is their management and what may be called their public relations, and one gets an idea of procedure from the *Coventry Leet Book*; for example:

1424. Wevers . . . Item. Arbitrati sunt et ordinaverunt quod dicti jorneymen et eorum quilibet solvet dictis magistris annuatim in futuro quatuor denarios ad opus de le pagent eorundem, et quod ipsi le jorneymen habeant cum magistris suis potacionem - sive collectionem [sicut] antea consuerunt, &c.—*Coventry Leet Book*, f. 27.

1441. Ordinatum est quod Robertus Eme et omnes alii qui ludunt in festo Corporis Xpisti bene et sufficienter ludant, ita quod nulla impedicio fiat in aliquo ioco sub pena xx s cuiuslibet deficientis ad usus muros levanda per majorem et camararios, &c.—Ibid., f. 102b.

1457. [The king came to Coventry on] Fryday the xj of Fevyere the yere reynyng of kyng Herry the sixt the xxxv^{ti}. . . . The quene [on margin]. On Corpus Xpisti yeven at nyght then next suyng came the quene [Margaret] from Kelyngworth to Coventre; at which tyme she wold not be met, but came prively to se the play there on the morowe; and she sygh then alle the pagentes pleyde save domes-day, which myght not be pleyde for lak of day. And she was loged at Richard Wodes the grocer, where Ric. Sharp some-tyme dwelled; and there all the pleys were furst pleyde. At which tyme the meyre and his brethern sende unto her a present which was sich as here suyth: That is to wit, ccc paynemaynes, a pipe of rede wyne, a dosyn capons of haut grece, a dosyn of grete fat pykes, a grete panyer full of pescodes and another panyer full of pipyns and orynges and ij cofyns of counfetys and a pot of grene gynger. And there were with her then these lordes and ladyes that here folowen: That is to sey, the duke of Bukkyngham and my lady his wyff and all ther childern, the lord Revers and my lady hys wyf, the lady of Shrowesbery the elder, and the lady of Shrowesbery the younger, with other mony moo lordes and ladyes. And the Friday then next suyng she remeved to Colshull to her mete and so to Eculsale to the prynce; at which tyme the seid meire and his brethern with right good feliship of the seid cite, which plesid her highnes right well, brought her to the utmast syde of theyre fraunchice where hit plesyd her to gyff them grete thank bothe for theyre present and theyre gentyll attendaunce.—Ibid., f. 173b.

1474. Hit is ordened at this present leete that every crafte with-in this cite com with their pageaunts accordyng as hit haith byn of olde tyme, and to com with their processions and ridynge also, when they byn required by the meir for the worship of this cite, peyne of x li. at every defalte.—Ibid., f. 227b.

1494. For-asmoche as the unyte, concorde, and amyte of all citees & comenaltees is princi-pully atteyned and contynued be due ministration of justice and pollytyk guydyng of the same; forseyng that no persone be apprised nor put to forther charge than he con-venyntly may bere and that every persone withoute favor be contributory after his substance and facultees that he useth to every charge had and growying for the welth and worship of the hole body; and whereso it is in this cite of Coventre that divers charges have be continued tyme oute of mynde for the worship of the same, as pagants and other, whech have be born be dyvers crafts whech crafts at the begynnyng of such charges were more welthy, rich, and moo in nombre then nowe be, as openly appereth; for whech cause they nowe be not of power to continue the seid charges without relief and comfort be shewed to them in that partie; and inasmuch as there be dyvers crafts in this cite that be not charged with like charges; as dyers, skynners, fysshemongers, cappers, corvisers, bochers, and dyvers other. Therfore hit is ordeyned be this present lete that the maire and viij of his counceill have auctorite to call all the seid crafts and other that be not charged to the forseid charges and them to adioyn to such crafts as be ouercharged with the forseid pagants uppon peynes be hym and his seid counceill to be sette. And if any persone refuse such unyon and contribu-cions, or such resonable measne to be taken be the discrescion of the seid maire and his counceill, such persone so refusing to forfet and paye such peyn in that partie so to be sette be the seid maire and his counceill. And that such resonable measne in the premisses to be taken be the seid maire and his counceill to be of like force and effect as yf it had be made at the present lete.—Ibid., f. 273.

1494. Also it is ordeyned, at the same lete, at the request of the inhabitaunts dwellyng in Gosseford strete, that the pageants yerely frohensfurth be sette and stande at the place there of olde tyme used and lymyt appoynted, uppon payn of every craft that doth to the contrary to lese at every defalt vj s viij d to the use of the cite, to be levyed and paide.—Ibid., f. 273b.

1507. Memorandum. That it is ordeyned at this lete that the craft and feliship of bakers shalbe contributories and charged from hensforth with the craft and feliship of smythes and to pay yerely to them toward theyre pagent at Corpus Xpisti tyde xiij s iiij d, and so to continewe from hensforth yerely. Ibid., f. 297b.

There are many other records from Coventry such as these, and similar ones also from York, Newcastle, Beverley, and other cities. Those printed above give a fair picture, although by no means a complete one, of the public aspect of the plays year by year. There are levies of expenses and attempts to equalize costs. The entry for 1494, for example, is rather fine in its justice and public spirit, and one may believe that it is characteristic of the sort of democracy practised in the Middle Ages. That of 1457 tells of a pleasant visit by Margaret, the unfortunate queen of Henry VI, to Coventry in order to see the plays, and of the simple and cordial honours paid her; also of her gracious reception of them. This was three years before the Battle of Wakefield. From 1494 comes one of the numerous adjustments made by the city authorities as to the stations or playing-places of the processional play, and there are many entries such as that of 1507 that have to do with the no doubt difficult matter of requiring crafts not responsible for pageants to make contributions to those that were. One of the interest-ing records, nowhere exactly paralleled, has to do with the appoint-ment of a pageant master. It is printed above from the lost accounts of the Smiths' Company as published by Thomas Sharp.[1] It shows how in one case many minor necessary details were attended to.

[1] *Dissertation on the Pageants or Dramatic Mysteries, Anciently Performed at Coventry, by the Trading Companies of that City*, loc. cit., p. 11; *Two Coventry Corpus Christi Plays*, loc. cit., p. 83. In the latter work, App. I and II, Sharp's collections from Coventry records, many of which are now lost, are reprinted. *The Coventry Leet Book* has been edited by Mary Dormer Harris, E.E.T.S., Original Series, cxxiv (1907), cxxxv (1908), cxxxviii (1909), cxlvi (1933).

V

Introduction to the Study of the English Religious Drama in the Middle Ages
The Chester Cycle

IN the study of the English religious drama we have set aside without prejudice *débats*, *estrifs*, dialogues, minstrelsy, monastic literary drama, the Feast of Fools, popular festivals, folk plays, ridings, mummings, and May games, because, although these activities are interesting and, like other social ways of men, were contributory in various ways to the medieval religious drama, they are not the thing itself and would never have become so. From this extra-dramatic point of view there are moreover several things of greater importance to us in our task of right understanding. These we shall have to treat summarily, but cannot wholly neglect. For the external and operative aspect of the medieval religious drama, which was communal, we need to know something about the church and its permeating and dominating activities, also something about guilds and trading companies and the government, even the politics, of medieval towns and cities, and the spirit of obedience that characterized the English community, particularly in the fourteenth and fifteenth centuries. To do this and to understand the plays themselves we shall need, not only to rid our minds of haste and sophistication, but to become, imaginatively at least, domestic, religious, rural, provincial, and peaceful in mind about these things. This is important, but perhaps may be left to casual inference from official records, from accidental bits of information that reveal motives, and especially from the plays themselves if they are read respectfully and patiently. These plays may sometimes seem almost childish, and at other times pompous, crabbed, or unskilful; but some knowledge of the spirit that created, developed, and enjoyed the plays may help us find the human level of their appeal. Medieval people prized the plays for the stories they told, and this is perhaps still the best gateway. The one subject we have emphasized so far in this book is the relation of medieval religious drama to liturgy or church service, and this, inadequate as it is, we have sought to justify by including the Latin liturgical drama in our subject. Indeed, we have said and shall endeavour to prove that the religious drama of the Middle Ages is from beginning to end a medieval institution in one piece.

The remains of this drama left us by the Renaissance and the Reformation remind one of the undestroyed parts of a badly bombed city of which a few fine buildings have been spared; also a few ordinary structures and a number of still valuable fragments. Specifically, chance has left us in English four full Corpus Christi cycles, a few fragments of cycles, and a small number of religious dramas that were never parts of the Corpus Christi play. These are all we have, and they are valuable in various ways. The Chester, York, and Wakefield cycles and the unlocated cycle in British Museum MS. Cotton Vespasian D. viii. are all extensive documents and in the field of Middle English literature all noteworthy in learning and culture, in vitality, and in religious earnestness. Each is possessed of special characteristics of the greatest interest. As regards the fragments of lost cycles, we have not been too fortunate. The Norwich and the Newcastle-upon-Tyne plays are not such as we would have chosen, but the two pageants from the lost Corpus Christi play of Coventry, supported as they are by abundant records, are in our present state indispensable. As to the independent plays—the plays of Abraham and Isaac, the Digby plays, the Burial and Resurrection preserved in a Bodleian manuscript, and the rather puzzling Croxton Play of the Sacrament—each of them has something to tell us about the nature and scope of the popular religious drama of medieval England.

We cannot, however, form a correct conception of our subject as a whole without counting our losses. The medieval religious drama in England has been too narrowly conceived of because chance has given us four great Corpus Christi plays with a good deal of information about them and has left us little about the great contemporary rival of the Corpus Christi play, namely, the Passion play of London and southern England. What for lack of information can hardly be imaginatively restored is the situation in London and the south of England, where the Passion play prevailed. In London in

1378 minor clergy of St. Paul's were presenting the 'History of the Old Testament' at Christmas. In 1384 a mystery play at Skinners Well lasted five days, and in 1409 we learn of a play there by certain *clerici Londoniae* that apparently lasted for five days and told 'How God created Heaven and Earth out of nothing, and how he created Adam and so on to the Day of Judgement.' It may be inferred that the Passion plays of southern England were played on stationary stages and that in London perhaps the performers were minor clergy. The 1409 play at Skinners Well seems to have been of full scope.[1] What relation, if any, it had to guilds and trading companies we do not know, although we know that London had its Corpus Christi procession and that guilds regularly went in it in a specified order of precedence. The London plays must have attained the height of medieval magnificence. We may conjecture with reasonable assurance that the Passion plays of southern England were in form somewhat like those of France and Germany. That is, they were plays, with or without Old Testament subjects, centring in the Passion and Resurrection, probably lacking plays of the Nativity and possibly lacking plays of the Final Judgement. We may also conjecture less certainly that such plays were like another drama on British soil, the tripartite play in the Cymric dialect of Cornwall, *Origo Mundi*, *Passio Domini*, and *Resurrectio Domini*, although the Cornish Passion play may have come from Brittany and not from the south of England. The loss of these great Passion plays from the most populous and dominant region of England forces us to conclude that the greater religious drama of the English Middle Ages was, neither quantitatively nor qualitatively, what it is ordinarily thought to have been.

The group of independent plays enables us to broaden our conception of the English religious drama of the Middle Ages by carrying it into towns and villages, and the sum total of dramatic activity may thereby be increased. Smaller places, lacking trading guilds and great wealth, may nevertheless have done their bit by presenting regularly plays of smaller compass, such as the Conversion of St. Paul, the History of St. Mary Magdalen, and the lives and martyrdoms of saints. That the provincial, often no doubt parochial, population and the members of schools and colleges did participate extensively in the

---

[1] Chambers, op. cit. ii. 379–82.

religious drama is beyond question. The records, often casually preserved, are fairly plentiful, widespread, and varied.

When we look at the religious drama from the point of view of
growth or development, certain facts and probabilities stand out as
significant. Indeed, it is possible to perceive certain definite stages of
change. In the thirteenth and earlier centuries we may be reasonably
certain, in spite of the paucity of English records and survivals, that
the dramatic practices of the continent of Europe prevailed also in
England. Europe was one community under the church, and the
indications are that there were in England liturgical plays of normal
forms in general use. When one considers such documents as are
known to exist, the status of other medieval arts in England, and the
religious activities of great English ecclesiastical centres, such as
York, Lincoln, and Norwich, we need not be too modest. Certainly
the Christmas and Easter cycles must have been very generally known,
in Latin and later in the vernacular. There were probably Old
Testament plays in various places besides London and probably
other liturgical plays not provided for at Christmas and Easter.
Whether there was originally in England a play dealing specifically
with the Passion is a matter of doubt, as also whether, apart from
London, there were plays of the Last Judgement.

At any rate, in the part of the field that concerns us most there
was in the second quarter of the fourteenth century a great event in
the world of the mystery play, namely, the institution of the Corpus
Christi play. It has been suggested above that, at that time, there must
have been in various northern, eastern, and midland cities a gathering
together of the whole religious story into one great series extending
from the Fall of Lucifer to the Final Judgement. The indications are,
certainly for York, that use was then made of plays already on hand,
although there and probably elsewhere it would have been necessary
in order to achieve completeness to borrow missing parts or to have
such parts composed anew according to a well-understood pattern.
Evidences derived from original or liturgical elements in various
Corpus Christi plays point, as we shall see, to great simplicity in
the Corpus Christi play at the time of its institution. The pattern to
be followed in the construction of a Corpus Christi play was everywhere available—in the church service, in the Scriptures, in many

learned works, and in various narratives in the vernacular. It is certain that in the fourteenth century, whether when the Corpus Christi play was set up or later we do not know, resort was had at York to the *Northern Passion*, a very simple poem in northern English that told the story of Christ's ministry, His Passion, and His Death and Burial.[1] It was translated from the French early in the fourteenth century and was extremely popular. It affected the York–Towneley cycle deeply, particularly of course the Passion group of plays—the Conspiracy, the Last Supper, the Agony and Betrayal, the Trial before Caiaphas, the Condemnation, the Bearing of the Cross, the Crucifixion, and the Death and Burial. Indeed, it is believed by both Miss Foster and Miss Lyle that the York–Towneley Passion group was originally composed on the basis of the *Northern Passion*. This poem has also influenced the Hegge plays of the Passion, although it is probably not the original source of that series.

This use of the *Northern Passion* is the beginning of a tendency in all Corpus Christi plays. We may believe that mystery plays before the institution of the Corpus Christi cycles were prevailingly simple and scriptural, and the *Northern Passion* itself follows the gospels closely. But with the next expansion that appears in the York–Towneley plays, certainly in the fourteenth century, we have the introduction of the New Testament apocrypha in the use by a reviser of certain plays of the *Gospel of Nicodemus* a poetical translation into northern English of considerable merit.[2] This suggests the basis of a great expansion undergone by the English mystery plays in the later four-teenth and the earlier fifteenth centuries. The apocryphal gospels in the Middle Ages might be described as sacred writings, and from no point of view can they be regarded as inconsiderable. With their ecclesiastical sanction and their vivid and earnest presentation of realistic and yet marvellous detail they offered a safe and interesting ground for the amplification of the mystery plays ready no doubt to

[1] *The Northern Passion*, edited by Frances A. Foster, E.E.T.S. (London, 1913, 1916), 81–101; Marie C. Lyle, *The Original Identity of the York and Towneley Cycles* (Minneapolis, 1919), pp. 4–29.

[2] W. A. Craigie, 'The Gospel of Nicodemus and the York Mystery Plays', *An English Miscellany. Presented to Dr. Furnivall in honour of his Seventy-fifth Birthday* (Oxford, 1901), pp. 56–61; *The York Plays*, edited by Lucy Toulmin Smith (Oxford, 1885), pp. lxviii–lxix; *The Middle-English Harrowing of Hell and the Gospel of Nicodemus*, edited by W. H. Hulme. E.E.T.S. (London, 1907), p. xviii; Lyle, op. cit., pp. 30–46.

advance beyond the limits of the liturgy. The dramatization of the New Testament apocrypha may therefore be thought of as a stage of growth. Of these writings the Gospel of Nicodemus is the most picturesque and was the most popular. It consists of the *Acta Pilati* and the *Descensus Christi ad Inferos*, joined rather inorganically together.

The former presents an account of the Trial, Condemnation, Crucifixion, and the Death and Burial of Jesus within the gospel account, but adds to it a great deal of legendary material mainly defensive of Pilate and explanatory of the life and actions of Joseph of Arimathea. The latter gives the circumstances of the Burial of Jesus in the tomb of Joseph and the Setting of the Watch at the sepulchre as well as the Visit to Hell. The northern poet followed, not the purer Greek text, but the Latin version with its various apocryphal expansions, such as the legend of the Oil of Mercy and the coming of Antichrist. The Harrowing of Hell was one of the most popular works of the whole Middle Ages, and it is impossible to be too posi-tive about it or the *Acta Pilati*, as the immediate source of particular works, for there attached themselves to the Gospel of Nicodemus a large body of subordinate apocrypha, many of which played an im-portant part in the late medieval drama. There are the Epistle of Pilate, the Report of Pilate to Tiberius Caesar, the Reply of Tiberius to Pilate, the Death of Pilate, the life of Joseph of Arimathea, and the Vengeance of the Saviour. The *Descensus* also had amplifications. The *Protoevangelium Jacobi*, also important among the apocrypha, comes from the second century and covers the events from the birth of the Blessed Virgin Mary to the Slaughter of the Innocents; Pseudo-Matthew, from the birth of Mary to the youth of Jesus. The Gospel of the Nativity of Mary gives her history before the birth of Jesus. The History of Joseph the Carpenter is a biography of St. Joseph thought to have originated in connexion with the feast of that saint. The Gospel of Thomas, one of the oldest and most popular of the New Testament apocrypha, enters with other apocryphal works strongly into the fifteenth-century plays of the Death and Assumption of the Blessed Virgin Mary. Finally, in the major group of New Testament apocrypha, mention should be made of the Gospel of the Infancy of Jesus, which covers the period from the Nativity of Jesus to his twelfth year. From it come the wonders and miracles of the sojourn in Egypt. The contents of these gospels will suggest how important they are in the growth of the mystery play, but they are by no means all, since there are about thirty other gospels and fragments, various apocryphal epistles and apocalypses besides the apocryphal Acts of the Apostles. To be sure, the immediate use of New Testament apocrypha as sources for mystery plays was characteristic of France rather than of England, but England was by no means immune. The result is that the whole subject of the sources of the medieval religious drama is one of great complexity, not so much as regards ultimate as immediate sources. The material was everywhere, and in that respect there is a circumstance that needs to be remembered. The fourteenth- and fifteenth-century redactors of English mystery plays seem usually to have followed vernacular and not Latin sources. To say therefore that such and such a play or episode comes from Peter Comestor, Nicholas de Lyra, or even *Legenda Aurea* is often not so much wrong as wrongly stated. It may well be true that the particular theme as dramatized appears in these learned works, but it is often impossible to say that it did not make its way to the mystery stage through some vernacular channel, for the greatest body of Middle-English literature is devoted to the presentation in English poetry or prose of the great mass of medieval Latin religious literature. One has to remind oneself that the story of man's creation, fall, and redemption with its multifarious amplifications was *the* medieval subject and that it was common property.

Not until after the York cycle had made its greatest use of the *Northern Passion* did it begin to revise certain plays from the apocryphal Gospel of Nicodemus. The change from simple gospel narrative to apocrypha is significant. This revision affected the First and the Second Trials before Pilate, the Harrowing of Hell, the Resurrection, and perhaps some others. It is, so far as we know, the herald of other redactions by the use of the New Testament apocrypha in this cycle and probably in others, and we may use it to mark a third stage in the growth of English mystery plays, the first being the liturgy and the second the establishment of the Corpus Christi play. This third stage we may think of as an expansion based mainly on the rather brilliant body of writings known as the New Testament apocrypha. There was some use of Old Testament apocrypha, but such use is relatively unimportant. This fact is an answer to those who talk vaguely about the secularization of the mystery plays. There were of course comic, even vulgar, interludes, but in the English mystery plays they are as nothing compared with the quite respectable and reverent apocryphal revisions. The materials out of which these amplifications were composed were to the minds of medieval people authoritative, sacred, and dramatically interesting. They were religious and not secular.

If the Corpus Christi cycles were more numerous than they are and at the same time showed the features of three out of four of the extant cycles, we might go one step farther and suggest still another stage of development in mystery plays before about the middle of the fifteenth century when the manuscripts of the York, the Towneley, and the Hegge plays were made. At York the latest redactor, as we shall see, was a writer of the traditional accentual alliterative verse. His quality is clearly marked; his interests were religious, his style of its kind excellent, and his dramatic talent noteworthy. At Wake-field the latest redactor was the so-called 'Wakefield Master', a genius in the use of language, rhyme, and stanza-form, an almost unequalled medieval wit and satirist, and yet capable of seriousness and tender-ness. In the Hegge plays the latest redactor was relatively a poor poet, but his intentions were perhaps also literary.

CRITICAL APPROACH TO THE SUBJECT

What was said in the Introduction to this volume about the religious drama as an expression of the medieval mind and disposition is necessary to any successful study of the subject. We must not look at medieval religious plays through modern eyes, confuse them with the drama of the Renaissance, or admire them for wrong or accidental or sporadic things. The earlier chapters of this book have given us much information as to the origins and early developments of medieval religious plays and groups of plays, and this background must be borne in mind, for it offers a constant and enduring frame of reference. The mystery plays after they fell into secular hands were not of course by any means faithful to their simple religious beginnings. They were full of aberrations, and their secularity grew as time went on. But they never lost their motive force essentially, much less completely.

When they did so, they were at their end, no longer medieval religious drama. It follows that we must not forget their religious purpose and must not view them as free enterprises in secular and individualistic dramatic art. We must also recognize a certain freedom to follow local traditions and influences while they adhered to their inherited dramatic prepossessions. And we must constantly bear in mind the great pattern of man's creation, fall, and redemption furnished by the services of the liturgical year with which the religious drama of the Middle Ages began. No doubt this original scheme was more or less legitimately amplified from the pages of Scripture and less legitimately amplified from the apocrypha and from legends of all sorts, but in general the ancient framework held.

In approaching the study of the English mystery plays chronology is also important. The matter is one of great difficulty, since records are scarce, and the work of scholars in the field is full of misapprehensions. Throughout the period of about 250 years—from the beginning of the fourteenth until slightly beyond the middle of the sixteenth century—religious plays were undergoing in various places and at various times continual amplification and revision. As the plays were revised and rewritten, they grew regularly farther from their Latin sources and also, let us say, farther from their simple vernacular beginnings. At the opening of the fourteenth century, and perhaps during a large part of that century, most of the mystery plays must have been scarcely more than amplified translations or paraphrases of Latin originals. They probably followed Scripture or liturgy closely, and they were written in old and simple metres and stanzas. In the long preservation of these poetic forms we find a useful key to the chronological development of the mystery plays.

Among the prevailing forms in English poetry of the thirteenth and earlier fourteenth centuries were octosyllabic couplets and quatrains, the latter rhymed alternately.[1] Neither was regular either in rhyme or in the number of feet to the line. For an example of the rhymed couplets of four feet take Jacob's prayer for guidance at the opening of the Towneley Jacob (VI):

> Help me lord, adonay,
> And hald me in the right way

[1] George Saintsbury, *A History of English Prosody* (3 v. London, 1923), i. 50–85 *et passim*.

To mesopotameam;
ffor I cam neuer or now where I am;
I cam neuer here in this contre;
lord of heuen, thou help me!
ffor I haue maide me, in this strete,
sore bonys & warkand feete.
The son is downe, what is best?
here purpose I all nyght to rest;
Vnder my hede this stone shal ly;
A nyght*is* rest take will I.

Illustrations of old quatrains may come from many places. The following, in which the Third Shepherd comments on the message of the angel, is from the *Pastores* (ll. 19–22) of the *Shrewsbury Fragments* and illustrates the old quatrain:

He said a barn schuld be
  In þe burgh of Bedlem born;
And of þis, myn*n*es me,
  Oure fadres fond beforn.

There was also the romance stanza that appears in Chaucer's *Sir Thopas*, the *rime couée*, which is rhymed aa⁴b³aa⁴b³ or aa⁴b³cc⁴b³. The following is from the Towneley Creation (I), ll. 49–54. God speaks,

Son & moyne set in the heuen,
With starnes, & planett*ys* seuen,
  To stand in thare degre;
The son to serue the day lyght,
The moyne also to s*er*ue the nyght;
  The fourte day shall this be.

An old form, similar to the *rime couée*, is the ballad stanza commonly used in the Chester plays and apparently still written there in the sixteenth century. It rhymes aaabaaab or aaabcccb, in which all lines are of four feet except the fourth and eighth which are usually of three feet. For example, a lament of Maria Magdalena in the play of the Resurrection (XIX) is as follows:

Alas! nowe lorne is my likinge;
For woe I wander, and handes wringe;

My harte in sorowe and in sickinge
   Is sadly set and sore.
That I moste loved of all thinge,
Alas, is nowe full loe lyinge;
Why am I, Lorde, so longe livinge,
   To lose thy luxom lore?

Another form that puts in an early appearance and has a caudal feature is of six lines rhyming aaabab, all lines being octosyllabic except the fourth and sixth, which have three feet or less. This stanza lived on in Scottish song and became celebrated in the hands of Robert Burns. The Towneley Resurrection (XXVI), lines 328–33, a stanza cancelled in the manuscript apparently because of its doctrine of the eucharist, is an example:

That ilk veray brede of lyfe
Becomys my fleshe in wordys fyfe;
Who so it resaues in syn or stryfe
   Bese dede for euer;
And whoso it takys in rightwys lyfe
   Dy shall he neuer.

Three other stanzas of frequent recurrence in the mystery plays may possibly need illustration. They are more elaborate, but it will be noted that they are built out of elements present in the early forms. First the so-called northern septenar stanza rhyming $ababababab^4cdcd^3$. The following is from a debate between Christ and Satan in the Harrowing of Hell (York XXXVII, Towneley XXV): Satan argues that the souls in limbo belong to him because of their sins:

A! þis wolde I were tolde in ilk a toune.
   So sen þou sais God is thy sire,
I schall þe proue be right resoune,
   Þou motes his men in to þe myre.
To breke his bidding were thei boune,
   And, for they did at my desire,
Fro paradise he putte þame doune
   In helle here to have þer hyre.
     And thy selfe, day and nyght,
      Has taught al men emang,
     To do resoune and right,
      And here workis þou all wrang.

Jesus replies that these matters were provided for in prophecy:

> I wirke noght wrang, þat schal þow witte,
>   If I my men fro woo will wynne,
> Mi prophetis playnly prechid it,
>   All þis note þat nowe be·gynne.
> Þai saide þat I schulde be obitte,
>   To hell þat I schulde entre in,
> And saue my seruautis fro þat pitte,
>   Wher dampned saulis schall sitte for synne.
>   And ilke trewe prophettis tale
>   Must be fulfillid in mee,
>   I haue þame boughte with bale,
>   And in blisse schal þei be.

Another stanza of some currency is that of the Proclamation of the Hegge play. It rhymes abababab⁴cdddc³:

> Of Abraham is þe fyfte pagent
>   & of ysaac his sone so fre
> how þat he xulde *with* fere be brent
>   & slayn *with* swerd as ʒe xal se
> Abraham toke with good A·tent
>   his sone ysaac & knelyd on kne
> his suerd was than ful redy bent
>   & thouth his chylde þer offered xuld be
>   Vpon An hyll full Ryff
>   than god toke tent to his good wyl
>   & sent An Angel ryth sone hym tyl
>   & bad Abraham a shep to kyl
>   And sauyd his chyldys lyff.

Finally, there are many complicated stanza·forms in the mystery cycles, and the most famous will serve our turn. The following lines are spoken by the Second Shepherd in Towneley *Pagina Pastorum* I when he offers the infant Jesus a ball:

> hayll, lytyll tyn mop/rewarder of mede!
> hayll, bot oone drop/of grace at my nede;
> hayll, lytyll mylk sop!/hayll, dauid sede!
> Of oure crede thou art crop/hayll, in god hede!
>   This ball
>   That thou wold resaue, —
>   lytyll is that I haue,
>   This wyll I vowche saue, —
>   To play the *with* all.

There is some recognizable progression in point of time among these metres and others. Indeed, there is a presumption, based as we shall see on the appearance of these early forms in simple and archaic plays and parts of plays, that these early popular metrical patterns (with their irregularities) were used in putting the Latin plays into Engish. Redactions, revisions, and complete rewritings of mystery plays were extensive and may be said to have been the general rule, but fortunately there are cases in all the cycles, and most obviously in the Coventry plays, where some of the oldest and most primitive parts of the plays were left unchanged for centuries. There was possibly something sacred about the old forms that caused them to be spared amidst the wholesale adornments and beautifications that beset and usually degenerated the mystery plays. The undisturbed portions are always essential parts of the plays concerned and, like the Latin plays themselves, close to Scripture or liturgy. In some cases, and perhaps as a whole, such casually preserved fossils give us a clue to the growth and development of the English mystery plays.

Closely in accord with the liturgical drama, these early forms, both in Latin and the vernacular, have a simple fidelity to religious story and religious feeling. All redactions of which we have any knowledge are in the direction of secularity—humorous, didactic, or narrative. Robert Croo, the Coventry redactor, rewrote about 1534 both the *Shearmen and Taylors' Pageant* and the *Weavers' Pageant*.[1] His revision was in some measure typical and in nothing more so than in the fact that his purpose was improvement. He did not rewrite the whole of these plays but only certain parts of them. He let the old central cores of the plays remain standing with few changes and composed amplifications of the plays in what was no doubt to him and his employers a more attractive style. It is easy to identify by their pomposity and their metrical confusion the parts that he rewrote. This conjecture was established by the author's discovery of two leaves of an earlier version of the *Weavers' Pageant*, themselves perhaps a century earlier than Croo's redaction. With the exception of Robert Croo at Coventry we have almost no external evidence, no records, no names of revisers, no knowledge of occasions when plays were or were likely

[1] J. M. Schipper, *Altenglische Metrik* (Bonn, 1881), i. 154 and i, sect. 171; *Two Coventry Corpus Christi Plays*, loc. cit., pp. xxiii–xxvi, xxxv–xxxviii, 119–22.

to have been revised, but we are nevertheless sure that plays were from time to time revised. The obvious and inescapable charac/teristic of such reworkings is that in general later revisions are farther from original sources than are first versions or intermediate versions. The narrative parts of the liturgy are the original sources, early vernacular plays and unrevised parts of certain plays are first versions, and rewritten plays and parts of plays are third, fourth, and it may be fifth versions.

The traces of such revisions of mystery plays are still to be seen in the two extant Coventry plays, and in some other plays, in the variety of metres, some historically older than others, used by revisers at different times, for such revisers seem to have employed metres and poetic styles current at various times during the two/and/a/half centuries when the mystery plays were undergoing growth and change. No hard and fast rules for determining dates can be derived from this fact, but in general some probable suggestions as to dates and relative stages of development can be found. For example, there seems to have been no currency of the Chaucerian stanza, that in which *Troylus and Criseyde* is written, before Chaucer's day. After that the stanza is widely current, although mainly in badly conceived and executed forms. Indeed, the metrical confusions of the fifteenth and early sixteenth centuries seem to point definitely to a post/Chaucerian stage or period in the history of English poetry.[1] It is also worth while in this connexion to call attention to ten Brink's opinion based on philo/logical grounds that the Towneley plays of Isaac and of Jacob show in their final form greater age than any other English mystery plays.[2]

Very primitive parts, both in form and contents, are, as beforesaid, still to be seen, along with obviously later additions, in the two pageants preserved from the Coventry cycle. There appear in the *Shearmen and Taylors' Pageant* in simple but not always regular octo/syllabic quatrains the following episodes that will be recognized as carrying the gist of the biblical story: the Annunciation, ll. 47–99; the Journey of Joseph and Mary to Bethlehem, ll. 168–203; the Angels and the Shepherds (in part), ll. 303–6, 321–4; the Coming

[1] Saintsbury, op. cit., 288–98.
[2] B. ten Brink, *History of English Literature*. English translation (3 v. London, 1883–96), ii. 244, and iii. 274.

of the Magi, ll. 529–32, 540–7; the Meeting together of the Magi, ll. 558–73, 582–9; the Summoning of the Magi to appear before King Herod, ll. 632–43, 652–5, 670–3; the Offering of the Magi of gold, frankincense, and myrrh, ll. 699–724; the Warning of the Magi by an angel to go home another way, ll. 733–44; Herod's plot to destroy the Magi, ll. 693–800; Herod's rage at their escape, ll. 802–13; Mary and Joseph warned to flee into Egypt, ll. 818–29; the Slaughter of the Innocents, ll. 830–46; the Escape of Joseph and Mary, ll. 884–91. A similar use of the octosyllabic quatrain can be seen in the first 814 lines of the *Weavers' Pageant,* and in that play also these stanzas carry the substance of the original play. Robert Croo, or any earlier redactor, might have so revised these plays that the metre, style, and tone of these parts would have been modernized beyond recognition, but the fact is that it was not done. That any fifteenth- or sixteenth-century reviser would have written these parts in an archaic style is an absurd hypothesis.

Another early metre that appears in the Coventry plays is a more or less successful attempt to write according to the rhyming scheme and metre of the eight-line ballad stanza prevailingly used in the Chester plays.[1] Throughout the two Coventry plays passages written in the Chester metre offer in general clear readings, and, although this metrical scheme is used to contaminate other metres, passages written in it seem usually to be uninterrupted. It may be, of course, since it is an old form, that some episodes were composed or translated originally into it. It is, however, interesting to note that many of the more humorous parts of the plays, including most of the Shepherds' play, parts of the Visit of the Magi, and nearly all of the dove episode in the Presentation in the Temple, with a majority of the excrescences of story and incident and many incidental speeches, are in pure or approximate Chester metre. A natural inference is that these two Coventry plays underwent an early and thorough-going redaction in this eight-line stanza or in approximations to it.

A third metrical form is a seven-line stanza rhyming ababbcc. It is of two sorts. The first is rhyme royal having five accents to the line.

---

[1] *The Chester Plays.* Edited by Thomas Wright, Shakespeare Society (2 v. London, 1843, 1847); edited by H. Deimling and G. W. Matthews. E.E.T.S. (2 pts. London, 1893, 1916); *The Play of Antichrist from the Chester Cycle,* edited by W. W. Greg (Oxford, 1935); *The Trial and Flagellation* (edited by F. M. Salter) *with other Studies in the Chester Cycle* (by W. W. Greg), Malone Society (London, 1935).

It is evidently post-Chaucerian and is used for the opening speeches of Isaiah, Herod, Simeon, and Anna. The other kind has only four accents to the line and is more puzzling. It usually makes sense and is used for normal dramatic discourse of a didactic nature. In both sorts the rhyme of the final couplet of the stanza is continued in the first and third line of the succeeding stanza, thus throwing together three lines with the same rhyme, a peculiarity that has caused the metre to be misunderstood and corrupted. Very great corruption, especially in the work of Robert Croo, does appear, and in general it may be said that the greater the metrical corruption the later the text is apt to be.

These illustrations drawn from the Coventry plays will serve to make clear a method of attack on the problem of the composition of the mystery plays. When such indications can be found and when they are supported by the presence of original and structural material, on the one side, or by excrescent and derivative material, on the other, they will be found to throw light on the composition and develop-ment of mystery plays and to help one to understand the long process by which English mystery plays gained in length and variety, but at the same time lost much of their original simplicity, beauty, and religious significance.

THE CHESTER PLAYS

The Chester cycle,[1] almost certainly the oldest Corpus Christi play in England, and certainly, as preserved, the one that retains most perfectly the original form and spirit of the Corpus Christi play, somehow escaped the excessive and unregulated changes under-gone by other cycles in pursuit of fifteenth-century modernization. Something in the situation at Chester or in an element of control exercised there kept them, for the most part, simple and religious. At first acted of course on Corpus Christi day, they were shifted probably by 1447 to Whitsuntide. Chambers[2] suggests very plaus-ibly that they were shifted in order to avoid interference with the Corpus Christi procession, which would thus be able to retain its religious character and to secure the undivided attention of the com-munity. The plays were acted on three successive days in Whit

---

[1] See p. 165, note 1.   [2] Op. cit. ii. 352-4.

week—nine on Monday, nine on Tuesday, and seven on Wednesday.
They were acted on heavy vehicles, usually described as carriages,
and travelled from one station to another through the city. The
description comes from the *Breviary of the City of Chester*, a collection
of information about Chester made in the late sixteenth century by
Archdeacon Robert Rogers and quoted above.[1] The starting-point
was the Abbey Gates, and the last station was at the Roodee. Salter
points out that, although this route was downhill all the way, it
took no less than seven men in 1572 to draw the Coopers' pageant
wagon. If the vehicle was to be used in the next day's performance,
as no doubt many of them were, it could be brought up at night over
a relatively short distance to the Abbey Gates for a new start.

There were towards the end twenty-four pageants. Manuscript H
shows the Flagellation and the Crucifixion as a single play, a circumstance that would reduce the total number to twenty-three. Salter[2] has
shown, however, that this is a very late combination, possibly in 1575
only, and Greg adduces evidence from the heading of the Peniarth
manuscript of the *Antichrist*, where that play is numbered XX, that
at some time late in the fourteenth century there were only twenty-
two.[3] There are two sets of banns, or public announcements, recited
on St. George's day by the town crier, who on his rounds was accompanied by the stewards of each craft or trading company. He also
read at the Roodee the mayor's annual proclamation against disturbers
of the peace at the time the plays were to be given. One of these sets
of banns, late and stupid, announces twenty-four pageants, but there
is an older set much more homogeneous with the cycle as we have it
that represents the cycle at an earlier stage and mentions twenty-five
pageants.[4] The extra pageant is thus described:

[In margin] Wyues
The wurshipffull wyffys of this towne
ffynd of our Lady thassumpcion
It to bryng forth they be bowne
And meyntene w^t all theyre might.

[1] *The Digby Plays*, edited by F. J. Furnivall, the New Shakespeare Society, reprinted
in E.E.T.S. (London, 1882), pp. xxviii–xxix; Chambers, loc. cit.; F. M. Salter, *The Trial
and Flagellation*, loc. cit., pp. 25–26, 121–63.　　　　[2] Op. cit., pp. 6–13.
[3] *The Chester Play of Antichrist*, loc. cit., pp. xiv, xx–xxi. Salter, loc. cit.
[4] *The Trial and Flagellation*, loc. cit., pp. 130–9. The late banns, published by Wright and
by Deimling, appear in British Museum MS. Harley 2150.

Greg argues[1] on the ground that the 'worshipful wives' did not form
a guild and that they gave a number of separate performances of the
play that it was not a regular part of the cycle, but it is said that they
are bound to maintain it, that it was for a long time acted as part of
the cycle, and that it became the prey of post-Reformation prejudice.
The Chester plays cover a large number of subjects, although the
treatments of most of them are brief. One play, for example, will often
present three or four subjects. The cycle also has its peculiarities, an
unusually large number of themes not appearing in any other English
collection. Most of these will be considered later.

An indication of local pride in the plays is an interesting story of
their origin, long treasured and often repeated. It has to do with the
translation, or, at any rate, the preparation in English from a foreign
language of the Chester plays. This widespread tradition assigned the
plays to Ranulf Higden (d. 1364), a Benedictine monk of St. Werburgh's Abbey in Chester, a well-known scholar who wrote his
Polychronicon by about 1327. This chronicle records the entire history
and geography of the world from the creation to Higden's own day,
and, as translated into English (1387) by John of Trevisa, a Cornish-
man and a Fellow of Exeter College, Oxford, it became a principal
instrument of historical instruction for generations. There is nothing
improbable about the date, which was 1328, or the assignment of the
English version of the Chester plays to Higden, especially since that
version from its beginning must have been an orderly and skilful
work. So unified in style and purpose was it that to their latest day
the Chester plays suffered less at the hands of revisers and redactors
than did any other known cycle of mystery plays.

Another name persistently associated with the origin of the Chester
plays is that of a famous mayor of Chester, John Arneway, called also
Hernway, mayor from 1268 to 1277. It is obvious that Arneway
could not have been concerned with an event that occurred in 1328
and that he could not have been associated with Ranulf Higden, who
did not take his monastic vows until 1299, so that one or the other
of the two features of the tradition must be wrong. Sir Edmund
Chambers made an ingenious explanation of the inconsistency by
observing that the mayor of Chester recorded for the years 1327 to

[1] *Bibliographical and Textual Problems of the English Miracle Plays* (London, 1914), pp. 28-29.

1329, covering the period in question, was Richard Erneis or Herneys and that the names Arneway and Herneis, both greatly varied in pronunciation and spelling, are sufficiently alike to be mistaken for each other. Since John Arneway was the more famous of the two mayors, the establishment of the Chester Corpus Christi play was popularly assigned to him. Mr. Arthur Brown has, however, advanced reasons for questioning the dates of Arneway's mayoralty. It appears from British Museum Additional MS. 29777 and from MS. Harley 2013 that Sir John Arneway may after all have been mayor of Chester in the years 1327–8. Brown shows also that the chronology supplied by Rupert Morris in his *Chester in Tudor and Plantagenet Reigns* is unreliable. This discovery does not, however, affect the traditional date for the establishment of the Chester cycle or their authorship.[1]

A third person connected by tradition with the enterprise of establishing the Chester Corpus Christi play was Sir Henry Francis, who by 1377 had become senior monk in the Monastery of St. Werburgh. An old and apparently reliable tradition says that Francis went thrice to Rome before he secured from Pope Clement, possibly Clement VI (1342–52), a grant of forty days' pardon to everyone who resorted to the plays in a peaceable manner, and ten additional days of pardon from the bishop of Chester on the same terms. There is, however, a late record (1628) that states that Higden himself went thrice to Rome before he could obtain the pope's leave to have the plays, which presented the substance of the Bible, in the English tongue. This is of course evidently a product of the anti-Catholic belief current in 1628 that the pre-Reformation popes and clergy sought to prevent the people from having access to the Scriptures in their own language. It seems therefore probable that it was Francis and not Higden who, after the plays were a going concern, went to Rome to obtain the pope's indulgence and that it was Higden, a properly qualified person whose name is persistent in the tradition, who is to be credited with translating the plays, and that the plays were ready for performance about

---

[1] Chambers, op. cit. ii. 348–56. The validity of Chambers's explanation is attacked by J. C. Bridge in *Journal of the Architectural, Archaeological and Historic . . . of Chester*, vol. ix (1903) and is apparently disregarded by F. M. Salter and Robert H. Wilson (cited below). See Arthur Brown, 'A Tradition of the Chester Plays', *London Mediaeval Studies*, vol. ii, pt. 1 (1951), pp. 68–72.

1328. It seems also clear that, according to the tradition, the guilds or trading companies of Chester were involved in the Corpus Christi play from its beginning. This feature of the tradition, since it appeals to local pride, would be very important in the spread of the plays to other cities.

We must be on our guard against the modern understanding of the operation and significance of translation or, indeed, of borrowing or what we should call plagiarism. The men of the Middle Ages lived in a world in which everything that could be known was already on record. There was no thought even of the possibility of creation out-right or of its desirability. The body of knowledge that men possessed was common property, and such originality in our sense as appeared was in some measure accidental or such as arose from the skill of the individual writer or his superiority in interpretation and illustration. One work therefore rested on another of the same kind, development might be described as incremental, and translation and authorship were scarcely discriminated the one from the other. Nevertheless, the question of whether or not the Chester plays were translated, adapted, or otherwise derived from French originals is one of great interest and importance, and we must give attention to it.

This tradition, many times repeated in the sixteenth and seventeenth centuries, says that Higden 'devised and made' or 'invented' the plays and that he 'redused yᵉ whole history of yᵉ bible into Englishe stories in metter in yᵉ Englishe tounge'; also that he was thrice at Rome before he could obtain leave of the pope to have them in the English tongue. It is clear from Chambers's most reasonable interpretation that it was Higden who prepared the plays and that it was Sir Henry Francis who visited Rome. It is also clear that the petition to the pope was not that they might have the plays in English, but that they might obtain a grant of indulgences to those who resorted to the plays in a peaceable manner. It is implied that translation is involved rather than new and fresh authorship, although most writers on the subject have apparently believed that Higden wrote the Chester plays *ab initio* and have failed to realize that these plays had been in existence sometimes for centuries. Higden must have been perforce mainly a translator and redactor.

If, as the tradition implies, the Chester plays were translated and, we may believe, adapted from a foreign language, from what language did they come? At that late date it could hardly have been Latin, for, as we have seen, religious plays had all been translated into vernacular languages, and no Latin plays of such scope and length are known ever to have existed. There would be a probability in favour of a French original, and evidences of such a French original for the Chester plays have been gradually and tentatively accumulated.

J. H. Markland (1818)[1] makes a general statement to the effect that there are resemblances between the English and the French mystery plays. This is repeated by Thomas Sharp (1825).[2] J. P. Collier (1831)[3] put forward a definite claim that the Chester plays were originally French and supported his claim by citing the fact that in the Chester plays there are a number of passages in French, also by calling attention to several parallels between the Chester plays and *Le Mistère du Viel Testament*,[4] which are about as close as any that have ever been cited. For example, in play IV, lines 337–40, is Isaac's speech to Abraham:

> Father, I pray you, hyde myne eyne
> that I se not your sword so kene;
> your stroke, father, wold I not seene,
> lest I against yt grill.

This is paralleled in *Le Mistère du Viel Testament*, lines 10227–30:

> Mais vueillez moy les yeulx cachier,
> Affin que le glaive ne voye
> Quant de moy vendres approchier;
> Peult estre que je foudroye.

Also this from the Balaam play in Chester (v. 177–9):

> am I not, Master, thyne owne Ass,
> to beare the whether thou woldest pas?
> And manye winters readye was.

---

[1] *A Dissertation on the Chester Mysteries*, Roxburghe Club, 1818; reprinted in Boswell–Malone, *Shakespeare* (1821), ii. 525–49.
[2] *A Dissertation on the Pageants or Dramatic Mysteries, Anciently performed at Coventry*, loc. cit. ii. 131–2.
[3] *A History of English Dramatic Poetry to the Time of Shakespeare* (3 v. London, 1831).
[4] *Le Mistère du Viel Testament*, loc. cit.

as compared with *Le Mistère*, lines 26,915–17:

> Ballaam, suis je pas ta beste,
> Sur qui tu as tousjours este,
> Tant en yver comme en este.

Thomas Wright in his edition of the Chester plays (1843) quotes Collier with tentative approval, as does A. W. Ward (1875).[1] Ten Brink with his usual insight declares that the resemblances between the Chester plays and the French mysteries can be 'scarcely by accident'.[2] A. R. Hohlfeld in an important study of the English mystery plays[3] goes still farther in his claim for a French original for the Chester plays. That was in 1889, and the next year appeared a very extensive study of the subject, possibly provoked by Hohlfeld, by H. Ungemacht.[4] He makes a general search for the sources of the first five Chester plays, and his work is not exclusively devoted to proving that these plays were translated from *Le Mistère du Viel Testament*, as is usually thought. In fact his work would have been much more valuable if it were. His book is vague and indefinite in method and gets into the region of medieval legendary and theological commonplace, where nothing very definite can be determined. Ungemacht and other writers who have considered the relation between the Chester plays and *Le Mistère* have failed to take into account the fact that *Le Mistère du Viel Testament* was a very different thing when it was put into print in 1500 from what it must have been at the end of the first quarter of the fourteenth century when it may have been translated into English and set up as the Chester cycle. We may believe that it was then much simpler, much shorter, and much more faithful to biblical or liturgical sources. Whereas the Chester plays in a provincial English medieval city have remained relatively faithful to the biblical story and simple in dramaturgy and style, *Le Mistère* has undergone that extensive amplification from which most mystery plays throughout Europe and, so far as we can tell, all mystery plays in France suffered between the early fourteenth

---

[1] A. W. Ward, *A History of English Dramatic Literature to the Death of Queen Anne* (2 v. London, 1875), i. 45.

[2] Op. cit. ii. 277.

[3] 'Die altenglischen Kollektiv=Mysterien', *Anglia*, xi (1889), 219–310.

[4] *Die Quellen der fünf ersten Chester Plays*, Münchener Beiträge 1 (Munich, 1890), pp. 116–18 *et passim*.

and the beginning of the sixteenth centuries. Therefore parallels in language between early forms and later forms must often have been obliterated almost completely, and only occasional passages can be expected to retain the marks of their origin. Ungemacht did not know this, nor have his critics known it. The question then is, what were the component parts of *Le Mistère du Viel Testament* in an earlier form, say that of the end of the fourth quarter of the fourteenth century? The answer is that these individual plays, not yet having undergone the almost incredible expansion and stylistic modification that French plays underwent mainly in the fifteenth century, were primitive in dramaturgy, simple in style, and still relatively close to biblical or liturgical sources. Ungemacht is therefore not to be criticized, although he did not know the significance of what he was doing, for finding parallels between perhaps a dozen lines in the Chester cycle scattered through 400 lines of *Le Mistère*, for this is the sort of thing that might be expected to happen when one version stood relatively still and the other was extensively rewritten.

Some of the parallels cited between the Chester plays and *Le Mistère* are close and probably valid indications that certain Chester plays were translated from an early form of *Le Mistère*, but no actual certainty can be arrived at from parallel passages in such a case as this, especially since both texts are derived ultimately from biblical or liturgical sources that could be counted on to produce parallels in any two mystery plays on a given subject. This point is made convincingly by A. C. Baugh in a general article on possible French influence on the Chester plays.[1] In order to arrive at proof or a very high degree of probability the argument from sign must be clear and definite. There must be special features, agreement in peculiarities of structure and event, in which the presence of identity or resemblance is clear. Professor Baugh recognizes this fact and studies unique episodes in the Chester plays in their relation to the French mysteries.

Among others he cites the play of Abraham and Melchisedek, unique in Chester among other English cycles. The fact that such a play appears in the greater French collections has little or no significance, since these French plays have been so expanded as to include

---

[1] 'The Chester Plays and French Influence', *Schelling Anniversary Studies* (New York, 1923), pp. 35–63.

nearly all the stories in the book of Genesis. It is more pertinent to ask how it came into the Chester cycle, where it is a very special feature of an original Old Testament group. All English cycles have of course plays or episodes that are special to them, but there is special significance in the fact that in both the Chester plays and *Le Mistère* the play is brought in in connexion with the story of Abraham and Lot. The Chester play, *Pagina Quinta de Mose et Rege Balak et Balaam Propheta*, agrees in unusual features with an episode in *Le Mistère du Viel Testament*, and this agreement, moreover, is supported by early documents in the liturgical drama. The Chester play of Balaam is really a prophet play of the same original type as the Rouen *Prophetae* and as that appearing in the Benediktbeuern Christmas play. It is well known that a tiny play of Balaam and Balak appears in the procession of the prophets and that Marius Sepet makes use of this fact to support his theory that the Old Testament plays came into existence by what Chambers calls budding out from the parent stem of the *Prophetae*. The scene of the prophets in the Benediktbeuern Christmas play, in which the number of prophets is abridged, retains, however, this same feature. The play in the Chester cycle has lost something in the earlier part of the *processus*, but at the end brings in an unmistakable group of Messianic prophets—Isaiah, Ezekiel, Jeremiah, Jonah, David, Joel, and Micah. Prophets would of course be less attractive to an audience than the speaking ass, and some of them have been lost. It is, however, to be noted that the Chester play still has a *Princeps Syna-gogae* who corresponds to the *Archisynagogus* of the Benediktbeuern play. The Chester play has also a scene of Moses receiving the Tables of the Law, which is apparently an unnoticed case of a scene budding forth from a *Prophetae*. Such a thing is not entirely without record, as appears in an entry discovered by Bishop Wordsworth in the Chapter *computi* of Lincoln Cathedral. As before noted, one Thomas Cham-berleyn is assigned tithes in the amount of 8*s*. 8*d*. for a spectacle (*visus*) at Christmas that was called *Rubum quem viderat*.[1] This back-ground of Latin drama makes it therefore highly significant that plays XXIX and XXX in *Le Mistère du Viel Testament*, which have been rewritten and very fully amplified, still retain this anachronistic

---

[1] Chambers, op. cit. ii. 377–8; C. Wordsworth, *Notes on Mediaeval Services in England* (London, 1898), p. 126.

association of Moses and the Tables of the Law with the play of
Balaam and Balak. The latter scene, which is based on Numbers
xxii, is introduced without warning near the end of a play on the life
and ministry of Moses, which is a dramatization of considerable parts
of the book of Exodus.

Another play, to which Baugh gives great importance in determining the relation between the Chester cycle and *Le Mistère*, is that
of Octavian and the Sybil, which forms a part of the sixth Chester
play. It is not found in any other English cycle, although it is common
enough in the French mysteries, appearing, as it does, in *Le Mistère du
Viel Testament*, the Semur Passion,[1] the Arras Passion, the two
Passion plays from Valenciennes, and the Rouen *Nativité*. A distin-
guishing mark is its association in Chester VI and in *Le Mistère* with
the legendary Temple of Peace in Rome. In *Le Mistère* (XLV) the
legend of Octavian and the Sibyl has been made into an elaborate
and learned independent play of the Conversion of Octavian with
much space devoted to the Roman Sibyls and their sayings. One of
these sybils, presumably the Erythrean Sibyl, appears of course in the
story of the Conversion of Octavian as it appears in the Chester play of
the Nativity, where it is properly treated as a New Testament subject.
Play XLV stands last in *Le Mistère*, and what seems to have happened
is that, in the great amplification carried out in the French cycle, the
subject was made into a drama separate from the Nativity, and, when
the Old Testament plays were cut off from plays of the Nativity, the
Passion, and the Resurrection, the revised and enlarged play of
Octavian and the Roman Sibyls was incorrectly left with the plays of
the Old Testament. In other words, the division of the original full
cycle was made at the beginning of the Annunciation, the first New
Testament subject. Of course, the fact that the sibylline prophecy was
an original feature of the *Prophetae* might have caused this to be done,
but the fact remains that Octavian in *Le Mistère du Viel Testament* has
been made into an Old Testament character.

Other unique features of the Chester cycle are the Woman Taken
in Adultery and the Healing of the Blind Man at the Pool of Siloam
in the composite play XIII, Christ at the House of Simon the Leper,
which includes also a very simple version of the Conversion of Mary

[1] *Le Mystère de la Passion en France*, edited by E. Roy (Dijon, 1903), pp. 58 ff.

Magdalen, a theme not elsewhere present in English cycles. As Baugh points out, these subjects are of common occurrence in France. This is also true of an episode in play XIV, Jesus in the House of Simon the Leper, namely, the Cleansing of the Temple. These and other special or unique themes present in the Chester cycle and in various *mystères* offer indications of close relations between the Chester plays and the French plays; but, since no obvious parallels among the French *mystères* have been found to plays in the Chester cycle except in the Old Testament group, it is hardly profitable to follow the subject farther. The closest analogues to the Chester plays seem to occur in the *Passion* from Arras and in the great work of Arnoul Greban. Indeed, in the latter case Baugh[1] has found remarkable correspondences between Greban's *Passion* and the Chester plays of the Creation and Fall of Man; in the scene of Cain and Abel in Chester II, the agreement is not only in scriptural subjects, but in no less than seven instances in which the subject-matter is not drawn from the Bible. A minor indication, not without value, of a French background for the Chester plays is seen in the often noted fact that in other English plays and in the apocryphal source the midwives in the Nativity are Salome and Zelumi, whereas in Chester and in the French plays they are Salome and Zebel or Tebel.

The passages in French that appear in the Chester plays are conventional, serving nearly always for the pompous and tyrannical utterances of great personages, such as Pilate and Herod, and such passages occur in other English cycles. There is no explanation of their use except the somewhat obvious conjecture that from old times French (and sometimes Latin) was thought of as satirically appropriate for supposedly great persons over-conscious of their own importance. The allusions to France, however, in the twelfth Chester play (ll. 251–2) and in the fourteenth (ll. 421–4) may have, as Baugh points out, some significance.

On the basis, then, not of parallel passages and general probabilities, but of agreement in unique matters of structure and contents, we may be sure that the Chester plays were translated and adapted from the French. We may go even farther and believe that the resemblances between the Old Testament plays of the Chester cycle and

[1] Op. cit., pp. 51–61.

the corresponding parts of *Le Mistère du Viel Testament* are too close to be matters of chance or of independent variation on the part of the Chester cycle. However, for this view to have the highest degree of probability, it is necessary to realize that the plays of *Le Mistère du Viel Testament*, now amplified to the last degree, were at an earlier time as simple and primitive as are the Chester plays now, or indeed more so. Allowance must be made for that great growth and develop/ ment undergone by the French *mystères* between the end of the fourth quarter of the fourteenth century and the beginning of the sixteenth century. After all, it is an accident of English provincial conservatism that the Chester plays are as simple as they are.

As a corollary to this well/established theory, not so well/authenti/ cated as one could wish, is the proposition that the particular French play translated and no doubt redacted by Ranulf Higden was of the Corpus Christi model, probably a Corpus Christi play itself, a play that extended in its scope from the Fall of Lucifer to the Last Judge/ ment. If that conjecture is sound, it would follow that that full/scope French play so translated and adapted must later in France have been cut in two, and the earlier part of it, dealing with Old Testament subjects, must have been used as the basis of *Le Mistère du Viel Testa/ ment*. The part not used in this way has never been found, but perhaps no one has ever looked for it. Of course one cannot be confident about this theory until such a French Nativity, Passion, and Resurrection has been identified. To have produced such an overwhelming redaction as that to which *Le Mistère du Viel Testament* has been subjected would have required the labours of special authors, who searched the Old Testament Scriptures and dramatized practically every subject they came to. They also introduced a certain amount of classical and apocryphal matter as well as homiletic and historical lore. In doing this they might have discarded the old plays *in toto* and begun afresh, but for some reason they did not do so. The primary features of an older cycle are left. Whenever in going through the great six/volume *Mistère* one comes upon matters belonging to the traditional drama, one is apt to find an older style in older metres— octosyllabic couplets and quatrains and *rime couée*, as also a closer correspondence with the Chester plays. It is no wonder that those who have difficulty in thinking historically, when they were told that certain Chester plays were translated from *Le Mistère du Viel Testament*, should have looked at the matter askance, for the Chester plays were obviously not translated from or modelled upon *Le Mistère* in its only preserved late form.

There are extant no less than five manuscripts of the Chester cycle as a whole, two manuscripts of single plays, and a small fragment of another play. They are described by Sir Walter Greg in detail.[1]

D. 1591. This manuscript was formerly in the possession of the Duke of Devonshire and is now in the Huntington Library. It is incomplete at the beginning, and at the end is signed 'By me Edward Gregorie scholler at Bunbury the year of our lord god 1591'. It is the oldest full manuscript in existence and is thought to preserve the older forms of the language with greater fidelity than the rest.

W. 1592. British Museum Add. MS. 10305. It is a small ornamented manuscript, each play, as if separately collected, being signed at the end 'per me Georgi Bellin'. Bellin was the official scribe for the guilds of the Coopers, the Ironmongers, and the Cappers and Pinners.[2] This manuscript was followed by Thomas Wright in his edition of the *Chester Plays* for the Shakespeare Society.

R. (Sometimes designated as *h* or K) 1600. British Museum MS. Harley 2013. This manuscript, which greatly resembles W, is a favourite with editors. It is also the work of George Bellin, who subscribes several plays 'per me Georgium Bellin 1600'.

B. 1604. Bodleian MS. S.C. 175. It is also perfect and at the end is signed '1604, per me gulielmum Bedford'. Like others of these manuscripts it has never been studied as a whole.

H. 1607. British Museum MS. Harley 2124. The manuscript is complete and was thought, somewhat paradoxically, by Deimling, the Early English Text Society editor, to present the cycle in an earlier form than any other in spite of its being the last to be written down. He is not in the case of certain plays, notably that of Balaam and Balak, to be considered as mistaken, since H preserves a text of that

---

[1] *The Play of Antichrist,* loc. cit., pp. xv–xxii; also *Bibliographical and Textual Problems,* loc. cit., pp. 34–38; F. M. Salter, *The Trial and Flagellation,* loc. cit., pp. 1–45 *et passim.*
[2] Salter, op. cit., p. 31.

play older in form than that of DWRB. Strangely enough, the same manuscript shows plays XVI and XVII in the very latest possible form, since these plays are there united into one, a union that Salter shows[1] is very late, possibly appearing only in 1575, the last year in which the Chester pageants were performed.

In addition to these complete manuscripts of the Chester cycle, there are also two manuscripts of single plays and one small fragment:

P. *c.* 1500. *Antichrist.* Hengwrt-Peniarth collection in the National Library of Wales at Aberystwyth. It is a vellum manuscript of very good workmanship, although it has suffered much from time and ill-usage. It is suggested by its editor that it is a prompt copy, but it seems more likely that it is an 'original' once belonging to the Dyers of Chester that had been superseded or lost.[2] It is probably the oldest manuscript of any Chester play preserved, and, taking advantage of the new point of view it affords, the editor made an elaborate study of the textual history of all six manuscript versions of the play of Antichrist and concluded that P is co-ordinate with the source of all the other five manuscripts, they being variously interrelated. In this and in the whole textual history of the play he is undoubtedly right. He decided, however, not unnaturally in view of a theory to be mentioned below, that the scheme of the relations of all the full manuscripts was that worked out for the Antichrist play.

C. 1599. This is a manuscript belonging to the Coopers' guild of Chester discovered by Professor F. M. Salter about 1933 or 1934 in the Coopers' Enrolment Book, 1597–1776. It is a copy of the Coopers' play of the Trial and Flagellation and is in the hand of George Bellin. Salter decided on the basis of his own study of variant readings that C does not fit in and agree with the scheme of the order and arrangement of the five complete manuscripts of the Antichrist, but has nevertheless an intelligible relation to other versions of the play as it appears in the full cycle. Salter's work is sound, and it offers a contradiction and partial refutation of the relation of the cyclic manuscripts generalized from the textual study of the Antichrist play. The validity of Salter's findings, however, was not admitted by Sir Walter Greg, and there the matter stands. The whole issue is laid out

---

[1] Ibid., pp. 6–13.   [2] *The Chester Play of Antichrist*, loc. cit., pp. xx ff.

quite clearly and frankly in the Malone Society's edition of the Trial
and Flagellation referred to above.

M. Early, but of uncertain date. It is a fragment 41 lines long of a
vellum manuscript of the Chester play of the Resurrection discovered
in the binding of a book. It is in the Manchester Free Public Library.
It too is contemporary with or earlier than the source of any of the five
full manuscripts and, like the Peniarth Antichrist, gives no trouble
as regards the relative priority of any one of the principal copies.

It is perhaps possible to find some way out of the impasse described
above. Greg[1] proceeds on the theory that there was in the hands of
the corporation at Chester a register of all the plays, an official manuscript of the whole cycle, not like the register at York into which at
one special time the individual York plays were collected from the
guilds and copied in their cyclic order as they came in, but an ancient
and authorized true copy from which the various Chester crafts
copied their plays. Salter also accepts this theory and speaks several
times of the 'Register of Plays kept in the Town Hall', indeed con-
structs his theory of the interrelations of the manuscripts of the Trial
and Flagellation on the assumption that there existed such an
authoritative register from which the greater number of the full
manuscripts were copied. This source was, he thought, much
emended and in parts illegible.[2] Chambers[3] merely says that an
'authoritative copy of the plays . . . seems to have belonged to the
city'. In point of fact the evidence supporting the belief that there was
an official register of the Chester plays is tenuous. It is obvious of
course that the corporation supervised the plays, perhaps with unusual
strictness. The smiths, for example, in 1575 submitted two alterna-
tive plays for the choice of the corporation. And we are confronted
by the fact that the Chester plays as compared to other cycles kept
more closely their older forms, a result that could hardly have been
achieved except by careful oversight. And yet evidence of the existence of a master copy is reduced to two records, neither of which is
completely convincing. The Peniarth manuscript of the Antichrist
play[4] has as its heading the name of the pageant, 'de falla . . .

---

[1] *Biliographical and Textual Problems*, loc. cit., pp. 44 ff.
[2] *The Trial and Flagellation*, loc. cit., pp. 28 ff.   [3] Op. cit. ii. 355.
[4] *The Chester Play of Antichrist*, loc. cit., pp. xx–xxii; *Bibliographical and Textual Problems*,
loc. cit., p. 27.

antechristi' and 'XXma', for *vicesima*. These markings are regarded as proof that the Peniarth manuscript had at some time been copied from a collective manuscript. This hardly follows, since the number of the pageant (officially important) as well as the title would have appeared had the play been a guild 'original' or copied from a guild original. Again, it is stated that 'on one occasion the smiths paid for permission to peruse the "original"'. 'Original' throughout the Chester records refers to the play-book owned by the company, and this record is capable of such an interpretation.

One might therefore call in question the statement that 'in the five collective manuscripts we clearly have texts of the whole cycle as officially recognized'. And if it is true that 'there is nothing in any of them to suggest that they were compiled, like the York "register", by transcribing a number of separate play-books in the hands of the various guilds', and that 'where divergencies of tradition appear, they seem to affect the whole cycle, not merely individual plays', one simply could not account for the differing and earlier version of the Balaam and Balak play mentioned above and for moralistic and homiletic bits appearing in manuscript H as compared to other manuscripts. Another hypothesis might better suit the facts, namely, that these manuscripts resulted from collection of plays still in the hands of the guilds in the late sixteenth century. If so, there must have been at least two independent collections, the one represented by H and an earlier one represented by DWRB. The evidence seems to be that these collections were made by amateurs and possibly for antiquarian reasons and that the individual scribes apparently felt at liberty to make such modifications as seemed best to them. This supposition would indicate that the work of both Greg and Salter is sound and that, if the textual history of each particular play in the cycle were subjected to the careful textual method outlined and followed by Greg, we should find a textual history for each play, some no doubt having a similar history, and that new and logical groupings would emerge.

British Museum MS. Harley 2150 is a collection of miscellaneous papers relating to the history of Chester. Among them is a copy of the 'comen bannes', that is, of the rhymed announcement or proclamation of the plays about to be played, with the contents of each play and the name of the trading company performing it. These banns, although dated by Chambers[1] about 1544–7, are said to be copied out of a lost document called 'The White Book of the Pentice' and are of a much earlier date, certainly before the Reformation. They give with few exceptions a straightforward account of the plays as we have them and may be said to be in the spirit of the cycle itself. They are written in the Chester ballad stanza, aaabaaab or aaabcccb. For an understanding of the Chester plays as they were performed for more than two centuries these banns must always be considered. Changes in the cycle after they were prepared are evidenced by the listing of a play of the Assumption of the Blessed Virgin Mary, as before mentioned, occupying the fourth place from the end of the cycle; also by a disruption of the metre that indicates that pageant number VIII, the Adoration of the Magi, was not originally provided for. It seems to be a case of the division into two parts of an original Magi play, perhaps in order to provide the vintners with a play of their own. The earlier part of the eighth play presents antique matter in a sound Chester style, but in lines 261 to 337 there appears additional, rather pompous matter in poorly managed Chester stanzas. These banns also show the Flagellation and the Crucifixion as separate plays.

Another Harley manuscript (1944), called a 'Breviary or some few Collections of the City of Chester', was made, as noted above, by Archdeacon Robert Rogers (d. 1595) and written up by his son David Rogers in 1609. It is an important document, since it contains the well-known description of the Chester pageants and their vehicles and follows it with a set of the later banns. These are written in awk-ward long-line stanzas intended to reproduce the Chaucer stanza. These pompous post-Reformation banns are accompanied by pious anti-papistical comments in prose, and the banns themselves end with an apology for the rude style of the plays and the unprofessional acting of the players.

THE PLAYS

The Old Testament group of Chester plays, in which have been found greatest resemblance to the French *mystères*, are, for the most

---

[1] Op. cit. ii. 350–1. See F. M. Salter, 'The Banns of the Chester Plays', *Review of English Studies*, xv (1939), 433–57; xvi (1940), 1–17, 137–48.

part, very faithful to Scripture. This is, however, not true of the first play, which deals with the Fall of Lucifer. That subject was not liturgical and indeed was relatively new. The whole subject of Satan as an embodiment of evil underwent careful theological treatment in the twelfth and thirteenth centuries by the greatest authorities of the time—Peter Lombard (d. 1164), St. Thomas Aquinas (d. 1274), Albertus Magnus (d. 1280), Alexander of Hales (d. 1245), and others. There was, however, no cultus of evil angels, and the Fall of Lucifer was comparatively simple. The account of the rebellion and fall of Lucifer in the *Historia scholastica* (1176?) is short and evidently an addition to the work, and the story in *Cursor Mundi* (c. 1300), although expanded and made picturesque, is still on simple lines. After the Dominican Iohannes Tauler (d. 1361) there was a cult that gave names, characteristics, and classification to evil angels as well as good. The first Chester play belongs to the older state of the subject. Only Lucifer and Lightborne are given names in the Chester play and these two are confused with each other. On the other hand, in the corresponding play in *Le Mistère du Viel Testament* —*Le Trébouchement de Lucifer*—the demons have been subjected to classification and have been given learned and interesting names. The angelic figures of the Chester play are presented with a knowledge of the Nine Orders of the Angels derived from *The Celestial Hierarchy* of Pseudo-Dionysius, but there is no particularization.

This play is written not in the Chester stanza (aaabaaab or aaabcccb) but in octosyllabic quatrains and double quatrains, eight-line stanzas with alternating rhymes. The two forms seem to be used discriminatingly, God and Lucifer using double quatrains and the ordinary angels and demons using quatrains. One feature of the style of this play has some importance for mystery plays as a whole. How old, one might ask, are the long-lined stately introductions to mystery plays? In this play they are obviously old and, since a similar feature is found in *Le Mistère*, they may go back to the beginning. *Deus Pater* speaks a total of 36 long alliterative lines rhyming in couplets or quatrains.

The Chester Fall of Lucifer is very simple, almost domestic, in action. After God's announcement of His power and glory, He reminds Lucifer and/or Lightborne of the honours He has bestowed upon them and warns them to be loyal. He goes away from home, and Lucifer begins to boast of his own beauty and to declare his intention of seating himself on the throne of God. The good angels are shocked at his behaviour as children in a family might be shocked at the behaviour of a particularly bad child. God returns and punishes Lucifer by casting him out of heaven. Thenceforth they lose their names and make their lamentations as Primus and Secundus Demon. A Latin note in the text of manuscript H refers intelligently to the sixth verse of the Epistle of Jude and to Isaiah xiv. 12 ff. God closes the play with a speech on pride and disobedience. Before He does so, He divides light from darkness, and a Latin note quotes Genesis i. 3. Latin stage directions and notes are given faithfully in manuscript H, but are often omitted in the other manuscripts or translated into English.

The second play, the Creation and Cain and Abel, is entirely in the Chester stanza and follows the Bible closely. There is an account of the creation proceeding day by day for five days. Then we are told in a stage direction (Latin in H and English in other manuscripts) that God goes from the place he was in to that in which he creates Adam, evidently a high part of the pageant. Biblical quotations (in Latin in H) follow from Genesis i. 26 and ii. 7. Adam is singularly reticent, and God creates Eve. Their creation finished, H provides quotations from the Bible—Genesis ii, Matthew xix, Mark x, Ephe-sians v, and 1 Corinthians vii. A stage direction then announces the entrance of Demon, who speaks at length and theologically. At the end of his speech we have surprisingly the 'Versus': *Spinx Volucris penna, serpens pede, fronte puella.* The temptation of Eve then begins, and the Demon speaks as *Serpens.* Eve yields without hesitation, and Adam eats without inward struggle or protest. They are both without any sophistication, and their only worry is their nakedness. They procure fig-leaves, and, when God enters, they are quietly submissive and merely utter a few lamentations. There is no interplay between them, and about their behaviour there is an unmistakable suggestion of little children who are scared. God clothes them in skins, admonishes them briefly, and departs, leaving them in charge of angels numbered *Primus, Secundus, Tertius,* and *Quartus.* Adam advances to the fourth chapter of Genesis and recounts his dream in which he beheld the glories of Heaven. Then Adam digs and Eve spins, and they teach their children like good parents. Cain and

Abel make their offerings. Cain quarrels with Abel and slays him and repents at once when God asks, 'Where is thy brother Abel?' Cain has to run away from home, and Adam and Eve sorrow like ordinary parents, not like voluble persons of the better class, but like repressed but respectable peasants who have never expected much from life. Again, there are Latin quotations from the Bible (omitted in other manuscripts) and Latin stage directions in H. It is not adequate to say that the scribe, James Miller, had an 'archaizing tendency', for this is the *res ipsa*.

The third play, the play of the Deluge, is written throughout in the Chester stanza and shows little evidence of amplification. There is only one small bit, two quatrains alternately rhymed, in another metre. In this the 'Good Gossopes' remark that, since the Flood is coming in, the best thing they can do is to have a drink. This is a very mild concession to comicality, especially if one remembers the great lengths in rebellion to which Noah's wife and her associates go in other Noah plays. Nevertheless the appearance of the theme of the recalcitrance of Noah's wife in the standard measure is an indication that from the beginning, however reverent and biblical the Chester plays were, there were elements of comicality in them. No play makes more naïve use of them than does this.

The fourth play, important mainly for its presentation of one of the best dramatic subjects in the whole cycle, namely, the Sacrifice of Isaac, begins with the blessing of Melchisedek bestowed on Abraham. Lot offers Melchisedek the bread and wine, and there follows between God and Abraham a dull dialogue on the Circumcision. Then, as a mere narrative incident, appears the story of the Sacrifice of Isaac. The choice of this great subject was merely formal, or accidental, since it was in the story of Abraham's life in Genesis; but, once chosen, its compelling interest caused it to spread widely. This might serve to rid us of the impossible idea of dramatic selection of subjects by authors. Isaac in the play is meek, submissive, and reticent. It is only his recollection of and longing for his mother, his asking that his eyes may be blindfolded so that he will not see the sword, and his desire to remove his clothes so that they will not get blood on them that offer a suggestion of the emotional possibilities of the theme. Isaac is a simple boy who carries the wood for the fire in a cheerful and upstanding way. The play is written throughout in Chester stanzas and seems little, if at all, changed from its primitive state. Of course all amplifications may not show, since it is clear that redactors of the Chester plays often made their revisions in the Chester stanza.

We have seen in the foregoing play how the presence of a theme of superior dramatic interest might make itself felt both by its own expansion and by its crowding out of less interesting matter. In the fifth Chester play of Balaam and Balak this tendency, we may believe, had begun to operate before the play was established in the Chester cycle. It has been said above that the play of Balaam and Balak was originally a *Prophetae* and that one manuscript (H) still retains at the end a considerable number of Messianic prophets; whereas in the other manuscripts (DWRB) the prophets have been discarded in favour of a rather innocuous continuation of the Balaam and Balak theme. Both Moses and Balaam, however, still utter their prophecies. The newer versions not only amplify the Balaam and Balak play by the substitution of 104 lines at the end, but they enlarge the play in other places—16 lines at the end of the Moses episode, 39 boastful lines for King Balak after line 116, 8 lines expressive of Balaam's disobedience before the angel appears in his way (after line 160), and an additional stanza of bad advice from Balak to Balaam after line 216. One can thus see a prophet play in the very last stage of conversion into a Balaam and Balak play. The play, even in the amplificatory parts, is written throughout in the Chester stanza.

The sixth Chester play is entitled *Pagina sexta de Salutatione et Nativitate Salvatoris Ihesu Christi*, but it contains a great deal more than is provided for in the title. In fact in this play we find a different, less purely scriptural, more legendary basis than is to be found in the Old Testament group. The manner remains simple enough. Manuscript H is well stocked with stage directions and scriptural quotations in Latin. The play presents brief and orderly versions of the Annunciation and the Visit to Elizabeth, an almost serious version of Joseph's Trouble about Mary in line with Scripture and untouched by the legendary accounts given in the apocryphal *Evangelium de Nativitate Mariae* and the *Protoevangelium Jacobi*. After that comes the extraordinary scene of Octavian and the Sibyl, whose likeness to *Octovien* in *Le Mistère du Viel Testament* has already been noted. The action of the scene is rapid and, in a simple way, very secular. Lines 177–304 are a development of Luke ii. 1 ff. There is a dialogue between Octavian and the Senators in which Octavian denies his godhead (ll. 305–52); they consult the Sibyl, who prophesies the birth of Christ (ll. 353–84). Preco, the officer of the emperor, summons Joseph to go up to be taxed. Joseph complains that he is a poor carpenter and unable to pay (ll. 385–428). Joseph ties his ox to his ass's tail, puts Mary on the ass, and proceeds to Bethlehem, arriving there at once. Mary, like a visitor from the country, notices the people. No lodgings are to be found, and Mary agrees to stay at the stable, for she recognizes that for Christ to be born between an ox and an ass will be the fulfilment of prophecy. Joseph seeks midwives in simple affection and solicitude. There then occur the painless birth and the appearance of the star; after that the miracle of the healing of Salome's withered hand according to the *Protoevangelium Jacobi*. There is next introduced the story of the miracle of the falling idols in the Temple of Peace in Rome (ll. 581–656). After the Nativity the Conversion of Octavian begins again and continues to the end. The whole construction is very puzzling. Actual Nativity plays are not liturgical, and yet in this case the Chester play presents a Nativity play as a central episode in a legend. It is the more perplexing because *Octovien* in *Le Mistère* has none of the features of a Nativity play.

The seventh play, the Adoration of the Shepherds, introduces a degree of complexity in its composition perhaps not elsewhere en, countered in the cycle. It seems to be a mixture of old and very old elements with possibly newer ones. The play begins in Chester stanzas, which are also scattered throughout, and interrupts them with large blocks of octosyllabic quatrains. There would of course be a temptation in a rural community to expand the roles of the shepherds in the direction of realism and humour. If we can show that these quatrains are used for these purposes and if we agree that the Chester metre is the standard original, we shall have a probable solution of the problem of composition. After the shepherds are introduced in the fields with their flocks in the first 48 lines, a long amplification mainly in quatrains begins and extends to line 310. There is introduced a clownish shepherd named Gartius, but the humour is normally restrained. The Chester stanza appears here and there, and a new style begins—3's instead of 4's—the rhyme pattern being, however, according to the Chester scheme. This continues, with some interruptions by quatrains and Chester stanzas, through-out the rest of the play. It happens that in other cases, such as the *Shearmen and Taylors' Pageant* of Coventry, the Shepherds' play also appears in a short-line ballad style. It is also to be noted that in some of the Latin plays the shepherds speak in a gay short-lined metre.[1] It may be therefore that in the composition of the original Shepherds' play in the Chester cycle an ancient style was carried over. The end of the play is metrically much confused. Manuscripts DWRB provide an evidently later insertion of 44 lines in Chester stanzas in which four shepherd boys present their gifts to the infant Jesus.

The eighth and ninth pageants were originally one play that has been divided between two crafts. The first, that of the vintners, deals with the Coming of the Magi, and in it, since there was hardly enough for a whole play, a supplement has been introduced. As it stands, it proceeds in orderly fashion in Chester stanzas for 260 lines. Then, by way of padding, it introduces a long passage (ll. 261–337) in rather poor Chaucer stanzas (five accents, rhyming ababbcc), which is meant to be an impressive debate between a learned Doctor and Herod, the Doctor uttering sound theology and Herod swearing by Mahound. There is no reason to regard the passage as new, and yet it cannot be earlier than the early fifteenth century when the Chaucer stanza was in vogue. The division of the play is provided for in the earliest banns and lists. After the debate the play proceeds to the end in normal style. The ninth play presents the offerings of the Magi and the frustration of Herod. There is only one quatrain in it, and that is devoted to a courteous leave-taking among the Kings.

The tenth play presents the anger of Herod, the Slaughter of the Innocents, the Flight into Egypt, and the return to Galilee. It is, on the whole, an orderly and restrained version. The fight of the mothers to protect their children from the soldiers is sufficiently lively, but has no such violence as the Digby Killing of the Children. There is some appearance of legendary matters in the play. The angel who has warned Joseph and Mary to flee into Egypt refers to the falling of the

[1] Young, op. cit. ii. 10, 19, 187–8.

Egyptian idols from the apocryphal *Infancy of Jesus Christ*, c. iv. Still more unusual is the appearance of the tradition that among the innocents slaughtered was a child of Herod's. (Wright attributes this to Macrobius, *Saturnalia*, lib. ii, c. iv, who reports it of Augustus as saying, when he heard the story, 'I would rather be Herod's pig than his son'.). The play has a sufficiently gruesome account of the death of Herod.

The eleventh play, called the Purification, has in it one feature of great interest. It presents a simple play of the Presentation in the Temple, 208 lines long. Then there is introduced an episode of Jesus with the Doctors in the Temple. That it is an insertion is clear from the fact that it is a shortened version of the same play in the York cycle and brings over with it the actual language of the original, rearranged in quatrains and double quatrains; also the concluding stanza of the play is in the Chester stanza, closes with the Presentation in the Temple, and shows no consciousness of the play of Christ and the Doctors. The fact that Jesus was forty days old in the Purification and a boy of twelve in the play of the Doctors did not worry the authors, and they are not alone in this. A precisely similar thing was done in the *Weavers' Pageant* of Coventry, where the York play was again borrowed. The two plays were juxtaposed in the Towneley cycle, but may have been separately acted.[1]

The problem of the origin of the Chester Corpus Christi play would be solved by the discovery of a pattern play in French, but so far we have only a model for the earlier part of the cycle. What is needed is some earlier and now lost cycle from which *Le Mistère du Viel Testament* was derived, but it should be a cycle that covered the Old Testament series of plays and proceeded through Nativity, Ministry, Passion, Resurrection, and Ascension to Doomsday. There is, however, in existence a very distant and primitive pattern for another great part of the Chester cycle to be found in the imperfect and rather confused contents of the Benediktbeuern Christmas play, which is made up of a combination of dramatic themes of the Christmas season that reappear in the Chester plays. This Latin play opens with a *Prophetae*, in which, however, only a limited number of

---

[1] *Two Coventry Corpus Christi Plays*, loc. cit., pp. xxviii–xxxiv; *The Trial and Flagellation*, loc. cit., pp. 101–20.

prophets appear. Among them is Balaam, *sedens super asinam*, and, although the ass does not speak, the angel with the sword appears, and the play may be described as an imperfect Balaam play in miniature. After a debate between St. Augustine and the prophets, on the one side, and *Archisynagogus,* on the other, there is an Annunciation and immediately after it a Visit to Elizabeth; then, in somewhat confused form, a *Pastores* and a *Stella*. At this point a stage direction says, *Herodes corrodatur a verminibus*. This would seem to be out of its proper order. Next come the Slaughter of the Innocents and the Flight into Egypt, which are followed by some secular matters and the Falling of the Egyptian Idols. Most interestingly, the play ends with the fragments of an *Antichristus*. This latter part Young refuses to accept as a portion of the Latin play, but his reasons are not convincing.[1] The fragmentary dialogue is there in association with the Benediktbeuern play, and it is not necessarily a fragment of the Tegernsee *Antichristus*. An Antichrist play, arising from the services of Advent, might be expected to attach itself, first of all, to the Christmas group. Finally, the Benediktbeuern Christmas play contains a version of the Fifteen Signs of Judgement from the Sibyl. The play is not only incomplete but confused, and yet it is possible to see in its general contents a remarkable parallel with the Chester plays, particularly in those themes in which the Chester plays are exceptional. We have seen how in the Balaam and Balak play a *Princeps Synagogae* appears as a debater and how a play of Balaam and the speaking ass has grown out of a *Prophetae*. We have seen also that the Chester plays have a Visit to Elizabeth or a Salutation immediately after an Annunciation and how the Sibyl has an important role in the Nativity and in the prologue to the Antichrist play. In the Chester Slaughter of the Innocents appear the Falling of the Egyptian Idols and a gruesome Death of Herod with the succession of his son Archelaus. In the last three plays in the Chester cycle we have an Advent play in three parts, although of course the fragmentary Benediktbeuern play furnishes only the fragment of an *Antichristus*. The inference from this comparison and parallel is that one of the component parts of the original cycle, probably French, from which the Chester plays were drawn was a Christmas play of

[1] Young, op. cit. ii. 463–8.

somewhat the same content and form as the Benediktbeuern Christmas play.

With the twelfth Chester play we encounter a series on the
Ministry and the Passion very different in their nature and much more
formal than those that have gone before. They are relatively bare in
their manner of treatment and have the characteristic of introducing
scene after scene in sequence without much provision for interrelations. These are original characteristics of Passion plays, and one
recalls the *Ludus breviter de Passione* from Benediktbeuern[1] and still
more the Benediktbeuern *Ludus de Passione*,[2] these plays being characterized by bareness and the enumeration of events. The same qualities
are seen in the St. Gall Passion play.[3]

The twelfth Chester play, which is regular in its use of the Chester
stanza, presents in a disconnected way the Temptation in the Wilderness (ll. 1–208) and the Woman Taken in Adultery (ll. 209–304).
The thirteenth pageant shows only slight variation. At the beginning
Christ speaks a sort of prologue of 35 lines in the Chaucer stanza.
After that there is a Healing of the Blind Man at the Pool of Siloam.
The episode is long (ll. 36–304) and contains unidentified legendary
matter. The blind man is given the name Chelidonius. At the end of
the first scene there begins without connexion a rather closely scriptural play of the Raising of Lazarus. It follows the well-known belief
that Mary the sister of Lazarus was Mary Magdalen the forgiven
sinner,[4] although in this play there is no treatment of the Repentance
of Mary Magdalen. That theme, however, appears in very mild form
in play XIV, Jesus at the House of Simon the Leper. After an
episode of Mary and Martha there is an Entry into Jerusalem and the
unusual scene of Christ's Cleansing of the Temple of the Money-
Changers, and also a Conspiracy. There is a remarkable uniformity
in style among these plays of the Ministry.

This indeed continues through the plays of the Passion, as does the
episodic or consecutive quality. The fifteenth play presents the Last
Supper with the Betrayal and the unusual episode of the Washing of

[1] W. Meyer, *Fragmenta Burana* (Berlin, 1901), pp. 123–4; Young, op. cit. ii. 513–18.

[2] J. A. Schmeller, *Carmina Burana*, loc. cit., pp. 95–107; R. Froning, op. cit., pp. 278–301;
Young, op. cit. i. 518–39.

[3] F. J. Mone, *Schauspiele des Mittelalters*, loc. cit., pp. 143 ff.; see also Creizenach, op. cit. i.
121–3.   [4] Young, op. cit. i. 534.

the Disciples' Feet; also the prayers of Jesus, the Capture, and the healing of Malchus' ear—all briefly treated and scriptural. The fifteenth play proceeds with the Trials, the Flagellation, the Bearing of the Cross, and, in manuscript H, the Crucifixion, which we know was originally an independent play. In the Crucifixion there is a *Planctus Mariae*, found even in the simplest Passion plays. The Crucifixion itself is a long play and in its atmosphere most interesting. It ends with the Death and Burial, and the dialogue of Pilate, Nico-demus, and Joseph of Arimathea goes as far in the delineation of character and the expression of individual thought as perhaps any-thing in the whole cycle. An unaccountable circumstance in this play is the appearance in its midst of a number of passages in the three-foot ballad stanza observed above in the play of the Shepherds. They appear as part of the Buffeting (ll. 49–120), the seizing of Christ's garments and the Scourging (ll. 313–84), and the nailing to the Cross (ll. 457–600).

The Harrowing of Hell in the Chester cycle (play XVII) is evenly written in the Chester stanza. It is rather primitive in form and in a simple way effective. The manuscripts other than H add an episode (ll. 261–320) presenting the cordial reception of the dishonest ale-wife in Hell, a subject found in German plays. In the Chester cycle the Harrowing of Hell occupies the logical, usually continental, position. That is, it comes before the Setting of the Watch. The Resurrection (play XVIII) is an almost perfect example of the species and yet is hardly English in the stress it puts on the Setting of the Watch and the anger of Pilate at the Resurrection of Christ (308 ll.). These matters are followed by a simple *Quem quaeritis*, and an odd meeting with Peter, whom Jesus reproaches for his Denial. It may have been suggested by Luke xxiv. 34. The nineteenth pageant is a *Peregrini* followed by Christ's Appearance to the Disciples in the Upper-chamber with the Incredulity of Thomas. So faithful is it that, if it were translated into Latin, it might be mistaken for a litur-gical play. This play is followed by quite simple and formal plays of the Ascension (XX) and Pentecost (XXI). The latter is the more vividly realized of the two plays, as appears in the sending out of the Disciples to carry the Gospel to the world. The play is also well supplied in manuscript H with scriptural quotations and stage directions in Latin and is very carefully constructed and explained. There is little variation of metre in either of these plays.

A unique and possibly most important feature of the Chester Corpus Christi play is the fact that its last three plays (XXII, XXIII, and XXIV) originally formed one eschatological drama. Evidences have been given above for believing that *Antichristus* and *Judicium* were originally and in some cases still are two parts of one play. As to play XXII, called 'The Prophets of Antichrist', it is merely an intro-duction to the major play. It borrows Ezekiel, Zachariah, Daniel, and Johannes Baptista from the list of the prophets, but uses them with a difference and with great perspicacity. They are no longer Messianic prophets, but prophets of the Second Coming and of the Doom. Great intelligence was exercised by the unknown person who wrote this prologic scene, although one hears it said over and over again that these prophets are merely taken over from the *Prophetae*. This prologue also introduces the figures of Enoch and Elijah, who under the reign of Antichrist were to suffer the deaths they had escaped in their lives on earth. There is also most appropriately a recitation of the Fifteen Signs of Judgement uttered by the Sibyl in the *Prophetae*, but far more appropriately used here. Beneath the whole unrecorded conception there is ancient and profound thinking on the cyclic level. This introduction and the two plays that follow it are splendidly conceived and well executed, perhaps the finest in the whole cycle.

It is easy to see why, in the establishment of a Corpus Christi play at Chester, one craft guild might have been well content to accept this prologic scene as its allotment. The Antichrist play itself is equally well executed and is metrically regular throughout. None of these three plays at the end of the cycle shows any sign of tampering. There may be some significance in the fact that the opening speech of Antichrist is in Latin instead of French, for these eschatological plays may rest originally on a lost liturgical play in Latin. The Antichrist play has great restraint, but at the end there is genuinely exciting dramatic action. The Kings are converted, Enoch and Elijah slain by Antichrist, and Antichrist himself, after stern denunciation, is struck down by the Archangel Michael. Two numbered demons come and carry off, not unwillingly, the body of their master to Hell. Enoch and Elijah rise from the dead and are carried to Heaven by Michael while there is sung the responsory *Gaudete, justi, in Domino*. The twenty-fourth and last play in the cycle presents the Last Judgement. It follows the Gospel according to Matthew faithfully, adds a small amount of traditional matter, and is clearly and neatly done. But the stiff ballad stanza and the provincial limitations of the spectacle are inadequate for the presentation of a theme that was taxing the skill of great sculptors and painters all over Europe. There is simple beauty in the gratitude of the saved souls. Two demons appear as accusers and speak pointedly and humorously as they claim their own. A pope and an emperor, both damned, utter the great defence of the wicked in the words of St. Matthew (xxv. 37–44): 'When saw we thee an hungred... and did not minister unto thee?' And the pleas of the other damned souls, including a false justicer, are very human. The play ends stiffly with the Four Evangelists, each of whom utters an eight-line stanza.

But, however inferior *Judicium* may have been to *Antichristus*, it was a *sine qua non* for the Corpus Christi play, and *Antichristus* was not. A Corpus Christi play had to end with the Last Judgement. Plays of the Last Judgement were relatively rare as compared with other plays of liturgical origin, and in this case we are supplied with one at an early date in Chester. Since Corpus Christi plays were at that very time being established in England, and since other English plays of the Last Judgement are built on the same lines as the Chester play, is it not at least possible that, when Corpus Christi plays were set up else-where, the authors may have adapted the Chester play as the last play in their cycle or at least have taken the Chester situation as a model? They would not need the *Antichristus*, or be intelligent enough to know that theologically speaking *Antichristus* and *Judicium* are merely parts of the same theme, although for local convenience they had been separated in the Corpus Christi play at Chester. These three eschatological plays at Chester, which show by their unity of conception and their workmanship that they were executed as one work, are the finest thing in the Chester cycle, and, if anything in the cycle suggests the hand of a superior person, such as Ranulf Higden, these plays do.

Chester is a city with an individuality, and has been such for cen-turies. One may also say that it has had a will of its own and possibly a gentle touch of self-satisfaction. Perhaps its situation on a sandstone bluff on the right bank of the river Dee affected its character. Its famous walls were built of its own red sandstone, and to be a walled city in the Middle Ages and later may have contributed something to a burgher-like independence. Chester was prosperous too in the fourteenth, fifteenth, and sixteenth centuries, and no doubt had a pride in successful business. It was the last city to be conquered by William the Norman, and its resistance to the parliamentary army under Cromwell was long and stubborn. It must have taken an unusually stiff and stern kind of conservatism to make the people of Chester protect their religious plays against the pious and often overworded stupidities of the fifteenth century and against the cock-sure loquacity of the early sixteenth. At any rate, they performed a miracle in keeping their plays, as a whole, unspoiled by modernity and in line with the intentions of those who had established them. The plays are still almost as simple as the Book of Genesis and the Holy Gospels, on which they are so largely founded. The cycle still shows that the people who played it and saw it might in some sort believe that they were honouring God and, if they resorted to the plays in a peaceable manner, might conscientiously claim a remission of forty days plus ten from the weary sentence they all expected to serve and no doubt deserved to serve in Purgatory.

It is not to be thought, however, that the Chester cycle did not undergo extensive revisions during its career. If the tradition of its origin in the early fourteenth century is true, the plays must have been fewer in number than they were during the sixteenth century, and in all probability they were more closely in line with the liturgical drama on which they were based. Salter calls attention to the fact that not only is the first play (on the Fall of Lucifer) written in the exceptional stanza form abababab but that form appears also in a number of other parts of the cycle.[1] The inference is that, since the style is the same, the passages are the work of the same reviser. But it is to be remembered that the Fall of Lucifer appears in *Le Mistère du Viel Testament*, where it shows certain resemblances to the Chester play and where it is also exceptional in metre. As to the later occurrences of the metre in question, the matter introduced rarely deals with original events but is in some measure excrescent. Salter also cites

[1] F. M. Salter, 'The Banns of the Chester Plays', loc. cit. xv. 451–2.

evidence that the metre of the late banns, composed in 1575 in an unmistakably bad style, reappears in lines 261–337 of play VIII (the Magi) and in lines 1–39 of play XIII (the Healing of the Blind Man and the Resuscitation of Lazarus). The same workman, Salter thinks, joined into one the plays of the Trial and the Crucifixion, transferred 100 lines from play XVIII to play XIX, and made some not identified changes in the play of Antichrist. There can be little doubt that these later revisions were made as Salter indicates.

A much more important redaction and apparently an early one was certainly based on the *Stanzaic Life of Christ*.[1] Miss Foster points out that a number of the Chester plays are closely paralleled in the *Stanzaic Life*. A further and more detailed study of the relation between the poem and the Chester plays by Robert H. Wilson makes it clear that we have to do with the revision of preexistent Chester plays or scenes.[2] In some cases, according to Wilson, there are minor changes and additions scattered over various plays and in others there are longer passages in which the parallels between the plays and the *Life* are abundant and unmistakable. When, however, these more extensive borrowings are considered apart from the plays most affected, the portions remaining untouched are in traditional form, and contain matter not in the *Stanzaic Life* but customary in mystery plays and of course originally derived from the liturgy. In a number of instances repetition of events and contradictions in detail show clearly that the matter from the *Stanzaic Life* was superimposed on plays of traditional origin and pattern.

The Chester plays most greatly affected are VI (the Nativity), VIII and IX (the Magi), XI (the Purification), XII (the Temptation), XVIII (the Harrowing of Hell), and XX (the Ascension). Of these the Nativity is typical of the revision, since it shows a number of brief parallels so close as to indicate actual borrowing. The first of the Magi plays seems to have taken over from the *Life* the incident of the disappearance of the star when the Magi reached Bethlehem. Otherwise, except for a number of possible minor borrowings, the Magi plays in the Chester cycle follow the course of the Latin liturgical plays of

[1] *A Stanzaic Life of Christ, compiled from Higden's Polychronicon and the Legenda Aurea*, ed. Frances A. Foster, E.E.T.S. (London, 1926), pp. xxviii–xliii.

[2] 'The Stanzaic Life of Christ and the Chester plays', *Studies in Philology*, xxviii (1931), 413–32.

the Adoration of the Magi. Play XI, the Purification, seems to rest heavily on the *Life*.[1] It borrows the miracle of Simeon's attempt to change the word 'virgin' to 'good woman' and the argument that the Blessed Virgin Mary does not need purification. The play shows an inconsistency in the number of doves offered in the temple. Wilson therefore argues rightly that the original source of the Purification in the Chester cycle was traditional and liturgical, citing the service of Candlemas at Padua.[2] In play XII the Expositor in explaining the theological signification of the Temptation follows a homily by St. Gregory[3] that is also followed by Higden in *Polychronicon*. This in turn appears in the *Stanzaic Life*, which is derived in part from *Polychronicon*. The Ascension (XX), although showing the influence of the *Life*, seems in its original form to have been a normal play on that subject, which was of course essential in cycle-building. Of the seven Chester plays most closely related to the *Stanzaic Life of Christ* the only one, according to Wilson, that might have been based solely on the poem is the Harrowing of Hell (XVIII), but even that is not to be too readily granted, since the Harrowing of Hell, as we have seen, is a very old subject going back to the liturgy and beyond and is, moreover, formal and definite in its events, so that all plays on the subject are much alike. The Chester cycle may very well have had such a play from the beginning. It will be remembered that at Chester many scenes were often crowded on one pageant. We may fairly conclude that the *Stanzaic Life of Christ* was not used as a source of new plays in the Chester cycle but for a recension of a full and normal Corpus Christi play. This poem is not a clear narrative like the *Northern Passion*, to which it is related, but is rather a storehouse of theological ideas and apocryphal events such as would lend itself not so much to original composition as to redaction for purposes of ornamentation and improvement. Miss Foster points also to probable influence from the *Stanzaic Life* on Abraham and Isaac (IV), Balaam and Balak (V), the Slaughter of the Innocents (X), and the Entry into Jerusalem (XIV), which is by no means improbable. Wilson thinks that the whole Chester cycle was rewritten at the time of the redaction. If, however, revision was in the hands of the

---

[1] Foster, loc. cit., pp. xxxv–xli. [2] See Young, op. cit. ii. 248–55.
[3] Migne, *P.L.* lxxvi. 1135–6.

individual guilds, as seems probable, such a complete rewriting is not likely.

The dates of the redaction in question are not definitely known, but one would guess that they were early. The *Stanzaic Life* comes from Chester itself, and the three manuscripts are all of the fifteenth century, but Miss Foster thinks on very good grounds that the poem was composed in the fourteenth century. The revision by the use of the *Stanzaic Life* had been carried through before the older banns were composed, and they came into being at some time before 1467. It is worth going into the matter of the relation of the Chester cycle to this religious poem with some care because of the mistaken practice of regarding the Corpus Christi play as composed bit by bit and play by play and not as made up originally by the putting together of a formal series of plays and subjects designed to tell the full story of the liturgical year.

VI

York–Wakefield Plays

THE York Corpus Christi play acted at York and the Towne-ley Corpus Christi play acted at Wakefield are nearly related not only in the ways in which all Corpus Christi plays are related but in actual texture and construction. Indeed, as we shall see, they had one and the same history during their formative period. They may also be regarded as significant literary achievements of the later Middle Ages so intimate, so genuine, and so expressive that one constantly regrets the loss of so many Corpus Christi cycles—those of Beverley, Norwich, Newcastle-upon-Tyne, and half a dozen other places—for, if we may judge also from Chester and Coventry, each cycle not only presented dramatically the whole plan of man's salvation, but presented it as it was locally understood. While the people were telling the stories of the Bible, they were telling their own stories.

The York and the Towneley cycles are preserved in two great manuscripts, both transmitted to us through channels we do not know, both incomplete, and both in the dialect of fifteenth-century Yorkshire. The manuscript coming from York itself has the clearer history and offers the fuller, more representative picture of the place of its origin. York was the capital of a British province under the Roman empire, a fortified outpost against the Picts and Scots. It was also the centre of the earliest British Christianity, a diocese as early as the fourth century, and an archdiocese as early as the seventh. It was also by that time a great educational centre. Alcuin, the greatest of English churchmen and the chief educational force in the Caro-lingian renascence, was born there about A.D. 735. The Cathedral Church of St. Peter, or, as ordinarily called, York Minster, has Saxon as well as Norman and later styles in its fabric. The ecclesiastical importance of York did not diminish as the Middle Ages advanced and was possibly at its height in the fifteenth century when the York plays were written down in the form in which we have them. Such a community origin ought to be reflected in this great popular theological creation and it is, for the York plays show both learning and dignity on a level perhaps not elsewhere seen.

The manuscript, British Museum Additional MS. 35290, earlier Ashburnham MS. 137, seems to be a register, or formal copy, made about 1430–40 for the corporation of the city from single plays in the hands of guilds or trading companies. That there were individual texts of plays in the hands of the guilds is attested by various records and by the survival of a copy of the Incredulity of Thomas formerly acted by the scriveners of York.[1] In the light of the religious importance of the city one would conjecture that the register was made in order to pre-serve the plays from fifteenth-century secularization and to save the city from scandal. But the task was never completed. The manuscript consists of 270 leaves of parchment of which 48 are blank, in some cases left so for the purpose of entering plays not on hand at the time the general copy was made. Two plays at the beginning were appar-ently missing, and, when they were later supplied, an unsigned quire of four leaves was placed in front. Some missing plays were never forthcoming. The handwriting, which is regarded as coming from the first half of the fifteenth century, is usually clear and workmanlike. Three plays, not newly composed, were copied in as late as 1558— the fullers' play of Adam and Eve in the Garden of Eden, an addition to the play of Cain and Abel, and the hatmakers', masons', and labourers' play of the Purification. At the end of the manu-script, in a hand described by Lucy Toulmin Smith[2] as of the end of the fifteenth century, is a part (47 ll.) of a play of the innholders on the Coronation of the Blessed Virgin Mary. After play XX, the Temptation in the Wilderness, are four blank leaves containing two lines only of the vintners' play of the Marriage at Cana, all that survives. Likewise, five leaves left blank after play XXIII for the ironmongers' play of Jesus at the House of Simon the Leper were

---

[1] Published from the Sykes MS. by J. Croft, *Excerpta Antiqua* (1797), pp. 105 ff., and by J. P. Collier in *Camden Miscellany* (1859), vol. iv.

[2] *York Plays. The Plays performed by the Crafts or Mysteries of York on the Day of Corpus Christi in the 14th, 15th, and 16th Centuries.* Edited by Lucy Toulmin Smith (Oxford, 1885), pp. 514–15; Chambers, op. cit. ii. 399–406, 409–512; J. E. Wells, *A Manual of the Writings in Middle English, 1050–1400* (New Haven, 1916); with nine supplements; Anna J. Mill, 'The York Bakers' Play of the Last Supper', *Modern Language Review*, xxx (1935), 145–58, and 'York Plays: the Dying, Assumption and Coronation of Our Lady', *PMLA*, lxv (1950), 866–76.

never filled. There are also in the manuscript various minor correc‚
tions and a few larger additions. Many of them come from 1568
when under stress of Protestant scruples the corporation ordered that
'the booke thereof be perused and otherwise amended before it were
playd'. The correction, indeed the abolition, of the plays is attributed
to the influence of Edmund Grindal, archbishop of York, and of
Matthew Hutton, the dean of the Minster. A complete overhauling of
the plays was projected for 1579, but fortunately not carried out, and
we have the plays pretty much as they were written down at some
time before the middle of the fifteenth century. Apparently the dean
and the archbishop, by 1579 Edwin Sandys, took the prudent course
of keeping the register in their own possession and temporizing with
the citizens, who obviously still wanted the plays performed.

The manuscript is a plain one, but well written in single column.
The rubrication consists of horizontal lines between speeches, strokes
through the first letters of lines of verse, and a few ornamental
capitals with spaces left for others. There is a not‚well‚understood
manuscript confusion in plays XXVIII to XXXV, which deal with
various episodes of the Passion. It has been plausibly suggested that
the scriveners' work was done for the city by the brothers of the Priory
of the Holy Trinity. The book was still at the priory in 1554, although
the institution had been dissolved in 1538.[1] Miss Smith conjectures
that, after the ecclesiastical authorities got the Register into their hands
in 1579, it passed into the ownership of successive members of the
Fairfax family. A member of this family gave it to Ralph Thoresby
in 1695, and when the Thoresby manuscripts were sold in 1764
Horace Walpole bought it for a guinea. It then passed through several
hands at increasing prices and finally came to rest for a long period in
the library of Lord Ashburnham.

A means by which a standard form of the York cycle may be
ascertained is an *Ordo paginarum ludi Corporis Christi* prepared and
signed in 1415 by Roger Burton, city clerk of York. It is in the *Liber
diversorum Memorandorum* among the York manuscripts.[2] There is also
a slightly later list, also signed by Burton.[3] The plays are placed in
their proper order in these lists, and in the earlier list each play has a

[1] L. T. Smith, op. cit., pp. xi–xii.   [2] Ibid., pp. xviii–xxviii.
[3] R. Davies, op. cit. pp. 233–5.

brief Latin summary of its contents. On the left-hand margin are the names of the guilds responsible for the plays, and this list of crafts has undergone some corrections in the later version. Fifty-one plays are enumerated in Burton's first list, and fifty-seven in his second. The number of plays in the manuscript is forty-eight, not counting the fragment of the Coronation of the Blessed Virgin Mary at the end. Number XVI in Burton's list, which deals with the subject of the Coming of the Magi, has been split into two since his time. Play XXII, the Marriage at Cana, was, as we have seen, never copied into the register, the same being true of Burton's number XXV, Jesus at the House of Simon the Leper. His numbers XXVI and XXVII have been combined and appear in the present cycle as XXIV, a play treating the Woman Taken in Adultery, the Accusation of the Jews, and the Raising of Lazarus with the story of Mary and Martha. Finally, there is a play omitted from the register, Miss Smith thinks accidentally,[1] numbered XLVIII by Burton and described in these terms: *Quatuor Apostoli portantes feretrum Marie, et Fergus pendens super feretrum, cum ij aliis Judeis cum uno Angelo.* It is of course the apocryphal story of the attempted desecration of the body of the Blessed Virgin Mary as it was being borne to burial.[2] It is thus possible to give a fair account of the York plays during the last century and a quarter of their dramatic life, and it will be seen that they were maintained in the somewhat prolix, and yet intelligent and reverent, state of the religious teachings of the first half of the fifteenth century.

Burton's list shows that the greatest period of the growth and expansion of the York cycle was before 1415, and for the tracing of it our definite materials are none too abundant. The city of York was large and rich, and the trading companies were numerous. Therefore the number of pageants necessary to supply the demands of guilds anxious and able to participate in the Corpus Christi play was correspondingly great. This means that subjects embracing more than a single episode were apt to be split into parts in order to accommodate more companies. There are in the York cycle no such groups of subjects in one pageant as we saw in the Chester cycle. One would expect them not to be long, and in fact they tend to be rather short.

[1] Op. cit., p. xxviii.
[2] See the apocryphal gospel *Transitus Mariae* and *Cursor Mundi* (ll. 20719–63).

The total length of the cycle was very great, and, since it seems to have been acted in a single day, there would be, even if the perform, ance began at dawn, a great deal to get through. As to the general situation, Miss Smith's statement is clear:[1]

> For, as business grew, a new craft would spring up, an old one decay and become too poor to produce its play, a new one must take its share; one craft trenching on the trade of another must share its burdens, sometimes two, or even three plays would be combined into one, sometimes a play would be laid aside and the craft to which it had been assigned must join in producing some other. A comparison of the different notices and ordinances of the companies relating to the plays explains many of the changes in the list.

In 1399 and in 1417 the city council in answer to a petition of citizens established twelve stations or playing, places—to begin at the gates of the Priory of the Holy Trinity in Mickel, gate, next at the doors of Robert Harpman, and of John Gyscburn, next at 'Skelder, gate, hend and North, strete, hend', next at the end of Conynge street towards Castle, gate, next at the end of Jubir, gate, next at the door of Henry Wyman, next at the Common Hall, next at the door of Adam del Brygs in Stayn, gate, next at the end of Stayn, gate at the Minster gates, then at the end of Girdler, gate in Peter, gate, and, lastly, upon the Pavement.[2] But later the number varied and ran as high as sixteen, and there seems to have been a lively competition in the later fifteenth and the sixteenth centuries for the privilege of having a station at one's door. From this the city derived some revenue.

The plays began with the Mayor's proclamation, and there is a text of it in Burton's own hand immediately after his list of pageants. It is quoted by Miss Smith[3] and it deserves to be repeated for the light it throws, not only on the control of pageants in York, but on the high ideals of performance that were entertained there. The proclamation was made on the vigil of Corpus Christi:

Oiez, &c. We comand of ye kynges behalue and ye Mair and ye shirefs of yis Citee yat no mann go armed in yis Citee with swerdes ne with Carlill, axes, no none othir defences in distorbaunce of ye kynges pees and ye play, or hynderyng of ye processioun of Corpore Christi, and yat yai leue yare hernas in yare Ines, saufand knyghtes and sqwyers of wirship yat awe haue swerdes borne eftir yame, of payne of forfaiture of yaire wapen and inprisonment of yaire bodys. And yat men yat bryngs furth pacentes

---

[1] Op. cit., p. xix.   [2] Ibid., pp. xxxii–xxxiii.
[3] Ibid., pp. xxxiv, xxxvii.

yat yai play at the places yat is assigned yerfore and nowere elles, of ye payne of forfaiture to be raysed yat is ordayned yerfore, yat is to say xl*s*. And yat menn of craftes
and all othir menn yat fyndes torches, yat yai come furth in array and in ye manere as
it has been vsed and customed before yis time, noght haueyng wapen, careynge tapers
of ye pagentz. And officers yat ar keepers of ye pees of payne of forfaiture of yaire
fraunchis and yaire bodyes to prison: And all maner of craftmen yat bringeth furthe
ther pageantez in order and course by good players, well arayed and openly spekyng,
vpon payn of lesying of C.*s*. to be paide to the chambre without any pardon. And
that euery player that shall play be redy in his pagiaunt at convenyant tyme, that is to
say, at the mydhowre betwix iiijth and vth of the cloke in the mornynge, and then all
oyer pageantz fast following ilk one after oyer as yer course is, without tarieng. Sub
pena facienda camere vi*s*. viii*d*.

With this is to be associated an order of council of April 3, 1476,
also indicative of careful supervision:

Þat yerely in þe tyme of lentyn there shall be called afore the maire for þe tyme beyng
iiij of þe moste connyng, discrete and able players within this Citie, to serche, here, and
examen all þe plaiers and plaies and pagentes thrughoute all the artificers belonging
to Corpus X^{ti} Plaie. And all suche as þay shall fynde sufficiant in personne and
connyng, to þe honour of þe Citie and worship of þe saide Craftes, for to admitte and
able; and all oþer insufficiant personnes, either in connyng, voice, or personne to
discharge, ammove, and avoide. And þat no plaier þat shall plaie in þe saide Corpus
X^{ti} plaie be conducte and reteyned to plaie but twise on þe day of þe saide playe;
and þat he or thay so plaing plaie not ouere twise þe saide day, vpon payne of xl*s*. to
forfet vnto þe chaumbre as often tymes as he or þay shall be founden defautie in þe
same.

The last provision of this ordinance has caused some perplexity. It
seems, however, merely designed to prevent popular actors from
engaging themselves to play more than two parts, presumably more
than one part in two different pageants, in any one day's playing.
Each part would of course be acted many times. The ordinance
provides for supervision over actors, acting, and the plays themselves.
There is also a unique appreciation of skill. The York plays themselves
show that they were held in line with Scripture, as were the Chester
plays, and made to avoid the rough vulgarity that sometimes appears
in other places. This steadiness in moral outlook and this attention
to public behaviour is a revelation of the merit of the York cycle.

There are preserved many records of the York plays, not so many
from the account books of guilds as from the regulations of the
municipality. Some of them are of great general interest. The first

mention of the Corpus Christi play of York is in a fine levied on the bakers in 1378, which was assigned 'a la pagine des ditz Pestours de corpore christi'.[1] The next is an order of council of 1394 that the pageants in the Corpus Christi play shall play in the places *antiquitus assignatis*, which would seem to say that, by that time, not only were the pageants an ancient custom, but the formal assignment of playing places was also an ancient custom. For the authoritative assignment of stations to be thus spoken of could hardly be a matter of less than thirty to fifty years, and if the plays were older than such action, the date of the institution of the Corpus Christi play at York would be very close to 1328, a year assigned by tradition to the Corpus Christi play at Chester. There was great activity in York in 1397 when Richard II came to York to see the plays.[2] An interesting circumstance appears in the records of 1426.[3] William Melton, a Minorite friar, tried to have the pageants postponed to the day after the Feast of Corpus Christi in order that the procession and the religious services of that day might have proper attention. He approved of the pageants but made a most reasonable appeal on grounds of piety. He failed, however, for the plays continued to occupy Corpus Christi day, and the procession and the ceremonies were postponed until the day after.[4] The city for a consideration supplied houses in which to store the pageants,[5] the guilds regularly appointed pageant masters and paid the costs of the plays, and, as at Coventry, there were many protests, adjustments, and special agreements.

The York cycle, long known to be in existence and occasionally mentioned, achieved publication in 1885 under the editorship of Lucy Toulmin Smith, an edition so full and careful that it has served well ever since.

The Towneley plays also survive in a unique manuscript of great interest and value. It is regarded with good reason as of the same kind as that of the York plays, namely, as a formal register of plays collected from the hands of individual trading companies who were responsible for their support and performance. Its survival also seems to have been more or less accidental, and to be due to the fact that it also had

[1] Ibid., pp. xxxii–xxxiii.
[2] Chambers, op. cit. ii. 402
[3] Davies, op. cit., pp. 243–4.
[4] Ibid., p. 245.
[5] Chambers, op. cit. ii. 403.

the good fortune to fall early into the possession of private persons who prized it or endured it throughout the long period when mystery plays were forgotten or despised.[1] The manuscript was first heard of in the library of John Towneley (1731–1813) of Towneley Hall, Lancashire, and was sold at a sale of Towneley manuscripts in 1814, when it was purchased for the Goldsmid library for £147. It was sold the next year to John North, and at the sale of his library in 1819 it went back into the library of Towneley Hall for the sum of £94. 10s. There it remained until 1894 when it was bought at another sale of Towneley manuscripts by Bernard Quaritch, the bookseller, for £620. Quaritch sold it in 1909 to Edward Coates, and in 1922 it was purchased for Henry E. Huntington and is now in the Henry E. Huntington Library and Art Gallery in San Marino, California.

The Towneley manuscript was handsomely bound, probably by Charles Lewis, while it was in the Goldsmid library. On the front cover is an elaborately tooled and gilded copy of the arms of Sir Louis Goldsmid. It is composed of 132 vellum leaves, some of which in various places show the effects of handling as if they had been used for the staging of certain plays. There are a number of costly gaps in the manuscript. Between plays I and II (modern numbering) twelve leaves are missing. They seem to have contained, if one may judge by the York cycle, a continuation of the first pageant to include the Temptation and Fall of Adam and Eve and their Expulsion from the Garden of Eden. The first Towneley play would therefore have been a long one containing, after the earlier pattern, a number of episodes. Two leaves are missing between plays IV (Abraham and Isaac) and V (Jacob and Esau). The loss amounts to about 110 lines of the end of play IV and the beginning of play V. There is an unex⁄plained defect at the end of play VII (*Prophetae*), the result of which is to leave that play incomplete. It breaks off before the end of Daniel's prophecy on folio 19*b*. That page is not completely filled, folio 20 is blank, and a former writing on folio 20*b* has been carefully erased. There is no clue to the puzzle, and the inference is that the scribe intended to copy in correct matter on the blank pages and never did

[1] Louis Wann, 'A New Examination of the Manuscript of the Towneley Plays', *PMLA*, xliii (1928), 137–52.

so. The prophet play introduces Moses, who recites the Ten Com-
mandments, David, and the Sibyl and breaks off before the prophecy
of Daniel is ended. The prophet play in the York cycle has been
reduced to a mere prologue to the Annunciation. It mentions the
prophecies of Amos, Isaiah, Joel, and John the Baptist, a selected list
and a modernized version that seems to throw no light on the lost
contents of the Towneley play. Two leaves are missing between plays
XVII (the Purification) and XVIII (Jesus before the Jewish Doctors), so that the end of the former and the beginning of the latter are
lost. This, however, is to speak in terms of the manuscript as edited,
since there is at least a reasonable chance that the two plays were
actually one, as at Chester and Coventry. Between plays XXIX
(Ascension) and XXX (*Judicium*) there is a great gap of twelve leaves
or about 1,500 lines, and upon the missing leaves there must have
been written a play of Pentecost and probably a play treating the
Death and Assumption of the Blessed Virgin Mary. This fact
suggests that the mutilation may have been wilful, although there
was no reason why the Pentecost play should have suffered. A play
of the Hanging of Judas (XXXII) at the end of the manuscript
(instead of in its proper place) is lost after 96 lines. This last play,
probably an addition such as was made in the York manuscript, is
written in a sixteenth-century hand, the rest of the Towneley manuscript being in a sound clerkly hand of about 1450.

The first publication of the mysteries in the Towneley Hall manuscript was by the Surtees Society in 1836, thought to have been edited
by James Raine or J. Hunter. It is, on the whole, a good text and is
provided with a short preface that traces the history of the manuscript,
but is able to give no information as to how it came into the possession
of the Towneley family. Francis Douce in 1814, in a catalogue prepared for the sale of the Towneley Hall manuscripts, being under the
old impression that mystery plays were acted by 'monks', made the
statement, still sometimes encountered, that the manuscript was
supposed to 'have belonged to the Abbey of Widkirk, near Wakefield in the county of York', where in early times was held an annual
fair. Douce later suggested that it was the Abbey of Whalley. The
Surtees Society preface, although it accepts the Widkirk attribution,
does not miss entirely the plain evidence afforded by the manuscript

that it belonged to the manorial city of Wakefield, since it notes that at the beginning of the first play in the hand of the principal scribe is: *In dei nomine amen. Assit principio, Sancta Maria. Meo. Wakefield*, and below this the word 'Barkers'. The preface interprets this as meaning that 'on some occasion this mystery was represented in the town of Wakefield by the Company of Barkers'. The writer of the preface also observes that at the beginning of the second play are the words 'Glover Pag.' and at the head of the third play (also in the hand of the original scribe) is the word 'Wakefield'; also that in the play of the *Peregrini* there is written below the title in a later hand than that of the scribe 'fysher pagent' and that the play of Pharaoh is marked at the beginning 'Litsters Pagonn' and further on 'lyster play'. This casual kind of marking in such abundance has great significance, but the writer of the preface failed to note it. He does not, however, miss some of the local allusions that have served to convince scholars that the Towneley manuscript is made up of a Corpus Christi play formerly acted at Wakefield.

He cites the familiar reference to Horbury, a village near Wakefield, by Primus Pastor in the play *Secunda Pastorum*, who in describing his search for his lost sheep says:

> I haue soght *with* my dogys
> All Horbery shrogys
> And of XV hogys
> ffond I bot oone ewe.

The preface also points out that, when the shepherds arrange a meeting, the place they appoint is 'the crokyd thorn'. There was, he says, a well-known 'Shepherd's Thorn' in Mapplewell near Wakefield. The writer had, of course, the main points of a case for locating the plays at Wakefield. A further bit of evidence of the same kind and very convincing was added in 1901.[1] In the second play Cain in line 367 says,

> bery me in gudeboure at the quarrell hede,

in which there is an obvious allusion to an open field or common in Wakefield still known as 'Goodybower'. In early times there was a quarry (*quarrell*) in Goodybower.

[1] Matthew H. Peacock, 'The Wakefield Mysteries', *Anglia*, xxiv (1901), 509–24.

It has been clear enough for a long time that the Towneley manu‑ script contains the plays anciently performed by craft guilds at Wake‑ field, but there were available no Wakefield records that showed that Wakefield had a Corpus Christi play, although one Wakefield player was known to have visited York.[1] The ancient city of Wakefield has very few records. There exist only a book of the Manorial Court Leet[2] and some fragmentary records of a Burgess Court. Wakefield was not a borough but a city under the control of a lord of the manor, and from that fact perhaps it happens that records are so few, although it is locally said that as late as about 1825 the city council caused or permitted the destruction of a quantity of old manuscripts. The records of the Burgess Court, however, make it perfectly clear that in 1554 and 1556 Wakefield had a Corpus Christi play performed by the trading companies of the city and played on movable pageants. The records are general enactments for the performance of the plays and the behaviour of the spectators:[3]

PAYNES LAYD BY THE BURGES QWEST AS FOLLOYT, IN ANNO 1554

Itm a payne is layd yt gyles Dolleffe shall brenge In or Causse to be broght ye regenall of Corpus Xty play before ys & wytsonday In pane . . .

Itm a payne layde yt ye mesters of ye Corpus Xti playe shall Come & mayke thayre a Count before ye gentyllmen & burgessus of ye toun before this & may day next. In payne of everye one not so doynge 20s.

PAYNES LAYDE BY THE BURGES ENQUESTE AT THE COURTE KEPTE AT WAKEFELDE NEXTE AFTER THE FEASTE OF SAYNTE MICHAELL THARCHAUNGELL IN THIRDE AND FOURTE YEARE OF THE REIGNES OF OUR SOVERAIGNE LORDE AND LADYE KINGE PHILYPPE AND QUENE MARYE, 1556

Itm a payne is sett that everye crafte and occupation doo bringe furthe theire pagyaunts of Corpus Christi daye as hathe bene heretofore used and to give furthe the speches of the same in after holydayes in payne of everye one not so doynge to forfett xls.

Itm a payne is sett that everye player be redy in his pagyaunt at setled tyme before 5 of ye clocke in ye mornynge in payne of every one not so doynge to forfett vjs. viijd.

---

[1] *York Memorandum Book* (1446): 'j ludento de Wakefeld vi. *d*.', quoted by Smith, op. cit., p. xxxviii.

[2] Published by the Yorkshire Archaeological Society.

[3] J. W. Walker, *Publications of the Yorkshire Archaeological Society*, Record Series, lxxiv (1925), 20–22. These discoveries of Dr. Walker's were reported by Matthew H. Peacock in letters to *The Times Literary Supplement*, 5 March 1925, and 7 June 1928. See M. G. Framp‑ ton, 'The Date of the "Wakefield Master"', *PMLA*, l (1935), 644–6 *et passim*.

Itm a payne is sett yt ye players playe where setled and no where els in payne of no (*sic*) so doynge to forfett xxs.

Itm a payne is sett yt no man goe armed to disturb ye playe or hinder ye procession in payne of everye one so doynge vjs. viijd.

Itm a payne is sett yt everye man shall leave hys weapons att hys home or at hys ynne in payne of not so doynge vjs. viijd.

Ye summe of ye expens of ye Cherche mester for ye Corpus Christi playe xvijs. xd.
    Item payd to ye preste xijd.
    Itm payd to ye mynstrells xxd.
    Itm payd to ye mynstrells of Corpus Christi playe iijs. ivd.
    Itm payde for ye Corpus Christi playe & wrytynge ye spechys for yt iijs. viijd.
    Itm payd for ye Baner for ye mynstrells vjs. viijd.
    Itm payd for ye ryngyng ye same day vjd.
    Itm payd for garlonds on Corpus Christi day xijd.

These entries are almost certainly evidence of an effort (made also at Lincoln and no doubt elsewhere) during the reign of Queen Mary to revive the mystery plays, as a means of restoring the customs of the old religion. The information is scanty, but it agrees with what we know of the regulations of Corpus Christi plays in other places, and it becomes certain that Wakefield had a Corpus Christi play and that it was a customary activity there.

We have long known that these two great North of England mystery cycles were closely related. They come to us, both of them, in advanced stages of growth, and we seek information as to what these cycles were like perhaps a hundred years or more before the manuscripts we possess were made. In point of fact, we are not without a slight piece of early evidence that can be made to yield a good deal of information. There is no reasonable doubt that the so-called *Shrewsbury Fragments* are parts of three York plays in a much earlier stage of their growth than that shown in the York manuscript. They must be at least 150 years older than the versions written into the York register, which versions must have been very different, let us say very much shorter and simpler and much closer to their liturgical origins; hence more like the fragments in the Shrewsbury manuscript. Indeed, it is a matter of chance and good fortune that these fragments happen to be recognizable at all as York plays. The *Shrewsbury Fragments*[1] were

---

[1] Young, op. cit. ii, 514–523; Manly, *Specimens*, loc. cit., i. xxvii–xxxvii; *The Non-Cycle Mystery Plays*, loc. cit., pp. 1–7; Adams, op. cit., pp. 73–78.

discovered in the library of Shrewsbury School and were published by
W. W. Skeat in *Academy*, 11 January 1890. Skeat noted certain
verbal resemblances to the York plays, particularly to the play of the
Shepherds, and more have since been added.[1] The Shrewsbury
manuscript is in a certain sense not a fragment at all, but the complete
role or player's part of an actor who played the Third Shepherd in a
Pastores, the Third Mary in a *Quem quaeritis*, and apparently
Cleophas in a *Peregrini* with his cues and those speeches spoken or
sung by all the shepherds, all the Marys, and both of the Disciples
and all the Disciples. As Young's edition shows, the plays were
closely connected with the service of the church and, indeed, may have
been played in the church itself. Certain parts are in Latin, and some
of these are annotated for singing; others seem to have been spoken.

Skeat observed a practical identity between the following eight-
line speech of the Third Shepherd in the Shrewsbury manuscript
and a speech of the Third Shepherd in York play number XV. The
former says:

> A! loke to me, my Lord dere,
>   Alle if I put me noght in prese!
> To suche a prince without(en) pere
>   Haue I no presand þat may plese.
> But lo! a horn spone haue I here
>   Þat may herbar an hundrith pese.
> Þis gift I gif þe with gode chere;
>   Suche dayntese wil do no disese.

The York Third Shepherd says:

> Nowe loke on me, my lorde dere,
>   Þof all I putte me noght in pres,
> Ye are a prince with-outen pere,
>   I haue no presentte þat you may plees.
> But lo! an horne spone, þat haue I here,
>   And it will herbar fourty pese,
> Þis will I giffe you with gud chere,
>   Slike novelte may noght disease.

Skeat also points out that the eighth line of the Shrewsbury speech,

> Þat may herbar an hundrith pese,

---

[1] Frances H. Miller, 'Metrical Affinities of the Shrewsbury *Officium Pastorum* and its York Correspondent', *Modern Language Notes*, xxxiii (1918), 91–95.

gives an original and correct reading, as witnessed by the alliteration, which it preserves. The York speech has been rewritten in a favourite twelve-line York stanza, eight octosyllabic lines rhymed alternately, by the simple device of adding a hexasyllabic quatrain with different alternate rhymes. After the repetitive fashion of these early plays, we may be sure that this speech was preceded by similar speeches of the First and the Second Shepherds. Does anybody doubt that, if their speeches had been preserved, they too would have agreed with the corresponding speeches of the other shepherds in the York play? If there is any doubt, note that the cue 'I mene' still stands in the York play. But this single speech by no means exhausts the resemblances between the Shrewsbury *Officium Pastorum* and the York Shepherds' play. Unmistakable parallels are to be observed between York ll. 69–71 and Shrewsbury ll. 16–19; York ll. 77–78 and Shrewsbury ll. 38–41; York ll. 79–81 and Shrewsbury ll. 31–32; and York ll. 84–85 and Shrewsbury ll. 33–34. In spite of the expansion of the York play and its change into a new metre, the Third Shepherd in the York play has the same role as the Third Shepherd in the fragment, utters the same thoughts, and uses many of the same words in the same patterns. It is therefore obvious that we have to do with two versions of the same play. Since York had such a play before the establishment of the Corpus Christi cycle[1] there can be no reasonable doubt that the player's part of the Shrewsbury *Officium Pastorum* preserves a bit of that play.

But what about the other roles provided for in the *Shrewsbury Fragments*? They are of the same form and kind, and one would think that they must have a similar origin. The problem of proving that they too are York plays is much more difficult, but, even so, a resemblance can be seen between them and corresponding parts of the York cycle. The York play of the Resurrection (XXXVIII) has been completely rewritten in the Burns stanza in a greatly expanded form by the use of the *Northern Passion*. In the fragment the Third Mary utters two laments, the first a quatrain in English followed by two octosyllabic couplets in Latin, the second the eight-line alternately rhyming stanza of four accents that appears in the *Officium Pastorum*. To her is assigned a lamentation for Christ's sufferings on the cross, the nails,

---

[1] Chambers, op. cit. ii. 399.

and the riven side in spite of His goodness as the Saviour. The York play is given over to Pilate and the Setting of the Watch and emphasizes the part of the First Mary, who seems to be Mary Magdalen. Nevertheless the Third Mary laments the actual killing of Jesus, and it is she who speaks, as in the *Officium Pastorum*, of the weight of the stone to be rolled away from the mouth of the sepulchre. The resemblance, except this slight evidence of similarity of function, is almost nil, for the play has been transformed under the influence of a literary source. As to resemblance of the player's part in the Shrewsbury *Peregrini* to the corresponding York play, the latter is one of those that has been rewritten in alliterative measure, probably late, and is therefore remote, and the Towneley play (XXVII) has gone through the same transformation as the York Resurrection; and yet, for what it is worth, the role of Cleophas is clearly the same. It is Cleophas who expresses fear of the Jews, dwells at length on the report of the Marys of their visit to the sepulchre, remarks on the disappearance of Jesus from their supper at the inn, tells of His breaking of the bread, and urges that he and his companion return and report to the Disciples what they have seen. Here again in the assignment of parts in the little drama and the great there is conformity. In any case, if the player's part in the Shrewsbury *Pastores* is part of a York play, it is certain that the parts of that same player in the other plays are also parts of York plays.

We may, in general, conjecture with fair safety that before the Corpus Christi play was established at York there was at hand a *Pastores* for inclusion in it, and, more doubtfully, a *Stella* (on the ground that the two plays, both belonging to the Christmas group, are always associated with each other); also a *Quem quaeritis*, a *Hortulanus*,[1] and a *Peregrini*. We may also conclude that these plays were first translated from the Latin into octosyllabic quatrains, and in an early expansion, preceding the composition of the Shrewsbury players' parts, they made use of an eight-line octosyllabic stanza rhymed alternately; further that, certainly in the case of the *Pastores* and possibly in others, this stanza was expanded into the northern septenar stanza by the addition of a quatrain of three accents to the eight-line stanza as it stood.

[1] Manly, *Specimens*, loc. cit. i, p. xxxi n.

There is only one theory that accounts completely for the likenesses and differences of the two cycles. Many alterations and developments had occurred during the fourteenth century and, as Burton's list of 1415 shows, the York plays had become a great and extensive cycle. At some time, probably before the year 1390, the York cycle was borrowed outright and set up at Wakefield, a city not far from York in the West Riding of Yorkshire. We know nothing of the circum-stances, but one would think that such a thing must have been with the consent of the city council of York. After the Wakefield cycle was established, the dramatic contacts must have been, so far as we can see, only casual. Each cycle went its own way and underwent many changes not reflected in the other. The final results are embodied in the two great manuscripts described above. The case for an original identity, when considered from the point of view of circumstantial evidence and the argument from sign, is very clear.[1] Indeed, it is inescapable that the two cycles were once, up to a certain point of development and a certain date, one and the same. One reasonably supposes that the cycle until the time of division had been developed at York, since York was a great ecclesiastical, educational, and com-mercial centre. No records throw light on the actual transaction or on the growth and development of the York cycle up to that time, and this is unfortunate, but one has a right to argue for truth on the basis of detail best explained by fitting and careful hypotheses or incapable of explanation on any basis except the terms of the hypothesis chosen and framed. One can thus by means of the completest possible know-ledge, great caution, and full attention to differing views arrive at high degrees of probability, and there need be nothing over-speculative about such a procedure if it is logically carried through and the work is sincerely done. We have two cycles of plays exactly alike in their

[1] This hypothesis was put forward and worked out by Dr. Marie C. Lyle as a Ph.D. dissertation under the direction of the author at the University of Minnesota. Her work was published as *The Original Identity of the York and Towneley Cycles*, published by the Univer-sity of Minnesota (Minneapolis, 1919). See Eleanor Grace Clark, 'The York Plays and the Gospel of Nicodemus', *PMLA*, xliii (1928), 153–61; Frances A. Foster, 'Was Gilbert Pilkington Author of the *Secunda Pastorum*?' *PMLA*, xliii (1928), 124–36; Grace Frank, 'On the relation of the York and Towneley Plays', *PMLA*, xliv (1929), 313–19; Marie C. Lyle, 'The Original Identity of the York and Towneley Cycles—A Rejoinder', *PMLA*, xliv (1929), 319–28. See also Sir Edmund Chambers, *English Literature at the Close of the Middle Ages* (Oxford, 1945), p. 36, who rejects all theories of a common origin of the York and Towneley cycles.

origins and in the sources of their earliest forms. This is checked by evidence that, up to a fairly advanced stage of growth and development, these cycles underwent similar treatments in matters of revisions. The likenesses are too many and too detailed, both structurally and as regards contents and sources of revisions, to be accounted for in casual ways.

It has been thought that the resemblances between the York and the Towneley cycles came about through the borrowing on the one side or the other of individual plays, or through literary influences and imitations, or by the use of common liturgical sources, and these conjectures are not necessarily entirely wrong. They might, most of them, be better described as partial truths. There is no reason to deny *in toto* the facts and judgements advanced by O. Herttrich,[1] Joseph Hall,[2] A. R. Hohlfeld,[3] Charles Davidson,[4] C. M. Gayley,[5] Frank W. Cady,[6] A. W. Pollard,[7] or by any of the more recent students of the subject. This is a simpler and more inclusive theory than those hitherto advanced. There are perhaps cases of interinfluence, special borrowing, and imitation, but the hypothesis that Towneley was taken over from York at a certain rather late stage of cyclic development explains the general situation and avoids most minor difficulties.

The obstacle that stands in the way of both the comprehension and acceptance of this theory arises from the remarkable growth of mystery plays in the fourteenth and fifteenth centuries, the consequent great activity in the revision, rewriting, and reassignment to trading companies, and many other changes that went on industriously at both York and Wakefield. At York plays were divided into two or more plays, some plays may have been added, and certainly a number must have been lost or discarded. At Wakefield too there was at least one extensive recension affecting a considerable number of the plays, that of the so-called 'Wakefield Master', and sometimes so thorough was the redaction that only faint traces survive of the older versions. The

---

[1] *Studien zu den York Plays* (1886).
[2] Article in *Englische Studien*, ix (1886), 448 ff.   [3] Op. cit.
[4] *Studies in the English Mystery Plays* (1892).
[5] *Plays of our Forefathers* (New York, 1907).
[6] 'The Liturgical Basis of the Towneley Mysteries', *PMLA*, xxiv (1909), 418 ff.
[7] *The Towneley Plays*, E.E.T.S. (London, 1897), introduction.

Towneley manuscript has, as we have seen, suffered serious injuries, and this circumstance does not make easier the task of seeing that cycle in its true relation to the York cycle.

In spite of these extensive changes, with the accompanying accidents and losses, six practically complete plays and a number of single speeches and passages in other plays remain identical in the two cycles. The plays are Pharaoh, Christ before the Doctors, Christ Led up to Calvary, the Harrowing of Hell, the Resurrection, and the Last Judgement. These plays are for the most part complete and in good literary form, and these circumstances may furnish a reason why they were spared. Their preservation was, however, a consequence of the local situations existing among the crafts in York and Wakefield. It will be seen that there is no one distinguishable common trait among these plays, either in style or in the tradition of mystery plays.

Secondly, there is a group of plays equally unrelated in grouping and theme that have been subject to revision in one cycle and not in the other. Those revised at York and not at Wakefield are the Fall of the Angels, the Creation of Adam and Eve, the Prophetic prologue to the Annunciation, Joseph's Trouble about Mary, the Magi, the Flight into Egypt, the Conspiracy proper, the Last Supper, the Agony and Betrayal, the Crucifixion, the Death and Burial, the Appearance to Mary Magdalen in the Garden, and the *Peregrini*. The plays extensively revised in the Towneley cycle and left in their older state in York are the Slaughter of the Innocents, the Incredulity of Thomas, *Pastores*, John the Baptist, and the Raising of Lazarus. Criteria for the determination of this situation are supplied in greater or less abundance by verbal parallels, the use of the rhymewords of the older version in the revised version, and various special characteristics carried over from the older form to the newer form. The simple and natural explanation of the interrelations of these pairs of plays is that one play in each pair has been subjected, according to current practice, to revision, and the other has not.

In the third place, there are, as might be expected, a considerable number of plays that, after the plays were carried to Wakefield, have been independently revised in both cycles. The result of this situation is of course to make it more difficult to see that any two versions of a given play that have been thus independently revised in both cycles were ever identical. Fewer original lines, words used in patterns, and identical rhyme-words have been carried over, whereas, when only one of the pair of plays has undergone revision, these signs are abund- ant and usually unmistakable. The plays in this category at York are from the Passion group, and the case is not clear, since many of them seem to have resulted from expansions of Towneley plays and new invention arising from them. It will be noted that nearly all of the York plays in this group are in alliterative verse, a form that seems to indicate late revision: Peter's Denial and Jesus before Caiaphas (XXIX), Pilate's Wife's Dream and Jesus before Pilate (XXX), Jesus before Herod (XXXI), Second Trial before Pilate, Remorse of Judas, and Purchase of the Field of Blood (XXXII), and Second Trial continued and Condemnation of Jesus (XXXIII). In the Towneley cycle also there are a number of these plays in which obliteration of resemblances is almost complete. They are mostly the work of the Wakefield Master: Cain and Abel (II), Noah (III), Abraham and Isaac (IV), Annunciation (X), Visit to Elizabeth (XI), Scourging and Condemnation (XXII), and Ascension (XXIX). This hypothesis is thus checked by the use in both cycles of late poetic and stanzaic forms.

Finally, there are plays in one cycle that do not appear in the other. The York cycle once contained plays on the same subjects as the Towneley Hanging of Judas and *Processus Talentorum*, but, as York records show, they had ceased to be acted. Four Towneley plays— Isaac, Jacob, *Prophetae*, and Octavian—all of which are on traditional subjects, do not appear in the York cycle. It is possible that they were lost from the York cycle through the poverty or failure of guilds to which they were assigned. A Temptation and Fall of Adam and Eve and an Expulsion from Eden, indispensable subjects, were, without a doubt, originally provided for in the Towneley cycle but were, as suggested above, lost from the manuscript as witnessed by the gap of twelve leaves that occurs after the first play. Similarly, the loss of twelve leaves after the Ascension would account for there being no plays in Towneley on Pentecost and the Death and Assumption of the Blessed Virgin Mary. Two plays in the regular sequence of the Passion, the First Trial before Pilate and the Trial before Herod, have been dropped from the Towneley cycle. That they were once there is clear, as Miss Lyle points out, from reference to these subjects in other plays of the Passion group. In York but not in Towneley appear also plays of the Nativity, the Temptation in the Wilderness, the Woman Taken in Adultery, and Pilate's Wife's Dream. The play of the Nativity proper is not provided for in liturgical drama, although obviously called for and supplied early in various forms. The York play, which is a mere addition to the Journey of Joseph and Mary to Bethlehem, may therefore be a late fabrication. The Temptation of Jesus, which is in the Burns stanza in York and therefore probably old, may have been lost in the Wakefield plays or may have been in abeyance or not available when the separation of the cycles occurred. The same thing may be said of the Woman Taken in Adultery, which is a subject often associated with the Raising of Lazarus, and a Lazarus play was certainly original at York. As for the last of these plays occurring in one cycle and not in the other, the York Trans-figuration (XXIII), it is an unusual subject and may well be a late addition to the York cycle.

If at an early time, not the earliest, the York cycle and the Towne-ley cycle were identical, and if we remember that after the cycle had been established at Wakefield under different management and with differing influences each cycle went its own irregular way in the matter of the revisions of various plays, it would follow that in some cases the one cycle and in other cases the other cycle would retain the older forms. Local circumstances in both places caused certain plays to be revised or rewritten and others to be left in their older states. In order to see this matter more clearly we are forced to a consideration of poetic style and stanza form. There are no records at all of the Wakefield plays until the very end of their career and few of any significance for the York plays during the great formative period of the fourteenth century. We can make some use of fourteenth-century sources of revisions and amplifications, but usually only very general ideas as to when they were used are possible. We have mainly metrics, which are at least an objective factor, to fall back on.

We know that as late as 1255 there were regularly performed at York a *Pastores* and a *Stella*, because in the cathedral statutes issued in that year the treasurer of the cathedral chapter was directed to provide annually 'stars' for plays on those well-known subjects, one for the shepherds and two for the kings:

Item inueniet [thesaurus] stellas cum omnibus ad illas pertinentibus, praeter cirpos, quos inueniet Episcopus Puerorum futurorum [for fatuorum?], vnam in nocte natalis Domini pro pastoribus, et ij^{as} in nocte Epiphaniae, si debeat fieri presentacio iij^{um} regum.[1]

We have reasonable grounds for inferring also that perhaps later in the thirteenth century York had early vernacular plays of the *Pastores*, the *Quem quaeritis*, and the *Peregrini*. This inference we have drawn above from the *Shrewsbury Fragments*. The fact that these plays, one of them certainly, were written in single and double quatrains suggests that those early simple verse forms were in use at York for early vernacular plays. It would be a thing to be expected that York would have had the ancient groups of plays at Christmas and Easter. We know that the Corpus Christi play was in process of institution after about 1318, and we must not forget that York was a dominant centre of religious culture.

We have no further knowledge covering the existence of very early plays at York, but there would be every reason to believe that in and around a great ecclesiastical institution like York Minster there would be no lack of plays on various themes from the *cursus* of the liturgical year. It would follow that simple and ancient metres would offer a suggestion as to what plays the York authorities had of their own, or at least had accessible, when they undertook the fabrication of a Corpus Christi cycle. The indications are that borrowing and special composition of plays were the exceptional things, and the compilers of cycles all over Europe seem to have kept what they already had. How else could one account for individual differences in the earliest forms from the beginning and for so little evidence (there is some evidence) of borrowing and imitation among groups of mystery plays? It would have been simpler and perhaps more satis-factory for York and Coventry to do what Chester did and borrow their plays from abroad, but they chose to follow a more normal medieval procedure.

There are, as we have seen, at least two other primitive English metres, besides the single and double quatrain, that we might expect

---

[1] Chambers, op. cit. ii. 399.

would make an early appearance, namely, the four-accented rhymed couplet and the *rime couée*. In point of fact there are some plays and parts of plays in the York or the Towneley cycle, sometimes in both, that appear to have been originally composed in these two early metrical forms. One makes this inference from the fact that such parts are often biblical or liturgical and are, indeed, the very cores or beginnings from which the plays must have grown. There was no reason and no available literary skill that would have caused later revisers and redactors deliberately to have composed these parts in primitive metres. Revisions and rewritings of York plays were numerous and drastic, but in spite of that fact some crucial and original scenes and dialogues escaped, and these old and simple parts can be best accounted for as remains of earlier and simpler versions of the plays in which they occur. We may follow this line farther by the tentative use of the hypothesis explained above, namely that at a certain time in a fairly advanced development of the York cycle it was borrowed, so far as we can tell as a whole, by Wakefield, so that at that time the York and the Towneley cycles were one and the same. The Towneley plays, although greatly changed, were apparently not so thoroughly and extensively revised as were the plays that remained at York. Therefore the Towneley plays would show and do show more of the early vernacular language and metre than do the York plays. We are thus enabled in certain instances to draw inferences from the Towneley plays as to what the earliest plays at York were about and in what metrical forms they were written.

There are indications that York had in a probably pre-cyclic stage and available for the building of the Corpus Christi cycle a group of Old Testament plays. Ten Brink, on philological and dialectal grounds, came to conclusions as to the date and provenance of certain Towneley plays that are too important in this connexion to be overlooked:

He says[1] in speaking of the Towneley plays of Isaac (V) and Jacob (VI) as one play:

This play has been handed down in the Towneley Collection: unfortunately it is mutilated at the beginning, and also divided into two parts: *Isaac* and *Jacob*. However, it originally formed, and, in fact, still forms, one drama, which was produced indepen-

[1] Op. cit. ii. 274 and iii. 244.

dently without regard to any cycle of mysteries, and indeed earlier than most of the others, probably than all the other parts of the cycle in which it was subsequently incorporated. All this can easily be proved by means now at the disposal of philology, but this is not the place for entering into the subject. Less certain is the local origin of the piece. The assumption that few of the rhyming words have been altered in their transmission could, for instance, allow for the supposition that the drama might have been produced in the north of the East-Midland territory, rather than in the southern districts of Northumbria, a supposition that would accord very well with many other peculiarities of the work.

In another place he adds:

In *Jacob* and *Esau* the dramatic art is still of a low standard: the situations are not made much use of; the characteristics show little depth or originality. The poet is full of reverence for his subject, and dramatizes faithfully what seems to him its most important traits, without putting to it much of his own originality.

Ten Brink's conception of the origin and growth of mystery plays is not the current one, certainly not the conception that underlies this book, but no one can deny the soundness of his judgement both as to the language and the dramatic primitivity of those plays.

There existed, probably at York, a play of the Creation and Fall of Man originally written in rhymed couplets and *rime couée*, a play of Cain and Abel in couplets, and, of course, almost certainly, a Noah in primitive metre, although the Noah plays in both cycles have undergone such thorough redaction that no traces of the original metre seem to be preserved. This may be regarded as an over-bold speculation, but other Old Testament plays universally associated with the Noah play were clearly once written in primitive metres, and the Noah play must have passed through such a stage and can be accounted for in no other way. There were in this hypothetical Old Testament group plays on Abraham and Isaac, Isaac and Rebecca, and Jacob and Esau. These three were in rhymed couplets and are partly so still. All three of them are preserved in the Towneley cycle, although they have been injured by the loss of leaves from the manuscript. If they existed in York, as they probably did, the last two mentioned have been abandoned and lost. It will be recalled that ten Brink regarded Isaac (V) and Jacob (VI) as one.

As to a play of the prophets, there was a *Prophetae* that has been lost in York or rather transferred and transformed into a prologue to the Annunciation. There is also a play on the subject of Octavian and the Falling of the Images in the Temple of Peace (no Sibyl) preserved in the Towneley cycle (IX). Both it and the Towneley *Prophetae* are written in *rime couée* and both are possibly original York plays. At any rate, the use of *rime couée* as an original metre is perceptible in both cycles in the series of plays that, like Octavian, lead up to the Nativity—Annunciation, Visit to Elizabeth, and Joseph's Trouble about Mary.

There was, too, as we know, a *Pastores* in quatrains and double quatrains and, one would think, a *Stella* also in that form. The York *Pastores* is in the northern septenar stanza, and, as we have seen, is immediately descended from the Shrewsbury *Officium Pastorum*. It has been rewritten by the Wakefield playwright in two versions. The *Stella* in York has been divided into two plays. The first of these belongs to the alliterative group, and the second is in northern septenar. The Towneley correspondent is in the Burns stanza, which is a puzzling circumstance. There was also a Flight into Egypt (exceptionally preceding a Slaughter of the Innocents) and a Slaughter of the Innocents. The former appears in the Burns stanza in Towneley and has been rewritten in York in a more elaborate form, $ababcc^4dd^2fefe^3$. The Slaughter of the Innocents appears in the York cycle in a fairly primitive form, $ababcddc^3$, and that, if one may judge by detailed resemblances, was the form elaborately rewritten by the Wakefield playwright. These plays are all on traditional liturgical subjects.

Other plays showing evidences of having been composed in English in the more primitive metres are the Raising of Lazarus, which seems to have been originally in couplets and double quatrains in the Towneley version, and appears naturally enough in York in the northern septenar; also the Ascension, which in York is written in orderly double quatrains, and in Towneley in a great variety of simple stanzas—quatrains, northern septenar, Chester stanza, and double quatrains, with even some of the work of the Wakefield playwright. Pentecost, probably lost from the Towneley manuscript, appears in York, like the Ascension, in double quatrains. We know from the *Shrewsbury Fragments* that there were probably early plays at York on the Resurrection and the *Peregrini* and that they were probably first written in English in quatrains and double quatrains. But an early great revision of the York plays affected, indeed overwhelmed, the simple early plays of the Easter group. It consisted in a thorough-going redaction of a large number of the plays on the basis of the *Northern Passion*.[1] The revision of the Resurrection group of plays was carried out in the Burns stanza. The principal events in the Resurrection group are *Quem quaeritis* (with or without the Setting of the Watch), *Hortulanus*, *Peregrini*, and the Incredulity of Thomas, such scenes being often included in one play of the Resurrection. In this case, the Resurrection proper appears in the same version in both the York and the Towneley cycles in the Burns stanza; *Peregrini* appears in that stanza in Towneley, as also do two stanzas pertinent to the *Hortulanus* in the Towneley Resurrection (XXVI); and the final episode of the series, the Incredulity of Thomas, appears in the Burns stanza in the York cycle. Thus a full Easter group exists in that form in one cycle conjointly with the other. Since an expanded form of the *Northern Passion* was used, the redaction may have been made about 1350, although the matter is of course vague.

There is little evidence that there was a Passion play at York before the establishment of the Corpus Christi cycle. The *Northern Passion* seems to have dictated the whole Passion group. Something like the original institution may be seen in the Wakefield plays, where the Conspiracy and the Crucifixion, both containing many episodes, with the Buffeting, Scourging, and Casting of Lots, cover the entire range, whereas in York the field has been divided into eleven plays. There are couplets and quatrains in the Towneley Conspiracy and a good deal of *rime couée* in the Towneley Crucifixion, so that there may have been a pre-cyclic Passion at York, although it is possible that the couplets came from the *Northern Passion*.

The whole issue is illuminated by two circumstances. The first of these is an extensive revision of the York–Wakefield plays under direct influence of the vernacular *Gospel of Nicodemus*. This, as we have noted, was discovered by W. A. Craigie and further developed by W. H. Hulme and others.[2] It is plain that this revision under the

---

[1] *The Northern Passion*, loc. cit. ii. 81–101; Lyle, op. cit., pp. 4–29; Frances H. Miller, 'The Northern Passion and the Mysteries', *Modern Language Notes*, xxxiv (1919), 88–92; F. W. Cady, 'The Passion Group in Towneley', *Modern Philology*, x (1913), 587–660.

[2] W. A. Craigie, loc. cit., pp. 52–61; *The Middle English Harrowing of Hell and the Gospel*

influence of the *Gospel of Nicodemus* was a matter of the elaboration of plays many of which had already been written or rewritten on the basis of the *Northern Passion*. Miss Lyle argues that, although the *Gospel of Nicodemus* forms the basis of the Harrowing of Hell and of the trial scenes before Pilate, it could not have been fundamental in the formation of the Passion group, since the group of Passion plays provides for many subjects directly from the *Northern Passion*. 'Such a situation', she says, 'seems to indicate that additional material from the *Gospel of Nicodemus* was incorporated in the York cycle in order to elaborate the simpler trial scenes based upon the *Northern Passion*.' She finds confirmation of this in Burton's list of York pageants, described above, in which the summaries of four of the five plays concerned follow the events of the *Northern Passion* and make no mention of those from the *Gospel of Nicodemus*, Burton's list being probably a formal one and out of date as regards the exact contents of plays. Hulme suggested that the northern septenar stanza entered the York cycle through the influence of the *Gospel of Nicodemus*, but this is questionable, since the measure was not uncommon and is an easy invention from the double quatrain. The York plays affected by the *Gospel of Nicodemus* are the Harrowing of Hell (XXXVII), Creation to the Fifth Day (II), Abraham and Isaac (X), Pharaoh (XI), prologue to the Annunciation (XII), *Pastores* (XV), Magi (XVII), Christ before the Doctors (XX), the Transfiguration (XXIII), Woman Taken in Adultery and Lazarus (XXIV), the Last Supper (XXVII), the Crucifixion (XXXV), Pentecost (XLIV). Various Towneley plays, including the Conspiracy, are of course also affected. These revisions, it may be believed, were all carried out before Towneley was separated from York.

The second matter of importance arises from the discovery by Jesse Byers Reese of a great revision of the York cycle in alliterative verse. It affects no less than fourteen plays, with a few bits in other plays.[1] The York plays in alliterative verse are Creation and Fall of Lucifer (I), the Coming of the Magi (XVI), the Conspiracy (XXVI),

---

of *Nicodemus*, loc. cit., p. xviii *et passim*; Lyle, op. cit., pp. 30–45; Clark, op. cit., pp. 153–61; Lyle, 'A Rejoinder', loc. cit., pp. 313–28.

[1] 'Alliterative Verse in the York Cycle', *Studies in Mediaeval Culture Dedicated to George Raleigh Coffman, Studies in Philology*, xlviii (1951), 639–68.

Agony and Betrayal (XXVIII), Peter's Denial and Jesus before Caiaphas (XXIX), Pilate's Wife's Dream and Jesus before Pilate (XXX), Trial before Herod (XXXI), Second Trial before Pilate continued and Condemnation (XXXIII), Death of Christ (XXXVI), Apparition to Thomas of the Blessed Virgin Mary (XLVI), *Peregrini* (XL), Death of the Blessed Virgin Mary (XLV). No evidence of this revision appears in the corresponding Wakefield plays, so that the alliterative plays must have been rewritten after the separation of the two cycles. Indeed, one may go farther and point out that Towneley plays I, XVI, XXVI, XXVIII, XXXVI, and XL are, for the most part, still in an older state, and the alliterative revision, as witnessed by verbal parallels, common rhyme-words, and similar structural features, was based on them as they stand. The reason why this interesting fact has not been discovered is, as the author suggests, that much alliteration is used in the York cycle for purposes of ornament, although in such cases the verse is syllabic as well as accentual. Reese's careful and skilful work has enabled us to see that these plays are written in the genuine alliterative style. They are of course a part of the Alliterative Revival, which is thought to have lasted from about 1340, the conjectural date of the *Alexander Fragments*, until about the middle of the fifteenth century. The rhyming of alliterative lines tells us nothing as to the date, since rhymed alliterative verse appears from about 1200 onwards. All that can be said is that a school of alliterative poets arose in the northern counties of England and in Scotland about the middle of the fourteenth century.[1]

There is reason to think that the thirteen York plays written or rewritten in a typically Middle English alliterative poetic style constitute the latest extensive redaction that that cycle underwent; also they are well worthy of consideration in and for themselves. This redaction seems certainly to be subsequent to the list made by Roger Burton and dated in 1415,[2] since there are characters and events in these plays, particularly those dealing with the Passion, that are not provided for in Burton's summaries.

---

[1] J. K. Oakden, *Alliterative Poetry in Middle English* (2 v. Manchester, 1930), pp. 153–200 *et passim*.

[2] L. T. Smith, op. cit., pp. xix–xxvii; Davies, op. cit., pp. 233–6.

The Conspiracy (XXVI), a play revised in York and not in Towneley, corresponds to only one part of the Towneley *Conspiracio* (XX), which has been divided into three plays in the York cycle: the Conspiracy proper, the Last Supper (XXVII), and the Agony and Betrayal (XXVIII).[1] In describing the York Conspiracy Burton merely enumerates the characters: Pilate, Caiaphas, two *milites*, three Jews, and Judas; but the York play as it stands has also Annas, who would seem to be demanded by the plot, and two soldiers and Judas, but no Jews. It has also a Janitor at the gate of Pilate's palace, who, like the Porter of Hell-gate in *Macbeth*, is of sufficient comic importance to have been listed if such a character had belonged to the play when Burton described it. On the other hand, the characters listed by Burton are practically the same as those that appear in the corresponding part of the Towneley play (ll. 1–313). For the Agony and Betrayal Burton again merely enumerates the dramatis personae, which are not the same as those that appear in the York play. Burton lists Pilate, a conspicuous character, who is, however, excrescent in the biblical story. The alliterative reviser follows Scripture closely: Pilate does not appear in the play, and one suspects that he has been dropped. In any case Burton calls for thirteen soldiers armed and has no Jews; whereas the play has four soldiers and four Jews. It also introduces an angel not in Burton's list.

The next four alliterative plays in the York cycle, Peter's Denial and Jesus before Caiaphas (XXIX), the First Trial before Pilate and Pilate's Wife's Dream (XXX), the Trial before Herod (XXXI), and the Second Trial before Pilate with the Condemnation (XXXIII), have been separately revised in both the York and the Towneley cycles, so that these York alliterative plays cannot be checked by their Towneley counterparts. One finds, however, some rather striking variations from Burton's list. For example, in York play XXX Burton makes no provision for Pilate's Wife's Dream, which would be, one would think, an altogether improbable omission had this episode been in the York play when it was described by Burton. Indeed, he provides for the first part of the play only, that is, the First Trial before Pilate. He has no *Uxor Pilati*, no *Ancilla*, no Beadle, and, most significant of all, no *Diabolus*. Again, the list provides for four

---

[1] Lyle, op. cit., pp. 77–83.

Jews, and the play has none at all. These plays, moreover, provide *Milites* instead of Jews as the chief tormentors of Jesus. Play XXX has two soldiers who seem to replace the two councillors of Burton's list. In the Trial before Herod (XXXI) it may be significant that Burton makes no mention of *tres Filii Herodis* who appear in the play, and again Burton fails to provide the Jews of the play. Further evidence that these three plays were in an earlier state when they were described in 1415 comes from the Second Trial before Pilate and the Condemnation, although the play as described by Burton was already an elaborate one. It then contained a scene of the Casting of Lots for the garments of Jesus that was evidently not rewritten by the alliterative reviser, since it appears in two small metrical bits at the ends of plays XXXIV and XXXV. York plays XXX to XXXV were affected by certain re-arrangements of the responsible guilds, so that Miss Smith[1] concludes that they were copied into the Register in a later state than they had been in when Burton listed them. The Towneley play *Processus Crucis* (XXIII), which includes not only the Crucifixion but the Death and Burial, shows an earlier form of York play XXXIV (the Cruci-fixion) and of play XXXVI (Death and Burial), a division into two plays already provided for by Burton, but nevertheless evidence of the lateness of the alliterative redaction. Of these two plays, originally one and still so in the Towneley cycle,[2] the latter has been rewritten in the alliterative style, and the former has not. Therefore one finds a closer agreement between play XXXVI and Burton's list than between XXXV and the list. In his summary of XXXV Burton does not mention Jacobus or Maria Salome, who appear in the York play, and in the play the *Servus cum spongea* has taken on the popular clown's name of Garcio.

There are slight indications of late revision in alliterative plays other than those treating of the Passion. It may, for example, be signi-ficant that in the Death of Mary (XLV) *duo Angeli* become *duae Ancillae*, three Jews become two, and two devils are reduced to one, and that in some other alliterative plays there are slight differences in dramatis personae from the characters listed by Burton. All in all, it may be considered practically certain that the rewriting in the alliterative style was done after 1415. There is even an indication that one part of it at

---

[1] Loc. cit. pp. xxii–xxv and notes.   [2] Lyle, op. cit., pp. 83–84 *et passim.*

least was done between 1415 and 1431. In the *York Memorandum Book* a record of the Goldsmiths' company shows that by the later date there were two Magi plays in the York cycle, whereas Burton's 1415 list shows but one. Of the two Magi plays in the York cycle as preserved, play XVI (the Coming of the Magi) opens with 58 lines in the alliterative style before the play changes into metre, and these opening lines may have been supplied at the time of the division of the one play into two. It remains puzzling of course that the rest of play XVI should be identical with lines 73 to 216 of the other Magi play.[1]

In the group of alliterative plays in the York cycle from the Conspiracy to the Burial (XXVI, XXVIII, XXIX, XXX, XXXI, XXXII, XXXIII, and XXXVI) it is possible to go farther and see that these excellent plays are probably the work of one author. It is worth doing because the man had a genius, or at least a noteworthy talent. The rhyme-schemes of stanzas used in the composition of these plays, though never exactly the same in different plays, and rarely consistently carried out in any one play, are generally similar throughout the series. The characteristic feature is the use of a long-lined alliterative double quatrain of four accents to the line, sometimes linked together in the middle by rhyme and sometimes rhymed alternately throughout the eight lines. In some plays the writer uses single quatrains, but in either case he usually follows the opening group with a *cauda* of varying length and of three accents to the line. The stanza form of play XXVI is $ababab^4cdcccd^3$. Such a style may not commend itself to one unused to Middle English alliterative verse and will almost certainly seem rougher than it is. For example, when Judas knocks at the gate of Pilate's palace (stanza 12), he says:

> Do open, porter, þe porte of þis prowde place,
> That I may passe to youre princes to proue for youre prowe.
> *Janitor.* Go hense, þou glorand gedlyng! God geue þe ille grace,
> Thy glyfftyng is so grymly þou gars my harte growe.
> *Judas.* Goode sir, be toward þis tyme, and tarie noght my trace,
> For I haue tythandis to telle.
> *Janitor.*   ꝫa, som tresoune I trowe,
> For I fele by a figure in youre fals face,
> It is but foly to feste affeccioun in ꝫou.

[1] L. T. Smith, loc. cit., p. 125 n.

For Mars he hath morteysed his mark,
Eftir all lynes of my lore,
And sais ȝe are wikkid of werk,
And bothe a strange theffe and a stark.
Judas. Sir, þus at my berde and ȝe berk
It semes it schall sitte yow full sore.

In Peter's Denial and Jesus before Caiaphas (XXIX) the stanza form is irregular, although the movement is the same throughout. The verse of the First Trial before Pilate and Pilate's Wife's Dream (XXX) is rhymed abab⁴cdddc³, a form that appears also in the *Peregrini* (XL) and in the Death of the Blessed Virgin Mary (XLV); also with only slight variation in the Fall of Lucifer (I). In the following lines from play I (stanza 12) Lucifer mounts God's throne and is suddenly dashed into Hell:

Ther sall I set my selfe, full semely to seyghte,
To ressayue my reuerence thorowe righte o renowne,
I sall be lyke vnto hym þat es hyeste on heghte; (*He seats himself.*)
Owe! what I am derworth and defte. Owe! dewer! all goes downe!
  My mighte and my mayne es all marrande,
  Helpe! felawes, in faythe I am fallande.
  Second falling Angel. Fra heuen are we heledande on all hande,
  To wo are we weendande, I warrande.

The Trial before Herod (XXXI) is written in stanzas of sixteen or more long lines curiously interwoven; indeed, the form is involved. The stanza form of play XXXII is also a puzzle. This play, like the preceding and the following plays, is of a deeply emotional nature. It presents the Second Trial before Pilate, the Remorse of Judas, and the Purchase of the Field of Blood. It opens in abab⁴cccd³, or something like it. Stanzas 5–15 and 35–39 in ababcdcd⁴ present interviews between Pilate, on the one side, and Caiaphas and Annas, on the other; also an odd little episode of an Armiger who wishes to sell a field. Stanzas 18–34 and 40–41 in ababcdcd⁴e²f³e² deal with the legend of the Bowing of the Standards from the Gospel of Nicodemus. The changes of stanza form within the play are thus connected with different themes and suggest piecemeal revision such as might have resulted from repeated contacts between a guild and a local poet. Play XXXIII, the rest of the Second Trial before Pilate, an excellent and well-unified play, is prevailingly, on the other hand, in ababbc-bc⁴dccd³, and the Death and Burial (XXXVI), also one of the writer's greatest achievements, is in a somewhat similar stanza, ababbcbcc³deee²d³. The dramatic quality of these stanzas is obvious. The first is stanza 28 of play XXXIII:

> *Pilate.* Why suld I deme to dede þan with-oute deseruyng in dede?
> But I haue herde al haly why in hertes ȝe hym hate,
> He is fautles in faith, and so god mote me spede,
> I graunte hym my gud will to gang on his gate.
> > *Caiaphas.* Nought so, sir, for wele ȝe it wate,
> > To be kyng he claymeth with croune,
> > And who so stoutely will steppe to þat state,
> > ȝe suld deme, sir, to be dong doune
> > > And dede.
> *Pilate.* Sir, trulye þat touched to tresoune,
> And or I remewe, he rewe sall þat reasoune,
> > And or I stalke or stirre fro þis stede.

The second is stanza 10 from play XXXVI:

> *Jesus.* Þou man þat of mys here has mente,
> To me tente enteerly þou take,
> On roode am I ragged and rente,
> Þou synfull sawle, for thy sake,
> For thy misse amendis wille I make.
> My bakke for to bende here I bide,
> Þis teene for thi trespase I take,
> Who couthe þe more kyndynes haue kydde
> > Than I?
> > Þus for thy goode
> > I schedde my bloode,
> > Manne, mende thy moode,
> > > For full bittir þi blisse mon I by.

It will be noted from these passages that this writer uses plain northern Middle English and shows none of the cumbersome Latinisms that beset the revisers of mystery plays in the fifteenth century. In the use of this plain northern speech he shows great skill, and his use of alliteration is truly ingenious. A slight experiment will show that his verse speaks better than it reads.

In these plays of the Passion group there is the favourable attitude toward Pilate that came from the Gospel of Nicodemus. The writer tends to lay the burden of showing cruelty to Jesus on *Milites* and not on the Jews. In this he follows Scripture, for a careful adherence to the gospel account of the Passion is another of his characteristics. He makes no revolutionary changes in events, but contents himself with an intimate realization of the stories he tells. He has also a strong sense of dramatic suspense and seems to carry it over from play to play. The Agony and Betrayal, for example, is a play of sustained power, in which one sees before one's eyes fear converted into resignation. The scene of the agonized Master in contact with the sleeping disciples presents a notable contrast, and nothing could well be more finely realized than the gentle remonstrance of Jesus. In play XXIX Peter's boast of faithfulness, very human, is gently rebuked by Jesus' prophecy, and dramatic suspense is the result. The passions of the play are also very real—the blind malice of Caiaphas and Annas, the coarse brutality of the soldiers, and the murderous mood of Judas. The interrelations of Caiaphas and Annas as priests, kinsmen, and politicians are clearly presented. Indeed, the author, always alive to matters of rank and position and aware of amenities, must have been a man of culture and intelligence. Play XXIX, and the same thing may be said of other plays, realizes the biblical story not only in a simple and direct way but with sensitivity to finer shades and relations. The episode of Peter's Denial (XXIX) carries on the suspense created in the Agony and Betrayal (XXVIII). The picture of Peter's lurking in the background beset by inquisitive women, his plausible recognition by Malchus (whose ear he had just cut off), Jesus' restrained reproach addressed to Peter, and the shrewdly set dialogues from Scripture may be said to demonstrate the fine quality of this redactor's dramaturgy. In the Buffeting in this play the stark cruelty of the soldiers begins. In play XXX, Pilate's Wife's Dream, which would seem to be an addition by this dramatist, is rather delicately done, especially in its treatment of Procula as a fine lady, but the episode is not carried through with much realization of its emotional possibilities, probably because there was no scriptural warrant for such a treatment. The sleepiness of Pilate's indolent son and the unexpected though probable fact that the Beadle is a Christian are clever minor features. In general, it will be noted, the play provides an excellent introduction to the Trial before Herod (XXXI), which play, however, is dramatically thin, but clever. Its feature is that Jesus, in spite of incredible mistreatment, maintains complete silence through-out the play. Play XXXII (the Second Trial before Pilate, the Remorse of Judas, and the Purchase of the Field of Blood) is, as indicated above, a rather terrible play. It tries to exculpate Pilate and stresses in bitter form the unreasonable malice of Caiaphas and Annas. The remorse of Judas when in his hopeless abandonment he throws down the purchase money seems almost perfectly dramatized. One wonders if the lost play put down in Burton's list between plays XXXV and XXXVI and entitled *Suspencio Jude* might also have been rewritten by this alliterative poet; if so, the loss is great. Play XXX (the Condemnation) is a drama of frightful cruelty exercised against Jesus, and one wonders how any modern person reading it sincerely could think that the English mystery plays had lost their tremendous religious and emotional appeal and subsisted mainly on their comicality. The *Mortificacio* (XXXVI) is a play of deep sadness and most impressive. 'His blood be upon you', says Pilate, and Annas replies, 'Let him madly mow on the moon.' Caiaphas says, 'Thou savedst others, save thyself.' Mary mourns for her son, and Jesus says, 'Man, see what bitter sorrow I suffer for thee' and 'I thirst.' Longinus at Pilate's command deals the stroke of mercy, and his reward is that he receives his sight. Pilate behaves graciously to Joseph of Arimathea, and Joseph and Nicodemus undertake the burial of Jesus like good neighbours.

As to the other alliterative plays, there seems little reason to draw a line between them and the Passion group and to attribute them to a different redactor. They too show adherence to Scripture and direct-ness of manner with the same intelligence, plain language, ingenuity in alliteration, the same simple yet emphatic humour, and the same ability to protract lines of interest.

One play does, however, stand out as the work of a different author or as the masterpiece of this one. It is play XLVI, the Appearance of Our Lady to Thomas. Its stanza differs somewhat from others, mainly in its greater perfection. There is little of the breaking down of the stanza into quatrains and double quatrains as in some of the plays. In this play we are carried consistently along in a form approximated elsewhere, $ababbcbc^4c^3ddd^2c^3$, but in this play possibly more smoothly

managed than in others. There are in it fewer of the blunt characteristics described above, although it too is a clear and simple play. It
merely seems gentler, more humane, and more beautiful. Thomas on
his way from India finds himself in the Vale of Jehoshaphat. He is
melancholy, discouraged, and alone. He mourns over the cruel death
of the good Jesus and the insults and tortures He has endured. He lies
down to sleep. At this low point there appears to him a vision of the
Blessed Virgin Mary with angels before her singing a Latin hymn
that begins, *Surge proxima mea columba.*[1] While the angels sing another
song, *Veni de libano sponsa veni coronaberis* from the Song of Solomon,
they bid Thomas arise, and, when he does so, he beholds the Virgin
in bright light borne aloft by the angels. She speaks to him with
infinite kindness and lets down to him her blue girdle, dispelling
his incredulity. She bids him carry the message of her ascension to
the other disciples. There is more music, and the vision vanishes.
Thomas hastens to meet the other disciples, and, when he meets them,
it is only to find that they distrust him, say he is a boaster, and reproach
him for his absence from the death-bed of the Virgin. He tells his
story and displays the girdle. They are convinced and, in the most
human way, they apologize to Thomas for having disbelieved in him.
All within this little play is sweet, friendly, and natural.

This alliterative reviser of so many of the York plays was apparently
familiar with the Gospel of Nicodemus and with the *Transitus
Mariae*, and there is no finer illustration of that fourteenth- and fifteenth-
century infusion of new blood into the mystery plays from the New
Testament Apocrypha than is his work, but he also returns to the
text of the New Testament itself and realizes it in his dramas. After
the meeting together of the disciples in play XLVI they go their ways
—Thomas to India, Peter to Rome, James to Samaria, Andrew to
Greece, and John to Asia Minor.

Redaction in the Towneley cycle after the separation from York,
compared to what took place in the York cycle, is, with one famous
exception, inconsiderable. There are evidences of minor revisions and
some greater ones may be unidentifiable, but there can be no question

---

[1] The hymn is apparently based on the *Transitus Mariae*. The music for it and the other
songs of the play is preserved in the Ashburnham MS.; reproduced by Lucy Toulmin Smith,
op. cit., pp. 517–24; also in photolithic plates.

about the work of the so-called Wakefield Master, who, as a writer of Middle English, is almost unique. A great controversy, waged over the Towneley cycle, concerns the authorship of the unwontedly spirited plays and parts of plays identified by the clever, complicated style in which they are written, the wit and comic ability they show, their homely realism, and their popular satire.[1] One writer, urged on by a laudable desire to discover the name of this unknown genius, selected the plainly written name 'Gilbert Pilkington' from among the many names that have been written on the Towneley manuscript and attempted to build up a case for Gilbert Pilkington as the author of the Wakefield group. He argued that the same man who was the author of these plays was also author of the *Northern Passion*, a probably unwise choice, and of the famous satiric romance *The Tournament of Tottenham*, a better idea. He was vigorously attacked, but it is rather a pity he had no evidence.[2] Whoever he was, the author of these plays was a genius. The author of the Wakefield group wrote a highly complex nine-line stanza described by A. W. Pollard by means of the symbols $\overline{aaaa^2 bbbb^2}c^1ddd^2c^2$, although some plays in other stanzaic forms, also complex, are thought to show his hand. Thirteen Towneley plays are affected, and five, Noah (III), *Prima Pastorum* (XII), *Secunda Pastorum* (XIII), Herod (XVI), and *Coliphizacio*, are in the favourite metre. C. M. Gayley in his *Plays of our Forefathers* (1907), impressed by the brilliant qualities of this greatest of revisers, called him 'The Wakefield Master'. Gayley praised particularly *Secunda Pastorum*, a clever, farcical play that has come to stand erroneously in the popular mind as typical of mystery plays, possibly because critics are unwilling that mystery plays should be what they were, namely religious plays, and want them to be, as they were not, farces, comedies, and romantic dramas.

To sum up what has been said in this chapter, at some time in the early fourteenth century the York authorities, whoever they were,

---

[1] Millicent Carey, *The Wakefield Group in the Towneley Cycle.* Hesperia, vol. xi (Göttingen, 1929).

[2] Oscar Cargill, 'The Authorship of the *Secunda Pastorum*', *PMLA*, xli (1926), 810–31; Frances A. Foster, 'Was Gilbert Pilkington Author of the *Secunda Pastorum* ?', *PMLA*, xliii (1928), 124–36; M. G. Frampton, 'Gilbert Pilkington Once More', *PMLA*, xlvii (1932), 622–35.

seem to have got together their simple plays, possibly supplied necessary scenes they did not possess, put them in the Corpus Christi
procession, and played them at certain places along the route of the
procession. The York sponsors probably provided pageant wagons,
for such vehicles seem to have been in use at Chester from the beginnings of the plays in 1328. These wagons and the plays themselves
were probably, as at Chester, assigned to the care of the craftsmen. A
fashion had been started, and one cannot think that the city of York
would have been long in following it or in bringing their Corpus
Christi play up to the Chester standard, if, indeed, York did not
precede Chester in this matter. One play we may be sure would have
been thought necessary at a very early time, and that is the play of the
Last Judgement. Such a play, relatively unaltered from an early form,
exists in the York cycle and, with characteristic tampering, in the
Wakefield cycle. The play is in double quatrains, eight-line stanzas of
four accents, rhyming alternately, a simple metre used in the early forms
of the York plays. If this play of the Last Judgement was suggested by
or imitated from the Chester cycle, there would have been no reason
for borrowing or imitating its companion play of Antichrist. The
Last Judgement was the necessary finale of a Corpus Christi play.

Of one thing we may be sure, and that is that at the time of the
setting up of the Corpus Christi play at York and constantly from
that time forward revision was rife. One of the first things done,
possibly though not certainly, soon after the cycle was established,
was the rewriting of the Resurrection group in the Burns stanza on
the basis of the *Northern Passion*. Also, probably very early since the
Passion is a necessary subject, came a grand revision, possibly a new
composition of a Passion group, this also done in close conformity
with the *Northern Passion*. Evidences of this revision or new composition appear in the whole group from the Conspiracy to the
Burial. It need not, however, be concluded that this was done once
and for all, since the *Northern Passion* was available for later use.
Passion plays were late developments in liturgical drama, and they
may not have been plentiful in England. At York it may have been
necessary to fill a great gap. A good deal of the pre-cyclic material
may have been in rhymed couplets, quatrains, double quatrains, and
rime couée, and revision both before and after the separation of the

York and Towneley cycles tended to obliterate these early measures but it did not wipe them completely out.

To what extent one has a right to regard plays appearing in a given early metre as contemporary with one another is of course uncertain, but there are cases that lend some plausibility to the idea that plays in the same metrical form may have been written or revised at about the same time. For example, the *Stella* (XVII) at York, once in quatrains and double quatrains, has been, like the Resurrection group, rewritten in the Burns stanza. This metre also appears in the Expulsion of Adam and Eve from Paradise, in the play of John the Baptist, and in that of the Temptation in the Wilderness. All are ancient and important themes and might have been selected by their guild owners at about the same time for revision in a newer and more attractive style. Likewise, there appear in the double quatrain not only the Last Judgement but parts of the *Hortulanus* and the whole of the Ascension. These are also important, indeed necessary, subjects in the building of a Corpus Christi play. It is possible that these plays not only go back to a very early time but that they actually show the same hand. The next great revision or set of revisions of the York cycle seems to have been prevailingly in the northern septenar stanza —eight lines of four accents and four lines of three accents, rhyming ababababcdcd. Revision in this stanza form affected many plays, many of them so important that Charles Davidson[1] regarded the plays appearing in the northern septenar stanza as constituting 'a parent cycle'. We know that the mystery plays did not grow out of any such heterogeneous subjects as these—Creation to the Fifth Day, the Building of the Ark, Noah and his Wife, the Waning of the Flood, Abraham and Isaac, the Annunciation, the Angels and the Shepherds (except the comic parts), the Coming of the Kings, the Adoration of the Magi, Christ before the Doctors, the Transfiguration, the Woman Taken in Adultery, the Raising of Lazarus, the Conspiracy (Towne-ley), the Last Supper, the Crucifixion, the Harrowing of Hell, and Pentecost. We know that the mystery plays originated as tropes or simple dramatic offices mainly connected with the services of Christ-mas and Easter and from other parts of the services of the liturgical year, such as Advent and Septuagesima. Nevertheless Davidson's

[1] Op. cit., pp. 137–53.

idea has been widely accepted—that or a less rational idea that the plays were written by individual dramatists with free selection of subjects from the Bible. In point of fact these plays composed in the northern septenar stanza point to a clearly marked set of revisions in the York cycle before the Wakefield cycle was separately established and after the main series of revisions based on the *Northern Passion* had been carried out. Possibly some of the plays in this stanza are of later composition, but they are, at any rate, revisions of older plays in a stricter conformity to biblical and apocryphal sources and, of course, written with the strong York sense of propriety and reverence. Most of the material for these revisions comes from the poetical *Gospel of Nicodemus*, itself composed in the northern septenar stanza. The plays in which the influence of the *Gospel of Nicodemus* appears are the First Trial before Pilate (XXX), the Second Trial before Pilate and the Condemnation (XXXII), the Harrowing of Hell (XXXVII), the Resurrection (XXXVIII), the Trial before Caiaphas and Peter's Denial (XXIX). As stated above, Miss Lyle argues plausibly that this additional material from the *Gospel of Nicodemus* was introduced into simpler, older plays rewritten earlier on the basis of the *Northern Passion*.[1] There are other York plays in this measure that may belong to the same period of revision and, for all we know, may be by the same authors. Some of them seem to show slight influences of the *Gospel of Nicodemus*. Such are the Creation to the Fifth Day (II), Abraham and Isaac (X), Pharaoh (XI), the prophetic prologue to the Annunciation (XII), the Shepherds (XV), the Magi (XVII), Christ before the Doctors (XX), the Transfiguration (XXIII), the Woman Taken in Adultery and the Raising of Lazarus (XXIV), the Crucifixion (XXXV), Pentecost (XLIV), and the Towneley Conspiracy (XX). A natural inference is that there were at York, probably after the middle of the fourteenth century, one or more dramatists deeply imbued with a serious religious spirit and familiar with the *Gospel of Nicodemus*, and that he or they were extensively employed in the revision and rewriting of plays. A number of the plays enumerated have, of course, undergone still further redaction.

Criticism of the York plays has naturally been greatly affected by Reese's discovery of an extensive rewriting of fourteen plays in

[1] Op. cit., pp. 30–45.

alliterative verse in connexion, we may believe, with the revival of
the alliterative style centring in the last half of the fourteenth century.
One can hardly identify a great metrist unless one knows the style in
which he wrote and judges his poetical skill according to the aesthetic
principles governing the style in which he wrote. What would rightly
be regarded as roughness and awkwardness in a syllabic style, let us
say of iambic pattern, may and, in the case of the alliterative plays in
the York cycle, actually does, turn out to be a proper, or indeed skilful, feature of alliterative verse such as that of *Piers Plowman* and *Sir
Gawain and the Green Knight* and other poems in the *Pearl* manuscript,
or *Chevalere Assigne* and *Pierce the Plowman's Crede*. There is, as we
have seen, great skill, genuine vigour, and no small amount of poetic
beauty in the alliterative plays of the York cycle, and there is much
else in other metres that is poetically admirable throughout the cycle.
By recognizing and approving the serious religious purpose and the
strong sense of propriety and reverence of the authors of the plays in
the northern septenar stanza and many of their revisions, one might
concede to them skill in a kind of poetry excellent in its expression of
the temper of an age. This will be open to those who are capable of a
sympathetic appreciation of the religious earnestness sought for and
often achieved. Another quality, not so hard to appreciate as is reverent
didacticism, is the embodiment of the feelings and thoughts of very
simple, often uneducated people, a quality we see most often in
sweet-tempered children. There is much less of this artless quality in
the York–Towneley plays than in the Chester plays, and it may be
said that, in their strict adherence to Bible and Apocrypha, the York–
Towneley plays give a possibly less convincing representation than
do the Chester plays of the Scriptures themselves—of the Gospels
and the Old Testament narratives. The redactor who used alliterative
verse described above is perhaps in his dramatization of the Bible the
greatest of all, but of course his plays are different in their attitude from
the more liturgical Chester plays. The whole matter of the literary
appreciation of the plays from York and Wakefield, and of other
medieval plays, rests on a knowledge of medieval people as well as
on a knowledge of the Bible and the liturgy.

VII

The Hegge Plays. Religious Drama at Lincoln

THE erroneous and misleading name of *Ludus Coventriae* given to the cycle of Corpus Christi plays in British Museum MS. Cotton Vespasian D. viii came about in an almost inescapable way. The use of it is nevertheless objectionable, and it seems better to call the cycle the Hegge (pron. hedge) plays after Robert Hegge of Durham who owned the manuscript before it was purchased, probably in 1629, by Sir Robert Bruce Cotton. It was the only manuscript of the kind as yet discovered and brought into notice and, as a part of the Cotton collection, it became widely known. It bore on the flyleaf a plain inscription in the hand of Richard James, Cotton's librarian, that said: *Elenchus contentorum in hoc codice; Contenta novi testamenti scenice expressa et actitata olim per monachos sive fratres mendicantes. vulgo dicitur hic liber Ludus Coventriae sive ludus corporis Christi. scribitur metris Anglicanis.* Coventry was known far and wide for the mystery plays performed there until 1580, and James's troublesome mistake was natural enough. Indeed, K. S. Block in her edition of the cycle for the Early English Text Society retains the name 'Ludus Coventriae' and justifies its retention by the belief that, so famous were the plays at Coventry, a 'Coventry' play had come to mean a 'Corpus Christi' play. But this was not the end of the trouble Richard James gave to students of English drama. He gave sanction to the baseless idea, destined to live on for centuries, that mystery plays were acted by 'monks' or 'friars'.

On the basis of these errors Sir William Dugdale in his *Antiquities of Warwickshire* (1656, p. 116) made his famous statement, almost that of an eyewitness, that entered into the accounts of the Hegge plays until almost our own time:

Before the suppression of the Monasteries, this City [Coventry] was very famous for the *Pageants* that were play'd therein, upon *CorpusChristi*day; which occasioning very great confluence thither from far and near, was of no small benefit thereto; which *Pageants* being acted with mighty state and reverance by the Friers of this House [the Grey Friars of Coventry], had Theaters for the severall Scenes, very large and high, placed upon wheels, and drawn to all the eminent parts of the City, for the better advantage of Spectators: And contained the story of the New-Testament, composed into old English Rithme, as appeareth by an ancient *MS.* [in bibl. Cotton. sub effigie Vesp. D. 9] intituled *Ludus Corporis Christi*, or *Ludus Coventriae.* I have been told by some old people, who in their younger years were eye-witnesses of these *Pageants* so acted, that the yearly confluence of people to see that shew was extra-ordinary great, and yielded no small advantage to this City.

Thomas Sharp, writing in 1825 in his *Dissertation on the Pageants or Dramatic Mysteries, Anciently performed at Coventry, by the Trading Companies of that City,* perceived that the Hegge plays 'were no part of the Plays or Pageants exhibited by the Trading Companies of the City', but he did not reject Dugdale's statement that the plays were acted by the Grey Friars. Halliwell, too, who edited the *Coventry Mysteries* for the Shakespeare Society in 1841, was under the impres-sion that these plays were 'acted by the Gray Friars of Coventry'. As soon as students of English dialects examined the Hegge plays, they saw that they had to do not with the Midland dialect of Warwick-shire but with a North-Eastern dialect probably of Lincolnshire. Ten Brink[1] saw this, and his findings were supported by M. Kramer in *Die Sprache und Heimat des sogenannten Ludus Coventriae* in 1892. But it makes the matter clearer to be able to see exactly how Dugdale's mistake occurred. There are in existence a considerable number of ver-sions of the Coventry manuscript Annals, two among the Corporation manuscripts at Coventry, and two at the British Museum, and at least one was burned in the library fire at Birmingham in 1879. One of the British Museum manuscripts, Harl. 6388, suggests the explanation of Dugdale's error. The manuscript was made by Humphrey Wanley in 1690 on the basis of eight versions of the manuscript Annals. Wanley says that in 1492 the King and Queen came to Coventry 'to see the plays at the Gray Friars', by which he means at the Grey Friars' Church, for there was abundant space in front of the church for the presenta-tion of the pageants. There was a station there for the pageants and the record merely means that Henry VII and his queen saw the Corpus Christi plays there just as Queen Margaret, wife of Henry VI, had seen the same municipal plays at a station in Earl Street in 1456.

[1] Op. cit. ii. 283.

The Annals that misled Dugdale had said 'by the Grey Friars', meaning at the Grey Friars' Church. In other words, Dugdale took the word 'by' in Viola's sense of agency and not, as he should have done, in Feste's sense of propinquity.

Cotton Vespasian D. viii is a thick paper volume of 225 leaves, measuring 8 by $5\frac{1}{2}$ inches. Several different kinds of fifteenth-century paper appear in the volume and, as described by Miss Block, throw some light on the make-up of the volume.[1] For example, the banns, or Proclamation, and all the plays as far as the beginning of The Conception of Mary, quires A and B, folios 1–40ᵛ, are written on paper with the *Bunch of Grapes* watermark (Briquet, *Les Filigranes*, No. 3055), a paper that appears again in quire O in an episode of Mary Magdalen in the play of the Last Supper. It is significant that the use of this paper continues until approximately the point where occurs the first great irregularity in the cycle, namely, the intrusion into the cycle of a St. Anne's day play, or play treating, mainly from apocryphal sources, the earlier life of the Blessed Virgin Mary. This St. Anne's day play, which is not substituted for but blended with plays on the subject in the original Corpus Christi play, occupies quires C to G inclusive and is written on paper with the watermark *YHS in a Sun* (Briquet, No. 9477), except quire E, an interpolation containing a dialogue between Joseph and the Generations of David. This paper, thought to be of later manufacture, has the *Pitcher* watermark. The use of *YHS in a Sun* continues through quire M (folio 135ᵛ), and at that point the second major interpolation begins, namely a Passion play in two parts, written for a stationary stage, but based on the Passion plays of an original Corpus Christi play. There are minor interpolations on different paper here and there in these larger divisions, but the main paper to the end of quire R has the *Bull's Head* watermark (Briquet, No. 14184). Quire S (beginning on folio 164, blank) changes the paper again at the beginning of the revised second part of the Passion play, which uses a paper with the *Two Crossed Keys* watermark, and the use of that paper ceases

[1] *Ludus Coventriae, or the Plaie called Corpus Christi*, ed. by K. H. Block, E.E.T.S. (London, 1922), pp. xi–xii. This cycle was also published by the Shakespeare Society in 1841 under the editorship of James Orchard Halliwell: *Ludus Coventriae. A Collection of Mysteries, formerly represented at Coventry on the Feast of Corpus Christi.*

with the end of the Passion and the beginning of the Setting of the Watch. This is only roughly true, since there have been numerous interpolations and transfers and some contrivance on the part of the scribe to make use of paper available at the end of the second Passion play. After the second part of the Passion play, in quires V and W, the *YHS in a Sun* comes back for the end of the cycle in all parts except folios 213–22, the play of the Assumption of the Blessed Virgin Mary, a play in a different handwriting from that of the principal scribe and plainly an interpolation, on a more closely woven paper, unique in the cycle, with the watermark the *Two-Wheeled Cart* (Briquet, No. 3528). It thus seems that, in spite of many minor interpolations on various papers, the *Bunch of Grapes*, the *YHS in a Sun*, the *Bull's Head*, and the *Two-Wheeled Cart* tell the general story of the composition of MS. Cotton Vespasian D. viii. A thing to be noted is that the Lamech episode or the Death of Cain in the play of Noah and other additions to the original cycle in tumbling or alliterative metre are not marked by any changes in the kind of paper.

Cotton Vespasian D. viii is written prevailingly in one very good fifteenth-century hand, varying somewhat from place to place owing to circumstances, such as haste or lack of adequate space, that can some- times be plausibly determined. Because the date 1468 appears in the scribe's hand on the play of the Purification, the manuscript has very properly been thought to have been written at that time or about that time. The Purification is an extraneous play added to the cycle, but on hand when the scribe was copying it. The manuscript as a whole is evidently a copy and partly a compilation, and the provisional dating is, as we shall see, no doubt correct enough. Other hand- writings, besides that of the scribe, appear in the manuscript. The chief of these is in the play of the Assumption of the Blessed Virgin Mary, which is written in an entirely different hand, more cursive and more difficult to read. Besides these two, there is, according to Miss Block's description,[1] a 'rough cursive hand' of about 1500 appearing in quire E, discussed above from the point of view of paper. There is also the hand of an important corrector and reviser not much, if at all, later than that of the main scribe. In it appear folios 95 and 96 inter- polated in the Magi play and containing, strangely enough, ancient

[1] Op. cit., p. xvi.

and necessary features of that play, namely, the presentation of the gifts of the Magi to the infant Jesus and the warning of the Magi by the angel to go home another way and thus escape the machinations of Herod. It looks as if these matters might have been accidentally omitted by the original scribe. This hand also appears in the inter-polated leaf (f. 112) that contains the beginning of the Baptism and in various corrections and minor additions. The manuscript has also many scribbles and defacements, but, except for a few pages at the end, it is complete. The fact that there is no name of town or city is puzzling and has given rise to many conjectures. At the end of the Proclamation or banns we find:

> A sunday next, yf þat we may,
> At vj. of þe belle we gynne oure play,
> In N. towne, wherfore we pray,
> That god now be ʒoure Spede.

It has also come to light from Miss Block's examination of the manuscript that folio 136, quire N, the beginning of the Demon's prologue to I. Passion Play, as Miss Block designates it, was once an outside leaf, a feature also observed with reference to folio 164, the first leaf of II. Passion Play. This seems to indicate that these two halves of the Passion, although written in the hand of the principal scribe, once had as manuscripts an independent existence—one would naturally think, for use in the separate performance of these parts of the cycle. The same thing seems to be true of folios 213–22, which, as before noted, contain the Assumption of the Virgin and differ from the rest of the cycle both in handwriting and the paper used.

THE BANNS OR PROCLAMATION

Perhaps the most striking thing about the Hegge plays, apart from the physical make-up of the manuscript, is the fact that, although the plays are provided with a full set of banns supposed to give the contents of the cycle pageant by pageant, these banns do not agree with the cycle as written. A somewhat obvious hypothesis, though slow to be accepted, is that the banns or Proclamation represent faithfully the cycle as it once was, but that the separate plays as they appear in Cotton Vespasian D. viii comprise revisions great and small made after the banns were composed. Why the scribe did not make over the banns to conform with the cycle he was about to copy we do not know. Perhaps his contract called merely for copying. He did make an attempt to correct the numbering of the stanzas in the Proclamation to make them agree better with the revised cycle, although he gave it up as a bad job; and he did distribute prologue numbers throughout the plays with reasonable exactitude. This hypothesis, that the banns represent an earlier form or stage of develop-ment of the cycle before revision and that the plays themselves present the cycle after it had been subjected to revision, was the subject of a study, too little known, by Esther L. Swenson, *An Inquiry into the Composition and Structure of Ludus Coventriae*.[1] The following pages, as well as some parts of Miss Block's introduction, draw to a consider-able extent on Miss Swenson's study, of which the present author was director.

The Proclamation seems to be the prologue to a normal, full, and interesting Corpus Christi play acted processionally, that is, pre-sumably on the customary movable pageants at stations at various places in some city one after another until the whole play was played. The word 'pageant' is used constantly throughout the prologue, but there are no mentions of any guilds or trading companies. The banns present every subject as an independent scene; and yet a question has arisen as to whether these pageants as described in the prologue were divorced completely from all features of a stationary stage. It is of course possible that one pageant vehicle after another might have been drawn into one area where a principal audience was assembled. It should be understood that these speculations refer to the cycle not as it is but as it is prefigured in the Proclamation in an earlier state than are the plays themselves, for of course the evidences for the use of a multiple or stationary stage are abundant in many pageants in the cycle itself. The question is whether the banns show any evidence of the use of one general stationary stage. Miss Block[2] thinks that pageants 15, 16 and 17, 27 and 29, and 31 and 32 form groups of interdependent plays with simultaneous action and thus indicate that the author of the Proclamation had in mind a standing and not a

[1] University of Minnesota. *Studies in Language and Literature*, No. 1 (Minneapolis, 1914).
[2] Op. cit., p. xxix.

processional play. This is of course true as regards the plays as we have them in the manuscript, but an examination of the stanzas in the banns reveals nothing beyond the multiple stage features that many plays acted on movable pageants possessed.[1] The first line of the description in stanza xxxi of the Proclamation, 'we purpose to shewe in our pleyn place', is not sufficiently definite to indicate the use of a general *platea*. One cannot rule out the possibility that pageants were drawn in sequence into a general area, but the Proclamation affords no evidence of it. The metre and stanza form of the Proclamation do show one irregularity that is reflected in the cycle and must therefore antedate the more important variations recorded below. The form appearing elsewhere in the Proclamation is a thirteen-line stanza rhyming abababababcdddc, all lines being usually of four feet, except the ninth and thirteenth, which vary from one to three feet. In place of this stanza the vexillators utter an ordinary quatrain each for the 13th and 14th pageants. The plays concerned are the Trial of Joseph and Mary and Joseph and the Midwives. These plays are different in tone from other plays recorded in the Proclamation, being more sensational and legendary.[2]

If one follows the banns strictly, one sees that they provided for a Corpus Christi play that presented the following subjects: 1. Fall of Lucifer. 2. Creation and Fall of Man. 3. Cain and Abel. 4. Noah. 5. Abraham and Isaac. 6. Moses and the Tables of the Law. 7. Prophets (Jesse Play). 8. Mary's Betrothal (two plays). 9. Salutation. 10. Joseph's Trouble about Mary. 11. Trial of Joseph and Mary. 12. Joseph and the Midwives. 13. The Shepherds. 14. The Magi. 15. Slaughter of the Innocents and Flight into Egypt. 16. Death of Herod. 17. Christ and the Doctors. 18. Baptism. 19. Temptation, with a Council in Hell. 20. Woman Taken in Adultery. 21. Lazarus. 22. Entry into Jerusalem. 23. Last Supper (including Judas' bargain with the Jews). 24. Betrayal. 25. Trial before Caiaphas and Peter's Denial. 26. Trial before Pilate. 27. Remorse of Judas. 28. Pilate's Wife's Dream and Second Trial before Pilate. 29. Crucifixion.

---

[1] Spencer, op. cit., pp. 168–208.

[2] Swenson, op. cit., pp. 32–33; Block, op. cit., pp. xxi–xxxi. For a study of the plays devoted to the Blessed Virgin Mary see Cornelius Luke, *The Role of the Virgin Mary in the Coventry, York, Chester and Towneley Cycles* (Washington, D.C., 1933). See also F. M. Salter, 'Old Testament Plays of Ludus Coventriae', *Philological Quarterly*, xii (1933), 406–9.

30. Longinus and First Harrowing of Hell. 31. Burial and Setting of the Watch. 32. Second Harrowing of Hell and Christ's Visit to his Mother. 33. *Quem quaeritis.* 34. *Hortulanus.* 35. *Peregrini.* 36. Incredulity of Thomas. 37. Ascension. 38. Pentecost. 39. Doomsday.

It is obvious from this list that the Corpus Christi play represented by the banns laid stress on episodes in the life of the Blessed Virgin Mary, not to the extent of the plays in the cycle as we have it, but to a degree unknown in any Corpus Christi cycle of which we have a record. It provides for a play of the Prophets, not of the ordinary kind, but the messianic Prophets transformed into a play of the Root of Jesse in which the prophecies are no longer of a Messiah but of the Virgin herself as the mother of the Saviour; there are also a play of Mary's Betrothal, in two parts, a Salutation, a Joseph's Trouble about Mary, a Trial of Joseph and Mary, and a play of Joseph and the Midwives. If this play should undergo, as it did, further expansion in this part by the addition or intrusion of a St. Anne's day play, or play dealing with the birth, girlhood, betrothal, and motherhood of the Blessed Virgin Mary, there would be at hand for several of the subjects involved two distinct and separate treatments of such subjects—one from the original Corpus Christi play and another from the St. Anne's day play. We shall see that the compiler of the cycle as we have it, although he might have chosen one or the other of the versions offered, tended to blend his two sources into composite plays.

THE HEGGE CYCLE

So far we have talked only about the Proclamation and what it reveals as to the composition and scope of the Corpus Christi play it sought to introduce and describe. It is now proposed to discuss the cycle, the plays themselves and their groupings, particularly as regards their many differences from the banns or Proclamation. It was, to begin with, a cycle of a pronounced Marian trend that was then revised and in part reconstituted in three major and various minor ways: first, by the intrusion of a series of St. Anne's day plays; secondly, by the re-embodiment within the main cycle of a minor cycle in two parts that dealt with the Passion, this Passion play in two parts having been built, with various additions, out of the Passion group of the original Corpus Christi play. This Passion play may have led for a time an independent dramatic existence. To these add, thirdly, a play of the Assumption of the Blessed Virgin Mary differing from the rest of the cycle in style, paper, and handwriting; also a play of the Presentation in the Temple. Lastly, add many minor revisions, mainly learned in style, dramatically unnecessary, and obviously theological. There have also been some transfers of materials from play to play; that is, there are places in which episodes that are called for by the Proclamation in certain plays are found in the cycle in other plays.

Before these statements are taken up in detail, there are two formal matters presented by Miss Swenson that demand attention. The first of these is metre. There is the metre of the prologue or Proclamation described above, a thirteen-line stanza rhyming abababababcdddc, which is to be regarded as old and possibly fundamental in the constitution of the original Corpus Christi play, since in it are composed not only the banns but those remoter, possibly less native, parts necessary for the building of the total Corpus Christi play; viz. a series of Old Testament plays the Fall of Lucifer, the Creation and Fall of Man, Cain and Abel, Noah—the Baptism and the Temptation, and, at the end, the Ascension, Pentecost, and *Judicium*. One need not believe that all passages in this form were written at one time, for this stanza was familiar to poets. The main part of Mary's Betrothal is in it, and it appears in a more or less fragmentary way in Joseph's Trouble about Mary, the Shepherds, the Magi, and the Slaughter of the Innocents.

The heart of the cycle, that which may perhaps be more characteristic of the place of its origin, appears in quatrains of four feet, fundamentally double quatrains linked by the rhyming of the fourth and fifth lines, although with this in almost all cases are simple quatrains, sometimes of five accents. In this metre is the whole, or the main parts, of the following plays: Abraham and Isaac, Moses and the Tables of the Law, Prophets, the Salutation, the Trial of Joseph and Mary, Christ and the Doctors, the Woman Taken in Adultery, Lazarus, the Last Supper, the Betrayal, the three parts of the Trial, Crucifixion (the first part), Burial, Resurrection (latter part), *Hortulanus, Peregrini*. This stanza form appears, usually in crucial parts, also in several other plays.

A third original metre in the cycle is a ballad stanza of eight lines in length, rhyming aaa⁴b³aaa⁴b³ or aaa⁴b³ccc⁴b³, which is the charac-teristic stanza form of the Chester plays. The scene of God's visit to Paradise in the play of the Fall of Man, an old and necessary feature of the story, is written in this form. The ballad stanza appears signifi-cantly, as probably ancient and original, in the plays of the Shepherds, the Magi, and the Slaughter of the Innocents; also in the Harrow-ing of Hell, the Setting of the Watch (and the Awakening of the Watch), and in the first part of the *Quem quaeritis*. With this rhyme-scheme appear also certain comic matters probably late. A few four-foot couplets appear in the Crucifixion and in the Trial plays, but they may be sporadic. The play of the Assumption of the Blessed Virgin Mary uses long, rather ponderous lines often in tumbling measure, and shows a variety of rhyme-schemes. Still another stanza, aa⁴b³aa⁴b³bcbc⁴, appears with some variations in the Purification and in the latter half of Joseph's Trouble about Mary.

The prologue stanza, the double and single quatrain, and the Chester stanza serve in general to indicate older parts of the cycle of the Hegge plays, but there is another metre that points almost un-failingly to the latest additions to the cycle. It is what Saintsbury[1] calls the 'tumbling alliterative', although it is sometimes not alliterative. This form is a result of fifteenth-century metrical confusion and, as a metre, it has a long history. It appears in the Coventry plays and in other cycles and is the favourite form for homiletic matter. In the Hegge cycle the tumbling measure, with or without alliteration, is used, with various rhyme-schemes, for various newer parts of plays, such as the Lamech episode in Noah, Contemplacio's speech in the Salutation, the cherry-tree episode in Joseph and the Midwives, Herod's first speech in the Magi, and Satan's prologue in Trial III. It seems to form the actual poetic substance of the following plays: Visit to Elizabeth, Council of the Jews, parts of the Last Supper, the Betrayal, Trial I and parts of Trial II, and the Incredulity of Thomas. One has a right to believe that plays and scenes written in tumbling measure are either additions to the original Corpus Christi play or are rewritings of older parts in a more modern-mannered style.

Another study of Miss Swenson's[2] that makes the structure of the

[1] Op. cit., i. 214-15.   [2] Op. cit., pp. 67-68.

Hegge cycle extremely clear has to do with stage directions. Apparently in the original Corpus Christi play of which the Hegge cycle is a revision the stage directions were prevailingly, perhaps exclusively, in Latin, and these Latin stage directions tend to remain in the cycle unless they have been interfered with by revision. In the seven plays from the Fall of Lucifer to the Prophets stage directions are entirely in Latin; so also are those of the four plays from the Trial of Joseph and Mary to the Magi, the six plays from the Slaughter of the Innocents to Lazarus, and finally, with a single exception, the eight plays from the second Harrowing of Hell to Doomsday. On the other hand, the stage directions of the Passion group from the Entry into Jerusalem through the Setting of the Watch, eleven plays, have either entirely or prevailingly very realistic stage directions in English. In other plays there is a mixture of English and Latin stage directions, and these plays, when examined, turn out to be those that contain both original materials of the Corpus Christi play as revealed by the Proclamation and new material not provided for in the Proclamation.

In the light of all these agreements and differences as thus explained we may conclude that Miss Swenson's thesis is proved, namely, that the Proclamation or banns enumerate the scenes as they were in an original Corpus Christi play of which the Hegge plays as we have them are a revision and amplification.

We saw when we looked at the Hegge cycle as a whole that the chief variations from the play described in the banns are these: the cycle has had intruded into it and in part blended with it a St. Anne's day play consisting of five scenes—the Barrenness of Anna, the Presentation of Mary in the Temple, the Betrothal of Mary, the Salutation and Conception, and Mary's Visit to Elizabeth. This we know from the prologue of Contemplacio and from other considera-tions. The Barrenness of Anna and the Presentation of Mary in the Temple, neither of which is represented in the Proclamation, are theological in tone, written in tumbling measure, and with some stage directions in English. The whole group of plays was obviously acted on a stationary, multiple-place stage. The Betrothal of Mary, on the other hand, does appear in the Proclamation, where it is divided into two pageants. The redactor has preferred to use, with certain ecclesiastical amplifications, the version provided by the

Corpus Christi play, which was in the prologue stanza. The Salutation and Conception shows the deeper religious tone of the St.
Anne's day play, has English stage directions, has two passages in
tumbling measure, and is apparently a blend of the two sources.
Joseph's Trouble about Mary was evidently brought over with few,
if any, changes from the Corpus Christi play. It is in the prologue
stanza. Mary's Visit to Elizabeth seems to be a play of mixed sources,
and it introduces an inconsistency, since it shows Mary not remaining with Elizabeth until the birth of John, but returning home
at once. The Trial of Joseph and Mary and Joseph and the Midwives are rather inharmonious plays that have stolen into the
cycle at some earlier time. It is of course entirely possible that the
Purification, a very good play, is a borrowing from the St. Anne's
day cycle.

    To speak so definitely of a St. Anne's day cycle or play when no
recognized example exists demands some explanation. The idea of a
service and then a play doing honour to the birth and childhood of
Mary must go back to that Presentation of the Blessed Virgin Mary
in the Temple discovered by Karl Young and printed and edited by
him[1] from the manuscript of Philippe de Mézières, but by what
varied roads or in what varied forms it reached England is unknown.
In its history and development it not only subdivided itself into two
or three plays, but also grew at the expense of plays traditionally
associated with the Nativity. One St. Anne's day play of unknown
provenance, of which only a single part exists, was evidently of
very great extent. I refer to the Digby *Killing of the Children*, which is
described as a part of a St. Anne's day play.[2] It announces itself in a
prologue by Poeta as played on the feast of St. Anne in her honour
and in that of the Blessed Virgin Mary. It says that last year they
played the Shepherds and the Magi, this year they will show the
Purification and the Slaughter of the Innocents, and next year they
will show Christ's Disputation with the Doctors. If Stow's note on
the manuscript, which says that the *Killing of the Children* is the seventh
play in the series, is correct, there would have been room in the earlier

---

[1] Op. cit. ii. 225–45.
[2] Chambers, op. cit. ii. 430–1; *The Digby Mysteries*, ed. F. J. Furnivall, E.E.T.S.
(London, 1896), pp. 1–23.

plays to treat, as the Hegge plays do, of the Barrenness of Anna and the Betrothal of Mary.

The second striking peculiarity of the Hegge plays is the appearance in the manuscript of a complete play of the Passion in two parts extending conventionally from the Entry to the Burial. The pageants described in the Proclamation have been revised and arranged in two groups for performance in alternate years. They have been provided with a special prologue spoken by a character called, like the Prologue to the Marian group, Contemplacio. It is evident that revision of the original Corpus Christi play had in the fifteenth century been proceeding in unusual ways and that at some time in the third quarter of the century there came into operation a motive for the restoration of the cycle to its complete form. In making this complete version the compiler did not restore the pageants treating of the Passion to their original state—perhaps he could not—but took them over bodily in the form into which for some special purpose they had been recast. In the light of the studies of Miss Swenson and Miss Block there seems no reason to question the fact that in the making of the special play of the Passion the playwright did not borrow a play from the outside but worked over into a new form the materials he had at hand in the Corpus Christi cycle.[1] The Passion I begins with a Lucifer prologue after a fashion known on the continent of Europe. Following that are the Council of the Jews, the Entry into Jerusalem, the Conspiracy, the Last Supper, and the Betrayal. Then Passion Play II begins with a speech by Contemplacio, who says they will continue where they left off last year and will proceed to show how Jesus was brought before Annas and Caiaphas, then before Pilate, and 'so forth in the passyon'. Although the end of the second Passion play is not clearly marked, Miss Block[2] shows that this play ends with the Burial and the Setting of the Watch and that the compiler has filled available space in the manuscript with matters serving to make the transition from the Passion to the largely unaltered plays treating of the Resurrection and subjects associated with it. It is noteworthy that the Harrowing of Hell was used after the Crucifixion in Passion Play II apparently in accordance with the belief that, as soon as it was

[1] Swenson, op. cit., pp. 26–31; Block, op. cit., pp. xxxii–xxxv, xlix–l.
[2] Op. cit., p. xiv.

liberated from the body, the *Anima Christi* would descend at once into Limbo in order to release the patriarchs from bondage. This does not, however, prevent the Harrowing of Hell from appearing in its more conventional position after the Setting of the Watch and before the Resurrection. In general, as pointed out by Miss Swenson,[1] the play of the Passion shows an extensive use of tumbling measure, has prevailingly English stage directions, and was obviously acted on a multiple stage.

The next most conspicuous feature among the variations of the cycle from the plays called for in the Proclamation is found in the introduction of a play of the Assumption of the Blessed Virgin Mary. It is, as we have seen, a clear case of the acquisition and the binding in of an independent manuscript. The Assumption of the Blessed Virgin Mary is from every point of view the most elaborate play in the cycle, full of great learning and theology. It is written, as before said, mainly in the fifteenth-century long line, usually of ten or more syllables, that Saintsbury[2] describes as 'ponderous lolloping doggerel'. It is not, however, bad of its kind. The stanzas follow a variety of rhyme-schemes, and it is to be observed that the play contains a good deal of Latin and that some simpler parts suggest that the story of the Death and Assumption of the Blessed Virgin Mary is as it appears in *Legenda Aurea*.[3]

That the Assumption of the Virgin once appeared in a less elaborate form is suggested by the opening lines of the play and by the style of some of the other formal parts. Two different stage directions in the Assumption of the Virgin call for the use of an organ, which is an indication that the play was played in a church. It also demands the use of two unusual pieces of stage machinery, namely, a single cloud and a double cloud to be used for the conveyance of the apostles from the ends of the earth to the bedside of the dying Virgin Mary. Other less obvious special features added to the cycle after the composition, not the transcription, of the banns have already been mentioned. We must, however, discuss the cycle from a different point of view in order to arrive at a fuller comprehension.

---

[1] Op. cit., p. 51 *et passim*.   [2] Op. cit. i. 214–15.

[3] *The Assumption of the Virgin, A Miracle Play from the N-Town Cycle*, ed. W. W. Greg (Oxford, 1915); Block, op. cit., pp. xix, lvii.

We have concluded that the Proclamation, or banns, of the Hegge plays as they stand in British Museum MS. Cotton Vespasian D. viii announced and summarized a Corpus Christi play. This fact carries with it implications that are sometimes overlooked or not understood. The Hegge plays belong to a different tradition, at least in part, from that of the York and the Chester plays. They have greater uniformity in tone and contents than the York plays, and they are much more theologically and moralistically ambitious than the Chester plays. They have been extensively and learnedly rewritten and show therefore possibly fewer traces of a liturgical origin. But that is only true with reference to their preservation of fewer identifiable early forms of liturgical plays. The very theological learning that made the Hegge plays what they are caused the retention of more Latin than is to be found in any other cycle, and much of that Latin is liturgical.[1] The Hegge plays nevertheless seem from internal evidence to have been put together out of a series of original simpler parts perhaps also with special inventions or borrowings in order to arrive at the completeness demanded by the Corpus Christi pattern. The Corpus Christi play outlined for us in the Proclamation and for the most part still preserved in the cycle itself had, as we have seen, one striking special feature, namely, an otherwise unequalled expansion of matters pertaining to the Blessed Virgin Mary. Not only was this true of the original Corpus Christi cycle, but, as we have seen, that cycle underwent still further amplification in matters pertaining to the Virgin at a later stage in their growth than is outlined for us in the Proclamation. One would think that both of these expansions must have taken place in some city where the Blessed Virgin Mary was especially honoured. There is even a third slight evidence of this trend. The banns suggest by an irregularity in their otherwise uniform style that two plays, the Trial of Joseph and Mary and Joseph and the Midwives, are amplifications of the favourite theme and had already been intruded into the Corpus Christi cycle when the banns were composed. They are either borrowings or the result of a slightly discordant addition by special composition. The former conjecture is the more probable of the two, since with all their crudity both of these plays contain simple

---

[1] Paul E. Kretzmann, *Liturgical Elements in the Earliest Forms of the Mediaeval Drama* (Minneapolis, 1916), pp. 30–34, 40, 71–72, 159–60, *et passim*.

and reverent traditional parts that may well have belonged to a Corpus Christi or a Saint Anne's day cycle.

To describe the sources of a Corpus Christi play is to involve one-self in a complex of matters almost impossible to discriminate into parts or to assign to definite works and authors. Primary sources were of course the Bible and the Apocrypha, but medieval theological learning was so diffused, so much of it carried in the memory and embodied in the service of the church, that it is often more than doubt-ful whether one has to do with an original or with a secondary source. In determining sources we have to reckon with much dissemination and popularization of religious knowledge and religious language. The first intermediary between the Scriptures and the plays was the liturgy, specifically the services of the liturgical year, and there is no reason to think that the use of the liturgy was confined to the earliest times. The services of the liturgical year were unchanged and because of their constant use still intimately in men's minds. The source material in the *lectiones* is more varied than is ordinarily thought— *lectiones* drawn from the Bible, from homilies, patristic teachings, legends and lives of saints and martyrs; also antiphons, hymns, psalms, canticles and their interpretations. Anyone who will take the trouble to examine the Sarum Breviary, for example, will see that the medieval breviary was a very rich book. Not all the men who sang the services in Latin were ignorant of what the Latin meant. At any time from the remote past until the fifteenth century this or that play or theme might be amplified from legends, doctrines, or tradi-tions—not from books only, but also from current, familiar beliefs of the medieval church—or resort might be, and actually was, had to religious works in the vernacular in poetry or prose. This amplifica-tion was a continuous process, and every dramatic theme or group of themes was liable, not to revolutionary change, but to an intended improvement in the form of revision, expansion, and ornamentation. In the circumstances surrounding the English Corpus Christi plays these modifications were largely local.

These ideas might be made clearer by a further attempt to determine what happened in England on the occasion of the establishment of the Corpus Christi play in the early fourteenth century. At Chester, as we have seen, the responsible persons seem to have derived, possibly actually translated, a Corpus Christi play from French sources. At York, so far as there are any indications, the Corpus Christi play seems to have been made up by joining together such plays as were available in and around the city of York. We have no knowledge of the origin of the Hegge cycle, but the principle of the preservation in primitive metrical forms of essential traditional parts is not without some significance. The liturgical cores of the *Pastores*, the *Stella*, and the Slaughter of the Innocents appear in the ballad stanza, aaa^{4}b^{3}aaa^{4}b^3 or aaa^{4}b^{3}ccc^{4}b^3. This may or may not be the original vernacular form of these plays, but it must be significant that we again find these subjects treated in an antique measure. This ballad form appears basically also in the Harrowing of Hell, the Setting of the Watch, and the Resurrection proper, all of which are very ancient themes, although *Quem quaeritis*, *Hortulanus*, and *Peregrini* appear in quatrains and double quatrains in the midst of other more complicated forms. We have thus some indication that the essential parts of the Christmas and the Easter groups are more ancient than other parts of the cycle. At least we may say that they appear in early metres and in relatively primitive forms.

The question of the origin of Passion plays in the English cycles is not easily answered. The case of the Chester plays gives no trouble, since the Passion group in that cycle are clearly of a continental pattern; indeed, they suggest the Benediktbeuern plays, the oldest known examples of Passion plays. But, as we have seen, the case of York–Towneley is not so clear, nor is that of the Hegge cycle. At the end of the fourteenth century, one may believe without great improbability, the religious drama of the North of England was far less highly developed than was at that time the religious drama of the continent of Europe. At least all the English references we have are to Christmas and Easter plays. We may therefore raise the question as to whether there were in the North of England and the Midlands Passion plays locally available. If there were not and if the pattern of the newly established Corpus Christi cycles demanded such plays, they would have to be specially composed. The order of events in the Passion was definitely established in the Gospels, in the liturgy, and in many works both in Latin and in the vernacular. The succession of events from Jesus in the House of Simon the Leper to the Burial was perfectly familiar.

In one work particularly they were, so to speak, pre-digested, since in it abundant detail was furnished and dialogue was provided for much of the story. That work was the *Northern Passion*, itself based not only on the Gospels and the New Testament Apocrypha but on many other works.[1] It has been shown that the *Northern Passion* entered into the composition of the Passion group in the York, the Towneley, and the Hegge cycles in a way so fundamental that it suggests not, of course, the invention of the Passion play but the writing of Passion plays according to an established pattern. Whether or not there was an already existent Passion play that underwent revision by the use of the *Northern Passion*, that poem was used in a way so thorough-going that few if any traces of an earlier play of the Passion can be discovered. It is even clear, as Miss Foster shows, that the writer of the plays was turning the couplets of the *Northern Passion* into quatrains. In the Hegge plays double and single quatrains prevail and are apparently fundamental from the Woman Taken in Adultery to the Burial, indeed to the *Peregrini*. Some parts of this writing may of course be more recent than other parts, but one may safely disregard minor variations. In any case, it will probably be agreed that the Hegge cycle, like others, went through the usual course of development from simpler beginnings to its latest form.

In one respect, already mentioned, the Hegge cycle in the form and scope in which it is outlined in the Proclamation was, as compared to other cycles whose contents are known, unusual. It contained a quite exceptional play of prophets and kings on the theme of the Root of Jesse. These prophets are no longer Messianic prophets, but prophets foretelling the advent of the Virgin Mary as the mother of Jesus. The speakers are thirteen kings provided for in the genealogy of the Blessed Virgin Mary and the same number of prophets. There is little difference in the words uttered by the kings and the prophets, since all speak prophetically of the coming of the Virgin. Sepet[2] declares that such kinds of prophet plays are known in France and cites a Corpus Christi procession at Mayenne in the seventeenth century that shows this form. The theme seems to have belonged in

---

[1] Foster, op. cit., pp. 47–80. See also Lyle, op. cit., pp. 4–29; Block, op. cit., pp. xlviii-li; Frances H. Miller, 'The *Northern Passion* and the Mysteries', loc. cit., pp. 88–92.

[2] Sepet, op. cit.; Block, op. cit., p. lii.

the first instance to art.[1] In art it was familiar as the Tree of Jesse or *Radix Jesse*, an allegorical depiction of the family tree of Christ based on Matthew i. 6–16. The genealogy took its beginning, however, not from Abraham, but from Jesse in accordance with Isaias xi. 1: *Et egredietur virga de radice Jesse, et flos de radice ejus ascendet.* The idea was imported from Byzantium in the eleventh century, and there are twelfth-century Jesse windows at Saint Denis, Chartres, and York. There is among others the quaint north (choir) window in the abbey church at Dorchester-on-Thames. The play in the Hegge cycle is therefore not, strictly speaking, a *Prophetae*. It calls itself Jesse or Jesse Root. That, however, it succeeded a *Prophetae* at some early time is suggested by its following in the cycle a play on Moses and the Tables of the Law, a play associated with the *Prophetae*.

The Proclamation in the original Corpus Christi cycle calls for a Betrothal of Mary, a Trial of Joseph and Mary, and a Joseph and the Midwives in addition to the customary Annunciation, Visit to Elizabeth (now obscured by revision), and Joseph's Trouble about Mary. The subjects, old as well as new, are more or less legendary, for, as the original series of liturgical subjects was expanded, the first resort was to the New Testament Apocrypha. There is nothing very difficult therefore about the sources of these plays. But when one comes to that set of Virgin Mary plays introduced into the cycle with the Saint Anne's day play, sources are drawn from wider afield and become, if not important, at least interesting and in some instances determinable. It is to be noted that, although the main parts of the additions to the cycle from the Saint Anne's day play are in quatrains and double quatrains or in the prologue stanza ($abababab^4c^3ddd^4c^3$) and also that the main parts of the Passion plays are in quatrains and double quatrains, the latest additions are in alliterative verse, and it is in them that sources are most definite and modern.

This tumbling, not usually alliterative, verse is used extensively for prologues and formal and connective passages, for the fitting in of the Saint Anne's day additions, and for a very considerable number of special episodes. The first of the latter is the Lamech episode in the Noah play. This has been described as being based immediately on

[1] J. K. Bonnell, 'The Sources in Art of the so-called *Prophets' Play* in the Hegge Collection', *PMLA*, xxix (1914), 327–40.

Comestor's *Historia Scholastica*,[1] and that may be true, but one must not dispense too readily with other sources in these amplifications. The Lamech episode appears also in *Le Mistère du Viel Testament* (viii, ll. 4566–4969) and in other continental plays and is to be found in the Cologne Breviary and in Genesis iv. 18–24. The following summary from Miss Swenson's study[2] will make clear the use of alliterative verse and usually the purpose of the use: slight instances in the Betrothal of Mary, Contemplacio's speech in the Salutation and Conception, the main part of the Visit to Elizabeth, the Cherry-Tree episode in Joseph and the Midwives, Herod's first speech in the *Stella*, most of the scene of the Council of the Jews, two scenes in the Last Supper (one of which deals with the institution of the Eucharist) the laments of the Women in the Betrayal, the main part of the First Trial (the prologue of the Doctor, Contemplacio's speech, some of Herod's speeches, some parts of the Trial, and Peter's lament), Jesus' speech to the Women in the Crucifixion, a scene between the Centurion and the soldiers in the Burial, and the whole play of the Incredulity of Thomas.

In the plays not called for in the Proclamation, and therefore presumably not parts of the original Corpus Christi play, there are indications of the use of special sources. These plays we have thought of as parts of a Saint Anne's day play introduced into and amalgamated with the Nativity subjects of the Corpus Christi play. If this hypothesis is correct, it would suggest that the Saint Anne's day play was a definite and probably relatively late composition that rested to some degree on current works of Mariolatry. As sources for these plays have been suggested Bonaventura, *Meditationes Vitae Christi*, and *The Mirrour of the Blessed Lyf of Jesus Christ*, with Nicholas Love's translation of the *Meditationes*,[3] and other works, but we may not ignore tradition. One should not forget Young's discovery[4] of a dramatic *Festum Presentationis Beatae Mariae Virginis*, a basic document for these plays of the nativity and girlhood of the Blessed Virgin Mary, nor that such plays are of fairly frequent occurrence. Whatever special sources may have been used in the composition of these plays in English,

---

[1] Migne, *P.L.*, clviii, 39–44; Block, op. cit., pp. lii–liii.
[2] Op. cit., pp. 64–66.
[3] Block, op. cit., pp. xxii–xxiv, xlv, xlvi, lviii, lx.   [4] Op. cit. ii. 225–45.

the probabilities are strong that the plays are within the bounds of the ecclesiastical tradition.

Besides these two great areas of revision, the birth and girlhood of Mary and the construction of a semi-independent play of the Passion, there were, after the composition of the banns, two independent and unrelated plays added to the cycle, namely the Purification and the Assumption of the Blessed Virgin Mary. Both, it will be noticed, honour the Virgin Mary. The former, a relatively simple play, is in a stanzaic form not otherwise appearing in the cycle, aa⁴b³aa⁴b³bcbc⁴. It is intruded between the Visit of the Magi and the Slaughter of the Innocents, where it interrupts the continuous action of those two plays. It seems to have been developed independently of the Christmas and Easter plays probably at the Feast of the Purification of the Blessed Virgin Mary, 2 February. There is a liturgical play preserved from Padua,[1] and the play of the Purification seems to have had a development independent of the cycles and to have been included in them at a fairly late date. This at least seems to be the only plausible explanation of the fact that plays of the Purification in the Corpus Christi cycles are always distinguishable in metre from the rest of the Nativity plays and seem to have no consistent place in the series of events.

The Assumption of the Virgin, described above as written on different paper and in a different hand, is nevertheless rubricated in the hand of the principal scribe and inserted in the cycle in its proper place before the *Judicium*. It was obviously bound in with the other quires of the manuscript. It has been described as based on *Legenda Aurea*; indeed, by Gayley, as based on Caxton's translation. Parts of it certainly are derived from *Legenda Aurea*, not, however, on Caxton's translation, but it is a mistake to regard the play as a new and special composition. It is an old subject and plays on the Assumption of the Virgin appear, or once appeared, in all cycles, in the Beverley list, and no doubt elsewhere. The play is also widely dispersed on the continent, and a play on the theme was acted in Lincoln Cathedral certainly from as early as the middle of the fifteenth century.

The conclusion to be arrived at from the foregoing sketch is that in the Hegge plays we have to do with a Corpus Christi play not

---

[1] Ibid. ii. 250-5.

essentially different in its scope and the history of its development from
other Corpus Christi cycles. To be sure, it has its special features,
but certainly, at least in the form outlined in the Proclamation, there
is nothing about it that would put it in another dramatic class or lead
one to think that it had other origin and growth than the accepted
ones for Corpus Christi plays, that is, simple beginnings and a gradual
incremental growth by revision into its final, highly developed form.
One might say that the special quality of the Hegge cycle is its learning expressed with great theological correctness and dignity. Its style
is for its time good. There is little ignorant misuse of words. The
verse, as a whole, is technically correct. The alliterative additions are
inferior to the fourteen York alliterative plays, and there is perhaps no
evidence anywhere of striking poetical ability. But for the serving of
its purpose the cycle may be said to be excellent. It professes again and
again that that purpose is the honour of God and His glory and greatness. If one is willing to accept it on its own religious terms, one
finds much to admire. There are, for example, a number of brief
poetical sermons that are not bombast, but excellent of their kind.
They make sense, and one might say that the Hegge plays are the most
intelligent of all the mystery plays. Jesus before the Jewish Doctors
does not merely create a sensation by reciting the Ten Command-
ments, but offers an explanation of the Trinity and the Incarnation
and their necessity. Episcopus in the plays of the childhood of Mary is
a very sensible character, and Mary's recitation of the Psalms as she
mounts the steps in the Presentation in the Temple (ll. 84–151) is very
prettily done:

> *Maria et sic deinceps usque ad finem xv^{cim} psalmorum.*

> The fyrst degre gostly applyed
> It is holy desyre with god to be
> In trobyl to god I haue cryed
> And in sped · þat lord hath herde me.
> Ad dominum cum tribularer clamaui; et exaudiuit me. . . .

> The twelfte is mekenes þat is fayre and softe
> In mannys sowle with-inne and with-owte
> Lord myn herte is not heyued on lofte
> nyn myn eyn be not lokynge a-bowte.
> Domine non est exaltatum cor meum; neque elati sunt oculi mei.

The Threttene is ffeyth þer with
with holy dedys don expresse
haue mende lorde of davyth
And of All his swettnes.
Memento domine dauid; et omnis mansuetudinis eius.

The ffourtene is brothyrly concorde i-wys
þat norchyth love of creaturys echon
Se how good and how glad it is
bretheryn ffor to dwelle in on.
Ecce quam bonum et quam jocundum; habitare fratres in vnum.

The ffyftene is gracyous · with on Acorde
whiche is syne of godly love semyth me
se now blysse oure lord
All þat oure lordys servauntys be.
Ecce nunc benedicite dominum; omnes serui dominj.

Episcopus. A gracyous lord þis is A mervelyous thynge
þat we se here all in syght
A babe of thre ʒer age so ʒynge
to come vp þese grecys · so vp-ryght
It is An hey meracle and by goddys myght
no dowth of she xal be gracyous.

The version of the Four Daughters of God or the Parliament of
Heaven, which follows that play, is by no means the worst rendering
of that familiar theme.[1] The appearance and the speeches of Mors in
the Death of Herod (ll. 207–84) are, to say the least, impressive, and
even the bombast of Herod[2] can be understood:

herodes Rex. Now kende knyghtys be mery and glad
With all good diligens shewe now sum myrth
Ffor be gracyous mahound more myrth never I had
ne nevyr more joye was inne from tyme of my byrth
Ffor now my foe is ded and prendyd as a padde
aboue me is no kynge · on grownd nere on ʒerth
merthis þerfore make ʒe and be ryght no thynge sadde
spare nother mete nor drynke and spare for no dyrthe
of wyne nor of brede
Ffor now am I a kynge alone
So wurthy as I · may þer be none

[1] Hope Traver, *The Four Daughters of God.* Bryn Mawr Monographs, No. 6 (Philadelphia,
1907), pp. 125–40 *et passim.*
[2] See R. E. Parker, 'The Reputation of Herod in Early English Literature', *Speculum,*
viii (1933), pp. 59–67.

þerfore knyghtys be mery echone
　　ffor now my ffo is ded. . . .
Mors. All men dwellyng upon þe grownde
Be⁓ware of me be myn councel
Ffor feynt felachep in me is fownde
I kan no curtesy as I ȝow tel
Ffor be a man nevyr so sownde
of helth in herte nevyr so wel
I come sodeynly with⁓in a stownde
me with⁓stande may no castel
　　　　my jurnay wyl I spede.
of my comyng no man is ware
Ffor when men make most mery fare
þan sodeynly I cast hem in care
　　　　and sle þem evyn in dede.

Thow I be nakyd and pore of array
and wurmys knawe me al a⁓bowte
ȝit loke ȝe drede me nyth and day
Ffor whan deth comyth ȝe stande in dowte
Evyn lyke to me as I ȝow say
shull all ȝe be here in þis rowte
Whan I ȝow chalange at my day
I xal ȝow make ryght lowe to lowth
　　　　and nakyd for to be
Amonges wormys as I ȝow telle
Vndyr þe erth xul ȝe dwelle
and thei xul Etyn both flesch and felle
　　　　As þei haue don me.

Both John the Baptist and Jesus are good preachers:

Johannes. Ecce vox clamantis in deserto.
I am þe voys of wyldirnese
þat her spekyth and prechyth yow to
loke ȝe for⁓sake all wrecchidnesse
fforsake all synne þat werkyth woo
And turne to vertu and holynese
Beth clene of levyng in your sowle also
Than xall ȝe be savyd from peynfulnese
Of fyere brynnyng in hell
If þat ȝe for⁓sak synne
hevyn blysse xall ȝe wyne
Drede ȝe not þe devyllys gynne
with Angellys xall yow dwell.

The Temptation, the Woman Taken in Adultery, the Raising of Lazarus, and other episodic plays are particularly good dramatizations of Scripture. The plays of the Passion, although no doubt inferior to the York plays on that theme, are serious treatments of a serious theme. Whatever literary credit may be due to clarity, good taste, restraint, and intelligence may be claimed, within limits, for the cycle as a whole.

The Old Testament plays, although very simple, are not without a characteristic sense of deeper consequences. The temptation and fall of Adam in the Fall of Man (ll. 221-72), for example, is perhaps as fine a treatment of that theme as appears in any of the English cycles:

> *Adam.* I dare not towch þin hand ffor dred
> of oure lord god omnypotent
> if I xuld werke after þi reed
> of god oure makere I xuld be shent
> If þat we do þis synful dede
> we xal be ded by goddys jugement
> out of þin hand with hasty spede
> cast out þat appyl a-non present
> ffor fer of goddys threte.
> *Eva.* Of þis appyl yf þou wylt byte
> goddys pere þou xalt be pyht
> So wys of kunnyng I þe plyht
> þis frute yf þou wylt Ete.
>
> *Adam.* If we it Ete oure self we kylle
> as god us told we xuld be ded
> to ete þat frute · and my lyf to spylle
> I dar not do aftyr þi reed.
> *Eva.* A ffayr Aungell þus · seyd me tylle
> to Ete þat appyl take nevyr no dred
> so kunnyng as god in hevyn hille
> þou xalt sone be with-inne a sted
> þerfore þis frute þou Ete.
> *Adam.* Off goddys wysdam for to lere
> and in kunnyng to be his pere
> of thyn hand I take it here
> and xal sone taste þis mete. *Adam dicit sic.*
>
> Alas Alas ffor þis fals dede
> my flesly frend · my fo I fynde
> Schameful synne doth us vn-hede
> I se vs nakyd be-fore and be-hynde

oure lordys wurd wold we not drede
þerfore we be now caytyvys vn-kynde
oure pore preuytes ffor to hede
Summe ffygge levys fayn wolde I fynde
Ffor to hyde oure schame. . . .

Eva. Alas þat evyr þat speche was spokyn
þat þe fals Aungel seyd on to me
Alas oure makers byddyng is brokyn
Ffor I haue towchyd his owyn dere tre
oure ffflescly eyn byn al vnlokyn
nakyd for synne oure sylf we se
þat sory Appyl þat we han sokyn
to deth hath brouth my spouse and me
Ryth grevous is oure synne
of mekyl shame now do we knowe
Alas þat evyr þis Appyl was growe
to dredful deth now be we throwe
in peyne vs evyr to pynne.

This belongs to an older period of the Hegge plays and has not been reworked by later and more learned revisers of the fifteenth century. It is crude and awkward, but it is sincere and it may represent for us an original quality of piety and genuine religious feeling that still distinguishes this cycle.

The same rather prosaic earnestness may be felt in others of these older plays, as, for example, in Cain's lament in the play of Cain and Abel (ll. 183–95):

Alas alas whedyr may I go
I dare nevyr se man in þe vesage
I am woundyn as a wrecch in wo
And cursyd of god ffor my ffalsage
Vn-profytabyl and vayn also
In felde and town in strete and stage
I may nevyr make merthis mo
I wot nevyr whedyr to take passage
I dare not here abyde
Now wyl I go wende my way
With sore syeng and wel away
to loke where þat I best may
Ffrom mannys ssyht me hyde.

An important confirmation of the opinion that the Hegge plays are permeated with the theological learning of the Middle Ages appears in an article by Dom Timothy Fry, O.S.B.[1] He studies the doctrinal contents of the plays, especially the dominance in the cycle of a particular patristic theory of the Redemption—in his words, 'Briefly, the theory supposes that when Adam and Eve fell into original sin, Satan was permitted to inflict death on them and on all mankind and hold them captive in hell. Christ, born of the Immaculate Virgin Mary, was not subject to the law of death. Satan, however, was deceived by the human nature of Christ, and, in bringing about His death, abused his power, and lost the souls in hell.' Thus, 'in the killing of an innocent and just man', Satan abused his delegated power and undid himself. Father Fry defines and traces the theory in the Greek and Latin Fathers and shows its variations even in St. Anselm and in Abelard. He does not say that this is the only doctrine of the Redemption to be found in the Hegge plays, but subjects the plays in the cycle to investigation and concludes that the abuse-of-power theory is dominant in the cycle, which it may well be. He finds many expressions and amplifications of the theory throughout the cycle, and it is to be noted that these usages appear abundantly in the fundamental and presumably older parts of the cycle, although they seem to find their clearest expression in those parts that show in their alliterative style and in their manifestly didactic purpose that they are revisional. There is no reason why such an interpretation as that provided for in the abuse-of-power theory should not have appeared in a very early, even liturgical, stage of development, and one can see not only that the idea is unifying but that it is dramatically potent. A greater marvel than any late composition by a single author would be a theological intelligence motivated by structural imagination that lasted from age to age in the development of a great cycle of mystery plays.

MEDIEVAL RELIGIOUS DRAMA AT LINCOLN

We have before us in Cotton MS. Vespasian D. viii a clearly marked document that must reflect its history. If we could find records from any medieval town or city in England that would reveal events

[1] 'The Unity of the *Ludus Coventriae*', *Studies in Mediaeval Culture dedicated to George Raleigh Coffman, Studies in Philology*, xlviii (1951), 527-70.

and situations capable of producing such casual and structural dramatic features as appear in the Hegge plays, we should probably know the place of the origin, performance, and growth of that Corpus Christi cycle.

To begin with, the dialect of the manuscript points straight to Lincoln; so much so that C. M. Gayley suggested that the Cotton manuscript was the lost playbook 'of some such town as Lincoln'.[1] It is possible to see in terms of very familiar delimitations of north-east Midland dialects that the assignment of the plays to Lincoln is not a mere speculation. For example, a line extending roughly westward from the mouth of the Humber marks the southern limit of the retention of O.E. ā (*mar* for *more*, &c.), a retention not observed in the Hegge plays. A line running slightly north-east and south-west (north of Lincoln) from about Skegness is the southern limit of the northern plural in -(e)s of verbs in the present indicative; also absent from the Hegge plays. A line extending east and west from the southern edge of the Wash (and of course south of Lincoln) is the southern limit of *sal* and *suld* for *shall* and *should*; this form of the auxiliary is the usual one in the Hegge manuscript. *Hem* for *them* does not occur north of this line and is not the customary form in the plays. This line marks also the southern limit of the -(e)s of the third person singular indicative of verbs, which is the regular form in the manuscript. With the dialect is to be associated a more particular consideration arising out of certain resemblances between the Hegge plays and *The Castle of Perseverance*. These resemblances are pointed out by W. K. Smart in the article referred to in the accompanying note.[2] Both the Hegge plays and *The Castle of Perseverance* contain the Parliament of Heaven, or the Debate of the Four Daughters of God, in very similar versions. Both have proclamations spoken by vexillators that leave the place of performance undetermined, and there is a resemblance between the vulgarities appearing in both. Smart shows that the reference by

[1] On the language of MS. Cotton Vespasian D. viii and its relation to Lincoln see B. ten Brink, *History of English Literature*, loc. cit. ii. 283 ff.; M. Kramer, *Die Sprache und Heimat des sogenannten Ludus Coventriae*, loc. cit., p. 69 *et passim*; Roger Sherman Loomis, 'Lincoln as a Dramatic Centre', in *Mélanges d'histoire du théâtre du Moyen Âge et de la Renaissance* (Paris, 1950).

[2] Traver, op. cit., pp. 125–40; W. K. Smart, '*The Castle of Perseverance*: Place, Date, and Source', *Manly Anniversary Studies* (Chicago, 1923), pp. 42–43.

Mundus in *The Castle of Perseverance* (l. 2422) to the 'galows of Canwick' connects *The Castle of Perseverance* with Lincoln, since Canwick had a gallows on a hill in plain sight of parts of the city of Lincoln.

There is also a general appropriateness in assigning the Hegge plays to Lincoln, since Lincoln was the cathedral city of one of the largest and most influential dioceses in England. It maintained a collegiate establishment for centuries and always had at hand from the earliest times until the sixteenth century a body of divinity students, choristers, canons residentiary, and higher clergy. Lincoln was thus a place of ecclesiastical culture such as was certainly needed for the production of the Hegge plays, which we have had reason to consider the most learned of the English cycles. Finally, Lincoln was a place especially dedicated to the worship and honour of the Blessed Virgin Mary. The great Lincoln cathedral is the church of the Blessed Virgin, and with the Virgin great honour was paid to her mother St. Anne. Special commemoration of St. Anne was added to the services of the hours and of the masses of the Virgin in 1383.[1] So absorbing was the indirect honour paid to the Blessed Virgin Mary through the honouring of St. Anne that in 1519 the Common Council of Lincoln notes that 'the great gild of the citie called our lady gild is fallen in decay and almost desolate for lake off gude order & for reformation'. They take action for its reformation.

There are other reasons for assigning these plays to Lincoln. It is known that Lincoln was a centre of ecclesiastical drama from very early times. Robert Grosseteste was bishop of Lincoln from 1235 until his death in 1253, and we have already referred to his series of disciplinary pronouncements about the drama. He denounced folk plays, miracle plays, the Feast of Fools, and other apparently disorderly practices, and sought to banish them not only from his cathedral but from his diocese.[2] Yet when William Courtney, archbishop of Canterbury, made his visitation of Lincoln in 1390, he found cause to complain about the presence of the same disorders. Chambers gives a summary of what has been known about religious plays at Lincoln,[3] which in turn rests to some extent on an article by

---

[1] C. Wordsworth, *Lincoln Cathedral Statutes*, loc. cit., pp. 541 ff.
[2] Chambers, op. cit. i. 321, 411, 891; ii. 100. [3] Ibid. ii. 322, 377-9.

A. F. Leach.[1] Further information mainly derived from the Acts and *Computi* of the Lincoln Cathedral Chapter is also available.[2] It appears that Lincoln had from very early times a rather full and in some respects unique group of purely liturgical plays. In 1317–18 vicars of the church were repaid for expenses for a play of the Three Kings (Magi) they had caused to be played at the Epiphany, a play also probably alluded to in the *Computi* in 1321–2. There are gaps in the accounts, but charges for the same play appear in 1384 and 1387. In 1321–2 appear expenses for St. Thomas Didymus, and there are frequent later references to such a spectacle. It was evidently a play of some interest, and Miss Shull is probably right in regarding it as presenting Christ's appearance to his disciples in the upper chamber, a scene usually attached to the *Peregrini*. The fact that it was played in the nave of the cathedral causes one to wonder whether it might not have been an early form of the Assumption of the Blessed Virgin Mary, a play recorded as performed there for three-quarters of a century following 1469, since in most versions of that play the incredulity of Thomas plays a conspicuous part. It is, however, to be remembered that the Hegge cycle has a full-length play of Christ's Appearance to Thomas. There are recorded in the *Computi* in 1384 expenses for a play of the Resurrection, and an entry of 1395–6 provides for a play of Pentecost. This suggests that there may also have been a play of the Ascension, since the two subjects go together.

We note also that there is to be found from 1393 to the very end of the records a long (usually annual) series of expenses for gloves at Christmas for Mary, Elizabeth, and the angel; and in 1396 and for some years afterwards gloves are provided for two prophets. Other names disappear, and the entry is formalized into gloves for Mary and the angel. This was evidently a play of the Annunciation, but it is perhaps not an ordinary one. The angel is probably Gabriel, and the presence of Elizabeth suggests also a visit to Elizabeth. As to the prophets, their presence suggests the idea that they may be prophets who foretold the birth of Mary as the mother of Jesus, a feature appropriate to Lincoln and present in the Hegge cycle. Chester had

---

[1] 'Some Early English Plays and Playgoers, 1220–1548', loc. cit., pp. 205–34.

[2] Virginia Shull, 'Clerical Drama in Lincoln Cathedral, 1318–1561', *PMLA*, lii (1937), 946–66.

had guild plays since 1328, and York plays were an old institution by the end of the fourteenth century. These later references must be to church plays, for the main body of Lincoln plays must have been turned into the vernacular long before 1393. It would appear from the chapter *Computi* that plays did not for that reason cease to be acted perhaps in liturgical forms in the cathedral church itself. The long continuance of an Annunciation at matins on Christmas morning suggests a Marian quality in the Lincoln ecclesiastical plays.

This trend is further illustrated by the most famous of the religious dramas in the cathedral church of Lincoln, a play of the Assumption of the Blessed Virgin Mary. The earliest expense account of the play appears in 1458–9, although there is no reason to believe that it was new at that time: *Et in regardo dato Johanni Hanson pro laboribus suis habitis circa Ascensionem factam in ecclesia Cathedrali ultimo Anno—xxvjs. viijd. Et in consimili regardo dato Stephano Bony vicario pro eius laboribus habitis circa visionem factam in Choro in die Natalis domini—vjs. viiid.* There are, as before said, numerous further references to this play of the Assumption of the Blessed Virgin Mary acted frequently in the nave of the cathedral.

The earliest reference to a Corpus Christi play in Lincoln is in 1471–2, but by that time the Corpus Christi play must have become an ancient institution. About the same time the Corpus Christi procession, if not the Corpus Christi play, was transferred to St. Anne's day (26 July). An entry in the cathedral chapter Acts of 1469 refers to the *visus* or sights of St. Anne's day, and early in the sixteenth century, after the corporation minute books begin, it is evident that St. Anne's guild had become all-powerful. On 18 July 1519 it is agreed by the Common Council 'that every man and woman in the city, being able, shall be brother and sister in St. Anne's Guild, and pay yearly 4*d*., man and wife, at the least'. Just when the transfer of the Corpus Christi procession to St. Anne's day was made cannot be told, but certain acts of the cathedral chapter and, one may say, the date of Cotton Vespasian D. viii suggest that the transfer of the procession and a union and amalgamation of plays had occurred by about 1468. An entry in the Chapter Acts seems pertinent.[1] On Saturday, the chapter day, 7 June 1483, the dean of the

[1] Ibid., p. 958; also Leach, op. cit., p. 225.

cathedral with his brethren, the precentor, the chancellor, the treasurer, and one Alford, standing according to custom before the west door of the choir, discussed the procession of St. Anne to be made by the citizens of Lincoln on St. Anne's day next, and decided that they would have the play (*serimonium*) of the Assumption or Coronation of the Blessed Mary repaired, got ready, and played and shown in the procession aforesaid, as usual in the nave of the said church (*et com-municantes una simul decreuerunt quod illud ludum siue serimonium de As-sumptione siue coronatione beate Marie erga dictum festum de nouo reparatum & preparatum habere uoluerunt ac ludificatum & ostensum in processione predicta prout consuetum fuerat in Naui dicte ecclesie*). They then discuss how the expenses of this enterprise may be met. There is no entry of such costs in the *Computi*, so that the chapter must have been fortunate in obtaining contributions. The entry seems to associate the play of the Assumption of the Virgin with the St. Anne's day celebration. It is to go in the procession, and that would have required the building of a pageant, and it is also to be played on that occasion in the nave of the cathedral church.

It seems definitely associated with the St. Anne's day celebration rather than with the Corpus Christi play. It is equally clear that the play is not to be played at any out-of-door station. Entries in the *Computi* for 1490, 1504, 1507, 1508, *et al.* show that the Assumption of the Virgin continued to be played in the nave of the church. The Corpus Christi play does not seem to have been played every year during this period, but the probabilities are that the cathedral play of the Assumption of the Virgin would become a part of it when it was played. This play appears in MS. Cotton Vespasian D. viii in a different hand from that of the principal scribe and on different paper, as we have seen, as if it had been introduced into the manuscript at the time, probably 1468, when the manuscript was made up; it is also to be observed that an organ is called for in the Hegge play, so that that play either was or had been played in church.

It is important (for certain reasons that will appear) to find out, if we can, whether the Lincoln mystery plays were processional and acted by craft guilds at various stations in the city, like those of York and Chester, or were possibly acted at one place on a stationary stage as we believe mystery plays in southern England to have been. The cordwainers' accounts are so far the only source of information we possess.[1] The topography of Lincoln, to anyone who knows it, is rather against the idea of pageants drawn from place to place, and there are no references in the acts of the Common Council of Lincoln after they begin in 1511 to the fixation by authority of any stations or playing-places, a matter carefully regulated at York, Chester, Coventry, and elsewhere. And yet the St. Anne's day *visus* or sights were, as we shall see, a matter of great concern to the Common Council.

This St. Anne's day procession was composed of pageants whose subjects were drawn from the Corpus Christi play, since we know that it presented the subjects of Noah, the Prophets, the Nativity, and, since there were two Marys for whom gowns had to be provided, the Resurrection. If it had in it these subjects, it presumably had the others. The procession was obviously a normal Corpus Christi procession and was, as regards its presentation, actually independent of the Corpus Christi play itself, since the pageants might go on even in years when no Corpus Christi play was played. As an absolute proof of this point, the *visus* were several times shown when the Pater Noster play was substituted for the Corpus Christi play. There is no evidence in the minute book that the city corporation, in spite of its preoccupation with the St. Anne's day sights, paid any expenses or exercised any special oversight, apart from the collection of funds, over the Corpus Christi play or, indeed, over the Pater Noster play. We know that there were at Lincoln a Corpus Christi guild and a Pater Noster guild, and it would almost certainly follow that these guilds concerned themselves with the management of the two great municipal plays, and yet the relations between the trading companies and the plays must have been close.

The cordwainers' company maintained and sent forth annually in the procession of St. Anne's day a pageant called the Pageant of Bethlehem. Among the entries in the account book of the company that refer to the pageant are the oaths provided for the graceman, out-brothers and sisters, the wardens of the guild, and the dean of the guild. Among the duties undertaken by the graceman are the dressing and arraying of the pageant and the unarraying and undressing of the same; also waiting on the pageant in the time of the procession until

[1] Hardin Craig, 'The Lincoln Cordwainers' Pageant', *PMLA*, xxxii (1917), 605-15.

it was done. Out-brothers and sisters undertake to go in the procession with the graceman and the fraternity from the Chapel of St. Thomas at the High Bridge of Lincoln to the cathedral church of Lincoln, where they are to offer one farthing, as the custom is. Wardens of the guild of the cordwainers bound themselves to help dress and 're-dress' the pageant and to go in the procession on St. Anne's day 'to the mother church of Lincoln and so down again'. Even the dean of the company must help prepare the Pageant of Bethlehem and wait on it in the procession.

An inventory, undated but apparently early, reveals the fact that the pageant was a formal ornamental structure. There were three linen cloths 'stained for damask works for Bethlehem' apparently intended to represent city walls; also a 'great gilded head set with seven beams and seven glasses for the same and one long beam for the mouth of the said head'. The beams seem to have been lights with glasses provided to cover them. There would have been no appropriateness in such a structure except as a sort of figure-head. There were also three great stars 'with their three glasses' and a cord for the stars. There is a suggestion of action in the cord, but none in another item of 'ij angels with sensers for the sam'. The angels were properties and belonged to the inventory. The annual accounts provide several times for the cost of mending their wings or arms. Finally, there was one cage 'for to ber dowes in'. No doves would be required in a normal play of the Shepherds, but doves would be a regular feature of a play of the Purification.

Among the customary annual expenses are 8*d*. for the storage of the pageant in the church of the Carmelite Friars. But near the end of the period, on 12 November 1539, there is an order of the city council 'that ther schalbe a large door mayde at the layt scowle hows that the pagents may be seyt in & euery pagent to pay yerly iijd. & Noy Schyppe xijd'. Lincoln trading companies did not own pageant houses, and that is one reason why we have so few guild records.

Other annual payments are for dinner for the shepherds in the procession of St. Anne and a payment to three of them of 18*d*. The records often list the payment of a penny for a cord, a penny-half-penny for a tackle, and payments for window glass, which entries seem to suggest the long and no doubt rough uphill pull from the

High Bridge to the Cathedral. There are frequent expenses for repairing and painting the pageant, and always 6*d*. for the 'portacio' of the pageant. There are never any expenses for rehearsals, nor is there any mention of a play-book or an 'original' such as one finds at Coventry and elsewhere, and as for actors, the matter is not clear. The cordwainers paid annually the sum of 18*d*. for the services of three shepherds, and they were costumed, for on one occasion the company paid for washing the 'herds clothes'. But the sum of 6*d*. apiece seems very small for playing as well as going in the procession. There are no other payments that might be for the services of actors. The very simplest form of a play of the Shepherds would demand actors to play the parts of Mary, Joseph, and at least two angels. No such payments were made by the cordwainers' company. There is, however, one entry that may give a clue to the mystery. In 1532 the accounts have this item: 'paid in expenses for the players ijd.' with this additional item: 'paid to the players above all that was gathered viijd.' This seems to say that the cordwainers paid players 8*d*. to make up for a shortage in the amount of the levy or gathering for the cost of the festival and that players in whom the cordwainers were interested took part in it. This suggests an explanation of the situa- tion. It is clear from their yearly expenses that the cordwainers did not regularly pay any part of the cost of a Corpus Christi play. Who, then, paid for these plays, provided for their casting and rehearsals, supplied the customary food and drink, and managed them? It is clear from an order of the Common Council of 21 March 1530 that it must have been the guild of Corpus Christi:

Also it is agried that euery person shalbe contributorye to the bryngyng fourth of Corpus Xpi gild and nott to deny the payments that thai shalbe sessed to pai by sutch as shalbe assigned to sesse euery crafte and other that shal haue profitt of the sam.

Elsewhere provision is made for the audit of the account. It must also be remembered that St. Anne's guild collected a great deal of money annually. If the records of these two guilds had been preserved, it is probable that one or the other of them would show the details of producing the Corpus Christi play—rehearsals, refreshments, and possibly matters pertaining to play-books and players' parts. We have the accounts of only one trading company, but it is clear that they at least did not pay for these things. And yet the pageants were important not only because their *visus* presented for those days a handsome municipal show but perhaps because they were intimately connected each with a particular play in the cycle and their equip- ment, so carefully attended to, had to be suitable for the plays as well as the procession.

The pageants, as stated above, were given most careful control and assistance by the Common Council. This may be gathered from the minute books of the municipal corporation, which begin with the year 1511 and record acts of the Common Council, the Secret Council, and the Court Leet.[1] We have learned that every man and woman, being able, within the city was required to be a brother or sister of St. Anne's guild and to pay annually 4*d.* at the least. Also every man in his degree must wait upon the mayor in the procession on St. Anne's day to the 'worship' of the city under penalty of 4*d.* Every occupation within the city was responsible for a pageant that it was regularly ordered to apparel and bring forth. These orders had by 1511 become routine matters, but we have seen how carefully they were observed by the craft of cordwainers. The corporation had an interest in the St. Anne's day sights both because of attention to public order demanded by so extensive an assembly in the community and because of the close connexion that existed between the mayor and the council, on the one side, and the guild of St. Anne on the other. Each mayor at the end of his term became graceman of St. Anne's guild, and likewise those who had occupied the office of sheriff, known as sheriff-peers, became wardens of the guild under orders to help the graceman in his business. They were required to give their attendance on the mayor on St. Anne's day and to wait at the hall until he arrived, also to provide 'a person in an honest gown' going in the procession 'among the prophets'. The aldermen them- selves were held responsible for one part of the procession, since they were required to furnish, either of their own or by borrowing, a gown for 'the kings' in the procession, to send forth in the procession a servant 'with a rochet upon him' bearing a torch to be carried in the procession about the sacrament, and to wait themselves upon the mayor. An order of 16 June 1518 directs under penalty every under-

---

[1] Most of the entries with which we are concerned are summarized in the 14th Report of the Historical MSS. Commission, Appendix VIII.

constable to wait upon the pageants of St. Anne's day by seven of the clock, and in another order constables and under-constables are directed not only to keep the people from the array but to take heed of such as wore garments in the procession; in other words, to see that the orders of council are being obeyed in matters of attendance and clothing.

The cordwainers started, as we know, from the Chapel of St. Thomas at the High Bridge at seven o'clock in the morning on the Sunday after St. Anne's day. That was the accustomed place and was presumably the place of assembly of all the pageants. The cordwainers' pageant proceeded to the Minster. Presumably the others did also. The question is, did they act plays on the way? Apparently they did not, for an act of the Common Council of 1524 seems to show that the procession arrived at the cathedral at ten o'clock, so that there would be insufficient time to enact plays between seven and ten in the morning. In fact, getting the pageants up the steep hill to the Minster would be all that could possibly be accomplished in such a period of time.

Also it is agreid that the ordynaunce for attendance on Mr maier to the Mynster schall stand in effect & strynght & euery man to be redy to gyff attendaunce so that Mr. Maier be at the Mynster afore x of the bell.

What happened at the Minster can perhaps be inferred. All the pageants would be there. It should also be remembered that all the citizens of Lincoln were, failing good excuse, obliged to be there. It may be said also that the only place in the old city of Lincoln where there could be such a concourse of people was the cathedral with its close and the vacant areas around it. It is surely no wild conjecture to suggest that the plays were acted there. One play we know was regularly performed on St. Anne's day in the nave of the cathedral church, that is, the Assumption and Coronation of the Blessed Virgin Mary. And we are not without another plausible piece of evidence that plays were to be seen at the cathedral. It comes from the *Computi* of the cathedral chapter.[1] In 1475 there appears in the *Curialitates* an item often repeated later:

In prandio dominorum canonicorum in festo Corpore Xpi, videntes ludum hoc anno xviiis. vid

[1] Shull, op. cit., pp. 946–66.

This shows the cost of a dinner for the canons, possibly a general term for cathedral ecclesiastics, while they were seeing a play of Corpus Christi. The expense incurred caused the item to appear in the *Computi*. If the dating by the feast of Corpus Christi is to be taken literally, it would indicate that the play retained its ancient date and was not acted in connexion with the St. Anne's day sights. A similar entry for 1477–8 tells us exactly where the canons were when they saw the play:

Et in convivio canonicorum existentium ad videndum ludum Corporis Xpi in camera Johannis Sharpe infra clausum v librae.

They met in John Sharpe's chamber within the cathedral close. The assembly at the *convivium* to see the play was considerable, since the cost was great. The entry of this expense appears in the *Computi* for 1473, 1474, 1480, 1482, 1486, 1489, and 1495. In fact, it is a regular expense. The entry for 1495 tells us that the canons with many other noble persons (*cum aliis nobilibus multis*) had not only dinner but supper at the great cost of 54s. 9d. In 1489 the canons saw not the Corpus Christi play but the Pater Noster play (*videntes ludum de le pater noster pley*). The same was true in 1482. It would seem to be unreasonable to question the fact that these ecclesiastics assembled year after year to watch a long play, such as the Corpus Christi play or the Pater Noster play, that was being played in the cathedral close at Lincoln.

Let us turn from the records of the Lincoln plays to examine the Corpus Christi play in MS. Cotton Vespasian D. viii for any signs that it belonged to Lincoln. The first consideration is a structural one. We know that when the pious fashion of paying special honour to St. Anne, the mother of the Virgin Mary, became dominant in Lincoln, probably before or by the middle of the fifteenth century, the Corpus Christi procession was shifted to St. Anne's day and became the St. Anne's day 'sights' and a great and carefully regulated and supported municipal spectacle at Lincoln. Such an event would naturally have an effect on the Corpus Christi play, for the procession and the play were closely related. The Hegge plays show an appro-priate and ingenious effect. We know that the procession as it passed through the streets, or rather up the hill, was not a processional play. Indeed, it is reasonably certain that the Corpus Christi play as well as the Assumption of the Blessed Virgin Mary was played at the cathedral. We have seen that an outline of an original Corpus Christi play is provided for us in the Proclamation or banns of the Hegge manuscript. So far as that original Corpus Christi play is concerned, it might have been staged on its own pageants perhaps in the cathe-dral yard. The Proclamation continually uses the word 'pageant'. But when we advance another step, as we have already done, we discover that that original Corpus Christi play has been made to include and in part was amalgamated with what we called a St. Anne's day play, or play dealing with the birth, girlhood, and be-trothal of the Blessed Virgin Mary, although the banns outlining the cycle in an earlier form do not include such an action or note such a change. If the Hegge cycle is the Lincoln cycle, we are obliged to conclude that, when the St. Anne's guild took over the Corpus Christi procession, they had a play of their own and that this play was combined with the Corpus Christi play, then in the state revealed by the Proclamation. There is no external evidence of this, but it would have been a natural thing to do in the circumstances, and, in any case, that is what the Hegge cycle shows with perfect clarity has been done. It may at least be claimed that that cycle reflects in its composition the union of a St. Anne's day celebration with a Corpus Christi celebration. This took place at Lincoln. Such an event is not customary or commonplace and reflects what we must believe was a highly special situation.

We have seen that the banns of the Hegge cycle were copied in an older, unrevised form. They make no mention of certain plays appear-ing in the cycle that have to do with St. Anne, give no correct description of what the Passion plays had become, and omit the plays of the Purification and the Assumption of the Blessed Virgin Mary, although in other presumably unaltered parts they give a faith-ful and correct summary of the plays concerned. If we devote our attention to the staging of those parts of the cycle not correctly described in the banns, or not described at all, we see evidences of the use of a fixed stage instead of a movable pageant. But in two cases pageants were actually rolled in and action took place on them. The play of Noah has these stage directions: *Hic transit noe cum familia sua pro navi quo exeunte locum interludii* and, at the end, *Hic recedat lameth et*

statim intrat noe cum navi cantantes. And at the beginning of the Trial of
Joseph and Mary we have: *Hic intrabit pagentum de purgacione Marie et
Joseph.* Hence two of the Hegge plays made use of movable pageants,
and there is no reason to think that others might not have done so,
in spite of the fact that some parts of the cycle were undoubtedly acted
on a fixed stage, since use is made of special structures from scene to
scene, as also of a *platea* or general playing-place. The following stage
direction from the Council of the Jews will make this clear:

> Here þe buschopys with here clerkys and the Pharaseus mett at the myd place and
> þer xal be a lytil oratory with stolys and cusshonys clenly be-seyn lych as it were a
> cownsel hous.

In other words, the Hegge cycle reveals just such a mixed and transitional state as that which must of necessity have existed in the latter
half of the fifteenth century at Lincoln.

There are other minor arguments from sign that seem inexplicable
on any other basis than that the Hegge plays belonged to Lincoln.
Two of them seem particularly pertinent. The corporation minute
book provides in 1521 and in several other years that the aldermen of
the city shall each provide a gown of silk for the Kings in the St.
Anne's day procession. This has been supposed to refer to the Three
Kings of Cologne in the Magi play, but there were only three kings
in the Magi play, and there were many more than three aldermen in
Lincoln. There seem to have been at least a dozen. The Hegge play
of the Prophets calls for thirteen kings as the progenitors of the Virgin
Mary. These kings must have gone in the procession, and they are
the kings who were to be clad in silken gowns, as they must have been
in the Jesse play, or Hegge play of the Prophets.

The following entry in the treasurer's inventory of 1536 in the
cathedral church of the Blessed Mary of Lincoln adds an interesting
detail to what has just been said, since an elaborate Jesse vestment
makes more certain the existence of a Jesse play at Lincoln:

> Item a Rede coope called the Rutte of Jesse of Rede velvett browdered wt Imagies of
> gold sett wt roses of perles wt a presyouse orfrey, havyng a morse of clothe of gold wt
> vj stones wantyng other ij havyng a hede sett yn gold the wyche hede hath now one
> stone.[1]

[1] See Herbert Hartman, 'The Home of the *Ludus Coventriae*', *Modern Language Notes*, xli
(1926), 530–1. The item is cited from *Archaeologia*, lii (1894), p. 24.

Further, there is preserved at the back of the corporation minute book[1] an inventory of stage properties supposed to have been used in the play of *Tobias* in July 1564. Some of them, however, seem to have belonged to the Corpus Christi play, e.g. 'hell mouth with a nether chap' and 'the citie of Jerusalem with towers and pynacles'. It will be remembered, incidentally, that the Virgin Mary died at Jerusalem. In another place, namely St. Swithin's Church, it is recorded that there remains 'a fyrmament with a fiery clowde and a duble clowde'. These clouds are strange properties, but the Hegge play of the Assumption of the Virgin offers a striking explanation of their use. Before her death the Blessed Virgin Mary desired to see the Apostles, who were abroad preaching the Gospel in distant lands. St. John suddenly appears and says (ll. 164–5):

> In pheso I was prechyng, a fer contre ryth,
> And by a whyte clowde I was rapt to these hyllis.

Later (ll. 255–8), after the rest of the Apostles have appeared, St. Peter says:

> In dyueris contreys we prechid of youre sone & his blis,
> Diueris clowdys eche of vs was sodeynely curyng.
> We in on were brouth before youre yate here i-wis,
> the cause why no man cowde telle of oure comyng.

The white cloud would be the fiery cloud and would be for one passenger. The double cloud would apparently accommodate more.

One thing that stands in the way of the acceptance of the Hegge plays as the Lincoln plays is the fact that the writer of the banns declares that the play will begin at six of the bell 'in N. town'. We know that a similar lack of definite location appears in the manuscript of *The Castle of Perseverance*, also believed on good grounds to be a Lincoln play. The scribal habit of designating places by N. (for *nomen*) instead of their names is not unknown elsewhere. For example, in *The Book of Margery Kempe* Lynn, the birthplace of Margery, is repeatedly written as N.[2] Besides, we do not know the plans that may have been in people's minds when the scribe wrote what he did. If he wrote it because the plays were sometimes acted at other places

---

[1] Historical MSS. Commission, Report XIV. Appendix viii, pp. 57–58.

[2] See *The Book of Margery Kempe*, ed. Sanford Brown Meech and H. E. Allen, E.E.T.S. (London, 1940), vol. i, p. 10, l. 34; p. 16, l. 29.

than the city to which they belonged, or because it was thought of as a possibility that they would be, such circumstances would not affect their connexion with Lincoln.

The foregoing argument that the Hegge plays are the Lincoln plays has some claim to be considered as more than a mere speculation. In the matter of dialect there is undisputed agreement. The learning, the theological culture, and the religious sincerity that appear in the Hegge plays could have been supplied by relatively few places in England in the fifteenth century and in none of them so character-istically as at Lincoln. The general structure of the Hegge cycle and its component parts reflect what we know about the history of mystery plays in the fifteenth century at Lincoln, where a Corpus Christi procession and possibly a Corpus Christi play were taken over or dominated by a guild of St. Anne. There are also a number of argu-ments from sign, two of which are so particularized that they look like finger-prints.

VIII

Single Mystery Plays and Parts of Cycles

THE COVENTRY PLAYS

THOMAS SHARP'S first publication of matter relating to the Coventry plays was made in 1817. A thin volume, of which only twelve copies were issued, has the title-page: *The Pageant of the Sheremen and Taylors, in Coventry, as performed by them on Festival of Corpus Christi; together with other pageants, exhibited on the occasion of several royal visits to that city; and two specimens of ancient local poetry.* The text of the pageant differs but little from that of the better-known edition of 1825. The remainder of Sharp's first book consists of entries copied from the *Coventry Leet Book.*[1]

Very little was as yet known about English mystery plays, although the description of the performance of the Chester plays in a *Breviary of the City of Chester* by David Rogers in 1609 and contained in British Museum MS. Harl. 2150 seems to have been known to Sharp and was of course generalized by him to apply to all Corpus Christi plays. Richard James's mistaken designation of the Hegge plays as *Ludus Coventriae* was still current and was to remain so for many years. A manuscript of the *Shearmen and Taylors' Pageant* and certain account books, no doubt still in the possession of the guilds, had been discovered in Coventry, and these formed the basis of Sharp's study of the Coventry plays. The trading companies, with but few of their ancient functions, had maintained their existence on an hereditary basis, because the guilds had owned land, sometimes the sites of their pageant houses, so that the heirs of the former members of companies found it profitable to continue their existence as corporate bodies. The discovery and publication of the *Shearmen and Taylors' Pageant* seem to have caused a good deal of antiquarian interest in the Coventry Corpus Christi play, which had been famous in its own day. Sharp knew little about the subject, for little was known by anybody. He

[1] Edited by Mary Dormer Harris, E.E.T.S., Original Series, cxxiv (1907), cxxxv (1908), cxxxviii (1909), cxlvi (1933).

was, however, a man of some position, who was acquainted with Sir Walter Scott. He was not a scholar in any strict sense, but was filled with antiquarian enthusiasm for the quaintness of old times and the plays of our forefathers. One suspects that the real discoveries and investigations of Coventry mysteries were due to William Reader, a printer of much modesty and good wits, as shown by his manuscript history of the guilds of Coventry and other documents from his hand that were in the Free Public Library of Coventry until the destruction of the old city in the Second World War.

In 1825 Sharp published his well-known *Dissertation on the Pageants or Dramatic Mysteries, Anciently performed at Coventry, by the Trading Companies of that City*. His book shows that he had before him at that time, besides the *Leet Book* (Coventry Corp. MS. A 3.) and the manuscript of the *Shearmen and Taylors' Pageant*, the accounts of the cappers, dyers, smiths, and drapers, and of Trinity and Corpus Christi guilds, with other less important manuscripts. His method was the selection of what he considered interesting illustrative details, and his object a general presentation of the subject of pageants and 'dramatic mysteries'. He drew for comparison on almost everything available to him that concerned English or continental religious drama, and a good many things that did not, and he attended chiefly to 'the vehicle, characters, and dresses of the Actors'. He published here a second edition of the *Shearmen and Taylors' Pageant*, and added sections relating to the Hox Tuesday play, the pageants exhibited on the occasions of royal visits to Coventry in the Middle Ages, the processions on Corpus Christi day and Midsummer's and St. Peter's eves, and on minstrels and waits. He even found room for the play of *Noah's Ship* from Newcastle-upon-Tyne. Matters relating to the Corpus Christi play are made up for the most part of citations from the account books to which Sharp had access.

In 1836 Sharp wrote a prefatory notice for the Abbotsford Club to an edition of *The Presentation in the Temple, as originally represented by the Corporation of Weavers in Coventry*. The manuscript of this weavers' pageant had, he tells us, been unexpectedly discovered in 1832. Sharp's prefatory notice was based on entries in apparently newly discovered books of the weavers' company. He follows the same plan as in the *Dissertation*, and he had gained further information about the location and ownership of pageant houses, which he also includes in the preface. This is the only instance at Coventry in which we have both the play and the accounts of the guild that acted it. The records are, however, imperfect and not happily selected, and the weavers' pageant is relatively unimportant. There are no accounts from the shearmen and taylors' company, and the rather fully pre-served records of the important dramatic activities of the smiths' company, the cappers' company, and the drapers' company have no plays with which the records may be compared.

The Coventry manuscripts that Sharp used for the *Dissertation*, which ought to have gone into the possession of the city of Coventry, passed into the Staunton collection at Longbridge House. There Halliwell-Phillipps in his *Outlines of the Life of Shakespeare*[1] made a few additional excerpts from them. The Coventry manuscripts came into the Free Reference Library at Birmingham, where in 1879 they were destroyed by fire. The last library catalogue of the Free Reference Library issued before the fire, 1875-7, shows a full list of 'Manuscripts relating to Coventry'. This includes, besides those mentioned above, a good many valuable documents, transcripts, and collections, but not the weavers' pageant or the weavers' account book. William Reader's manuscript history of the guilds of Coventry and other documents at Coventry enabled the author to find out that the weavers' company still exists under the name of the Broadweavers and Clothiers' Company. The manuscript of the *Weavers' Pageant* was accordingly found in the possession of Mr. A. Seymour, secretary of this company, and is now in the Muniment Room, St. Mary's Hall, Coventry. It is a codex on parchment consisting of seventeen folios, one missing, written by Robert Croo in 1534. Along with this manuscript were two loose leaves in what seems to be a fifteenth-century hand on torn paper, illegible in places, but certainly fragments of a purer and an earlier version than Croo's. The weavers' account book used by Sharp was not then to be dis-covered. Because of the loss of the Coventry manuscripts and the relative unavailability of Sharp's books, the records he quoted are col-lected in the Early English Text Society edition of the Coventry plays.[2]

---

[1] Brighton, 1881, 1882; other editions to the seventh (2 v. 1887).
[2] *Two Coventry Corpus Christi Plays*, loc. cit.

The number of crafts that supported pageants at Coventry was fewer than at most places where there are records of Corpus Christi plays, and combinations of crafts and union of subjects seem to have characterized the Coventry Corpus Christi play. The following act of the Coventry Leet was passed in 1445 to determine the order in which the trading companies should ride in the procession on the morning of Corpus Christi day; it shows that the whole number of companies taken into account was seventeen: 'Pur le ridyng on Corpus xpi day and for watche on midsomer even: The furst craft, fyshers and cokes; baxters and milners; bochers; whittawers and glovers; pynners, tylers, and wrights; skynners; barkers; corvysers; smythes; wevers; wiredrawers; cardemakers, sadelers, peyntours, and masons; gurdelers; taylors, walkers, and shermen; deysters; drapers; mercers.'[1] This was doubtless an order of precedence already long followed; it is repeated in 1447 under this heading: *Et quod le ruydyng in festo Corporis Christi fiat prout ex antiquo tempore conserverint.* The fullers were made a separate craft in 1447, and there were doubtless other changes, but the number was never very large. Of course a company usually included several minor crafts whose occupation was more or less closely connected with that of the principal company. It would seem that when these lists were issued there may have been as many as seventeen pageants maintained in the Coventry play, since the original reason for taking part in the Corpus Christi procession, or 'riding', at Coventry would have been the possession of a pageant and a play. But the records show that some of the trading companies had no plays of their own, but contributed to the support of plays maintained by other companies. Indeed, in my study of the Corpus Christi play at Coventry only ten companies could be shown to have been responsible for plays. There is other evidence that the number of pageants available for use on occasions of celebration was limited to ten. This introduced a serious difficulty. Since the total number of pageants, and therefore plays, seemed to be so few and since the subjects of all plays that could be determined were New Testament subjects, I concluded reluctantly that there were in the Coventry cycle no plays on Old Testament subjects. My reluctance has increased since those days, and I feel sure that without Old

---

[1] *Coventry Leet Book,* f. 122; Harris, op. cit. i. 220.

Testament plays there could have been no Corpus Christi play at Coventry or elsewhere.

Of course Old Testament plays might have existed in very early times and have been discontinued, since there was a great deal of changing about and of fluctuating financial status among Coventry guilds. But so close was the control of guilds and pageants by the city council, as recorded in the *Coventry Leet Book,* that it is difficult to see how such discontinuance could have escaped notice. Of course the references to pageants in the *Leet Book* begin in 1424, when the Corpus Christi play was already an ancient institution, but, in any case, one cannot believe that a Corpus Christi play could have maintained its integrity and significance without at least a play of the Creation and Fall of Man. When I wrote I was still hampered by a too literal acceptance of Sepet's theory of the origin of Old Testament plays from the *Processus Prophetarum,* and that idea, in so far as it refers to the plays of the patriarchs, is erroneous. The best that can be said is that my conclusions were arrived at unwillingly. I am not, however, disposed to reject my idea that at Coventry the *Processus Prophetarum* did not exist as a separate play, but that the prophets were distributed throughout the plays. But, as to Old Testament plays, the difficulty still exists.

There is, however, one possibility. The opinion that there were, during the period for which records exist, only ten pageant vehicles and only ten plays in use at Coventry may be wrong, but the evidences seem to point plainly to that conclusion. The Coventry plays were, in any case, unique in the fact that they did not deal in single episodes.

The city corporation of Coventry, as witnessed by the enactments recorded in the *Leet Book,* was vigilant in the matter of compelling all crafts that had no pageants of their own to become contributory to crafts that had and thus pay their fair share of the costs of the plays. The corporation was very much in earnest about the matter. There are two general enactments in April and at Michaelmas 1494, and another briefer one in 1533. The former mentions the dyers, skinners, cappers, corvisers, butchers, and 'dyvers other' as contributing nothing to the cost. It provides for their assignment by the mayor as contributory to crafts that had pageants. The move met with success, and the later entry mentions as non-contributory only the fishmongers, bowyers, fletchers, and 'suche other'. The records show that most of the delinquent crafts, indeed all known crafts, were made to contribute to pageant-producing companies. One must conclude that all of the Coventry trading companies, with a few possible exceptions, are accounted for. It turns out that the companies responsible for pageants in the late fifteenth and early sixteenth centuries were ten.

The following list will show the responsible companies and their subsidiaries for the production and support of the Corpus Christi play: *Cappers*. Sharp had in his possession a book of accounts of the cappers' company that went back to 1485. Until 1530 the cappers had been contributory to the girdlers' pageant, and in 1529 an act of leet gave them possession of the weavers' pageant. This act, however, was not carried out, since the weavers' own records show that they had the same pageant both before and after 1529. The next move of the cappers, who had grown rich from the sixteenth-century fashion of wearing caps, was to associate themselves with the cardmakers and saddlers. This is recorded in an act of 1531. They began to exhibit their newly acquired pageant in 1534, and it is the record of their performance of the play that was in Thomas Sharp's possession. The pageant was of course much older, and enactments of the leet tell us that the cardmakers, saddlers, ironmongers, painters (after 1436), and masons (after 1444) constituted one company. At one time or another contributors to the pageants were the carvers, skinners, barbers, and the surgeons to barbers. The records are so ample that it is easy to tell that the cappers' pageant presented a great group of subjects—the Resurrection and events before and after it.

Drapers. We know little about this company except that it was a rich and politically important company, that it was responsible for the pageant of 'Doomsday', and that it included, besides the drapers, linen-drapers, haberdashers, grocers, and salters.

Girdlers. No records are extant, and we do not know what play they played, or how they were constituted; but it is on record that the cappers, fullers, and painters contributed to their pageant.

Mercers. The mercers constituted a rich and important company, and we have no record of any crafts contributory to them. As we shall see later, it is probable that they presented a pageant of the Assumption of the Blessed Virgin Mary.

Pinners, needlers, tilers, and wrights. This company maintained a pageant, the subject of which is doubtful or unknown. The carpenters and the coopers were contributory to them, and after 1547 the coopers took the lead in the matter of the pageant.

Smiths. The guild was made up of smiths, goldsmiths, pewterers, cutlers, wiredrawers, and (after 1507) bakers and apparently cooks. According to their petition, dated on the Conversion of St. Paul, 1527–8, they had taken over the cutlers' pageant and had continued it only for the mayoralty of Giles Allesley. They then prayed to be discharged of it. The leet refused to grant their petition and ordered them under heavy penalty to continue to present the pageant, a fortunate decision for us, for the records of the smiths go back to about 1450 and are most abundant. There are probably no such records of guild plays to be found anywhere. Their play, which dealt with the Passion, is unfortunately lost, but it is possible to learn a great deal about its contents and equipment. The smiths had a large number of contributory crafts—including fishers, cooks, baxters and milners, and tallow chandlers.

Shearmen, tailors, and walkers. This company, from whom we have preserved one of the most interesting of all mystery plays, makes no appearance in the *Leet Book*, and this makes one wonder if there may not have been other pageants now lost that were unobtrusively maintained and of which we have no knowledge whatever.

Tanners or *Barkers.* This company certainly supported a play of which we have no knowledge. To it the corvisers and shoemakers contributed.

Weavers. We have the weavers' play, and Sharp gives us miscellaneous excerpts from their records.

Whittawers. This company seems also to have included glovers, fellmongers, and parchment-makers. They maintained a play about which we know nothing. The butchers and the needlers seem to have been contributory.

A piece of confirmatory evidence that the pageants were ten in number is found in the fact that, when Queen Margaret was received in Coventry in 1456, the year after the first battle of St. Albans, ten pageants are mentioned. In the *Leet Book* 'pageant' means the vehicle on which the plays were acted, and ten pageants were used.

Nine were needed for the Nine Worthies, and one was left over and stood within the gate at the east end of Bablake Church. The Coventry pageants were few in number as compared with other known cycles, and each pageant seems to have presented a whole group of subjects. The grouping of many subjects on one pageant certainly characterized the whole cycle. *The Shearmen and Taylors' Pageant*[1] presents these subjects: the Annunciation, the Visit to Elizabeth, Joseph's Trouble about Mary, the Journey to Bethlehem, the Nativity proper, *Pastores*, Magi, the Flight into Egypt, and the Slaughter of the Innocents. It is a simple and yet complete Nativity play on traditional lines. *The Pageant of the Weavers*, also preserved,[2] is made up of two subjects, both of which are probably extraneous, since the subjects treated are not originally parts of a Corpus Christi play. The first of these, the Purification or Presentation in the Temple, is obviously a late addition in the York–Towneley plays and in the Hegge cycle, and possibly, although doubtfully so, in the Chester cycle. The other component element of the weavers' play, Christ before the Doctors, is an outright borrowing, directly or indirectly, from York–Towneley. Halliwell-Phillipps quotes an ordinance of the company showing that the weavers had a play as early as 1453, and that is a likely time for such borrowings.

The lost pageant of the smiths was, as the records show, a full-length Passion play that extended from the Entry into Jerusalem at least as far as the Crucifixion. Whether or not it included the Burial one cannot tell. The lost cappers' pageant, which was taken over from the cardmakers in 1531 to 1534, was a play of the Resurrection that extended from the Setting of the Watch to the *Peregrini*. It may also have included Christ's Appearance to the Disciples in the Upper Chamber, a subject closely connected with the *Peregrini*. The mercers almost certainly presented the Assumption of the Blessed Virgin Mary. This is indicated by the importance of the subject at

[1] Ed. Sharp, loc. cit.; W. A. Marriott, *A Collection of Miracle Plays or Mysteries* (Basle, 1838); Craig, op. cit.; Manly, *Specimens*, loc. cit.; A. W. Pollard, *Fifteenth Century Verse and Prose* (Westminster, 1903); Adams, op. cit.

[2] Ed. J. B. Gracie with a Prefatory Notice by Thomas Sharp for the Abbotsford Club (1836); F. Holthausen, *Anglia*, xv (1902); Craig, op. cit. The earliest edition of any part of the *Ludus Coventriae* with some detail with regard to plays at Coventry is to be found in J. Stevens, *Appendix to Dugdale's Monasticon* (1722), vol. i.

Coventry and the local pre-eminence of the mercers' company. When the Princess Mary came to Coventry in 1525, she saw the mercers' pageant play being finely dressed in the Cross Cheaping.[1] This, although a mere agreement of names, carries some weight when we compare it with the special entertainments provided for Margaret, Edward, and Arthur. Besides this, and more important, is the fact that the mercers' company seems to have been a fraternity in honour of the Assumption of the Blessed Virgin Mary. The arms of the company painted on the wall of the mercers' room in St. Mary's Hall, Coventry, are: gules, a demy Virgin Mary with hair dishevelled crowned, rising out and within an orb of clouds, all proper; motto, *Honor Deo.* St. Mary's guild, or the Merchants' guild, founded in 1340, had annual meetings in St. Mary's Hall at the Feast of the Assumption. St. Mary's, St. John the Baptist's, and Trinity guilds were formally united in 1392, and they seem to have been always associated with the guild of Corpus Christi and were finally amalgamated with it in 1534. It seems from all the records that these guilds were always in control of the mercers and drapers.[2] Some entries of expenses on Corpus Christi day from a lost corporation manuscript[3] indicate that there was a pageant of the Assumption in the Corpus Christi procession. There are charges for food: 'peny bred for the apostells vjd, beiff for the apostles viijd; to the Marie for hir gloves and wages ijs, for beryng the Crosse and candelsticks the even and the day viijd, to the Mr to offer xijd, the Marie to offer jd., Katharine and Margaret iiijd, viij virgyns viijd, to Gabriell for beryng the lilly iiijd, to James and Thomas of Inde viijd, to x other apostles xxd.' From an inventory of jewels (1493) in the same manuscript we have, according to Sharp, 'a girdull of blue silk harnest with silver and gilt weyng cord and all iiij unc. et dim., a girdull of rede silk harnest with silver and gilt weyng cord and all vj unc. iij qrt.'. These last entries and several others about payments and properties for Mary on Corpus Christi day prior to 1534 seem to indicate that the presentation of the Assumption in the Corpus Christi procession had been controlled by the Corpus Christi guild

---

[1] Quoted by Sharp, op. cit., p. 162, from Coventry Corporation MS. A. 6.
[2] See Mary Dormer Harris, *Life in an Old English Town* (London, 1898), chapters vii and xiii.
[3] Quoted by Sharp, op. cit., p. 162.

even before the amalgamation of the guilds; but the connexion with the mercers' company would not in any way be affected, since the mercers controlled the guilds as well as the corporation. Finally, it is known from records and certain brief allusions that the drapers' company, the second company in importance in Coventry, acted the play of the Last Judgement.

This leaves the subjects of four pageants unidentified, namely, those of the whittawers, the barkers or tanners, the girdlers, and the pinners, needlers, tilers, and wrights. In my earlier treatment of the subject[1] I was, I now think, misled by an entry, quoted in Sharp[2] from the 'rules and orders of the company of pinners and needlers' of 1414, which recited '*inter alia*, that the said craft are to bear the charges and reparations of "her pagent callyd the takyng down of God fro the cros"'. The company was a big one with many contributors, and, in view of the tendency of the Coventry plays to combine many themes in a single pageant, it seems improbable that the pageant of the pinners and needlers presented only the story of the Burial. The record, which is early, probably represents an earlier state of the cycle when the units were smaller and the number of pageants probably greater. As to the scene of the Burial, the great smiths' pageant may have handled that theme along with its many others. The cappers' pageant, also an inclusive play, had an elaborate Setting of the Watch and a Harrow-ing of Hell. The two pageants came close together, and there is hardly room for a pinners and needlers' pageant between them. We do not know how the pageants may have been allotted and divided at so early a date in Coventry as 1414, but with reference to the pinners', needlers', and tylers' pageants there is a possible way out. In 1414 the pinners' pageant was referred to as the Taking down of Christ from the Cross, but in 1435 the pinners and needlers were given joint responsibility for an unnamed pageant with the tilers. In 1453 these crafts were given the wrights' pageant, with the wrights made con-tributory to it. This would indicate that, if the subject of the original pageant of the pinners had not been changed, at least two more subjects were added to it. We have seen that from the point of view of the records the pinners had at one time a play of the Burial, and

---

[1] Craig, op. cit., pp. xi–xix.
[2] Op. cit., p. 78; Craig, op. cit., p. 103 n.

no two additional themes could have been added to it, since the Burial was a single episode between the Crucifixion of the smiths and the Setting of the Watch of the cappers. If, for example, the tilers' play had occupied the whole fraternity and had dealt, let us say, with the Creation, then the wrights' play, which they got into their posses-sion in 1453, might have dealt with Adam and Eve with or without Cain and Abel, and an Old Testament play of characteristic scope would have been provided. This principle might have applied in other situations.

We have thus a residue of four pageants whose subjects are un-known, and, when we ask what other groups of subjects would be needed to complete the New Testament story, there is only one area that seems definitely vacant, namely, the ministry of Jesus, let us say the Baptism, the Temptation, Jesus at the House of Simon the Leper, and the Raising of Lazarus. John the Baptist was a popular saint in Coventry. There was a church of St. John the Baptist, and when Queen Elizabeth, wife of Henry VII, visited the city, there was some dramatic performance before that church. However, if the subject of the pageant of the pinners, needlers, and wrights is counted as unknown and if one other pageant was devoted to a group of New Testament themes, there would still be three pageants that may have presented Old Testament subjects. There would be needed a pageant of the Creation and Fall, with or without the Fall of Lucifer. Such a pageant might and probably would, as in the Chester cycle, have included the story of Cain and Abel. A Noah play would be, one would think, inevitable, as also a play of Abraham and Isaac. The play of the prophets, if one may judge by the two plays preserved, was broken up and distributed, and the three Old Testament topics mentioned would seem to be the lowest possible terms, although any play centring in one of them might, in accordance with the grouping tendency of the Coventry cycle, have included a variety of associated themes. There is thus a possibility of there having been Old Testa-ment plays in the Coventry cycle, and this would meet the demands of the form of the Corpus Christi play that there should be such Old Testament plays.

The tendency of the Coventry Corpus Christi plays to combine into larger groups of subjects may be seen in *The Shearmen and Taylors'*

Pageant itself. Up to line 474 we have a play of the Nativity and the Shepherds, but with Herod's French prologue beginning at line 475 there opens a Magi play that continues with the Flight into Egypt and the Slaughter of the Innocents. Not only is each of the two parts made up of a group of subjects, but it is manifest that at some earlier time each part was a separate play. It happens that we can tell with some assurance that the second of these combined pageants was originally that of the shearmen (and possibly the fullers). The shear/men and taylors' guild, a guild of the Nativity, called also St. George's guild, was licensed in the reign of Richard II. In 1392 there is mention of the 'tailour pageant howse', and before the forma/tion of the shearmen and taylors' guild the tailors and the shear/men, whose occupations were not at that time separate from that of the fullers, may each have had a pageant of their own. More than this, there is reason to connect the shearmen (and fullers), but not the tailors, with the Visit of the Kings; for when fulling had become a separate occupation from cloth/shearing, and the fullers had formed a company of their own, the fullers were granted in 1439 the privilege of using a common seal with the shearmen.[1] This seal may be regarded as the original property of the shearmen. It represents the Virgin Mary seated and crowned with the Infant Jesus in her lap, receiving gifts from the Magi. The inscription in capital letters and round the margin, according to Fretton, is 'sigillu' co'e scissor' fullonii frat'nitat' gilde natiuitat' d'ni de Coventre'.

There is another matter bearing on the possible presence of Old Testament plays at Coventry to which I was at one time disposed to give more weight than perhaps it deserves. The records of the cappers' company[2] which, it will be remembered, indicate that that guild played a play of the Harrowing of Hell, also show that there was some representation of Adam and Eve. We have these entries of expenses: 'it. pd for a pece of tymber for an apeltrie ijs iijd, it. pd for ij cloutes, a clamp and other yron work about the apeltre xijd'; and in an in/ventory of goods belonging to the cappers' company of 1597 there appear 'Adams spade' and 'Eves destaffe'. It is not unusual in Passion

---

[1] W. G. Fretton, *Memorials of the Fullers' Guild.* Birmingham and Midland Institute, *Transactions* (1877).

[2] Sharp, op. cit., pp. 42–64; Craig, op. cit., pp. 93–98.

plays on the Continent to find considerable dramatic development of the stories of the patriarchs in connexion with the Harrowing of Hell. In other words, these plays introduced a good deal of Old Testament material in this way into their cycles. In the case before us, however, there are in the cappers' accounts no recorded payments to Adam and Eve or to any patriarchs. Their stories therefore cannot have been dramatized at any great length in the cappers' pageant.

The *Weavers' Pageant* of Coventry in the scene of Christ's Disputation with the Doctors shows interesting links with the plays on the same theme in the York, Towneley, and Chester cycles.[1] The text as it appears in the York cycle is evidently closest to the original form, and, because it is there complete and in its proper place, it is pretty clear that the Doctors' play was originally a York play. But of course the main body of the play as it appears in the Towneley cycle may be of equal antiquity, since this was one of those plays carried from York to Wakefield that remained relatively without change in both cycles. The original metrical form is the twelve-line stanza widely used in the York plays (abababab⁴cdcd³). It is to be noted, at the outset, that the Doctors' scene in both the Chester cycle and the Coventry weavers' pageant is united with the Purification. It follows next after the Purification in the Towneley cycle, but the loss of two leaves in the Towneley manuscript at the end of the Purification and the beginning of the Doctors' play prevents us from knowing what was the original situation in that cycle, and in the York plays the Purification is out of its chronological position in the manuscript.[2] No explanation of the association of the Doctors' play with the play of the Purification has been provided.

The scene of Christ's Disputation with the Doctors begins in the weavers' pageant with line 722, and the opening of the play differentiates it slightly from the York and Chester versions, which both begin with Mary's discovery that Jesus is missing. The play in the Towneley cycle, defective at the beginning, has been in the earlier part rewritten in quatrains, but a parallel between the weavers' pageant and the York and Chester plays begins with line 3 in York, line 219 in Chester, and line 718 in the weavers' play. The Coventry version,

[1] See Craig, op. cit., pp. xxviii–xxxiv; W. W. Greg, *Chester Play Studies*, Malone Society (Oxford, 1935), pp. 101–20.   [2] *York Plays*, loc. cit., p. 433 n.

although it agrees certainly, but roughly, with York–Towneley in many lines, groups of lines, and rhymes, has been expanded rather stupidly, and the York–Towneley stanza has become degenerated. Indeed, it looks as if the maker of the Coventry scene did not under-stand the structure of the York stanza. In the Chester play agreements in language and rhyme with York–Towneley, when they occur at all, are close, but the original lines have been pieced together and usually made over into quatrains, no very difficult thing with the York twelve-line stanza. It seems to have been borrowed from York–Towneley possibly before these two cycles were separated. The Coventry version, certainly originally borrowed from York–Towneley, since it is actually a degenerated version of the same play, is in such condition that it is hard to tell what text it came from or what intermediaries there may have been between the Coventry scene and its source.

As to stations, or customary playing-places, in the city of Coventry, there is some uncertainty. I conjectured in my earlier study that there might have been ten such stations, one in each of the ten city wards. Six are mentioned in the records, and they seem to have been in different wards: Jordan Well, Newgate, Earl Street, Bablake Gate, the Cross in Cross Cheaping, and Gosford Street. There was also dramatic activity at the Grey Friars' Church and at the Conduit in Smithford Street. But for the playing of these long plays all in one day ten stations seem too many. There is a small piece of evidence that suggests fewer performances. The drapers' company in their play of Doomsday burnt three worlds, not ten. There might have been only three places in the city where the world could be safely burnt, but for a full performance the burning of these worlds would seem to be necessary.

The last year in which the Corpus Christi play was played in Coventry was 1580, but in 1584 the crafts joined together in a great new dramatic effort intended no doubt to take the place of the famous and profitable Corpus Christi play. They chose a subject familiar on the continent of Europe, the Destruction of Jerusalem, and the smiths paid 'Mr Smythe of Oxford' the considerable sum of £13. 6s. 8d. for 'writyng of the tragedy'. Whether that was his full payment or merely the smiths' part of the expense is not known. The guilds held many rehearsals, spent a great deal of money, and evidently took great

pains with the new play, but they only repeated the performance once
and then not immediately. It was played processionally on movable
pageants as the Corpus Christi play had been, and it is an illumin-
ating exercise to see how the story of the Destruction of Jerusalem as
narrated by Josephus was handled for processional performance.

At least two other aspects of the Coventry Corpus Christi play
ought to be mentioned. If we may judge from the two examples
preserved, they escaped to a surprising degree the usually harmful
effects of modernization. This is a fair assumption when one considers that both pageants were subjected to the ignorant, inept, and
pompous ministrations of Robert Croo, the only redactor of pageants
of whom there is any record at Coventry. The *Shearmen and Taylors'
Pageant* is said at the end to have been 'newly correcte be Robart
Croo', who finished his work on 14 March 1534. The *Weavers'
Pageant* is written in Croo's hand and is dated 2 March 1534. He
supplied two leaves for the lost playbook of the smiths' company,
and in 1557 was paid xxs. for 'makyng of the boke for the paggen'
for the drapers' company; he also played God in that pageant (iijs.
iiijd.), supplied 'a hat for the Pharysee' (vijd.), and made three worlds
(iijs. viijd). It is even possible by a comparison of Croo's text with
that of the two leaves of a fifteenth-century version mentioned above[1]
to form an idea of what Croo did. He spoiled a good deal of the
verse, mixed up the stanza forms, and used many large words; but
he devoted himself mainly to homiletic passages and let the stories
alone. This is fortunate from several points of view. Generally
speaking, the older and simpler the texts of mystery plays the better;
the better because in this way the religious symbolism of the liturgical
drama and the simple beauty of the biblical stories were left intact.
The *Shearmen and Taylors' Pageant* and, to a less degree, the *Weavers'
Pageant* in their dialogue, action, and representation are still in their
main parts much as they were when they passed from Latin into
English. Free from comicality and bombast, the parts of these plays
that tell the story are still in simple language and ancient stanza forms
and preserve the reverent tone of the liturgical drama. These two plays
from Coventry reveal in miniature the history of the mystery play in
England.

[1] Craig, op. cit., Appendix iv, pp. 119–22; also pp. xxxv–xxxviii.

The two metrical forms at the command of the original authors or translators were, as we have seen, first, four-foot quatrains. In this form appear in the *Shearmen and Taylors' Pageant*, always in close conformity to liturgical scriptural sources, the cores of most of the principal episodes. The next most significant metre, perhaps the original stanza of the *Pastores*, is the Chester ballad stanza, rhyming aaabaaab or aaabcccb, or sometimes a corrupt form of it. Many of the most humorous parts of the plays, including parts of the Shepherds' scene, some parts of the Magi, and the dove episode in the Presentation in the Temple, as well as a majority of the excrescences of the stories, are in pure or approximate Chester metre. From the beginning the liturgical drama had many lyrical or didactic passages, and in these Coventry plays they appear mainly in a seven-line stanza rhyming ababbcc. This is in two forms: the rhyme royal with five accents to the line (used in the opening speeches of Isaiah, Herod, Simeon, and Anna), possibly the later of the two; and another seven-line stanza with the same rhyme-scheme with only four accents to the line. This has been extensively used in the Presentation in the Temple and in Christ before the Doctors, and rather scantily in the *Shearmen and Taylors' Pageant*. The metres of the Coventry plays afford us a sort of dim record of their literary and dramatic history.

In the second place, the Coventry plays, so far as one can judge from the examples preserved, seem to retain a medieval quality. They are simple, direct, and naïve. They mingle gaiety with reverence, and their comicality is of a rustic, peasant sort, not pretentiously or wittily vulgar. These plays are lively and full of action, and these qualities can be conjectured of all the plays of which there are records. The accounts show interesting, suggestive, and rather startling accessories employed in the staging of plays at Coventry, so that it is still not difficult to see why the Coventry Corpus Christi play was famous. In the smiths' pageant the pillar and the cross were gilded, God's coat was of white leather (six skins), Herod carried a falchion, Pilate a pole-axe, the Devil's head was painted and often needed repairs, there was much machinery, and there was a truss with a new hook for the hanging of Judas. In the cappers' accounts there was provided a hell-mouth, and the Devil had a specially constructed padded club, which, according to Sharp, was preserved until the nineteenth century. The drapers' accounts excel all the others in their mysterious interest. There were many demons (dressed in orange and black to represent flames), white and black souls, a Pharisee, an earthquake in a barrel, and three worlds to be consumed by fire.

The Coventry plays, as far as preserved, are the least learned, show the least clerical or ecclesiastical influence, and are the most popular of all the mystery plays of which we are able to form an opinion. But they have the merits as well as the defects of these qualities. They were no doubt funny, and yet the two surviving examples reflect in a convincing way the religious faith of simple medieval people. The records of the smiths' and the cappers' companies indicate uproarious farce. The frequent renewal of Pilate's club and the mending of Herod's head are recurrent expenses, and the Herod scenes of the *Shearmen and Taylors' Pageant* have a bad pre-eminence in low comedy surpassed only by the Digby *Killing of the Children*. The cultural level is low. The speeches of prophets and other didactic persons are formal and unintelligent, the worst being the speeches attributable to Robert Croo.

Herod is the most notorious of mystery play characters, and Hamlet's 'out-heroding Herod' has made him proverbial. The following scene in Croo's outlandish spelling is presented as an example:

> *Nuncios.* Hayle, kynge, most worthist in wede!
> Hayle, manteiner of curtese throgh all this worlde wyde!
> Hayle, the most myghtyst that eyuer bestrod a stede!
> Hayle, the most monfullist mon in armor man to abyde!
>   Hayle, in thyne hoonowre!
> Thesse iij kyngis that forthe were sent
> And schuld haue cum ageyne before the here present,
> Anothur wey, lorde, whom the went,
>   Contrare to thyn honowre.
> *Erode.* A-nothur wey? owt! owt! owtt!
>   Hath those fawls traytvrs done me this ded?
> I stampe! I stare! I loke all abowtt!
>   Myght I them take, I schuld them bren at a glede!
> I rent! I rawe! and now run I wode!
> A! thatt these velen trayturs hath mard this my mode!
>   The schalbe hangid yf I ma cum them to!

Here Erode ragis in the pagond and in the strete also.

E! and thatt kerne of Bedlem, he schalbe ded
And thus schall I his profece for-do.

How sey you, sir knyghtis? ys not this the best red,
Thatt all yong chyldur for this schuld be dede?
Wyth sworde to be slayne? (ll. 768–788)

But we get a gentler impression of the play from the following bit
(ll. 168–83) from the journey of Joseph and Mary to Bethlehem:

Josoff. But now to Bedlem must I wynde
  And scho my-self, soo full of care;
And I to leyve you, this grett, behynd, —
  God wott, the whyle, dame, how you schuld fare.

Mare. Na, hardely, husebond, dred ye nothyng;
  For I woll walke with you on the wey.
I trust in God, all-myghte kyng,
  To spede right well in owre jurney.

Josoff. Now I thanke you, Mare, of youre goodnes
  Thatt ye my wordis woll nott blame;
And syth that to Bedlem we schall vs dresse,
  Goo we to-gedur in Goddis wholle name.
                    (*They pretend to make a journey.*)

Now to Bedlem haue we leygis three;
  The day ys ny spent, yt drawyth toward nyght;
Fayne at your es, dame, I wold that ye schulde be,
  For you groue all werely, yt semyth in my syght.

NORWICH WHITSUN PLAYS

There was at Norwich in the later Middle Ages a Corpus Christi
play that had been transferred to Monday and Tuesday after Whitsunday. The procession was still held on Corpus Christi day, and the
Norwich trading companies were expected to display their pageants
in it. In 1527 the guilds were made responsible for the expenses of
their plays as well as of their pageants in the procession. The Norwich
records, though relatively few, are interesting.[1] The Assembly Book
of the corporation provides, for example, an explanation of the

---

[1] Chambers, op. cit. ii. 386–9; H. Harrop, 'Particulars concerning Early Norwich
Pageants', *Norfolk Archaeology*, iii. 3 ff.; *The Non-Cycle Mystery Plays*, loc. cit., pp. xxvi–xxxv.

enactment just mentioned. The guild of St. Luke, itself composed of a number of trading companies, had apparently until the year mentioned been responsible for the cost and probably the management of the Corpus Christi play. On 21 September 1527, St. Luke's guild petitioned the Assembly to the following effect:

> Where of longtime paste the said Guild of Seynt Luke yerly till nowe hath ben used to be kept and holden within the citie aforesaid upon the Mundaye in pentecost weke at which daye and the daye next ensuyng many and divers disgisyngs and pageaunts, as well of the lieffs and martyrdoms of divers and many hooly Saynts, as also of many other light and feyned figurs and picturs of other persones and bests; the sight of which disgisings and pageaunts, as well yerly on the said Mondaye in pentecost weke in time of procession then goyng about a grett circuitte of the forsaid citie, as yerly the Tuysday in the same weke [serving] the lord named the Lord of Misrule at Tumlond within the same citie, hath ben and yet is sore coveted, specially by the people of the countre...

The petition then calls attention to the fact that the city has profited by the resort of people to see these sights and says that the entire cost has been borne by St. Luke's guild, which is 'almost fully decayed'. It therefore asks an order 'that every occupation wythyn the seyed Citye may yerly at the said procession upon the Mondaye in pentecost weke sette forth one pageaunt'. It was agreed that each craft should play 'one such pageaunt as shalbe assigned and appoynted by Master Mair and his brethern aldermen, as more playnly appereth in a boke thereof made'. Then follows the list of subjects and crafts quoted below.

The connexion between the Norwich guilds and the Corpus Christi procession and play was of course not new. Harrop cites an order of the Assembly of 1489 to the effect that on Corpus Christi day the thirty-one guilds of the city shall go in procession before the pageants 'ad Capellam in Campis Norwici modo sequi'. The order of the Assembly above quoted seems best explained as merely intended to relieve the guild of St. Luke of the expenses of the play. There is no reason to doubt that the guilds had long owned their pageants and gone in procession as at other places.

The one play of the Norwich cycle extant, the so-called *Grocers' Play*, or *The Creation of Eve, with the expelling of Adam and Eve out of Paradise*,[1] has been almost accidentally preserved along with certain

---

[1] Waterhouse, op. cit., pp. 8–18; Manly, *Specimens*, loc. cit.; Adams, op. cit., pp. 88–93.

accounts of the grocers' company that refer to it. The original manuscripts of both the play and the *Grocers' Book* have been lost, and the
only source of information is what is described as a somewhat
inaccurate eighteenth-century transcript of the play and of certain
records from this book. Robert Fitch, a Norwich antiquary, published in *Norfolk Archaeology*, volume viii (1856), two versions of the
Grocers' Play, the better one dating from 1533, although fragmentary;
the other a post-Reformation redaction dating from 1565, strictly
scriptural and not bad of its kind, but not the *Grocers' Play* as it was
acted during the Middle Ages. The earlier text, so far as it is preserved, is mainly in seven-line stanzas of the Chaucerian pattern; the
later, usually with the same rhyme-scheme, is in longer and more
ponderous lines that have the rhythm of alliterative verse but not its
alliteration. With the texts of the play are extracts from the lost
Grocers' Book that begin in 1533 and give details about the pageant,
including an 'Inventory of particulars appertaining to the Company
of the Grocers, A.D. 1565'. From this some transcriptions have
already been given. These items Fitch derived from the eighteenth-
century transcript described above, which, according to Waterhouse,
is still in existence.

The assignment of plays made by the city assembly in 1527 furnishes
what is apparently a complete enumeration of the Norwich pageants
in that year. There is a list of twelve plays and opposite each title are
the names of the trading companies, in one case as many as seventeen,
made responsible for the performance and support of the play:

1. Creation off the World	7. Moises and Aaron with the Children of Israel & Pharo with his Knyghts
2. Helle Carte	8. Conflict off David & Goleas
3. Paradyse	9. The Berth off Christ with Sheperdes & iij Kyngs of Colen
4. Abell & Cain	10. The Baptysme of Criste
5. Noyse Shipp	11. The Resurrection
6. Abraham & Isaac	12. The Holy Gost

The Corpus Christi play here outlined seems to belong to a different
tradition from any elsewhere recorded in England and probably had
a special liturgical basis. The Old Testament plays are normal,
except for the inclusion of an elsewhere unknown subject of David

and Goliath. The Christmas group, crowded as at Coventry on one pageant, is followed by a John the Baptist play. An altogether odd and unaccountable thing is that there is no play of the Passion. There is a Resurrection and a Pentecost, one may even suppose that there was an Ascension, but there is no play of the Last Judgement. Even supposing that at an earlier time St. Luke's guild or the crafts themselves may have presented a number of plays not continued by the order of the Assembly, it is incredible that, the cycle having once had plays of the Passion and Doomsday, these plays should have been discontinued, since both are crucial features of the Corpus Christi play. It must be that the Norwich cycle originated from such subjects as were at hand. Groups of plays dealing with Old Testament subjects, with the Nativity, and with the Resurrection would be a good beginning, and a single play of John the Baptist need create no surprise in any English centre. But it is doubtful if Norwich ever had a play of the Passion or of the Last Judgement. One may, more-over, presuppose no small degree of independence in the medieval city of Norwich, which was an important place that ranked in com-merce with London, York, and Bristol. That Norwich was also a place of great ecclesiastical importance its many very old churches and its great twelfth-century cathedral still bear witness.

Waterhouse is of the opinion that the Norwich plays were per-formed not at various stations throughout the city but at one fixed place like those at Reading, Shrewsbury, and Edinburgh. If, how-ever, we may judge from the *Grocers' Play*, they were certainly per-formed on movable pageants. The records are too few to indicate that there were no stations about the city for the acting of plays. The sort of thing that must have happened in many places with the breakdown of the Corpus Christi play after the Reformation and the coming of modern times is so well illustrated by an extract from the lost *Grocers' Book* that it is worth quoting. It describes the decay and destruction of the apparently magnificent pageant vehicle of the Norwich grocers. We have seen from an entry quoted earlier from the *Grocers' Book* that the pageant was 'a Howse of Waynskott, paynted and buylded on a Carte with fowre whelys'. The pageant was fitted with a square top, and the top was ornamented by means of a griffin and a large iron 'fane' or pennant holder at one end, with eighty-three

smaller vanes. They had what are described as 'perfumes' or 'fumiga-
tions' apparently for use with the griffin. The pageant had also a tree,
which it was the custom of the company to decorate with oranges,
figs, almonds, dates, raisins, plums, and apples. There was also
provision of flowers with coloured thread to bind them. The most
notorious of all the properties of the grocers' pageant was 'a Rybbe
colleryd Red'. But the *Grocers' Book* recorded the decay of all this
magnificence:

Item, yt is to be noted that for asmuch as for þe space of 8 yeris ther was neyther
Semblye nor metynge, in the meane season þe Pageante remaynynge 6 yeris in þe Gate
howse of Mr. John Sotherton of London, untyll the ferme came to 20s.; and bycause
the Surveiors in Mr. Sotherton's tyme would not dysburs ani moni therfor, þe
Pageante was sett oute in þe Strete & so remayned at the Black fryers brydge in open
strete, when bothe yt was so weather beaten, þat the cheife parte was rotton; wherupon
Mr. John Oldrich, then Maior þe yer 1570, together with Mr. Tho. Whall, Alderman, offred yt to þe Company to sell for the some of 20s., and when no person would
buy yt for þat price and þat yt styll remayned, & nowe one pece therof rent of & now
another as was lyke all to come to nothinge, Nicholas Sotherton, then offycer to Mr.
Maior, was requested to take yt in pieces for þe dept dewe to hym for þe seyd howse
ferm therof for 6 yeres aforesayde, at 3s. 4d. a yer, who accordinglye dyd take down þe
same & howsed yt accordinglye.

There is some suggestion of popular interest in the titles of the
plays as given in the Assembly list. The *Grocers' Play* is put down as
'Paradyse', and we know from their records how earnestly they tried
to make it a paradisiacal spectacle. If we judge from the efforts of the
grocers, we can understand why the Fall of the Angels should be
described as 'Helle Carte'. No doubt medieval diablerie found
obvious expression in that pageant. There is also something suggestive
in the title of the seventh pageant: 'Moises and Aaron with the Children of Israel & Pharo with his Knyghts.' The Magi are described traditionally as the 'iij Kyngs of Colen', and the Pentecost play is put down
simply as 'The Holy Gost'. But, unfortunately, in the two versions of
the *Grocers' Play* preserved we get, apart from a few stage directions,
little that is suggestive of the old time and the Middle Ages. The
older fragmentary version is for the most part in rather poor Chaucerian stanzas, and the heart of the play is lost. The style in which it is
written indicates that it is fifteenth- or early sixteenth-century work.
The only original virtue it has is a naïve quickness and objectivity.

Satan has few wiles. Eve yields immediately to temptation, and Adam follows her lead without hesitation or compunction. The later version is respectable, but commonplace. It is closely scriptural, but is metrically and dramatically unskilful. The redactor usually follows the Chaucerian rhyme scheme, but his lines are cumbersome and have, as above noted, the rhythm of alliterative verse without the alliteration. The writer introduces as a modernistic, but by 1565 belated, feature the characters Dolor, Misery, and the Holy Ghost, the last mentioned being there for the purpose of consolation and the bringing of the good tidings of salvation.

NOAH'S ARK; OR, THE SHIPWRIGHTS' ANCIENT PLAY OR DIRGE
Newcastle-upon-Tyne

Such is the title given by Henry Bourne, curate of All Hallows Church in Newcastle-upon-Tyne (in a book published four years after his death), to the only surviving pageant of the Corpus Christi play anciently performed by the guilds or trading companies of that city.[1] His book was *The History of Newcastle-upon-Tyne* and was published in 1736. In it he included the only known text of this play, and a very bad text it is. Whether Bourne copied an original manuscript himself or worked from a transcript is not known. His original is lost. The language, which of course was northern English, is ignorantly modernized, so that it is often unintelligible. There are also some omissions in the manuscript. But the play became known early and was sufficiently quaint and lively to attract attention. In 1789 John Brand reproduced Bourne's text in his *History and Antiquities of Newcastle-upon-Tyne*, and in 1825 Thomas Sharp included it in his *A Dissertation on the Pageants or Dramatic Mysteries, Anciently performed at Coventry*. In 1897 F. Holthausen published in *Göteborgs Högskolas Årsskrift*, volume iii, a critical text of the shipwrights' play based on Bourne's text, an honest and useful, although not very perspicacious, piece of work. With it he published a good deal of information about the Newcastle plays. Finally, R. Brotanek made an ambitious and ingenious attempt to restore the text to the northern English of the early fifteenth century. The best edition, however, is that of the *Non-Cycle Mystery Plays*, edited by Osborn Waterhouse.

[1] Chambers, op. cit. ii. 385; Waterhouse, op. cit. xxxv–xliii, 19–25.

Waterhouse makes no attempt to restore the original language, but by use of various emendations and his own observation he presents a satisfactory text.

The subject of the play is the first part of the Noah story, the Build-ing of the Ark, and the play is simple, spirited, and naturalistic. The principle metre is quatrains of four accents to the line and alternately rhymed. It has a gratuitous introduction of the Devil in order that he may tempt Noah's wife to recalcitrance. Noah's wife, as well as the Devil, is, traditionally speaking, an excrescence in the play, and both are probably introduced in order to enlarge the first scene of the Noah play into a satisfactory pageant. There must, of course, have been in the cycle a following pageant dealing with the embarkation, the experiences in the Flood, and the safe landing. Such partitions of plays, well known in the history of the York cycle, were made, no doubt, to provide pageants for crafts that had none, and that may have been done in this case. If so, the scene lopped off from the opening of the play would need to have its interest increased, and to that end perhaps the reviser took over from the Temptation of Eve the Devil, whose method and behaviour are quite the same in this appearance as they were traditionally in the earlier one. Noah's wife belongs properly to the second part of the Noah play, but she is advanced into the scene of the Building of the Ark, no doubt to lend human interest to that undramatic episode. These conjectures are supported by the fact that, in the parts in which these newcomers appear and speak, not quatrains but longer and more varied stanzas are used.

There are said to be in existence somewhat extensive records of the trading companies of Newcastle-upon-Tyne that contain references to the guild plays, but they do not seem to have been collected and published. Waterhouse gives the fullest excerpts available. There exists no formal list of the individual plays of the Corpus Christi cycle at Newcastle, but, since the records of the guilds often mention the names of the plays for which they are responsible, it is possible to tell the subjects of twelve different pageants. 'The Creation of Adam' was acted by the bricklayers and plasterers, 'Noah's Ark' by the shipwrights, 'The Offering of Isaac' by the slaters, 'The Deliverance of the Children of Israel out of the Thraldom, Bondage and Servitude of King Pharao' by the millers, 'The Three Kings of Cologne' by the goldsmiths, plumbers, glaziers, pewterers, and painters, 'The Flying of our Lady into Egype' by the bricklayers and plasterers (who were also responsible for 'The Creation of Adam'), 'The Baptizing of Christ' by the barbers and chirurgeons with the chandlers, 'The Last Supper' (by inference from guild records) by the fullers and dyers, 'The Burial of Christ' by the house-carpenters, 'The Descent into Hell' by the tailors, and 'The Buriall of our Lady Saint Mary the Virgin' by the masons. It is also provided that the merchant ven-turers' company were to be responsible for five plays, and there are some guilds that may have had plays, the titles of which we do not know. There was thus provision for a fairly extensive Corpus Christi cycle at Newcastle-upon-Tyne. Waterhouse estimates it perhaps too conservatively at twenty-two to twenty-five in all. There seems to be no reason to think that these Newcastle plays were not acted procession-ally on movable pageants as they were at Chester, York, and Beverley. In fact there is an entry in the books of the fullers and dyers that records a payment 'for the carynge of the trowt and wyn about the toun'.

The shipwrights' play is so naturalistic and lively in spite of its unimportant subject that one must regret that there are not other survivals of this northern cycle. The lore of shipbuilding and the tools employed in that trade, doubtless most familiar in Newcastle, are convincing, and Noah's reluctance at his age of 600 years to enter into a new occupation was in the circumstances that must have existed in Newcastle no doubt highly amusing.

ABRAHAM AND ISAAC—MANUSCRIPTS FROM BROME HALL AND FROM DUBLIN

Genesis xxii. 1–19, the story of God's command to Abraham to offer up his beloved son Isaac as a burnt offering, became the source of one of the most popular of all mystery plays. There are seven different versions, counting that in the Cornish *Origo Mundi*, pre-served in England and as many more now lost. Such plays were abundant in France and Germany. The subject with its strongly Christian teaching appealed to Protestants as well as Catholics, and Theodore Beza's *Abraham sacrifiant* (1550) went through many editions and translations. This popularity has been attributed by critics and historians of the drama to literary choice but was in fact originally accidental. The subject is in its very nature so appealing that, at one time dramatized as a mere part of biblical story, it eventually won its own currency. The life of Abraham—his calling, his journey to Egypt, his separation from Lot, God's promise to him, his blessing by Melchisedek, the rite of circumcision, the story of Hagar and Ishmael, his investiture of Isaac, his death, and on into the stories of Isaac and Jacob—found its liturgical place in the services of Quinquagesima and Quadragesima. In the first dramatization of these subjects there was naturally no discrimination among them, since the purpose was religious and not dramatic, so that the Sacrifice of Isaac merely took its place as an episode in the history of the patriarchs. This fact is clearly reflected in *Le Mistère du Viel Testament* and in the Chester plays. The first ideal was merely religious completeness, but the story of Abraham's sacrifice ceased to be an episode and became a theme. What greater extension the Chester play of Abraham, Melchisedek, and Lot may once have had one does not know, but in its preserved form it is in a transitional state, still a mere succession of biblical events with one of them outgrowing the rest. It is, for example, not the more important dispute with Lot (Gen. xiii. 7–12) that appears, but Abraham's rescue of Lot from captivity (Gen. xiv. 14–16). The blessing of Abraham by Melchisedek with the gift of bread and wine is important theologically rather than dramatically. Certainly the same thing may be said of the rite of circumcision, treated in the Chester play of Abraham and Isaac relatively at great length. Following it is the story of the proposed sacrifice of Isaac still in precisely biblical terms but with little touches of emotional appeal here and there that show that the subject in its own right has begun to make itself felt.

This is said as if the Chester play were certainly very old, whereas the earliest manuscript we have dates from 1591. We are forced into a paradoxical situation when we say that the oldest English version of the play of Abraham and Isaac is in the newest manuscript, but the conservative medieval city of Chester chose to protect its Corpus Christi play against modernization for more than 250 years, and the Chester play of Abraham and Isaac is the most primitive one we possess on the subject. We need not, moreover, be too uncertain about the matter, for the source, form, language, and spirit of the Chester play attest its antiquity. In order to write such a play *de novo* an author would not only have to stick to the Vulgate text and record rather indiscriminately what he found there, but he would also have to be a man living in a provincial English city early in the fourteenth century and would have to be under the sway of a still potent liturgical tradition. *Le Mistère du Viel Testament* was printed by Pierre Le Dru about 1500 in a greatly expanded form, and we are concerned with the scene of Abraham and Isaac as it appears in that cycle.[1]

We need also to call attention to another French play of the Sacrifice of Isaac republished in Rothschild's edition of *Le Mistère du Viel Testament*.[2] It is *Le Sacrifice de Abraham à huit personnages*, a separate play of Abraham and Isaac printed at Paris in 1539. The editor recognized the intimate relation of this version to that which appears in *Le Mistère du Viel Testament* and reprinted with some collations and below his text extensive parts of the 1539 play.[3] The charm of the subject caused it at some time not necessarily after 1500 to become a separate play, and in this operation *Le Sacrifice de Abraham à huit personnages* has been amplified from the type still preserved in the Chester play and in *Du Sacrifice d'Abraham*, the seventeenth play in *Le Mistère du Viel Testament*. Sarah, the mother of Isaac, has become an important character in the play. She is not even mentioned in the twenty-second chapter of Genesis, and in the Chester play she is present only in the minds of Abraham and of Isaac, and the same is true of *Du Sacrifice d'Abraham*.

In England we have to do with only certain Abraham and Isaac plays. In the York–Towneley complex one may recognize as original a simple scriptural play. The York version has been vigorously re-written after the separation of the cycles. The Wakefield version, much simpler in style and contents, may retain parts of the original play.[4] It shows some puzzling resemblances to the Chester version, but in general does not seem to be of the same type as the Chester play. The Abraham and Isaac play in the Hegge cycle, scriptural and simple, does not seem, so far as one can see, to be related to the group of which the Chester play is the centre.

[1] *Le Mistère du Viel Testament*, loc. cit. ii. 19–77.
[2] On this subject see Waterhouse, op. cit., pp. l–lii.
[3] See 'Du Sacrifice d'Abraham', *Le Mistère du Viel Testament*, loc. cit. ii. 28–79.
[4] Lyle, op. cit., pp. 96–97.

The popularity of the play of Abraham and Isaac is indicated by the preservation of two independent plays neither of which has been connected with any known Corpus Christi cycle. The first of these is a play on the subject in the library of Trinity College, Dublin. It is often called the 'Dublin' play, and until its dialect was studied and until more was known about the lost Dublin plays it was thought of as part of a lost Dublin Corpus Christi play. It is in a manuscript made up of a variety of writings and labelled *Tractatus Varii*,[1] which is known to have been given to the library by Archbishop Ussher (1581–1656). The manuscript was apparently written late in the reign of King Henry VI (1422–61). Since it contains in the principal handwriting of the manuscript a list of the mayors and bailiffs of Northampton, it has been thought to have originated in that Midland English town, especially since the dialect in which the play is composed is appropriate to the region of Northampton. The play has no markings and no local references, and no records of mystery plays at Northampton have been discovered. All that can be said is that the play was eventually copied into the collection by a person sufficiently interested in Northampton to make a list of mayors and bailiffs of that place.

The Abraham and Isaac in the Dublin manuscript has dignity and no small amount of spirit. The stanza forms are fairly elaborate and are thought of by Waterhouse as appropriately varied for the expression of character and situation. However this may be, the familiar Chester ballad stanza (aaa⁴b³aaa⁴b³ or aaa⁴b³ccc⁴b³) appears in the heart of the play and carries the burden, a thing that would indicate age, original simplicity, and later revision. Early in the play, and occasionally in other places, longer and more complicated stanza forms appear, usually the stanza of the Proclamation in the Hegge cycle, *The Castle of Perseverance*, and other works. The metrical state of the Dublin play suggests a dramatic, if not cyclic, history. It is of the same temper as the Chester play but of a different type. There are occasional parallels, but they are too distant for one to be able to say that the play in the Dublin manuscript was derived from the Chester play. A contention introduced by Brotanek[2] has a good deal to

---

[1] See Waterhouse, op. cit., pp. xliii–xlviii, 26–36.
[2] *Anglia*, xxi (1898–99), 21–55.

commend it. He shows that the structure and movement of the play resemble *Le Sacrifice de Abraham à huit personnages* (1539) mentioned above as reprinted by Rothschild in *Le Mistère du Viel Testament*. The play in the Dublin manuscript, like that French play, introduces Sarah as an important speaking character. It seems probable that the play in the Dublin manuscript goes back to an early and simple form of the French version, but whether it came by way of Chester or by a different route at a different time cannot be told.

The other play of Abraham and Isaac, named after Brome Manor in Suffolk, is one of the most widely known of all mystery plays. It was also discovered in a commonplace book, written between 1470 and 1480, and was published twice by Lucy Toulmin Smith, editor of the *York Plays*, once in *Anglia* (v. vii. 36) and again in *A Commonplace Book of the Fifteenth Century* (1886), and since by various other editors.[1] The Brome Abraham and Isaac is obviously a skilfully developed version of the Chester Abraham and Isaac. The matter would never have been in doubt if scholars had been willing to allow for the continual revisions of mystery plays that went on throughout their career. Scholars have tended to think of each version of a particular work as the original creation of some author whose name they would like to know and have tended to forget the habits, the religious purposes, and the anonymity of the Middle Ages. The revision and expansion of the Chester play into the Brome play have been brilliantly done. A good deal of the play has been rewritten in alternately rhyming quatrains of four, sometimes five, stresses. Some longer stanzas appear, among them a not unfamiliar combination of the quatrain with the Chester stanza with the rhyme-scheme abaab. The prevailing form, however, is the Chester stanza, and it is significant that the Brome play and the Chester play actually run parallel in language and rhyme for 119 lines, with, however, some slight differences. One wonders how historians of the medieval English drama think those lines from the Chester Abraham and Isaac got into the Brome Abraham and Isaac. These 119 lines are not by any means the only verbal and poetical resemblances between the two plays, for both Chester words and Chester rhymes have been

---

[1] Manly, *Specimens*, loc. cit., pp. 41–57; Waterhouse, loc. cit., pp. xlviii–liv, 36–53; Adams, op. cit., pp. 117–24.

retained in the revision in considerable numbers here and there throughout the Brome play, and the lines that are common to the two plays are the very framework of the story. Without them there is no play.

THE DIGBY PLAYS

Very little seems to be known about the history of Bodleian Digby MS. 133 and almost nothing about the provenance of the plays it contains.[1] We can, however, see that without these plays our ideas of the variety presented by the English mystery plays would be greatly limited. The manuscript contains four plays, as follows: (1) the Conversion of St. Paul, written in one hand (A) throughout, except for an insertion (f. 45) in another hand (B) of a scene between Mercury and Belial. (2) St. Mary Magdalen, written in hand B. (3) the Slaughter of the Innocents and the Purification (called by Furnivall *The Killing of the Children*), written in hand A. (4) A fragment of the morality, *Mind, Will, and Understanding*, which occurs in complete form in the *Macro Morals*. The fragment and the complete morality play are said by Furnivall to be written in the same hand. These plays have various annotations in later hands. Particularly, the first play has written against the prologue of Poeta the name 'Myles Blome-fylde'. The initials 'M.B.' appear also at the beginning of the second play. This Miles Blomefield was a monk of Bury and an alchemist born in 1525.[2] There is no reason to think that he was more than an owner of the manuscript, but his residence suggests an East Midland associa-tion for the manuscript. At the end of the Slaughter of the Innocents and the Purification occurs the plain statement, as yet unexplained, 'Ihon Parfre ded wryte thys Booke'. It is in a later hand. The play is dated in two places 1512. (5) To these four plays in Digby MS. 133 Dr. Furnivall added in his edition of the plays for the New Shakespeare Society another play, the Burial and Resurrection, from Bodleian MS. e Museo 160, f. 140 ff., with the statement that this manuscript once formed a part of Digby MS. 133. Dr. R. W. Hunt, Keeper of Western Manuscripts, Bodleian Library, who was kind

---

[1] *The Digby Mysteries*, loc. cit.

[2] K. Schmidt, Berlin dissertation and *Anglia*, vii (1885), 371 ff. For Miles Blomefield see *D.N.B.*; *Fulgens and Lucres*, ed. F. S. Boas and A. W. Reed, introduction; *The Times Literary Supplement*, 10 Sept., 9 Oct., 5 Nov., 1925.

enough to compare the two manuscripts, could find nothing to support Dr. Furnivall's statement. The manuscripts are not written in the same hand.

These plays were never parts of Corpus Christi cycles or great Passion plays, but are probably, with the exception of St. Mary Magdalen, plays from smaller towns or cities that had been developed slowly *in situ* for long periods, perhaps centuries, since they present ancient and originally liturgical subjects. Secondly, it is to be noted that, with the exception of the Conversion of St. Paul, they are composed of more than one subject and are thus, in an incipient way at least, small cycles. Schmidt assigns them all to the East Midlands and qualifies his statement by saying that the Conversion of St. Paul had a southern scribe; St. Mary Magdalen, a Kentish scribe; and the Slaughter of the Innocents, a southern scribe. The Burial and Resur-rection he regards as a mixture of Northern and East Midland dia-lects. But such definite assignments on the basis of dialect are, for early sixteenth- or late fifteenth-century documents, quite unsure. Besides, the element of ancient descent continually interferes with the identification of these later dialects. It merely seems probable that the Digby plays are of East Midland origin.

1. *The Conversion of St. Paul*

The Feast of the Conversion of St. Paul is celebrated on 25 January and there is a Latin liturgical play on the subject, clearly connected with this feast, in the Fleury Playbook.[1] The Fleury manuscript is dated in the thirteenth century, and this Latin play shows clear signs of having arisen in the normal way from the services of the Feast of the Con-version of St. Paul. It ends with the *Te Deum*, and that circumstance would associate it with Matins. It tells the story faithfully as it is recorded in Acts ix. 1–27 and in the *lectiones* read in the service of the day. This liturgical play is most abundantly provided with stage directions. *Loca* and *sedes* are called for, and the action is divided into scenes according to place. It opens in Jerusalem, where Saul, yet to be called by the name of Paul, is engaged with the aid of his soldiers in persecuting the Christians. He is noisy and boastful. He hears that the Christians have fled to Damascus and obtains authority from the

[1] Young, op. cit. ii. 219–24.

high priest, *Princeps Sacerdotum*, to pursue them to Damascus. A *sedes* is provided for the high priest. On the way to that city he hears the voice from heaven and is stricken down and blinded. He is converted. The next place of action is Damascus, where there is a *locum* for the house of Judas to which St. Paul is taken and a *sedes* for Ananias, whom the Lord now addresses, bidding him visit and succour Paul. Ananias then instructs and baptizes Paul, who begins to preach the Gospel. He meets the high priest and makes known his views. The high priest is offended and seeks Paul's life, but Paul escapes by being let down over the city wall in a basket. He returns to Jerusalem, where he meets Barnabas and is introduced into the company of the Apostles.

This summary of the plot comes from the Fleury play, but it might have come from the late English play we have under consideration, which is, in the serious action, exactly the same as the Latin play. In spite of the lapse of time and of amplification and degeneration, the descent of the English play from the liturgical play is clear. A play of the Conversion of St. Paul was spread over Europe and eventually appeared in this late form in English. It led an independent life and seems never to have been absorbed into any of the great cycles. Plays on the subject in both France and Germany confirm its isolation.

There is even a preservation in the English play of the general *mise en scène* of the original—stations (*loca* or *sedes*) and the use of a *platea* or place in the action. It has been inferred, not perhaps wrongly, that the Conversion of St. Paul belonged to some small town or city, for in the performance the audience moved with the players from one station to another and back again. Consider, for example, these stage directions and indications of action: 'here entryth saule goodly besene in the best wyse lyke an aunterous knyth.' 'Here cummyth sale to caypha and anna, prestes of the tempyll.' Before the comic scene between the Servant and the Stablekeeper: 'here goyth sale forth a lytill a-syde for to make hym redy to ryde.' Then 'Her sale rydyth forth with hys seruantes a-bowt the place. owt of the place.' The audience is urged by Poeta 'to folow and succede with all your dyligens this generall processyon'. Then 'ffinis istius stacionis et altera sequitur'. 'Here commyth saule rydyng in with hys seruantes'—not into a station but into an open place. 'Here commyth a feruent with gret tempest and saule faulyth down of hys horse. that done, godhed spekyth in hevyn.' After that: 'Here the knyghtes lede forth sale in-to a place and cryst apperyth to annanie.' 'Here Ananias goth toward saule.' After Ananias has baptized Saul: 'ffinis istius secunde stacionis et sequitur tarcia.' Poeta speaks of 'thys pagent at thys lytyll stacion'. Caiaphas and Annas confer, and then 'Here to enter a dyvel with thunder and fyre and to avaunce hym selfe sayyng as folowyth and, hys spech spokyn, to syt downe in a chayre.' There follows an extended devil scene. The devils vanish away, and appa-rently at the same station: 'Her apperyth saule in a disciplis wede sayng'. Saul, now Paul, preaches. He goes without change of station to the priests, announces his conversion, and angers them. They shut the gates of the city and plan to destroy Paul. An angel warns him, and he declares he will escape over the walls. Poeta announces that Paul will go to Jerusalem. There seem to be three separate playing-places, and the play is rather primitive in spite of a good deal of pretentious machinery in the form of prologues and comic scenes. The audience moves through a town or city in a sort of procession, a circumstance which suggests that in this play are still retained the features of the very earliest processional drama.

We must not overpraise the Digby Conversion of St. Paul. As an open-air spectacle, with St. Paul dressed like an 'aunterous' knight and on horseback and with crowds moving behind him from station to station, it must have been gay enough, but the play is degenerate in the worst fifteenth-century way. The language is verbose and pompous to the point of unintelligibility. Now and then in the action there are echoes of an earlier and better form of expression, but, in spite of its preservation of the theme of its original, it is as a religious play vastly inferior.

2. The Slaughter of the Innocents and the Purification—'The Killing of the Children'

This, the second play in the Digby manuscript, was briefly dis-cussed in connexion with the Lincoln plays. It was there pointed out that the Slaughter of the Innocents and the Purification form together one section of a St. Anne's day play, a cycle of considerable extent having originally to do with the birth and earlier life of the

Blessed Virgin Mary, but in this case so expanded as to include the whole body of the Nativity plays. A note in a hand identified as John Stow's[1] says 'the vij booke', a probably correct indication of the number of parts into which the Blessed Virgin Mary–Nativity was divided for annual presentation. This is probably the penultimate performance in the series, and one may conclude that it required eight years to play the entire cycle.

In his opening speech Poeta, after declaring that the play is in honour of the Blessed St. Anne, mother to our Lady, says:

> The last yeer we shewid you in this place
> How the shepherdes of Cristes birthe made letification,
> And thre kynges that come fro ther Cuntrees be grace
> To worshipe Iesu, with enteer deuocion;
> And now we purpose with hooll Affeccion
> To procede in oure mater as we can,
> And to shew you of our ladies purificacion
> That she made in the temple, as the vsage was than.

And also the story of how Herod had killed the children. In the epilogue Poeta says,

> And the next yeer, as we purposid in our mynde,
> The disputacion of the doctours to shew in your presens.

Like the Conversion of St. Paul this play is late and has degenerate features. There is a dance of 'virgines' at the end, Herod is a roaring boaster, and he is provided with a comical knight Watkyn, who is beaten in battle by the mothers of the slaughtered infants, although they are armed only with distaffs. This character and episode rank with the Towneley *Secunda Pastorum* as a limit of secularity and show the introduction of farce into a mystery play. The double play of the Slaughter of the Innocents and the Purification is written for the most part in cumbersome double quatrains often with five accents to the line. The simpler and more ancient parts of the play are, however, in neater double quatrains of four stresses to the line. The situation is not unlike that of the *Weavers' Pageant of Coventry*, in which a long-lined late metre has intruded upon a rather better earlier metre with the same rhyme-scheme. If these St. Anne's day plays were written and

---

[1] Op. cit. ii. 430–1.

partly compiled in the fifteenth century, as seems probable, they were later revised in a worse metrical style of greater pomposity. There are almost no indications of the way the play was staged, but there seems to be no reason to think that the stage could have been other than a multiple stage with various assigned *loca*. The scene shifts from Jerusalem to Bethlehem, and then we have this stage direction: 'Here mary and Ioseph shall go out of the place and the goddes shall falle and then shall come in the women of Israel with yong children in ther armys and than the knyghtes shall go to them sayng as foluyth.' Note also this stage direction: 'here shal Symeon bere Iesu in his armys goyng a procession rounde aboute the tempill.' At other places Mary and Joseph go 'toward the temple' and 'from the tempill'. It therefore seems clear that there was a playing-place, a temple, and probably other *loca*.

3. *St. Mary Magdalen*

The Digby play of St. Mary Magdalen follows in general the legend of St. Mary Magdalen as we have it in the *Golden Legend*, and yet it would be wrong to say that the *Golden Legend* is its original source. That source is a liturgical play dealing with Mary Magdalen and principally with the Raising of Lazarus as it appears in the Fleury Playbook[1] and the Benediktbeuern Passion play.[2] The *Lazarus* of Hilarius treats only the Raising of Lazarus and is not therefore in the full line of the succession.[3] The Lazarus from the Fleury Playbook and the Benediktbeuern *Ludus de Passione* combine the story of the repentance and salvation of Mary Magdalen with the story of the resuscitation of Lazarus whom tradition represented as her brother. Although the story of Mary Magdalen is the smaller part of these Lazarus plays, it outgrew because of its sensational quality the story of Lazarus. These Latin plays form the basis of the story of Mary— her seduction, her life as a prostitute, and her forgiveness by Jesus. One would say that in order to achieve a form such as that of the English play the simple, more biblical play was immersed in the long romantic legend that had grown up around St. Mary Magdalen's name—how she was the daughter of Cyrus, a great king, how the devils conspired

---

[1] Young, op. cit. ii. 199–211.   [2] Ibid. i. 518–36.
[3] Ibid. ii. 211–19.

against her and brought about her seduction, and how, after the events of the liturgical plays, she wrought miracles, converted the king and queen of Marseilles, was fed in the wilderness by angels, and, dying, ascended into heaven. Strangely enough, the original of the English play of St. Mary Magdalen is obvious from the style and metre of the play. The romantic parts from the *Golden Legend* are in pretentious language and usually in the awkward double quatrains common to many of the later mystery plays; whereas the older traditional parts are in quite simple quatrains or eights, of usually four stresses to the line. Such parts are the scene of Mary and Martha in the house of Simon the Leper, and the Raising of Lazarus as recorded in the New Testament; also the scenes of the *Quem quaeritis* and the *Hortulanus*, for these two episodes were apparently parts of the original simple play. The long sensational play has at its centre simple verna-cular forms of certain ancient liturgical plays.

There is among the English mystery plays no play of more extensive development, both in contents and staging, than that of St. Mary Magdalen, and it is indeed a wonder to observe what amplification and redaction have done to these simple beginnings. Dr. Furnivall in his edition of St. Mary Magdalen for the New Shakespeare Society has divided the play into two parts to correspond with the action, but there is really no ground for such a division. The play is continuous in action, a most varied and improbable story, and is one of the best examples of a play played on a stationary stage. This stage was apparently round, like that of *The Castle of Perseverance*, with spectators viewing it from all sides.[1] Within the enclosure were a large number of *loca* or *sedes*. They include the Castle of Magdalen, thrones for the Imperator (Tiberius Caesar), Herod, and Pilate, a stage for the prince of devils with Hell beneath it, Jerusalem, an arbour, a tavern, the house of Simon the Leper, a sepulchre for Lazarus and the *sepulchrum* of Jesus used in the *Quem quaeritis* and the *Hortulanus*, a palace for the king of Marseilles, a heathen temple, a heaven that could open, a lodge for Mary Magdalen in Marseilles, another castle, a rock, and a wilderness. There is also an actual ship plying to and from Marseilles and passing in and out of the 'place'. All in all, it is the most elaborate of all known medieval stages in England. Because

---

[1] See Adams, op. cit., p. 225 n.

of the length and costliness of the play one would think that it must have belonged to a city of some size.

In the characters there is a corresponding variety. There is Cyrus, father to Mary Magdalen, Martha, and Lazarus; the World, the Flesh, and the Devil with other devils; Lechery and a Gallant, who seduces Mary Magdalen; Martha and Lazarus; Jesus; the king of Marseilles, who is a boaster; a Priest and a priest's Boy, who performs a mock Mass; a Fisherman, with a Boy named Grobbe. The Fisherman sings a song.

Not less striking is the sensational and widely extended course of the action. The Imperator is Tiberius, who calls for silence in the prologue and is in league with Herod and Pilate. Cyrus blesses his three children (Mary, Martha, and Lazarus) and dies. The devils hold a council, as a result of which Lechery and a Gallant corrupt Mary Magdalen. She awaits her lover in an arbour, where a Good Angel speaks to her. She goes to the house of Simon, anoints the feet of Jesus and dries them with her hair. She is forgiven by Jesus, and eight devils are beaten for letting her escape. Then comes the resuscitation of Lazarus. At this point the king and queen of Marseilles are merely introduced. Jesus gives an account of how he has harrowed Hell, and this is followed by a *Quem quaeritis* and a *Hortulanus*. Thenceforth the scene is divided between Marseilles with its heathen temple and Jerusalem, and in the parts played in the latter place there is a good deal of very puzzling matter, probably old, connected vaguely with the death of Christ. In it Pilate and Herod are speakers. There is even a suggestion of an Ascension. After this the scene turns finally to Marseilles and follows the events of the *Golden Legend*. Mary Magdalen with divine assistance converts the king and queen of Marseilles. They go in the ship to Jerusalem, so that St. Peter may baptize them. Mary goes into the wilderness where she is fed by angels. She is visited by Jesus, dies in blessedness, and there is rejoicing in heaven. It is to be noted that the play is marked at the end as an original, which may mean that it was the formal copy of a play belonging to a city or guild.

BURIAL AND RESURRECTION

Plays of the Resurrection proper almost certainly continued to be played in Great Britain, France, and Germany as separate dramas throughout the period of the mystery plays. No doubt they always combined a considerable group of the scenes associated with the central event of Christ's rising, and were not always united with plays of the Passion and certainly not combined with great cycles. Such plays are referred to in the records at Bath (1482), Leicester (1504–7), Morebath (1520–74), Reading (1507, 1533–5), and Kingston (1513–65). Chambers[1] expresses the opinion that we cannot be sure in these cases that the Resurrection was not played in connexion with the Passion, and some of them, if more information becomes available, may turn out to have been so combined. The joining of these subjects was customary, but, when they were united, they usually took the name of the Passion, which was the more commanding subject. The fact of the existence of the Bodleian Burial and Resurrection indicates that there were Resurrection plays entirely independent of the Passion.

To be sure, this play is not in the popular tradition, but a sort of literary exercise. Yet it was intended to be played at Easter. A note preceding the prologue[2] makes the intention of the writer clear: 'This play is to be playede on part on gudfriday after-none, & þe other part opon Esterday after the resurrectione. In the morowe, but at be-gynnynge ar certene lynes which [must] not be saide if it be plaiede, which . . . .' Before the prologue is the statement: 'The prologe of this treyte or meditatione off the buryalle of Criste & mowrnynge therat.' At a number of places in the play[3] the text reads like a narrative and not like a drama, and yet the Burial and Resurrection is made up throughout of traditional matter in traditional form. The first part, intended to be enacted on Good Friday, begins with an elaborate *planctus* of the Three Marys and Joseph of Arimathea, more elaborate than anything else of the sort to be found in the English mystery plays. After that Nicodemus arrives, and the body of Christ is taken down from the cross. There is then another extended *planctus* of Mary, the mother of Jesus, and the body is then laid away in the tomb supplied by Joseph of Arimathea.

The second part, intended to be enacted on Easter morning, is a *Quem quaeritis*, with, however, considerable amplification. The Marys

---

[1] Op. cit. ii. 129.   [2] *The Digby Mysteries*, loc. cit., p. 171.
[3] Ibid., p. xii; Chambers, op. cit. ii. 432.

visit the sepulchre, there is a lamentation of the disciple Peter with consolation by Andrew and John, a *Hortulanus*, and a second appear-ance of Christ to the Marys in which He tells them again that He has released the patriarchs from Hell.

There is no comicality in the play, and the extremely religious quality of the Burial and Resurrection suggests that it is a late rewriting of a play of the Resurrection that had been developed within a church and never subjected to secularity. The stage directions are in Latin, and the *mise en scène* is such as would have been furnished by the interior of a church—the cross, the tomb, the garden. There is some use of church music within the play, and at the end there is an accu-mulation of the ancient antiphons, responses, and hymns that accom-panied the earliest forms of the Resurrection drama. They include *Victimae paschali laudes, Dic nobis, Maria, quid vidisti in via, Credendum est magis soli Mariae veraci quam Iudaeorum turbae fallaci, Scimus Christum surrexisse,* and *Tu nobis, victor rex, miserere.*

Neither metre nor language is elaborate in the Burial and Resurrec-tion, which is pious and modest in tone. The action is recorded mainly in a simple, ancient metre, *rime couée*, aabccb. This gives way in places to the eight-line ballad stanza employed in the Chester plays, aaab-aaab or aaabcccb. If the play were a recent composition, a literary exercise, a mere meditation, it would hardly have employed these ancient metres or stuck so closely to the ancient traditional events. The lamentations, of which there are many, tend to appear in double quatrains, ababbcbc, and the number of accents to the line varies usually according to pattern from three to five. In general the metres are not late, and there is little of that breaking down of the line that characterizes late mystery plays, particularly in homiletic parts. The metres of the traditional parts are simple and early, the greatest ampli-fication being the extended *planctus* or complaints. The play shows none of that forgetfulness of religious purpose that appears so fre-quently in the mystery plays of the fifteenth and sixteenth centuries. Indeed, in its own reverent piety it is very fine.

IX

Miracles and Moralities

MIRACLE PLAYS

AS a means of convenient distinction we have been using the word 'mystery' to designate that group of religious plays of the Middle Ages that are based ultimately on Scripture and arose from the services in the *cursus* of the liturgical year and the word 'miracle' to denote those that treat of the lives and martyrdoms of the saints. In our study of the St. Nicholas plays, the only Latin saints' plays that have been preserved, we concluded that these plays originated from the liturgy as additions to the church services rather than as the inventions of dramatists for dramatic purposes. Mystery plays and miracle plays thus originated in exactly the same way and were results of exactly the same artistic religious impulse. The lives and experiences of the saints were, in the church services and in the thoughts of the medieval church, of equal sanctity with the lives and experiences of patriarchs, prophets, and disciples, and there was originally no distinction between the liturgical plays of St. Nicholas and those of St. Thomas and St. Paul. The distinctions are matters of later growth, if, indeed, in the Middle Ages they were ever definitely made. By their position in the services of the year saints' plays were isolated and by their nature much more individual and varied, so that there were fewer inducements to combine them into cycles and parts of cycles.[1] It is a pity that we have left only liturgical plays dealing with St. Nicholas, for we may be sure there were other liturgical plays, now lost, based on the lives of other saints. For example, there

---

[1] On miracle plays see Karl Young, *The Drama of the Medieval Church*, loc. cit. ii. 307–60, and 'Concerning the Origin of the Miracle Play', *Manly Anniversary Studies* (Chicago, 1923), pp. 264–8; Chambers, op. cit. ii. 97, 123, 427, *et passim*; Creizenach, op. cit. i. 105–7, 233 ff., 259 ff., *et passim*; Petit de Julleville, *Les Mystères*, loc. cit. i. 95–106, ii. 221–350, 466–564, *et passim*; Adams, op. cit., pp. 51–69, 243–62; G. R. Coffman, *A New Theory of the Origin of the Miracle Play* (Chicago, 1914); 'The Miracle Play in England', *Studies in Philology*, xvi (1919), 56–66, and various articles in learned journals; J. M. Manly, 'The Miracle Play in England', *R.S.L.*, ser. 3, vol. vii (1927), 133–53.

is the record of a play of St. Catherine performed at Dunstable in Bedfordshire at the end of the eleventh or the beginning of the twelfth century, with a very pretty story attached to it.[1] Geoffrey, a Norman, was at Dunstable expecting to be employed as a teacher in the school. He there, as we say, produced a miracle play of St. Catherine. In providing costumes for his players he borrowed certain copes from the sacristan of St. Alban's Abbey. These copes were unfortunately burned while in Geoffrey's possession, and he was so smitten in his conscience that he became a monk and by 1119 had become abbot of St. Alban's. This was a miracle play of very early date and was, of course, in Latin. It is not as if it were an isolated occurrence, since there were many later St. Catherine plays in Great Britain and on the Continent. There was an early play of St. Martial at Limoges in 1290 and in 1302 by the 'bourgeois de Cahors, dans le cimetière Saint-Martial, près de la croix de pierre dudit cimetière', and an early play of St. Catherine at Lille (1351). The miracle of Théophile appears at Aunai (Eure-et-Loire) as early as 1384.[2] There is also a fragment of the popular play of St. Dorothea dated in 1340,[3] and we know from the life of St. Thomas Becket by William Fitzstephen (*fl.* 1170–82) that miracles of holy confessors were customarily performed in London in the twelfth century: *Londonia pro spectaculis theatricalibus, pro ludis scenicis, ludos habet sanctiores, representationes miraculorum quae sancti confessores operati sunt, seu representationes passionum quibus claruit constantia martyrum.*[4]

The greatest development of miracle plays was, of course, in France, and there are preserved two early vernacular plays that seem to be of fundamental importance in the growth of the form. There is *Le jeu de Saint Nicolas* by Jean Bodel of Arras in Artois, author of *La Chanson des Saisnes*. It is dated in the thirteenth century and is a spirited performance. Bodel did not, of course, invent this play, which is an amplified version of *Iconia Sancti Nicolai* that had already

---

[1] Chambers, op. cit. ii. 266; Matthew Paris, *Gesta Abbatorum S. Albani*, ed. H. T. Riley, Rolls Series, i. 73.

[2] Julleville, *Les Mystères*, loc. cit. ii. 2–6; Frank, *The Medieval French Drama*, loc. cit., pp. 106–12.

[3] Creizenach, op. cit. i. 128–30; ed. H. Schachner, loc. cit., xxxv, pp. 157–96.

[4] Chambers, op. cit. ii. 379–80; J. C. Robertson, *Materials for the History of Becket*, Rolls Series, iii. 9.

appeared in the twelfth-century version attributed to Hilarius[1] and in the famous Fleury Playbook of the thirteenth century.[2] As we shall see, records of St. Nicholas plays in England are not numerous, but a general notoriety for this particular St. Nicholas play is suggested in Hamlet's warning to the Players against 'o'er-doing Termagant'.[3] The pagan who had left his goods in charge of his idol only to have them carried away by thieves and has had them restored to him by St. Nicholas beats the idol, and an actor concealed within it makes a great outcry.

There is also *Le Miracle de Théophile* by a Rutebeuf about whom little is known. The play comes from Paris and is dated between 1255 and 1280.[4] This drama is important because it may have established the pattern for the very numerous *miracles de Notre Dame*. Théophile was an unfortunate priest who, threatened with the loss of his ecclesiastical charge and the consequent disgrace, pledges his soul to the Devil in return for the fiend's assistance. After seven years he repents of his bargain and through the intercession of the Blessed Virgin Mary escapes the clutches of Satan and achieves salvation. Théophile is not a sceptic like Johannes Faustus but is in great trouble and sincere in his desire to escape disgrace. It is interesting, however, to observe that Théophile operates by the help of a magician who has power over Satan. There is characteristically also a bishop who aids Théophile in obtaining absolution. The play, which is 666 lines long, is vivacious in its presentation of the story in such matters as the despair of Théophile, his lifting up his eyes to the image of the Virgin, and Satan's discouragement at the loss of his victim. The play also shows a feature characteristic of miracle plays in its undramatic protraction of the play after the main action is over, since Théophile's penance and his public confession are carefully provided for. One cannot of course say that *Le Miracle de Théophile* is the earliest miracle play of the Blessed Virgin Mary, but it certainly furnishes the pattern that was followed with such extraordinary activity in the fourteenth

---

[1] Bibl. Nat. MS. lat. 11331, *Hilari Versus et Ludi*; Young, op. cit. ii. 337–43.

[2] Orléans, Bibl. de la Ville, MS. 201; Young, op. cit. ii. 343–57; Jean Bodel, *Le Jeu de St. Nicolas*, ed. F. J. Warne (Oxford, 1951); introduction, notes, and bibliography.

[3] *Hamlet*, III. ii. 15.

[4] Julleville, *Les Mystères*, loc. cit. i. 95–114; Traduction nouvelle avec notes par A. Jeanroy (Paris, 1932); *Le Miracle de Théophile*, édité par Grace Frank (Paris, 1925).

century in France. The famous fourteenth-century manuscript in the
Bibliothèque Nationale contains forty miracles of the Blessed Virgin
Mary.[1] It is very mixed in contents and draws from a wide range of
subjects. A few of them (such as the Nativity of Jesus) are biblical,
some (such as *Berthe et Pepin* and Robert the Devil) are from the
romances, many are legendary, and there is a large number of
ordinary *fabliaux* made over into Marian miracles. There were other
miracles of the same general sort in France in the fourteenth and
fifteenth centuries,[2] and there is a grand body of thirty-five or forty plays
about individual saints, not, however, gathered into a cycle, but
widely dispersed.[3] French production of miracle plays was perhaps
a dozen times greater than that of any other country, but there were
considerable numbers elsewhere.

Miracle plays of course became very numerous in the whole area
and in Britain, and there entered into them a variety in the choice of
subjects unknown to the mystery plays, which were by tradition and
perhaps by regulation held to a list of biblical subjects extensive, to be
sure, but varying from place to place, mainly in minor features. Some
saints' plays were undoubtedly old and were liturgical in origin, but,
when the pattern had established itself, there was a freer choice of
dramatic subjects, many under local influence, and the great period
of expansion was no doubt in the vernacular and covered a
long period of time. An extended study of miracle plays, both
English and continental, might result in a discrimination between
early, vernacular, and possibly liturgical subjects, on the one hand,
and, on the other, later plays, the subjects of which were more freely
chosen. Many miracle plays show evidence of revision, and such
evidence may also be a clue to age. The subject is complicated, but
not hopeless. There are so few remains of the miracle play in English
that a proper understanding of the origin and growth, with their varying phases, of the miracle play is a matter that belongs to the field of
continental literature. On the basis of English plays and references to
plays one would be disposed to think that in England the fifteenth

---

[1] Bibl. Nat. 819 and 820, 2 v., *Miracles de Nostre Dame par personnages*; Julleville, *Les Mystères*,
loc. cit. ii. 226–36; *Miracles de Nostre Dame par personnages*, publiés par Gaston Paris et
Ulysse Robert. Société des Anciens Textes (Paris, 1876–).

[2] Julleville, *Les Mystères*, loc. cit. ii. 335–50.

[3] Ibid. 466–568.

century was the period of the greatest exploitation of the miracle play, but such plays must always have been sparse and primitive compared to those that were acted in France.

The late Professor J. M. Manly,[1] observing the wider range and variety of subjects in miracle plays than in mystery plays, made a suggestive inference as to the miracle play as a preparation for the growth and development of the English romantic drama of the sixteenth century. He takes as examples the saints' plays mentioned in the churchwarden's meagre accounts from St. Michael's Church in Braintree, Essex. There were plays of St. Swithin (1523), St. Andrew (1525), and Placidas *alias* St. Eustace (1534) acted there, and Manly shows what a wealth of human material the legends of these saints contain—adventure, danger, sentiment, pathos, and character. Such qualities in their variety, he says, were common to miracle plays and to medieval legends. They also reappear in essence in Tudor drama.

We have seen how in the case of the Digby play of St. Mary Magdalen a vast body of matter from the *Golden Legend* itself has been made to envelop a simple and ancient mystery play made up of the liturgical themes of the Conversion of St. Mary Magdalen, the Raising of Lazarus, the *Quem quaeritis*, and the *Hortulanus*, so that the Digby St. Mary Magdalen is only quantitatively and revisionally, not originally, a miracle play. Indeed, the only complete and typical miracle play preserved in English is the *Play of the Sacrament*. It is found in Trinity College, Dublin, MS. F. 4. 20, and is dated in the latter half of the fifteenth century.[2] A set of banns spoken by two *vexillatores* tells the story and ends as follows:

> And that place yow, thys gadering þat here ys,
> At Croxston on Monday yt shall be sen;
> To see the conclusyon of þis lytell processe
> Herteley welcum shall yow bene.

The name Croxton appears in many places in the Midlands and the East Midlands, so that no particular Croxton has been identified.

---

[1] 'The Miracle Play in England', loc. cit.
[2] Waterhouse, op. cit., pp. liv–lxiv, 54–87; Manly, *Specimens*, loc. cit. i. 242–76; Adams, op. cit., pp. 243–62.

Another local allusion to 'Tolcote' and 'Babwelle Mylle' points to the vicinity of Bury St. Edmunds in Suffolk.[1]

The play tells the story of how Jonathas, Jewish merchant, gets possession of the Host, persecutes it, and endeavours in vain to destroy it. He puts it into a cauldron and an oven, and, as he proceeds, his hand is withered. Christ appears in a vision and speaks to Jonathas, who repents his wickedness. He puts his hand into the cauldron again, and it is made whole. He goes then to a bishop and is baptized. This tale, a specimen of medieval anti-Semitism, is widely distributed over Europe and was no doubt perennial in its recurrence. It appears in the *Croniche* of Villani in 1290, and we are told at the end of the English play, 'Thus endyth the Play of the Blyssyd Sacrament, whyche myracle was don in the forest of Aragon, in the famous cite of Eraclea, the yere of ower Lord God M'cccc.lxi, to whom be honower. Amen!' This at least tells us that the colophon cannot have been written before 1461, although the manuscript is perhaps later than that. A closely related version forms the subject of a French miracle play, *La Sainte Hostie*, printed twice in the sixteenth century without date.[2] The French play is 1590 lines long and has twenty-six characters. The story was a Parisian miracle and was well attested as genuine, although of course an old theme. It seems to be the same version as the English Sacrament play, but has different details and ends much more severely. A poor woman has pawned her cloak to a Jew. Before the feast of the Passover she begs him to return the cloak, which she needs because of the cold. The Jew agrees to do so on condition she will bring him the consecrated wafer she has received at Mass. She does this, and the Jew proceeds to persecute the Host. He carries through the same series of tortures as in the English play. The Jew's wife and children beg him to desist, and his daughter tells a Christian woman what is going on, who in turn tells the priest. Officers come, and the Jew is arrested, tried, and burnt at the stake. His family turn Christian and are saved. This is the proper end of the story, but the play with the tiresome technique of the miracles goes on with the story of the poor woman who had

---

[1] Cited by Whitley Stokes, who edited the play for the *Transactions of the Philological Society* (1860–1), Appendix.

[2] Julleville, *Les Mystères*, loc. cit. ii. 574–6.

given the Jew the wafer. She becomes a servant at a hostelry at Senlis, where she has an illegitimate child which she murders. Her crime is discovered, she confesses and is put to death.

The English play of Jonathas the Jew is clearly composed in double quatrains of four stresses linked together by rhyme, ababbcbc. The linking, however, is not uniformly carried out, so that a good many quatrains stand by themselves; it rarely joins speeches by two different speakers or bridges stage directions. In longer speeches it is used with fair consistency, and in some cases three quatrains are thus joined together. There can be no doubt that this is the original metre of the play. There is, however, some original use of a longer, more pompous stanza, heavily alliterated, a thing to be expected for the speeches of bombastic characters. This appears in the opening speech of Aristorius, the Christian merchant, and in other parts of the play where assumed importance is to be represented. But the main plot of the play, in spite of possible incon-sistency in the use of independent quatrains and a tendency to ponderousness, may be considered as composed in double quatrains linked by rhyme, with, however, some use of separate quatrains. This is important in analysing the play, since it marks out very clearly certain additions and revisions. These can usually be identi-fied by the appearance of the familiar ballad stanza aaabcccb or some approximation to it. It is a fair supposition that, when the original play was written, probably not before 1461, it was an awkward, but normal and consistent, piece of fifteenth-century play-writing. It will be observed that the banns, which are written throughout (with one exception) in linked double quatrains, tell the original tale and make no mention of the folk-play subject of the doctor and his boy. The banns were evidently written to introduce and summarize an original miracle play of serious import. That the episode of the quack doctor is an addition to the original play is evident from the fact that it appears in the ballad stanza and in a livelier style than the rest of the play.[1] This addition has appropriately or traditionally a comic proclamation written in rhymed tumbling measure of four accents, the rest of the episode being in the ballad stanza. This excrescence is indeed a tiny folk play inserted in the main story. It accomplishes

[1] See lines 445–572.

nothing, and at the end the doctor and his boy are beaten away by the four Jews. The allusions to 'Tolcote' and 'Babwelle Mylle' occur in the proclamation of the doctor's boy, a thing that may pertain to the location of the folk play rather than the miracle. The ballad metre, however, appears in other places, where it serves to amplify an older text. As originally written the Play of the Sacrament was no doubt bad enough, but it was serious and had the gentle features of admitting the Jews to salvation and of showing mercy on proper penitence to the rich merchant who had basely sold the Host to Jonathas and whose case was much less excusable than that of the poor French woman who had pawned her cloak.

One dramatic fragment remains to be considered because it presents a perplexity. There is in the Bodleian Library[1] the part of a single actor in what may be a lost miracle play. The name of the character speaking is Dux Moraud. The word 'Moraud' has been associated without any satisfactory ground with *Maraude*, meaning 'vagabond' or 'pillager'. Otherwise there is no interpretation of the name. In the beginning of the part Dux Moraud in a conventionally boastful speech bids an audience refrain from any 'yangelynges' and assures his auditors that he will 'Schewe resounes here to youre pay'. These speeches give full assurance that we have to do with an acted play. There are no stage directions and nothing to guide one but inferences from Dux Moraud's speeches. The manuscript has been learnedly edited by W. Heuser.[2] It is a narrow parchment roll, 4 feet 2 inches long by about 4 inches wide, and thought by Madan to have been written in the fourteenth century. This narrow strip has been cut from the margin of an assize roll, or document containing the record of periodical sessions of superior courts in the counties of Norfolk and Suffolk. This roll is dated in the thirteenth century, and one gets from it only the suggestion that the court document was mutilated and the strip used for a player's part in one of those counties. There is nothing in the language of the fragment to contradict this supposition. The speeches are written in *rime couée* with some longer stanzas of longer lines in the boastful speeches of Dux Moraud.

---

[1] F. F. Madan's *Catalogue of Additional Manuscripts*, No. 30519.

[2] 'Dux Moraud, Einzelrolle aus einem verlorenen Drama des 14. Jahrhunderts', *Anglia*, xxx (1907), 180–208.

The play turns out to be a dramatization of the theme of the incestuous daughter, and, through Heuser's industry, it is possible to trace
this theme through a number of versions. It is not the familiar theme
of what might be called the incestuous father,[1] but independent and
of different origin.[2] The most primitive of the versions cited by Heuser
from *Scala coeli*[3] betrays its origin. Jacobus de Vitriaco tells how a
certain young woman who was sinfully involved with her father was
reproached by her mother, whom she killed, and, when the crime
was known to her father and he rejected her on that account, she
killed him while he slept, then became a prostitute. This is merely the
record of a sordid crime. This conception appears in amplified form
in *Gesta Romanorum*, where it is entitled 'Of a repentant harlot'.[4] The
tale is completely secular, but in other versions it has taken on a
religious colouring. In one of these in Herolt's *Promptuarium Exem-
plorum*, MXX, the daughter, fearing exposure, poisoned her mother
and, being rejected by the father, poisoned him. In the midst of her
desperation she heard a sermon on salvation from sin by divine
mercy; whereupon she repented, confessed, was baptized, and saved.
This, it will be noted, puts stress on the salvation of the daughter.
Another version of thirteenth-century origin from Thomas Canti-
pratanus is the story of confession, but is too vague for one to be
certain that it is the story of the incestuous daughter. In it, however,
the father's salvation is the only issue. A far more highly developed
form of the story is printed by Heuser from Rawlinson MS. 118 and
is actually the same story as that of *Dux Moraud*.[5] In this the daughter
is the main figure. She is tempted by the Devil, wins her father's love,
and bears him three children, all of whom she destroys. The mother
discovers the crime and leaves them, but is pursued by the daughter
and murdered. The father goes to Holy Church, repents and confesses.
He is assoiled of his sins and agrees to go on pilgrimage to the Holy
Land. He returns to the daughter and rejects her love. She reproaches

---

[1] Julius Zupitza in *Sitzungen der Berliner Gesellschaft*; *Archiv für das Studium der neueren Sprachen und Literaturen*, lxxxii (1889), 204; C. H. Hartshorne, *Ancient Metrical Tales* (London, 1829).

[2] This form appears in *Sir Degaré, Emaré*, and in *Les Mystères de Notre Dame*, No. 29, *La Fille du Roi du Hongrie*.

[3] F. 48ʳ; Hugo Gering, *Isländische Legenden* (Halle, 1882-4), ii. 395.

[4] Ed. S. J. H. Herrtage, E.E.T.S., Extra Series, xxxiii (1879), No. 72.

[5] With variants from Cambridge MS. Ff. v. 48.

him for the sins he has caused her to commit and at night she cuts his throat.

In the preserved speeches of *Dux Moraud* the father, after a conventionally boastful utterance, addresses his wife affectionately and bids her farewell, hoping she will soon return, and professes piety. He next seduces the daughter. His wife returns and discovers the sin. Dux Moraud fears she will betray them and encourages the daughter to slay her mother, which she does. The daughter has a child, and the father encourages her to slay it. He then rejoices in his sin and boasts loudly in long lines. Then the church bell rings. He goes to church and returns penitent, sends for the priest, confesses his sins, receives absolution, and tells the daughter he has renounced sin and worldly wealth and will travel on account of his wicked fame. The daughter evidently kills him, for, as he dies, he asks forgiveness for her 'for the trespass that thou hast done me', and prays that she may repent. There is no indication as to whether or not the daughter was saved, but, since the subject was brought up in a miracle play, the probabilities are that she was. Prayer for conversion would presuppose conversion, and such plays attended carefully to all details. In spite of the judgement passed on the age of the manuscript one would think that this play belonged to the fifteenth rather than the fourteenth century. *Dux Moraud* is almost certainly the fragment of a miracle play, but with some reservations. There is no mention of any saint or of the Blessed Virgin Mary, but it belongs to a play of conversion from sin to salvation quite like some French miracle plays in its style and its *mores*.

A very great doubt as to whether or not we have to do with a fragmentary miracle play attaches itself to the *Interludium de Clerico et Puella*.[1] We have only the beginning of the piece, but the entire story is made clear by a closely related version in the poem *Dame Siriz*, which is later and seems to be based on the so-called play or, more probably, on a version of it.[2] The story of the 'Weeping Bitch' to

---

[1] See *Reliquiae Antiquae*, ed. T. Wright and J. O. Halliwell (2 v. London, 1841, 1843), i. 145–7; Chambers, op. cit. ii. 324–6; W. Heuser, 'Das Interludium de Clerico et Puella und das Fabliau von Dame Siriz', *Anglia*, xxx (1907), 306–19. Heuser announced the rediscovery of the manuscript in British Museum Add. MS. 23986.

[2] *Anecdota Literaria*, ed. T. Wright (London, 1844), 1 ff.; Maetzner, *Altenglische Sprachproben* (Berlin, 1867), i. 103 ff.; J. Zupitza, *Alt- und Mittelenglisches Übungsbuch*

which these poems are devoted offers most unpromising material out of which to construct a miracle play, and, granting the ingenuity of the writers of miracle plays in transforming preposterous subjects into examples of heavenly grace, one is prevented from entertaining the idea that such a thing was done in the lost part of the *Interludium de Clerico et Puella*. *Dame Siriz* is later than the *Interludium* and, as said above, based on it or another form of it. The two pieces are quite alike in form and content, and, although *Dame Siriz* has been amplified in *rime couée*, the original couplets of the *Interludium* still appear, not only in the earlier parts where the versions can be compared, but farther on in *Dame Siriz* where these couplets, and not *rime couée*, carry the main features of the story to the end. Critics have been misled by the use of the word 'interludium', which meant merely an entertainment of any sort intruded into the midst of a feast. It had no exclusively dramatic application until the time of J. P. Collier, who used it to designate a body of transitional dramatic writings of the earlier sixteenth century. The *Interludium de Clerico et Puella* is most probably to be regarded as a dialogue or *débat* of more than usual narrative point. The attractive notion that *fabliaux* were dramatized into farces, a thing that would have been natural enough and very pleasant, unfortunately has no clear examples, except possibly *Pierre Pathelin*, to show that it was ever done in the Middle Ages. There were apparently no popular secular plays current in England in the fourteenth century.

Finally, this search for every trace of the miracle play in medieval England may be brought to a close with a mere suggestion. It is that the folk play of St. George may be an infinitely degenerated survival of a medieval miracle play on St. George. The subject of that play, we may infer from a small number of continental examples, was the story as recorded in the *Golden Legend*.[1] A terrible dragon that lived in a swamp had laid waste the country of Libya. A pestilence was spread by its breath; it had to be fed with two sheep a day, and, when the sheep gave out, it was necessary to feed the dragon on

(Leipzig, 1915); G. H. McKnight, *Middle English Humorous Tales* (Boston, 1913), 1 ff.; A. S. Cook, *A Literary Middle English Reader* (Boston, 1915), pp. 141–58.

[1] Creizenach, op. cit. i. 231–2; C. R. Baskervill, 'Mummers' Wooing Plays in England', *Modern Philology*, xxi (1924), 225.

children. They were drawn by lot, and ultimately it fell to the king's daughter. The maiden was elaborately dressed and carried to the swamp. St. George rode by and learned what was about to happen. He pierced the dragon with his lance, placed the maiden's girdle about the dragon's neck, and she led it home like a lamb. The people of the city were converted to Christianity, and the dragon's head was severed from its body. St. George also fought certain heathen warriors vaguely suggestive of Captain Slasher, the Turkish Champion, and the Giant Blunderbore. It must be remembered that St. George was many times wounded, indeed destroyed, and then resuscitated, and this just possibly may have furnished a prototype for the Noble Doctor. There are several allusions to a maiden who has been saved. For example, in the Lutterworth play Prince George says,

> I am Prince George, the champion bold,
> And with my sword I won three crowns of gold;
> I slew the fiery dragon and brought him to the slaughter
> And won the King of Egypt's only daughter.

The matter is of no importance unless it might suggest the end of the vast degeneration that medieval religious plays underwent throughout their later history.

There are various references to St. George plays in Great Britain, and most of these we may certainly take as miracle plays rather than as folk plays. There was such a play at Lydd in Kent in 1455–6;[1] also at New Romney in the same county, where it is recorded that a certain chaplain from New Romney went to Lydd in 1490 to see such a play with the expectation of reproducing it in Lydd.[2] There was a play of St. George in Lanark, Scotland, in 1507,[3] and on 20 July 1511 a play of St. George as a holy martyr was played at Basingbourne in Cambridgeshire.[4] St. George appeared in the procession at Aberdeen in 1531,[5] and there are other references. For example, there is a payment by the council at York for St. George to be

---

[1] Chambers, op. cit. ii. 386; Hist. MSS. Commission, v. 521.
[2] Chambers, ibid.; Coffman, 'The Miracle Play in England', loc. cit., p. 61.
[3] Anna Jean Mill, *Mediaeval Plays in Scotland*, St. Andrews University Publications, No. 24 (Edinburgh, 1927), p. 261.
[4] Coffman, 'The Miracle Play in England', loc. cit., p. 64.
[5] Mill, op. cit., p. 125.

'brought forth and ryde as hath been accustomed'. St. George would hardly have been in these processions if there had not been a St. George play at such places, and Coffman interprets the following York entry of the same date as indicative of such a play: 'to the waites for ryding and playing before St. George and the play.'[1] Even these references are few when one considers the popularity of St. George in England. The figure of St. George, the patron saint of soldiers, was magnificent, with or without the dragon, and his brave resistance before his martyrdom to the many attempts of the tyrant Dacian to destroy him offered, we may be sure, splendid opportunities for dramatic action.

Miracle plays could never have been so numerous in Great Britain as they were in France, and yet the number must have been very great, particularly, if one may judge from extant records, in Scotland. The close intercourse between Scotland and France in the fifteenth century may have led to the introduction of miracle plays into Scotland. There are claims put forward in various places that the lives and martyrdoms of holy saints and confessors were regularly performed. Plays about certain saints were no doubt particularly numerous and the variety also seems to have been great. St. Catherine, as we have seen, was performed at Dunstable in Bedfordshire about the year 1100, and a play of St. Catherine is mentioned in the London Chronicle for the year 1393.[2] St. Catherine with three tormentors appeared in the Corpus Christi procession at Hereford in 1440,[3] and a costume for her was provided for the Corpus Christi procession at Dundee.[4] A play of St. Catherine, miswritten in certain manuscript annals as 'St. Crytyan' or 'St. Christian', seems to have been regularly performed at Coventry in Little Park Street in the fifteenth century.[5] There was also a play of St. Catherine at Edinburgh.[6] A play of St. Catherine was widespread in France[7] and was known in Germany.[8] The story, which records the brave resistance of the virgin to the tyrant Maxentius, her refusal to worship pagan gods, and even

---

[1] Coffman, op. cit., p. 64.
[2] Chambers, op. cit. ii. 380; Coffman, 'The Miracle Play in England', loc. cit., pp. 56–66.
[3] Chambers, op. cit. ii. 369. [4] Mill, op. cit., p. 173.
[5] Craig, op. cit., pp. xix–xxi. [6] Mill, op. cit., p. 225.
[7] Julleville, _Les Mystères_, loc. cit. ii. 181.
[8] Creizenach, op. cit., i. 128–30 _et passim_.

to become the tyrant's wife, was probably popular in schools, since it provided great opportunity for disputation.

A play of St. John the Baptist is recorded three times in Scotland,[1] and the saint was of course extremely popular in England, where the Baptism was a usual subject in the mystery cycles. As to St. Nicholas, his play must have been in wide use in Great Britain, although the references are not numerous. In a Trinity College, Cambridge, manuscript (B. 14. 39) there is a sermon on the anniversary of St. Nicholas that mentions a St. Nicholas play to follow it.[2] St. Nicholas was in the Aberdeen procession in 1531, and there are numerous references to St. Nicholas plays in Scotland.[3] St. Andrew, of course, appears in Scottish records and at Braintree in Essex.[4]

Of miracle plays on less familiar subjects there are recorded a great variety in England and a still greater variety in Scotland. In England we find St. Christiana at Bethersden in Kent (1552), Sts. Feliciana and Sabina at Shrewsbury (1516), St. Clotilda at Windsor (1430), St. Margaret and St. Lucy at St. Margaret's Church, Southwark, St. Mary Magdalen at Thetford Priory, Norfolk (1503-4), and at Oxford (1506), St. Tewdricus at Carnarvon,[5] and plays on St. Thomas Becket at King's Lynn (1385-6) and possibly at some other places.[6] There is also the play of St. Meriasek (Mereadocus) of the early sixteenth century, *The Life of St. Meriasek, Bishop and Confessor* in the Cornish language, at Camborne in Cornwall, one of the few British miracle plays that have been preserved.[7] There is the interesting group from Braintree in Essex—St. Swithin, St. Andrew, and St. Eustace;[8] also the puzzling list from Lincoln about which

---

[1] Mill, op. cit., pp. 173-5.

[2] Carleton Brown, 'An Early Mention of a St. Nicholas Play in England', *Studies in Philology*, xxviii (1931), 594-601.

[3] Mill, op. cit., pp. 313, 314, 315 ff.

[4] Ibid., pp. 173, 311; Chambers, op. cit. ii. 342.

[5] Described by Coffman (op. cit., p. 60) as from a manuscript of Reginald Cholmondeley, entitled *Sanctus Tewdricus sive Pastor bonus, Rex et Martyr*; no date given.

[6] For the foregoing references see Chambers, op. cit. ii. 133, 245, 248, 381, *et passim*; Coffman, 'The Miracle Play in England', loc. cit., pp. 61-63 *et passim*.

[7] Chambers, op. cit. ii. 435-6; Coffman, 'The Miracle Play in England—Nomenclature', *PMLA*, xxxi (1916), 448-65 (see also p. 462); *Beunans Meriasek. The Life of St. Meriasek*, edited with translation and notes by Whitley Stokes (1872).

[8] Chambers, op. cit. ii. 342; Coffman, 'The Miracle Play in England', loc. cit., pp. 133-53; Manly, 'The Miracle Play in England', loc. cit.

more will be said later—St. Lawrence, St. Susanna, St. Clara, and St. James. The almost unaccountable thing is that so far no clear traces have been found in Great Britain of miracle plays of the Blessed Virgin Mary.

THE CREED PLAY OF YORK AND THE PATER NOSTER PLAY

Two plays, both apparently of cyclic proportions and both scantily reported, appear in the York records, the Creed play and the Pater Noster play. The former is elsewhere unknown, but we know that there were Pater Noster plays also at Lincoln and at Beverley. Such information as we have is so interesting that one ardently desires more (and less vague) knowledge, particularly because what we have seems to open a field of expansion and variation in the medieval drama, namely the appearance in England by the application of theological and traditional ideas to the plays of such dramatic groupings as occurred so freely in France. It would not do to say that these were combinations of miracles and moralities, since, although abstractions and concrete events seem to have been mingled together in these two plays, the plays themselves must have been either miracle plays or morality plays.

From the application of the name 'Creed' play we get an idea of the field covered. We know that the play must have had to do with the ancient tradition of the composition of the Apostles' Creed, a tradition that goes back certainly to the fourth century and is generally believed by scholars to be much older than that. The doctrine of this tradition is that on the day of Pentecost the eleven apostles met together and, after choosing Matthias to fill the vacant place of Judas Iscariot, composed the Apostles' Creed. To the creed each apostle contributed one tenet.[1] A pseudo-Augustinian sermon of the sixth century tells us which article of the creed was contributed by each of the twelve apostles: Peter, 'I believe in God, the Father Almighty'; John, 'Maker of heaven and earth'; James, 'And in Jesus Christ, His only-begotten Son, our Lord'; Andrew, 'Who was conceived of the Holy Ghost, born of the Virgin Mary'; Philip, 'Suffered under Pontius Pilate; was crucified, dead and buried'; Thomas, 'He descended into Hell; the third day he rose again from the dead'; Bartholomew,

---

[1] Migne, *P.L.* xxxix. 1034; see also Rufinus, ibid. xxi. 337.

'He ascended into heaven, and sitteth on the right hand of God the Father Almighty'; Matthew, 'From thence he shall come to judge the quick and the dead'; James, son of Alphaeus, 'I believe in the Holy Ghost, the Holy Catholic Church'; Simon Zelotes, 'The communion of saints, the forgiveness of sins'; Jude, 'The resurrection of the body'; Matthias, 'The life everlasting.' The Creed play must then have concerned itself with the twelve apostles and their relation to the Apostles' Creed, but, since the Creed play at York was very long and was acted on at least twelve movable pageants, it cannot have been a mere assembly and consultation. Some structural idea must have divided it into parts.

The records tell us something about the play. In 1408 a guild of Corpus Christi was founded at York, not in order that it might manage the Corpus Christi play, which had long been in charge of the city council and the individual trading companies, but to attend to the procession on Corpus Christi day and no doubt to promote the religious services of that day. In 1446 William Revetor, a chantry priest, member and warden of Corpus Christi guild, bequeathed to the guild the book of the Creed play with books and banners belonging to it and with the stipulation or request that the play be performed through the city every tenth year.[1] And the Creed play was performed about Lammastide every ten years presumably from 1446 onwards. Five performances are recorded. The first of these was in 1483, out of its temporal sequence and put on in honour of King Richard III, who was in York about his second coronation. The last was in 1535, when the Creed play took the place of the Corpus Christi play, although it was not suffered to do so in 1545. The Corpus Christi guild was suppressed in 1547, but the books of the Creed play remained in the possession of the Hospital of St. Thomas. In 1568 the city council, no doubt anxious to have a municipal play of some sort, sought to have the Creed play performed again, and the books were sent to Dean Matthew Hutton of York Minster to be passed upon. The dean in a letter still preserved advised against the performance of the play, saying, 'that is shuld not be plaid, ffor thoghe it was plawsible to yeares agoe, and wold now also of the ignorant sort be well liked, yet

---

[1] *Register of the Gild of Corpus Christi*, ed. R. H. Skaife, Surtees Society (1872), pp. 24, 294.

now in this happie time of the gospell I know the learned will mislike it.' There are no further records of the book of the play.[1]

An inventory (1465) of the guild of Corpus Christi gives some of the details about the Creed play:[2],

> Liber vocatus Originale continens Articulos Fidei Catholicae in lingua anglicana, nuper scriptum appreciatum x^{li}.
> Et alius liber inveteratus de eodem ludo c^s.
> Et alius liber de eodem anglice vocatus Crede Play continens xxij quaternos.

A book of 22 quires or 88 leaves would indicate that the Creed play was of very considerable length. Lucy Toulmin Smith is of the opinion that both the Creed play and the Pater Noster play were played on separate pageants, as was the Corpus Christi play. Presumably there would have been twelve pageants in the Creed play, but there is also the possibility that one episode may have required more than one pageant. The inventory shows also a large number of banners and properties such as would have been customary for the decoration of pageants. Among the properties are:

> Et xij rotulae nuper scriptae cum articulis fidei catholicae, apprec' iijs. iiijd.
> Et una clavis pro sancto Petro cum ij peciis unius tunicae depictae, apprec' xijd.
> Et x diademata pro Xp'o et apostolis cum una larva et aliis novem cheverons, vjs.

Davies suggests that the play fell into twelve scenes, in each of which one of the apostles took a leading part, and Chambers supports this conjecture by reference to a letter of King Henry VIII to the justices of York. The king has taken offence at a riot that took place 'at the acting of a religious interlude of St. Thomas the Apostle on the 23rd of August now last past . . . owing to the seditious conduct of certain papists who took part in preparing for the said interlude'. The king orders the justices to imprison any persons who in 'performing interludes which are founded on any portions of the Old or New Testament' use language tending to a breach of the peace.[3]

On the bases of these all too scanty records one might find a clue to the contents of the Creed play from the legendaries. For example, the *Northern Legendary*[4] begins with the lives of the twelve apostles:

---

[1] See L. T. Smith, op. cit., pp. xvi, xxx; Chambers, op. cit. ii. 404–6. Both accounts rest on Davies, op. cit., pp. 266–9.   [2] Chambers, op. cit. ii. 405.

[3] Chambers, loc. cit., pp. 405–6; *Letters of the Kings of England*, ed. J. O. Halliwell (1846), i. 354; Davies, op. cit., pp. 251–2.

[4] Ed. W. M. Metcalfe, Scottish Text Society (3 v. Edinburgh, 1896).

Andrew (30 Nov.), missionary to Asia Minor, crucified in Greece on an X-shaped cross; Thomas (21 Dec.), missionary to India, martyred at Meliapur, many picturesque events; John (27 Dec.), varied experience, died in old age at Ephesus; Matthias (24 Feb.), martyr, various stories in *Legenda Aurea*; Philip (1 May), martyred at Hieropolis in Phrygia; James the Less (1 May), elaborate story in *Legenda Aurea*; Peter (29 June), missionary at Antioch and at Rome, martyred under Nero; James the Greater (25 July), missionary to Spain, martyred under Herod Agrippa; Bartholomew (24 Aug.), missionary to North India, flayed to death in Armenia, crucified, like St. Peter, head downwards; Matthew (21 Sept.), missionary to Ethiopia, martyr; Jude (28 Oct.), martyred in Persia with St. Simon Zelotes. Even these brief notes from the lives of the apostles in the *Northern Legendary* give some idea of the dramatic possibilities of these themes.

Les Actes des Apôtres, a gigantic French cycle attributed to Simon and Arnoul Greban, although of course merely an extensive amplification, offers little help in determining the original form of the play of the lives of the apostles.[1] There was a probably simpler play on the subject at Aix as early as 1478. The long play does, however, retain certain fundamental features. It begins with the selection of Matthias as the twelfth apostle, follows that with the descent of the Holy Spirit, then takes up the lives and adventures of the apostles one after another. It is filled with extraneous episodes and saturated with a great variety of diablerie. Its vast bulk (61,908 lines) and its incredible amplification make it difficult to do more than trace the lives and martyrdoms of the Twelve Apostles. It is noteworthy that *Les Actes des Apôtres* begins with a Pentecost play, following an Ascension, and contains a Death and Assumption of the Blessed Virgin Mary, circumstances that seem to point to the place in the liturgical year at which the play of the Acts of the Apostles originated. We may reasonably conclude that the Creed play at York was a play of this kind and, if so, infinitely simpler than the French example. It would therefore have been a cyclic miracle play rather than a morality.

Before taking up the subject of the Pater Noster play[2] it is necessary

---

[1] Raymond Lebègue, *Mystère des Actes des Apôtres* (Paris, 1929).

[2] See Chambers, op. cit. ii. 120, 154, 377–9; Leach, op. cit., pp. 206–23 *et passim*; Karl Young, 'The Records of the York Play of the Pater Noster', *Speculum*, vii (1932), 540–6.

to remind ourselves that there has been great confusion in the minds of students of the drama as to the nature of the morality play. This confusion has come about through a vague idea that the presence of allegorical figures in any play makes of it a morality play. This is absurd on the face of it, for nearly all medieval literature has, or is apt to have, in it allegory and allegorical figures. A morality play is a dramatized allegory, and the mere presence of allegorical figures or episodes does not make an essential mystery play or miracle play into a morality. An ancient mistake arising from this confusion has rendered scholarly thought vague on the subject of the origin and nature of the morality play.[1]

Let us begin with the earliest reference to the Pater Noster play at York. Wyclif says in *De Officio Pastorali* (1378)[2] 'herfore freris han tauȝt in Englond the Paternoster in Engliscsh tunge, as men seyen in the playe of Yorke'. This is rendered more intelligible by two other early references: the preamble to the return of the ordinances of the guild of the Lord's Prayer in 1389 states that 'once upon a time, a Play setting forth the goodness of the Lord's Prayer was played in the city of York; in which play all manner of vices and sins were held up to scorn, and the virtues were held up to praise'. Secondly, a *computus* of the guild of the Lord's Prayer for 1399[3] contains the settlement of a debt owed by one John Downom and his wife for their entrance fee to the guild: *Sed dictus Iohannes dicit se expendisse in diversis expensis circa ludum Accidie ex parte Ric. Walker ijs. jd. ideo de praedicto petit allocari.* The request was apparently granted and the debt was cancelled. The word *Accidia* means Sloth, one of the Seven Deadly Sins, and it is plain that one part of the Pater Noster play dealt with the subject of sloth and was called by its Latin name. Also why the whole play is called a Pater Noster play becomes plain, since an ancient tradition provided that each of the seven petitions of the Lord's Prayer was a means of salvation from a particular one of the Seven Deadly Sins. Equipped with these bits of information and seeing the word 'Accidie', an allegorical character, scholars at once concluded that the York Pater Noster play was a morality play and that Wyclif's

[1] Chambers, op. cit. ii. 151–7; W. R. Mackenzie, *The English Moralities from the point of view of Allegory* (Boston, 1904), *passim*.
[2] *English Works*, E.E.T.S. (London, 1880), ch. xv, p. 429.
[3] *English Gilds*, ed. Toulmin Smith, E.E.T.S. (London, 1870), p. 137.

was the earliest known reference to a morality play. This belief is still widely held. It is nevertheless extremely hard to see how such a play could have been composed in series and acted processionally or, if it was, how the parts could have had any dramatic content and how it could have fulfilled the conditions indicated for Pater Noster plays at Lincoln and Beverley.[1]

The current conception of the Pater Noster play at York, Beverley, and Lincoln is that it was the first morality play and was somehow a representation of a conflict of the virtues and vices for the soul of man, a conflict made familiar by the *Psychomachia* of Prudentius (*c.* A.D. 400). We learn from the article in the Furnivall Miscellany by A. F. Leach, above referred to, that there were eight pageants at Beverley in 1469, one for each of the Seven Deadly Sins and an additional one called 'Viciose', which last name is probably to be regarded as a plural and as meaning *vitia* as distinguished from *peccata*; also that the Beverley play was processional like the Corpus Christi play, was supported by the craft guilds, who are assigned so many to each pageant, and was acted at approximately the same series of stations about the city as was the Corpus Christi play. It is not easy, as said above, to see how the theme of the *Psychomachia* could have been presented cyclically and processionally in a drama. That the conflict is the same no one would doubt, but in Prudentius we have a series of Homeric debates between pairs of contrasted figures, such as *Ira* and *Patientia*, *Superbia* and *Humilitas*, and so on. The theme in this form is, moreover, elsewhere unknown in the English morality play; nor do any of the other morality themes, such as the Debate of the Four Daughters of God, the Dance of Death, the Pilgrimage of the Life of Man, or the Besieged Castle, fit in with the outlines of the Beverley performance.

Accounts from Lincoln, small in number as they are, suggest another solution of the problem of the Pater Noster play. Leach brought to light among the rolls of Bishop Lexington's Episcopal Register a set of local annals with lists of mayors and bailiffs of Lincoln and notices of some events. Among the entries are mentions of the performance of plays. The Corpus Christi play is mentioned twice; a *Ludus de Pater Noster* (1397-8), which is marked 'liv anno',

[1] See article by the author, *The Nation* (New York), civ, 3 May 1917, 563-4.

which would date its beginning in 1343–4; *Ludus de Pater Noster* (1410–11); *Ludus de Pater Noster* (1424–5); *Ludus Sancti Laurentii* (1441–2); *Ludus Sanctae Susannae* (1447–8); *Ludus de Kyng Robert of Cesill* (1452–3); *Ludus de Sancta Clara* (1455–6); *Ludus de Pater Noster* (1456–7). According to Chambers,[1] Canon Rock also from the same document records at Lincoln a *Ludus de Sancto Jacobo*, and at York, where there was also a Pater Noster play, there was willed to the Corpus Christi guild in 1446 a *Librum de Sancto Jacobo in sex paginis compilatum*. With reference to the latter it may be remarked that if this play of St. James was composed in six pageants, it and others of these saints' plays may have been of considerable size.

There is something formal about this list of saints' plays. The saints mentioned, except St. Lawrence, are not Lincoln saints, and the subjects throughout suggest resistance to various ones of the Seven Deadly Sins. King Robert of Sicily, although not canonically a saint, was so conspicuous for his victory over Pride that he may well have been admitted to a company of saints who had each overcome a deadly sin. Saint Clara overcame Gluttony; Saint Susanna, Lechery; St. Lawrence, Avarice; and, without a too great stretch of the imagination, St. James may be said to have won a successful battle against Wrath. May not these saints' plays, which, if we may judge from the St. James play at York and from their standing forth as principal plays in the manuscript annals, were of considerable length, have been constituent parts of the Pater Noster play? At Lincoln they were apparently of sufficient extent to be substituted for the Pater Noster play itself. It may be only a coincidence, but the days of St. Lawrence, St. Susanna, and St. Clara are successive from the 10th to the 12th of August as if they had been traditionally associated with one another by some common characteristic.

Further slight support comes from York, where in 1455 Robert Lasingby left by will to the fabric of his church of St. Dionysius a *ludum originale Sancti Dionysii*. If, as is at least possible, St. Denis is to be united with this sin-resisting company of saints, it will be remembered that he waged warfare against Envy. Finally, when the religious guilds of York were nearly all suppressed, the last two performances of the Pater Noster play at York were in the hands of the

---

[1] Op. cit. ii. 378; Leach, op. cit., p. 223.

still unsuppressed guild of St. Anthony, and if for the sake of completeness one might be permitted to hazard a final guess with reference
to a subject about which there is so much guesswork, one might
conjecture that St. Anthony was the seventh and last subject,
especially since his life seems to exemplify with great aptness resistance
to that spiritual slackness that was known as Sloth.

Even on this showing one might be permitted to call in question the
hasty conclusion that the Pater Noster play was a morality play, and
put forward the more careful conjecture that it was a composite of
miracle plays joined together by the theme of resistance to the ravages
of sin with the aid of the divinely efficient clauses of the Lord's
Prayer. Further light may yet be thrown on the perplexity. A Pater
Noster play is mentioned in French records, and information about
it may possibly be found. Now that we have called in question the
opinion that the Pater Noster play was the first morality play, we
may endeavour to suggest a more plausible theory of that origin.

It only remains to tell the story of the loss of the York Pater Noster
play, and that story will probably apply to all the others. The
Pater Noster play was played at York in 1558 instead of the Corpus
Christi play. In 1572 the book of the play was submitted to the
Lord Mayor of York to be perused, amended, and corrected, no
doubt by ecclesiastical deputy, and the play was played that year, its
last performance; for in 1575 Archbishop Grindal requested that
the copy of the play be delivered to him, apparently for further correction and amendment. The request was complied with, and this
curious and no doubt interesting play has never been heard of since.
The owners were willing to have the book reformed and they asked
for it back, but presumably in vain.

THE MORALITY PLAY

It is true that a morality play is a dramatized allegory and that no
drama is a morality play unless it has this characteristic feature, but
even this statement leaves the subject vague. Abstractions cannot
express dubieties of mind and struggles of conscience, for they are
not human beings. Mankind in the abstract must behave positively
and objectively in accordance with an embodied concept of human
nature and human action. Therefore when Temptation invites *Homo*

or *Humanum Genus* to yield, he does so without inward struggle, because his *genus* habitually does just that, and, when Repentance asks him to return to his better nature, this abstraction is suddenly and immediately in a state of repentance, leaving individual struggles to individual human beings. His course of life is also both formalized and predetermined. He is born in innocence, although conceived in sin, but his nature obliges him to yield to temptation and plunge into sin; from sin he may or may not emerge into salvation.[1] This formal conception is in line with true belief in religion and is founded upon it. A corollary had long ago been deduced to the effect that man in the abstract is a bone of contention between victorious sins and persevering virtues. Another ancillary, but inevitable, boundary was the certainty of death and of damnation unless the mortal accept the grace provided by divine Atonement. Even the problem of why God should show mercy to sinful and ungrateful man was subject to formal consideration in terms of the abstract. Divine compassion was an act of free grace, and from early times it had been perceived that the tenth verse of the eighty-fifth psalm afforded a perfect statement of God's position with reference to the disposal of sinful man: 'Mercy and truth are met together; righteousness and peace have kissed each other.' Out of this was built an adjunctive allegory of wide dissemination—the Parliament of Heaven or the Debate of the Four Daughters of God. Since it was a part of God's mercy that man should not enter upon or pursue a life of sin without warning from on high, use was made of the doctrine of attendant spirits, and Humanity was supplied with a Good and a Bad Angel, the former to guide him to virtuous action and the latter to urge him on in his sinful way. In this group of allegories, large and small, the Middle Ages may be said to have expressed the bounds and the substance of their largest faith and to have expressed the creed of the true believer. But this allegory composed of these major and minor parts and representing the state of man was not the only one current in the Middle Ages. There were also the themes of life as a pilgrimage and of man as one who dwelt in a castle under siege by armies of sins and vices, and there were perhaps others of general scope. Each has its own history, and, as the later Middle Ages and the Renaissance discovered,

[1] See M. W. Bloomfield, *The Seven Deadly Sins* (East Lansing, Mich., 1932), *passim*.

allegory is endless and every moral aspect of human existence can be allegorized, but in this study of the moral play we must perforce limit ourselves to early and initiatory aspects of the subject. Indeed, we must go farther and confine ourselves, not too strictly, to a distinctive type of the morality that apparently originated in England and, so far as we can see, followed a pattern different from that of the medieval moralities of the Continent. The word 'morality' to denote plays of this kind has been in use since the fifteenth century, and that word and the term 'moral play' connoted ethical and religious pur-pose. *Moralité* in French was a broader and vaguer term that applied to social custom and behaviour. It seems to have been equivalent to *sottie* and is different from the English word.

We might base our conception of the English morality play on brief outlines of a few examples, some of which will need to be taken up later in detail. Let us begin with what is perhaps the most primi-tive and perhaps the oldest, *The Pride of Life*. In it the King of Life defies Death in spite of the warnings of the Queen and the Bishop. The King calls in the aid of Health and Strength and sends his mes-senger to challenge Death to combat. In the duel Death is victorious, and the soul of the King of Life is given over to fiends. He is saved by the intervention of the Virgin, and at the end is a familiar debate between the Body and the Soul as to which of them is guilty of the disaster. *The Pride of Life* is essentially a play on the certainty of death. *Mankind* (*c.* 1475) is a badly degenerated play, its characters absurdly reduced in numbers, and the play itself lewdly vulgarized for the amusement of rural audiences; but it may be much older than its manuscript and originally much more serious in purport. Mankind meets mere vices—Nought, Newguise, and Now-a-days—and is overcome by a mere clown, Titivillus. In the end he is saved by Mercy. *The Castle of Perseverance* (*c.* 1405) is the most extensive and com-plete, indeed, the most learned, of English moralities. It follows *Humanum Genus* from infancy to old age. Tempted by the World, the Flesh, and the Devil with the Seven Deadly Sins, *Humanum Genus* yields to evil, then repents and takes refuge in the Castle of Perseverance. He withstands the siege well, but in old age yields to Covetousness. He is slain by Death and his soul carried off to hell. The Four Daughters of God debate his case before the heavenly throne, and God decides in favour of Mercy and Peace. In *Wisdom*, or, as it is usually called, *Mind, Will, and Understanding*, the characters are the faculties of the soul, but the situation is perfectly general. The three faculties are seduced by Satan, but *Anima* is saved through the mediation of Wisdom, who is Christ. *Everyman* in its simplicity and typicality suggests great age, but the version is late.[1] Like *The Pride of Life* it is a universalized allegory of the Dance of Death. *Nature* (*c.* 1530) by Henry Medwall presents man as a gage in a conflict of reason and passion. *Mundus* wins him and puts him in the service of the Seven Deadly Sins, but in later life Man, according to allegorical pattern, repents, returns to Reason, and achieves salvation. In *The Nature of the Four Elements* (*c.* 1519) by John Rastell Humanity wavers between Studious Desire and Sensual Appetite. Nature indicts Humanity, who repents and reforms. In the brilliant and amusing *Hyckescorner*, an oldish play printed by Wynkyn de Worde about 1512, Pity acts as umpire and advocate of peace in the warfare between Virtues and Vices and gets put in the stocks for her pains, but after her release Pity converts Free Will and Imagination. Finally, *Mundus et Infans*, an anonymous play printed in 1522, is strictly typical of English moral plays and is one of the most ingenious. It proceeds in truly allegorical fashion by change of names. The abstract hero is first Infans, at seven he is Wanton, at fourteen Lust and Liking, at twentyone Manhood. When he yields to sin and goes to London, he becomes Shame, and, after a life of sin there, is called Age. He is then in despair and seeks for death, but Perseverance rescues him and his name is changed to Repentance.

These and other English moral plays have the one universal plot described above. It is the plot of the microcosm over against that of the macrocosm to the representation of which the mystery play, based on the church services of the liturgical year and extending from Creation to Doomsday, is devoted, and the value and significance of the English morality is by this comparison greatly enhanced. Its principle is universality, and that principle is deducible from the vast history of man's fall and redemption.

The current view of the origin of the morality play may be expressed

---

[1] *The Summoning of Everyman* passed through four editions between 1509 and 1519, two by Pynson and two by J. Skot.

in the words of Sir Adolphus Ward:[1] 'If, then, the love of allegory which had been early implanted in the English people, and the impulse given to this predeliction by French examples both in literature and on the stage in the period between Chaucer and the renascence be remembered, it will not be difficult to account for the growth, side by side with the biblical and saintly religious drama, of a species differing from it in origin, except as to their common final source, and varying from it in method, and, as time went on, more or less in character also. Nevertheless, the growth of this didactic species accompanies that of the plays following, with more or less digression, the biblical narrative, or dealing with lives of saints or the aftereffects of their martyrdoms in the form of miracles, and continues to affect these sister species in many instances, or actually in some cases to intermingle with them.' This is reasonable and true, but it is not enough; it does not provide for an actual event. Chambers[2] also speaks truly and reasonably. He mentions the *Roman de la Rose*, the figures of *Heresis* and *Ypocrisis* in the Tegernsee *Antichristus*, Mercy and Truth, Righteousness and Peace in the Parliament of Heaven, *Sapientia* and *Contemplacio* in the Hegge cycle and cites a possible allusion to the *danse macabre* in those plays, and, finally, the *Psychomachia* of Prudentius, all of which are cases in point, but none of which is a drama of the state and fate of mankind. G. R. Owst,[3] impressed with the close resemblance between the moral plays and medieval sermons in allegorical matters, suggests that the origin of the morality plays lies in the homily, and who can doubt that the suggestion for the first morality play may have come from a sermon? But sermons are not plays, nor are debates and casual narrative or expository allegories. In Manly's important essay on the theory of chance variation in literary species[4] there is the suggestion that the morality play arose from the chance combination of allegory with the dramatic method. Whether or not the first sporadic example is ever found, the truth of the matter must lie here.

The theory of the origin of the morality play that carries greatest conviction would regard it as a dramatic treatment of the Dance of

[1] *Cambridge History of English Literature*, Vol. v, pp. 24–25. [2] Op. cit. ii. 151–4.
[3] *Literature and Pulpit in Mediaeval England* (Cambridge, 1933).
[4] J. M. Manly, 'Literary Forms and the New Theory of the Origin of Species', loc. cit., pp. 577–95.

Death. W. Seelmann[1] attempts to prove that the *Lübecker Totentanz* and *La danza general de la muerte* are actually morality plays. He shows incidentally that both are based on a fourteenth-century French original that was later worked over into *La danse macabre*; also that the writing precedes and is the basis for the woodcut illustrations of *La danse macabre* and also of course for numerous other pictures including those of Holbein.[2] Seelmann goes very far towards proving that these 'dramatic' versions of the Dance of Death were actually morality plays; indeed, all they lack is an abstraction as hero. The performances took place in a church and, like the liturgical drama, were religious in spirit and purpose. They were played upon a stage provided with *loca*. There was a door or sepulchre into which the victims of Death disappeared, with a pulpit in front of the stage from which a priest gave warning to the congregation of the certainty of death to all and spoke of the necessity of preparation for the ordeal of death by the accumulation of good works. Proper costumes are provided for the characters, and Death, when he appears on the scene, is made to resemble a corpse or a skeleton. Death summons Pope, Emperor, King, and the lower orders of society, and with each victim as he or she appears Death dances to the door of the sepulchre. There is dialogue, impersonation, and action of a sort, so that the Dance of Death is a dramatic spectacle, a procession, and a ceremony, but is perhaps not a true drama and could not be until its energy was changed from static to kinetic. It was close to the borderline and needed only the histrionic impersonation of an abstraction already implicit in the great theme itself. The development of the Dance of Death into a morality play was easy and obvious, but we do not know, and perhaps shall never know, when that development took place. We do, however, know exactly what took place from at least two English plays on the theme of the Dance of Death.

These two plays are *Everyman*[3] and *The Pride of Life*. There is a

---

[1] *Die Totentänze des Mittelalters*. Verein für niederdeutsche Sprachforschung, *Jahrbuch*, Nr. 17 (1892); Waterhouse, op. cit., pp. lxx–lxxii.

[2] See L. P. Kurtz, *The Dance of Death* (New York, 1934).

[3] There exists a Dutch version of *Everyman* called *Elckerlijk*, and there has been an extensive controversy over which of these plays is the original and therefore whether the play belonged originally to England or to Holland. Opinion seems to favour a Dutch origin. See *inter alia* J. M. Manly, 'Elckerlijk–Everyman: Question of Priority', *Modern Philology*, viii (1910); W. Creizenach, *Cambridge History of English Literature*, Vol. v, p. 59 n., where attention is

simplicity about *Everyman* that makes one think that in some form it may be far older than the date of its publication by Pynson in the early sixteenth century. It makes use of a parable told in the legend of *Barlaam and Josaphat* about a man with three friends only one of whom, symbolizing his Good Deeds, is willing to accompany him before the throne of judgement. The use of this suggests not primitivity but some literary development. Yet *Everyman* is so definite and so severe a presentation of the coming of death that it may be older than *The Pride of Life*. It is nevertheless possible to see in the latter play something that looks transitional and therefore primitive.

The Pride of Life appears in a puzzling and difficult manuscript in the Irish Record Office in Dublin. It is written in two different hands on the back of and on blank spaces within a roll of accounts of the Priory of the Holy Trinity, Dublin, for the year 1343. The copying is thought to have been done in the early fifteenth century, but, as we shall see, the play shows signs of being much older. There are several serious gaps in the copy, and the end of the play is missing, but fortunately the play has a prologue by the aid of which the action of the whole play can be determined. The plot of the play is summarized above, and it is clear that *The Pride of Life* bears strong resemblance to the Dance of Death not only in the central idea that death is a universal conqueror but also in the warnings given and in an ultimate dependence on the mercy of God and the intercession of the saints. *The Pride of Life* introduces a personal idea of sin and negligence, but does not carry it very far. The King of Life is very proud, but there are no definite impersonations of sins as his corrupters or as enemies to his salvation. In these respects it is like the Dance of Death. The strife for the King's soul, moreover, as revealed in the prologue, seems to be not between good and evil but between life and death. The King of Life in *The Pride of Life* is but a shade removed from a king in the Dance of Death who must, king though he is, submit to all-conquering Death. The metre of the play is extremely simple, quatrains of four (sometimes three) accents to the line throughout the play, which, indeed, seems in dramaturgy as well as style to be very old. The play was apparently written in the South of England,

called to the work of de Raaf; E. R. Tigg, 'Is *Elckerlijk* prior to *Everyman*?', *Journal of English and Germanic Philology*, xxxviii (1939), 568–76.

but greatly modified by northern speech when, and possibly before, it was copied. *The Pride of Life* was performed on a stationary stage with fixed properties. The King of Life has a *tentorium* into which he retires, and there is a *sedes* for the Bishop. The indications are that it was played out of doors.[1]

This play and *Everyman* present in a simple form the type of morality play that was dominant in England, that is, a play in which there is a contest for the soul of a representative of all mankind. At a later time, when the practice of making morality plays had established itself, other allegorical themes and various modifications of the principal theme manifested themselves, but these two plays seem simpler and possibly older than any others. On the present showing one would think that the most plausible conjecture as to the origin of the English morality play is that it was a dramatic development of the Dance of Death. The case for this possible origin of the English type of moral play is weakened by the fact that the *danse macabre* theme, although always present by implication, is by no means so dominant as the theme of man's struggle for salvation.

For our knowledge of English morality plays in their early forms we are largely dependent on one manuscript formerly in the collection of Cox Macro (1683–1769) and now in the Folger Shakespeare Library in Washington, D.C. The moral plays in this manuscript were published by the Early English Text Society under the editorship of F. J. Furnivall and A. W. Pollard in 1904. The plays, or some of them, had been published before. There are three of them, and, as will be seen, they do not seem to have any connexion with one another.

The Castle of Perseverance is dated by Furnivall and Pollard in about 1425 and has been located with great probability by W. K. Smart at or near Lincoln.[2] This allocation is based on dialect and other considerations, particularly on an allusion to the gallows of Canwick, a notorious place of execution actually within sight of some parts of the city of Lincoln. Smart would date *The Castle of Perseverance* about 1405. All morality themes, except the Pilgrimage of the Life of Man, have been ingeniously worked into the service of this play, and this

[1] Waterhouse, op. cit., pp. lxiv–lxxiv; Chambers, op. cit. ii. 436.

[2] '*The Castle of Perseverance*: Place, Date, and Source', *Manly Anniversary Studies*, loc. cit., pp. 42–53.

fact of itself is an indication that the play originated in a cultural centre such as Lincoln. There is the Struggle of the Virtues and Vices for the soul of *Humanum Genus.* There are a Good and an Evil Angel arrayed against each other, as in *Doctor Faustus*, the one striving to convert *Humanum Genus*, the other to make him continue in the ways of sin. The World, the Flesh, and the Devil, assisted by the Seven Deadly Sins, fight against Confession, Penitence, Absolution, and the Six Heavenly Graces. *Humanum Genus* is besieged in the Castle of Perseverance, from which the besiegers are thrown back by showers of roses, symbols of Christ's Passion. Death claims *Humanum Genus*, and at the end there is the Parliament of Heaven or the Debate of the Four Daughters of God in which, with *Pater sedens in trono* as presiding judge, Justice and Truth prosecute *Humanum Genus* before the bar, and Mercy and Peace defend him.

The *mise en scène* of the play is of the greatest interest, and the manu-script is provided with a well-known crude drawing that shows the playing-place and its equipment. The former was circular with a ditch or barrier about it. In the centre of the circle was the Castle of Perseverance with Mankind's bed beneath it. At the foot of the bed is the cupboard of Covetousness, for, when all other sins have failed, old men fall victims to that. At the south rim is the scaffold of the Flesh (*Caro*), on the west the scaffold of the World (*Mundus*), on the north that of Belial, on the north-east that of Covetousness, and on the east the scaffold of God. The *platea* of course is extensive. Below the drawing are notes of costume and action, very quaint and rather funny. *The Castle of Perseverance*, like the Hegge plays, has banns that announce a performance at 'N town' at nine o'clock in the morning.

Mind, Will, and Understanding, more properly designated as *Wisdom*, is a literate play well informed in the lore of psychology and theology. It has been briefly summarized above. There are in it a number of allusions to London, and London would have been an appropriate place for it to have originated. Schmidt,[1] however, thinks on rather narrow evidence that the dialect is that of the East Midlands. Most of the allusions are to courts and abuses, such as the Holburn Quest, where the jurymen are Wrong, Sleight, Doubleness, Falsehood,

[1] K. Schmidt, loc. cit.

Ravine, and Deceit. Pollard thinks these allusions are of the sort that country people would make to London, but they are perhaps too intimate for that. W. K. Smart in an important monograph[1] points out that the play requires a large cast and expensive costuming and is in general on too high a level to have been intended for a strictly popular audience. He thinks the play may have been directed against a growing tendency for monks to desert their monasteries. The date assigned to the play is about 1460, and Smart agrees with this. In the action of the play Lucifer corrupts the three principal powers of the soul—Mind or intellect, Will or passion, and Under-standing or intuition. Wisdom, who represents the active power of Christ, reconverts these faculties of the soul, who, being saved, give praise to Christ. The drama is over-worded and is not dramatically effective, but it is neatly constructed and is intelligent in the learning it uses as its basis. It will be remembered that the first 754 lines of this play appear as a fragment in Digby MS. 133.

Mankind, in its present state at least, is a play of the utmost ignorance and crudity, but it shows some signs of having seen better days.[2] Smart's study of the allusions in the play, although many of them are so corrupt as to be scarcely recognizable, nevertheless suggests that some learning and intelligence went into the original composition of *Mankind*. The play has apparently been carried on the road for one does not know how long by a low-class company of strolling players, players whose appeal was to the uneducated and the vulgar. It was acted apparently in an inn-yard by a company too small to present it fully, so that it is badly abridged. Mercy, who is possibly the only one left of a group of virtues, contends for the soul of Mankind against a disproportionate number of evils and enemies. Devils and vices were comic. Mischief is the leader of the band, and is assisted by Nought, Newguise, and Now-a-days, and particularly, later, by a devil Titivillus. Titivillus is the grand attraction, and before his appearance a collection is gathered among the spectators under threat that, unless money is forthcoming, this main attraction will not appear. Parts are doubled, and it seems possible that some have been done away

---

[1] *Some English and Latin Sources and Parallels for the Morality of Wisdom* (Menasha, Wis., 1912).

[2] W. K. Smart, '*Mankind* and the Mumming Plays', *Modern Language Notes*, xxxii (1917), 21–25; 'Some Notes on *Mankind*', *Modern Philology*, xiv (1916–17), 293–313.

with, since there are only seven actors in all. The play is ignorant, corrupt, probably degenerate, and vulgar to the point of obscenity, and yet it is possible that it was a typical English morality play, not perhaps of the fullest scope, but a play with a bias toward social satire. It is difficult to see it in its present form as an original composition either of a rural poet or of a man with any pretence to education. If changes have been made, they were of course introduced by the necessities of staging with a small troupe and by a comic appeal to yokels and the toughs of small towns. One is disposed to think it possible that *Mankind* was not composed for such audiences. The manuscript is dated by Furnivall and Pollard at about 1475, but the play may be much older than the manuscript and might, in an original state, have been a typical morality. Even this poor thing ends with a prayer that God will grant the audience eternal life. The dialect is thought to be East Midland, and there are allusions to towns in Norfolk, Suffolk, and Cambridgeshire, the last mentioned being most numerous.

In consequence of the fall of Adam man is destined to die in sin unless he be saved by the intervention of divine grace and by repentance. It is the presentation of man in this situation in perfectly general terms that is the essence of the English morality play. St. Augustine has a notable phrase,[1] *Merito autem non videretur iniustum . . . si non esset ipsa universa ex Adam massa damnata.* The concept of justice with which man is confronted is a part of the larger concept of divine justice stemming from God and exemplified in the creation of the universe. This is the constant position of St. Thomas Aquinas and other theologians.[2] When sin exists in man it is a completing element, so that man not only desires the temporary good but hates the permanent good; but man may have his will purged by the infusion through divine grace into his soul of the four cardinal virtues and the three theological virtues, so that he comes to desire the permanent good. This is a statement, imperfect no doubt, of the theological principle of the typical English morality play.

[1] Letter to Optatus, Migne, *P.L.* xxxiii. 859.
[2] See *Summa Theologica*, i^a-ii^{ae}, question 87, article 3, the body of the article and the reply to objection 3; ibid., Supplement, question 99, article 1. On original sin and eternal punishment see ibid., i^a-ii^{ae}, question 87, article 5. These references the author owes to Father J. B. Dwyer, S.J.

But this characterization of the English moral play cannot be made without some consideration of Continental moralities. The argument turns out to be negative but not without strength, since there are no such plays on the Continent at any early time. There seems to have been no German morality as such. The word *Moralität* was applied to *Fastnachtspiele*, comic plays for Shrove Tuesday performance. There are no moralities recorded or preserved from Italy. Holland, if one excepts *Elckerlijk*, had nothing significant. Dutch moralities seem to have been written on set subjects for prizes, apparently in answer to proposed questions; such as, What is the greatest service that God has brought forth for the happiness of man? Spain seems to have had no fully developed medieval morality. There are plenty of Spanish moralities of the fifteenth and sixteenth centuries written by professional playwrights in obvious imitation of an established form. Spanish plays of the sort show contamination, *autos* (miracles) with *farsas* (moralities), and only the feature of allegory distinguishes Spanish morality plays from comedies.

One gets into the habit of thinking that almost everything artistic or literary in the English Middle Ages comes from France, but, although there are scores of French *moralités*, there seems to be no evidence that the particular universal type of morality play that is dominant in England made its appearance in France at any time early enough to have been the original invention. There are no very early morality plays preserved in any country—none that can be safely dated earlier than the end of the fourteenth century. In France there is a reference in 1426 to a lost play about the Heart and the Five Senses, a subject indicative of specialization of the form. *Bien-Avisé, Mal-Avisé* is dated in 1439, but seems to have been played in 1396.[1] It presents two contrasted careers—the Good Boy-Bad Boy theme— and is a forerunner of a later morality by Simon Bougouyn, *L'Homme juste et L'Homme mondaine*, acted before Louis XII. *L'Homme pécheur*, also a late play, tells the story of wayward youth and its defection, with a salvation not unlike that of the English plays. *Les Enfants de Maintenant*, fifteenth century, is elaborate and sophisticated, so is Adrienne de la Vigne's *Honneur des Dames, franc Vouloir, Cœur loyal, Danger, Envie, Mallebouche* (c. 1500). Of the three plays from the Chantilly

[1] Julleville, *Répertoire du Théâtre comique* (Paris, 1886), pp. 39–41, 67–73.

manuscript,[1] *La Moralité de l'Alliance de Foy et Loyalté* contains elements both of the pastoral and of the Nativity play and is a political allegory in the cause of peace. *La Moralité des sept Péchés Mortels et des sept Vertus* is in the form of a pageant of the Seven Deadly Sins and their opposing virtues, and the only action is the somewhat improbable one of the conversion of the sins by the virtues. *La Moralité du Pélerinage de la Vie Humaine* treats a theme not known to have been treated in England. It and many of the French dramas are genuine morality plays, but the English type with Mankind as its hero is not found. There are cases, of course, in which English and French moral plays are quite of the same kind.

We shall not in this chapter even attempt to suggest the widely diversified forms taken on by later English moralities or the great influence they exerted on Tudor Drama.

---

[1] *Mystères et Moralités du manuscrit 617 de Chantilly*, ed. Gustave Cohen (Paris, 1920).

X

The Reformation, The Renaissance, and the Medieval Religious Drama

MYSTERY AND MIRACLE PLAYS

THERE is no doubt that Father Harold C. Gardiner, S.J., is right in his contention that Reform was the chief enemy of the mystery plays and that it more than any other agency brought about their downfall.[1] One may go farther and say that it was anti-papacy in a virulent form. But there were other agencies besides anti-papacy at work. The Scottish Privy Council and of course the General Assembly of the Kirk with, we may believe, many pietistic individuals and communities in both Scotland and England disapproved of the presentation on the stage of sacred events. This opinion is perfectly expressed, for example, in an Act of the General Assembly of 1575:[2]

> Forasmuche as it is considered that the playing of clerk-plays, comedies or tragedies, upon the canonicall parts of the Scriptures, induceth & bringeth with it a contempt and profanation of the same, it is thought meete and concluded, that no clerk-plays, comedies or tragedies, be made upon canonicall Scriptures, other New or Old, in time coming, other upon the Lord's Day or upon a worke day: that the contraveeners, if they be ministers, be secluded from their functions, and that others be corrected by the discipline of the kirk.

Even this order does not express disapproval of plays as such, an attitude, contrary to popular opinion, very late in making its appear-ance and, indeed, not noticeable in England until 1577.[3]

There must also have been some defection, in England as on the Continent, from the traditional mystery and miracle plays because

---

[1] *Mysteries' End: An Investigation of the Last Days of the Mediaeval Stage* (New Haven, 1946); with bibliography.

[2] Quoted by Gardiner, op. cit., p. 89, from D. Calderwood, *A History of the Kirk of Scotland* (Edinburgh, 1843), p. 345.

[3] William Ringler, 'The First Phase of the Elizabethan Attack on the Stage, 1558–1579', *Huntington Library Quarterly*, v (1942), 391–418.

of the introduction by the Renaissance of the finer dramatic art of the comedies of Terence and Plautus and the tragedies of Seneca.[1] After all, except in certain provincial English cities where the plays were securely established and connected with the social and commercial life of the communities, there may have been some dis-continuance of religious plays as if from loss of interest. No mystery plays are known to have been performed at Beverley after 1541, none at Canterbury after 1520, and at Lincoln and London there seems to have been no traditional dramatic activity after the brief revival in the reign of Queen Mary. This is not to say that at the great provincial centres of the medieval religious drama—York, Chester, Coventry, Norwich, and others—the plays were not clung to with great tenacity and strong affection by the citizens. It is only suggested that in such places the Middle Ages were slow in 'waning'.

It is also at least questionable whether Elizabeth's government was from the beginning bent on the destruction of the popular religious drama of the Middle Ages. In so far as the plays taught and fostered Catholicism they must always have been under suspicion, for one must not forget the bitter enmity of the Queen's government and the greater number of her subjects against Rome and that it was a time of struggle on both sides, the Queen herself after 1570 being under excommunication. This struggle culminated in the rebellion of the Northern Lords in 1569, when no quarter was given by the Queen's government to her enemies. Therefore at certain times, particularly in the north country in the 1570's, there was certainly strong and determined effort by Her Majesty's Commission for Ecclesiastical Causes, with the co-operation of the officials of the church, to put down the plays, not primarily because they were plays, but because they were thought to be papistical in their influence. As we shall see, not all Protestants were opposed to religious plays, and, as we already know, the mystery plays were not primarily doctrinal and did not derive their popularity from their systematic support of the Catholic Church, since they were religious in their origin and nature rather than ecclesiastical.

[1] C. H. Herford, *Studies in the Literary Relations of England and Germany in the Sixteenth Century* (Cambridge, 1888), chapter iii, pp. 70–164; Creizenach, op. cit., ii. 1–181, 369–505; iii *passim*; P. Bahlmann, *Die lateinischen Dramen von Wimphelings Stylpho bis zur Mitte des sechzehnten Jahrhunderts, 1480–1550* (Münster, 1893), *passim*.

The story of the suppression of the religious plays is much the same for all the cities of which we have any record. At Chester the process was complicated and protracted. There the Whitsun plays were regularly performed, but probably not annually. There is some evid' ence for plays in 1546, 1551, 1553, 1554, 1560, 1561, 1566, 1567, 1569, 1571, 1572, 1574, 1575, and possibly in other years during the latest period. Interest was apparently strong and that the mystery plays were not quickly forgotten seems to be indicated by the fact that no less than five manuscripts of the Chester cycle were copied out between 1591 and 1607.

In 1571, during the mayoralty of John Hankey, the plays were performed at Chester, although a letter forbidding them was sent, presumably to the mayor and his brethren, by Edmund Grindal, Archbishop of York, but, as recorded in a document quoted by Ormerod,[1] 'this year the Whitsun plays played & an inhibition was sent from the Archbishop to stay them, but it came too late'. To this is added the statement 'this year the mayor would needs have the plays go forward, against the wills of the bishops of Canterbury, York and Chester'. Mayor Hankey was summoned before the Privy Council where he seems to have had some difficulty in clearing himself, for as late as 1575 he seems still to have been in need of exculpation. In 1574 Sir John Savage was mayor of Chester, and during his term the plays were played in spite, says Ormerod,[2] of 'an inhibition of the primate's letters from York and from the Earl of Huntingdon'. The Earl of Huntingdon was Lord President of the North and a loyal supporter of the policies of the Privy Council. Archbishop Grindal's motives, in the light of his history, are not to be taken for granted on the basis of these acts. He was no doubt ready enough to suppress the plays, but he did not see eye to eye with the Privy Council and, indeed, in 1577 was suspended for his refusal to enforce the Queen's mandate suppressing prophesyings. As Gardiner notes,[3] Savage was summoned to appear before the Privy Council on the very day he ceased to be mayor of Chester. Nothing

[1] Gardiner, op. cit., p. 80; G. Ormerod, *The History of the County Palatine and the City of Chester* (3 v. London, 1882), i. 235.
[2] Gardiner, op. cit., p. 81; Ormerod, op. cit. i. 236; Historical MSS. Commission, vol. viii, pt. 1, pp. 263 ff.
[3] Op. cit., pp. 81–82.

seems to have been done about the case against him, which was that he 'caused to be plaied the accostomed pageons . . . of himsellf to satisfie his owne will & pleasure & contrary to his othe & dutie without the assente or consente of the rest of his brethrene . . . to the greate costes & charges, losse & harme of the citizens & inhabitaunts of the said citie & to their no little impoverishmente'.[1] The answer to this false and disingenuous charge is given in a letter from the mayor of Chester, Henry Hardware, to the Privy Council.[2] It expresses the exact truth. The letter is dated 21 November 1575, and bears witness to the fact that Savage had acted

only accordinge to an order concluded & agried upon for dyvers good & great considerations redoundinge to the comon wealthe & benefite & proffitte of the saide citie in assemblie there holden accordinge to the auncient and laudable usages & customes there hadd & used fur above mans remembrance by & with the assente, consente & agreament of his saide then brethrene, the aldermen of the saide citie & of the comen counsell of the same.

The charges against former mayor Hankey were also included in the defence of Sir John Savage. At any rate, the opposition of the authorities had apparently become so great that the Chester cycle was never played after 1575.[3]

The circumstances of the suppression of the York plays are well known because of the work of Lucy Toulmin Smith.[4] The operation was more tortuous and possibly more tactful, but equally effective.[5] There were three cyclic plays to be suppressed at York, and the hostile, but pious, ecclesiastical authorities took them one at a time. The earliest manifestation of a purpose of revision and removal of papistical matters was in 1561, when 'it was agreed that the Corpus xpi play shalbe played this yere with good players as hath ben accustomed, except onely the pageants of the dyeing, Assumption and Coronacion of our Lady'.[6] The serious attack, led apparently by Dean Matthew Hutton, opened in 1568 against the Creed play. Dean Hutton, as

[1] Quoted by Gardiner, op. cit., p. 82, from R. H. Morris, *Chester in Plantagenet and Tudor Reigns* (Chester, 1893), p. 321.

[2] Ibid.

[3] F. M. Salter, *The Trial and Flagellation with Other Studies in the Chester Cycle*, loc. cit., pp. 13, 25, *et passim*.

[4] *York Plays*, loc. cit., p. xvi *et passim*; see also Chambers, op. cit., ii. 404 *et passim*.

[5] Gardiner, op. cit., pp. 73–79.

[6] Ibid., p. 68 n., quoting York *House Books*, vol. xxiii, f. 10, 27 March 1561.

Gardiner points out,[1] was one of the members of the Commission for Ecclesiastical Causes in the North. The city corporation had decided to have the Creed play enacted that year instead of the Corpus Christi play. Davies says that the council determined to send the book of the play to Dean Hutton to get his advice, a thing that seems probable, although Gardiner says conjecturally[2] that Dean Hutton 'called for and perused the book'. The Dean's report is preserved in the form of a letter in which he says,[3]

> . . . as I find so manie things that I muche like because of th' antiquities, so I see manie things that I cannot allow because they be disagreeing from the sinceritie of the gospell, the which things, yf they should either be altogether cancelled or altered into other matters, the whole drift of the play shuld be altered, and therefore I dare not put my pen unto it, because I want both skill and leasure to amende it, thoghe in good will I assure you yf I were worthie to geve your lordshipp and your right worshipfull counsel, suerlie mine advise shuld be that it shuld not be plaied, ffor thoghe it was plawsible to yeares agoe, and wold now also of the ignorant sort be well liked, yet now in the happie time of gospell, I knowe the learned will mislike it, and how the state will beare it, I know not.

Granted the Dean's partisanship and his religiosity, it is not a bad letter. He at least saw that the play could not be amended without being spoiled. Would that his interest in 'antiquities' had been sufficient to make him preserve the book! The council heeded his advice and decided to have no play that year. It is said puzzlingly 'the booke of the Cred play to be delyvered in agayn'. This seems to indicate that the corporation meant that the manuscript of the play should be returned to their possession and placed with the Master and brethren of St. Thomas's Hospital 'whoo have the custody thereof'.[4] In the light of what happened to other play-books the probabilities are that the original of the Creed play was never returned to its owners.

With reference to the suppression of the York Corpus Christi play one must not in the presence of the records forget the influence, perhaps centuries old, of the ecclesiastical body of York on the corporation that controlled the play. Without the co-operation of the

---

[1] Op. cit., p. 72, where Patent Rolls, 10 Elizabeth, pt. 2, are cited—Public Records Office, Serial No. C 66/1042.

[2] Davies, op. cit., pp. 267–73; Gardiner, op. cit., p. 74, where he quotes York *House Books*, vol. xxiv, f. 104ᵛ.

[3] Davies, ibid. The original, Gardiner tells us, is in York *House Books*, vol. xxiv, f. 106.

[4] Gardiner, op. cit., p. 74, quoting York *House Books* as above.

York clergy the Corpus Christi play could never have reached and maintained so high a standard of learning and propriety as it reveals. If simply read, the action of the council following their failure to secure approval for the Creed play in 1568 seems to express a respectful attitude. They state that the citizens were 'much desyerous to have Corpuschrysty play this yere', but 'the council woll not agree, but that the booke thereof shall be perused and otherwise amanded before it were played'. Although the Corpus Christi play was probably not played in 1568, it was played in 1569, and, indeed, a series of light revisions appear in the manuscript of the York plays and apparently date from the revision called for. There are about fifty of these emendations recorded by Lucy Toulmin Smith,[1] who regarded the handwriting as of the late sixteenth century. The revisions are, for the most part, mild and doctrinal and seem to be corrections made at this time, possibly at the direction of Dean Hutton. This is made probable by the fact that the question had not as yet become bitterly partisan or national in its bearings. After the rebellion of the Northern Lords in 1569 there may have been for a time insufficient assurance in the public mind to have the plays called for, as there was certainly less chance for the acquiescence in the enterprise of either political or ecclesiastical officials. The popular demand for the plays manifested itself again in 1575,[2] when the council, noting that the archbishop had in his possession some of 'the play bookes as perteyn to this citie', requested that he would 'apoynt twoe or thre sufficiently learned to correcte the same, wherein by the laws of this realme they are to be reformed'. It was evidently the policy of the dean and the archbishop to do nothing about it, for, when in 1579 the council expressed a desire to have the Corpus Christi play performed, the book was still unrevised, and the obedient council made provision that 'first the booke shalbe caried to my Lord Archebisshop and Mr. Dean to correcte, if that my Lord Archebisshop doo well like theron'. Miss Smith was of opinion that no revision was made at that later time, which is of course a very fortunate thing. The original or register of the York Corpus Christi play and perhaps other documents must have been delivered to the

---

[1] Loc. cit., pp. xv–xvi; also p. 93 (in the Annunciation), p. 138 (in the Flight into Egypt), p. 177 (in the Baptism).

[2] L. T. Smith, op. cit., p. xvi, who quotes Davies, op. cit., pp. 267–8, 271–2.

archbishop or the dean and presumably from that time withheld from the corporation. It was no doubt a most disingenuous and yet politic method of disposing of the play. It will be recalled that Lucy Toulmin Smith[1] suggests very plausibly that the great book fell into the hands of some member of the Fairfax family.

The Pater Noster play was played in 1572 after having been 'perused, amended and corrected'. Father Gardiner, referring to the York *House Books*, states that 'the Archbishop was not satisfied but demanded a copy of the play'.[2] The council accordingly agreed to deliver 'a trewe copie of all the said bookes even as they weare playd this yere'. This seems to account for the disposition and probably the loss of the mysterious Pater Noster play, but, as Gardiner truly remarks, the mere reformation of the plays was not what was really desired by those in authority.

A document of this period is for the first time brought to light by Gardiner.[3] It is of great interest, since it reflects the official activity of the Archdiocese of York in the suppression of mystery plays and gives us the only information we have about the contemporary situation at Wakefield. It is from the records of the Diocesan Court of High Commission.[4]

xxvij° die Maii Anno dni 1576 corā Com̄ ecclē Ebor. Corā Mrr. Matthew Hutton, John Gibson et W° Palmer Commissionarii et in pr mei Willim Fothergill notarii publici. This daie upon intelligence geven to the saide Commission that it is meant and purposed that in the towne of Wakefeld shalbe plaid this yere in Whitsonweke next or thereaboutes a plaie commonlie called Corpus Christi plaie which hath bene heretofore used there, wherein they are done t' understand that there be many thinges used which tende to the derogation of the Majestie and glorie of God, the prophanation of the sacramentes and the maunteynaunce of superstition and idolatrie, the said Commissioners decreed a lettre to be written and sent to the baylyffe, burgesses and other the inhabitantes of the said towne of Wakefeld that in the said playe no pageant be used or set furthe wherin the Ma'ye of God the Father, God the Sonne, or God the Holie Ghoste or the administration of either the Sacramentes of baptisme or of the Lordes Supper be counterfeyted or represented, or anythinge plaied which tende to the main-

---

[1] Op. cit., pp. xii–xiii.

[2] Op. cit., p. 75, with citations of York *House Books*, vol. xxv, folios 6 and 19.

[3] Op. cit., pp. 77–78. He makes acknowledgement for the discovery to the Reverend A. Raine of York, who in turn accredited it to his father, Canon J. Raine.

[4] Described (Gardiner, op. cit., pp. 77–78) as *Court Book 1575–1580*, f. 19 (unpaginated).

tenaunce of superstition and idolatrie or which be contrarie to the lawes of God and [cancelled] or of the realme.[1]

Gardiner points out that the manuscript of the Towneley plays has been corrected in several places in passages of theological import,[2] a circumstance that lends an additional shade of probability to the no longer seriously questioned belief that the Towneley manuscript is the original of the Wakefield plays.

As to the prohibition of the pageants of Coventry, it is difficult to make out a case for official repression. Coventry was not under suspicion of papistry and had for generations been an extremely independent city, never ecclesiastically dominated. In 1561 the citizens of Coventry protested against the suppression of the Hox Tuesday show and urged the intelligent reason that there was no papistry or superstition in it. It is not now possible to tell with certainty in what years the Coventry Corpus Christi play was acted, but the accounts of the smiths' and the cappers' companies with a few scattered records in the *MS. Annals* seem to indicate that the plays were acted pretty much as was customary until about 1579. Thomas Sharp, who had seen many records now lost, was of the opinion that there were no Corpus Christi plays from 1580 to 1583 inclusive. What happened about 1579 or 1580 we do not know. There may have been ecclesiastical or governmental interference, of which, however, we have no trace; or, if the impression of one who has spent much time in the study of Coventry records can be trusted, it may be that the Protestantism of Coventry was not too well satisfied with the old guild plays. The citizens of Coventry nevertheless liked plays and, being very much in earnest about the profits brought to the city by the plays, they decided to do something fine and very modern. They therefore paid a considerable sum to 'Mr. Smythe of Oxford' for writing for them a new play, *The Destruction of Jerusalem*. Mr. Smythe may very well have known of plays on this subject in France and may have modelled his drama on them. He had, however, one original task imposed on him.

---

[1] Father Gardiner is disposed to see in the cancellation of 'and' and the substitution of 'or' an evidence of governmental action, but it may be only a change to a more customary form of official expression.

[2] See *Towneley Plays*, ed. A. W. Pollard, loc. cit., p. 201, where stanza 25 has been struck through probably because of a mention of the Seven Sacraments; further possibly doctrinal corrections appear on pp. 203 and 316.

He had to present the story from Josephus processionally. From the few indications of the names of characters that survive in the smiths' accounts, he may have done his work very well. His play was called a 'tragedye', by which of course was merely meant that it was a serious drama. We have no means of knowing how the play was received, but we do know that the new play cost the guilds a great deal of money. That circumstance would have deterred them from repeating it too often. No great popular interest could have been quickly built up on the basis of a far-off history full of strange names and unfamiliar events. No doubt Coventry citizens preferred the old plays, for familiarity was the very basis of the enjoyment of mystery plays. Three songs at the end of the *Shearmen and Taylors' Pageant* under the name 'Thomas Mawdycke' are dated in 1591, and Chambers[1] argues quite plausibly that some attempt may have been made to revive the Corpus Christi play in that year. But by that time the leet had probably come over to the side of modern culture and perhaps ecclesiastical opinion, and that body resolved on 19 May 1591,[2] 'that the destruction of Jerusalem . . . at the request of the Comons of this Cittie shal be plaied on the pagens on Midsomer daye & St. Peters daye next in this cittie & non other plays'. The last four words of this order may have nipped in the bud the project of singing Thomas Mawdycke's songs in the *Shearmen and Taylors' Pageant*. There was certainly still some hope among the guilds of Coventry, for in 1587 the weavers built at very considerable expense a new pageant-house in Mill Lane.[3]

The downfall of the pageants at Norwich as reflected in the records of the grocers' company[4] is almost pathetic, and Father Gardiner cites[5] somewhat similar cases from Newcastle-upon-Tyne, Doncaster, and Kendal. Lincoln, a strong centre of the established church, gave up its plays early, and after their revival in the reign of Queen Mary they do not appear again. In 1564 the Lincoln corporation provided 'that a standing play of some story of the Bible shall be played two days this sumertime'. The story of Tobias was accordingly played that

---

[1] Op. cit. ii, 361–2.
[2] *Coventry Council Book A* 14 (a), f. 216; cited by Gardiner, op. cit., p. 85.
[3] *Two Coventry Corpus Christi Plays*, loc. cit., p. 108.
[4] Waterhouse, op. cit., pp. xxvi–xxxv.
[5] Op. cit., pp. 86–87.

year at Broadgate and was repeated in 1567. Some of its properties appear in an inventory of 1569.[1]

The records of the suppression of the medieval religious plays indicate that people in many English provincial cities were much attached to them and gave them up with reluctance, indeed were persistent in their efforts to keep them alive. Ordinary people were of course not sufficiently learned to be aware of doctrinal issues. The mystery plays were not theological or propagandistic; they were religious. They sought from the beginning to tell the truth as they believed it to be and to give instruction in the means of salvation. Perhaps the plays written to honour the Blessed Virgin Mary might raise an issue that even ordinary people would understand, but even these plays, which were sweet and human, were sufficiently innocuous from a theological point of view. The plays were in their essence simple stories of patriarchs, prophets, the family and friends of Jesus, His ministry, His disciples, and His sacrifice. They probably had little sectarian effect in their teaching. Their offence was that they formed a rallying-point for those who not only preferred the old customs but the church that had fostered them.

It is a mistake to over-simplify the downfall of the mysteries. They were medieval in their essence, and the Middle Ages were passing away. The modern world did the mystery plays great harm before it finally suppressed them. Queen Elizabeth and her government certainly did not hate the mystery plays and form a long and patient plot for their destruction when the time became ripe. The mystery cycles seem for a long time to have been pretty much left alone, and a good many of them seem to have died out of themselves, and that death was no doubt no great cause of grief to those who took the Protestant side in the long period of religious war, both hot and cold, that went on throughout the middle of the sixteenth century. There is no evidence that the Protestants at first, or as Protestants, objected to drama. To be frank about the matter, they objected to Catholicism, and, so far as biblical drama is concerned, it was not dependent for its future on the medieval mystery plays. Indeed, before the downfall of the mystery plays, biblical drama had entered on a career of incredible extent. This great movement occurred in France and in German-speaking

---

[1] Historical MSS. Commission, vol. xiv, pt. 8, p. 25.

lands. It was manifest also in England, although to a much slighter degree. That needs to be described and will be better understood after a brief consideration of what happened on the continent.

One of the most popular dramas in the whole of dramatic history was *Abraham sacrifiant* (1550) written by Théodore de Bèze (1519–1608), French Protestant theologian and, after Calvin, leader of the Reformation in France.[1] In plot it follows the lines of the medieval play, which followed the Scripture, but avowedly attempts to enrich 'nostre langue' with the dramatic art of Greece and Rome. It went through numerous editions in French, and there were many publications of the play in Latin, Italian, German, and Spanish. Arthur Golding translated it into English in 1575. It is to be thought of as the model for many of the numerous dramas, mainly on Old Testament subjects, that flooded the continent for the next fifty years after its composition. The story of Isaac and Rebecca was also widely used as a dramatic subject, as also the stories of Isaac and Ishmael and of Jacob and Esau. Other popular subjects were Adam and Eve, Cain and Abel, the Deluge, and the Building of the Tower of Babel. Perhaps the most popular subject of all was the history of Joseph. *La Vendition de Joseph* was one of the most popular of French *mystères*. Sixt Birck, after his famous *Susanna* (1532), wrote his 'comedy' of *Joseph* (1535), which went through fifteen editions in Latin alone. It is thought by Creizenach[2] to have preceded the equally popular Latin play on the same subject by Cornelius Crocus. Other Joseph plays were writen by Diebolt Gart (1540), Peter Jordann (1540), and Macropedius (1540).[3] There were also Joseph plays in Latin by Andrew Diethero (1544), Martin Balticus (1556), and Aegidius Hunnius, and these are by no means all. The French *Vendition* had a long and vigorous life, and there were twentyfive or more French plays on Joseph, as many in Italian, and many in Spanish, Dutch, German, and other languages. The story is not half told. Samson, Saul, Susanna, and Esther were important dramatic subjects. David with the various events in his career appears in many dramas in many languages. Xystus Betuleius, or Sixt Birck, wrote his *Sapientia Solomonis* in 1547 to be followed with a wide dissemination of Solomon

[1] Creizenach, op. cit. ii. 456–8.   [2] Op. cit. iii. 321–2 *et passim.*
[3] Ibid. ii. 111–16.

as a dramatic subject. A play of Job exists in Bibliothèque nationale MS. fr. 1774 and is dated 1478 and another manuscript of a play on the same subject is dated in 1490. The play was popular as a *mystère* and appears in *Le Mistère du Viel Testament*. Later the subject became still more popular in France, and many dramas on Job were printed in French, Latin, and Spanish. In this and in many other cases there is an unquestionable continuity between the mystery plays and the new Latin dramas. All the authors did was to change the form by dividing into acts and scenes and by introducing choruses and rhetori⁄ cal speeches. The model was most commonly Terence, then Plautus, and later Seneca. The play of Tobaeus was popular throughout the later sixteenth century in all European languages. Naogeorgus wrote his Latin play of *Hamanus* in 1543, and that subject became well known. Of plays on Judith there are eight versions in Latin, twenty in French, twenty⁄six in Italian, twenty⁄three in German, and numer⁄ ous versions in Spanish and other languages. An equally wide range can be claimed for the play of Esther, which appeared in Latin, French, Italian, Spanish, Dutch, German, Greek, Swedish, Polish, Czech, and Hebrew, and even in English.

It may be remarked that the model of these biblical dramas was usually Terentian and that the word 'comedy' is very loosely used, apparently referring to borrowed Terentian technique. It was applied to dramatic plots that did not turn out badly. Many of the dramatists wrote on secular as well as religious subjects, and an idea of the situation may be gained from the contents of two early collections, both known in England, where the mystery plays were still undis⁄ turbed and flourishing. The first of these is *Comoediae et Tragoediae aliquot et Novo et Vetere Testamento desumptae*, published at Basel by Nicholas Brylinger in 1540. It contains *Acolastus* by Gulielmus Gnaphaeus, *Joseph* by Cornelius Crocus, *Samaritanus Evangelicus* by Petrus Papeus, *Ovis Perdita* by Jacobus Zovitius, *Susanna* by Sixt Birck, *Pammachius* by Thomas Naogeorgus, *Christus Xilonicus* by Bartholomaeus Lochiensis, *Hecastus* by Macropedius, and two *fabulae lepidissimae*. The other collection is *Dramata Sacra, Comoediae atque Tragoediae aliquot e Vetere Testamento desumptae*, published by Joachim Oporinus at Basel also in 1540. It contains *Susanna* and *Joseph* as above, *Ruth* by Jacobus Zovitius, *Eva*, *Judith*, and *Sapientia*

Solomonis by Sixt Birck, *Hamanus* by Naogeorgus, *Pedonothis sive Heli*, *Immolatio Isaaci*, *Protoplastus* (the Creation), and *Nomothesia* (in which God succours Moses in the wilderness) by Hieronymus Ziegler, another *Joseph* by Andreas Diethero, *Jobus* by Johannes Lorichius, *Beel* by Martin Ostermincher, and *Zorobabel* (book of Esdras) by Johannes Entomius. In these lists there is no Prodigal Son play, although such plays were very numerous and form an important element in the sixteenth-century biblical drama in England. Neverthe-less both of these collections were known in England and, although no great amount of influence on English drama has been traced, nearly all of it is connected with subjects, if not plays, in these collections.

Still another much later collection shows the greatest influence of all. That is *Terentius Christianus* by the Haarlem schoolmaster Cornelius Schonaeus (1540–1611). A collected edition of *Terentius Christianus* appeared in Cologne in 1592, but many of the plays are much older.[1] The plays are *Tobaeus* (1568), *Saulus Conversus* (1570), *Nehemias* (1570), *Naaman* (1572), *Josephus, Juditha, Susanna, Daniel, Triumphus Christi, Typhus, Pentecoste, Ananias, Baptistes, Dyscoli, Cunae, Vitulus, Pseudostratiotes*. Three plays from *Terentius Christianus—Tobaeus, Juditha*, and *Pseudostratiotes*—were published, apparently for use in schools, in London in 1595 and 1620, in Cambridge in 1635, and in London in 1652 and 1674.

The plays enumerated, even the earliest, are a not readily separable part of the history of Terence, Plautus, and Seneca in the rise of Renaissance drama in Italy, France, and Germany, and with this vast subject we are not immediately concerned. It is interesting, for example, that Conrad Celtes, author of *Ludus Dianae*, discovered and edited (1501) the Terentian plays of Hrotsvitha, tenth-century Bene-dictine nun of Gandersheim in Saxony, and that her plays were influential, and it is significant that the neo-Latin plays of the Renaissance were scholastic and not popular in their origin and patronage and are therefore widely different from the medieval religious drama. And yet there is a close community of subjects between the sixteenth-century Latin drama and the mystery plays. But it is obvious that in them we have to do with the Renaissance and

---

[1] For bibliographical detail see 'Terentius Christianus and the Stonyhurst Pageants', *Philological Quarterly*, ii (1923), 56–62, by the present author.

not with the Middle Ages. The continuity in France is clear, since separate plays on freely selected biblical subjects had come into existence without the aid or interference of Latin comedy. In Germany that is not the case, for there is a gap between the older mystery plays and the new Latin drama of the sixteenth century. Satire and controversy enter freely, and, although subjects were drawn from medieval plays, the Latin drama itself differs from them in form, spirit, and appeal. There is nevertheless a continuation of the mystery plays that is worth tracing.

We may neglect Wimpheling's *Stylpho* (1470), Reuchlin's *Sergius* (1498), and the brilliant satirical dramas of Nicodemus Frischlin and set aside for later remark the fact that Chilianus Eques wrote a 'comedy' on the ancient theme of St. Dorothea (1506). We omit also the inevitable fact that early in the sixteenth century Aretino's Latin play *Poliscene* (1509) and other Latin plays by Italians were translated into German and concern ourselves briefly with what is sometimes called 'Christian Terence'. Three eminent Hollanders, all schoolmasters, George Macropedius, William Gnaphaeus (or Fullonius), and Cornelius Crocus, were the pioneers. Herford[1] thinks that their motive was to save the Latinity and intimacy of Terence and at the same time protect their pupils from his vulgarity and worldliness. Gnaphaeus wrote the all-important play of *Acolastus* (1534), a sort of school book of Terentian Latin in the form of a very good play, that made itself widely felt on the Continent and, perhaps particularly, in England, where it was translated by John Palsgrave in 1540.[2] Cornelius Crocus produced one of the many plays of *Joseph* (1535), a superior play in an intelligent classical tradition, rivalling in that respect the plays of George Buchanan. Macropedius, much the greatest dramatist of the three, left behind him a brilliant comedy called *Asotus* (1537), not by any means the first, but one of the most popular and influential, of the Prodigal Son plays. Sixt Birck was a German-speaking Swiss humanist of bold romantic and political interests. That so few traces are to be found in England of his *Susanna* (1532), his *Beel* (1535), his *Children of Eve* (1539), his *Ezechias* (1536),

---

[1] Op. cit., pp. 84–85.

[2] See the edition of *Acolastus: The Comedy of Acolastus*. Translated from the Latin of Fullonius by John Palsgrave, ed. P. L. Carver, E.E.T.S., Original series, No. 202 (London, 1937).

Joseph, Sapientia Solomonis,[1] and his *Zorobabel* is as surprising as it is disappointing. The influence of Naogeorgus (Thomas Kirchmayer) was, however, clearly felt, not apparently so much in his *Esther, Haman, Jeremias,* and *Judas Iscariot,* or his striking allegorical drama *Mercator,* as in his Antichrist play *Pammachius* (1538). That play was performed at Cambridge in 1545 and, on John Bale's own testimony, translated and adapted by him in his play *Kynge Johan.* Herford[2] speaks of a gradual shift in this Latin drama to secular subjects and tragic treatments, a thing that would seem to be reflected in Great Britain.

As a matter of general interest and as the last descendant of the medieval religious drama, it might be noted that the extensive Jesuit school drama of the seventeenth and eighteenth centuries is apparently an immediate descendant of the religious and moral portion of the drama we have just reviewed and that it preserved for a century and a half the familiar forms and subjects of the sixteenth-century Latin plays. This Jesuit drama had perhaps little influence in England, although the subject has been but little studied, but it does, in a sort of atavistic relation, become the principal heir of the mystery plays. The fact of the connexion is apparent on the face of it and becomes obvious by a comparison of the two collections, that of Brylinger and Oporinus, described above, with the extensive collections of Jesuit plays and the still more extensive collections of dramatic programmes that have been preserved from the schools and colleges of the Society of Jesus.[3] At least three of the authors of plays in the earlier collections were Jesuits.

The Jesuit school drama was carefully regulated. The plays had to be in Latin, not given too frequently, and on moral or sacred subjects. The choruses or interacts (in Latin) must observe decorum. No female person or feminine dress might be introduced, a rule that was,

---

[1] Played before Queen Elizabeth, 1555/6; see Creizenach, op. cit. ii. 86 n.

[2] Op. cit., pp. 95–96.

[3] P. Bahlmann, *Die Jesuiten Dramen der niederrheinischen Ordensprovinz.* Beihefte zum Central-blatt für Bibliothekswesen, Bd. vi, Hefte 15–18, pp. 1–352 (Leipzig, 1896–7), where there is a large bibliography of printed dramas, collections of programmes, &c.; also the same author's *Das Drama der Jesuiten,* Euphorion, ii (1895), 271–941, and his *Die lateinischen Dramen von Wimphelings Stylpho* cited above; H. Holstein, *Die Reformation im Spiegelbilde der dramatischen Litteratur des sechzehnten Jahrhunderts* (Halle, 1886); see also Creizenach, *passim.* The biblio-graphy is extensive. See 'Jesuit Drama' in *The Oxford Companion to the Theatre* (Oxford, 1951).

however, relaxed at the beginning of the seventeenth century.[1] As time went on the Jesuit plays grew more operatic and pretentious, but always maintained a carefully dignified tone and pattern. The subjects are biblical, legendary, classical, allegorical, and now and then at rare intervals controversial. The subjects tend to be repeated, and the form and style are, in general, not immediately Terentian. In most respects the Jesuit school drama may be regarded as the truest pro-jection of the mystery plays into the modern world.

The English field presents little unity of pattern. John Bale (1495–1563), converted Carmelite friar and ardent anti-Catholic contro-versialist, has left a list of his own plays in his *Illustrium Majoris Britanniae Scriptorum Catalogus* (1548). Before fleeing into Germany in 1540 after the fall of his patron Thomas Cromwell, Bale had for several years at least been writing religious dramas, most of them on the traditional subjects of the mystery plays. He enumerates twenty-two plays (with one repetition). Four of them in addition to his contro-versial drama on King John have been preserved. Bale's plays, even the lost ones, were in English, since he describes them as *in idiomate materno comedias sub vario metrorum genere.* They are as follows:[2]

1. Lib. 14. Vitam D. Ioannis Baptistae.
2. Com. 1. de Christo duodenni.
3. Com. 2. de baptismo & tentatione.
4. Com. 1. de Lazaro resuscitato.
5. Com. 1. de consilio pontificum.
6. Com. 1. de Simone leproso.
7. Com. 1. de coena Domini & pedum lotione.
8. Com. 2. de passione Christi.
9. Com. 2. de sepultura & resurrectione.
10. Lib. 2. super utroque regis coniugio.
11. Lib. 2. de sectis Papisticis.
12. Lib. 2. erga Momos et Zoilos.
13. Lib. 2. Proditiones Papistarum.
14. Lib. 1. contra adulterantes Dei verbum.
15. Lib. 2. de Ioanne Anglorum rege.
16. Lib. 1. de imposturis Thomae Becketi.
17. Lib. 1. de magnis Dei promissionibus.

[1] G. M. Prachtler, *Ratio Studiorum et Institutiones scholasticae Societatis Jesu* (Berlin, 1887).
[2] Chambers, op. cit. ii. 446–7; *The Dramatic Writings of John Bale*, ed. J. S. Farmer (Oxford, 1939); J. W. Harris, *John Bale* (Urbana, 1940).

18. Lib. 1. de predicatione Ioannis.
19. Lib. 1. de Christi tentatione.
20. Lib. 1. Corruptiones legum divinarum.
21. Lib. 1. Amoris imaginem.
22. Lib. 4. Pammachii tragoedias transtuli.

Bale's titles reveal two purposes. One is the Protestantizing of the mystery plays. Not only do Nos. 2 to 9, some of which were in two parts, cover the ground of a Passion play, but No. 17, called in English *God's Promises*, is a sort of prophet play. The other purpose, which is anti-Catholic controversy, is revealed in the titles of Nos. 11, 13, 14, 16, 20, and others. Of four plays, in addition to *Kynge Johan*, all are said on their title-pages to have been compiled in 1538, and that is probably true of the first three: *God's Promises* (London? 1577), *John Baptist* (n.d., possibly printed abroad), *Temptation* (the same), *Three Laws* (the same and London, 1562). Chambers[1] calls attention to the fact that the *Three Laws* contains allusions to King Edward VI and to the Lord Protector and must therefore at least have been revised after 1547. It is practically a morality in form, is far advanced in anti-papistical controversy, and seems to show the influence of the contemporary Latin drama of Germany, particularly perhaps of *Pammachius*. Bale had begun with the simple mystery-play technique, which may be described as merely telling a story on the stage by means of impersonation and dialogue, and it may be, since he was in exile in Germany for some years after 1542, that in the *Three Laws* he shows the effect of contact with the Continental Latin drama. There can be no question about *Kynge Johan*. That play was preserved in a Chatsworth manuscript (now in the Huntington Library) and was first published by J. P. Collier for the Camden Society in 1838.[2] It is customary to mention Sir David Lyndsay's *Satire of the Three Estates* in connexion with Bale's play, because Lyndsay's vast and varied morality is also political on an international scale, but there appears to be no relation between them. In point of fact Bale's *Kynge Johan* is

---

[1] Loc. cit., p. 449.

[2] *Kynge Johan* is included in Manly, *Specimens*, loc. cit. vol. i. A facsimile of the manuscript appeared in Bangs *Materiellen*, vol. xxiv (1909). The play was also issued in the publications of the Malone Society in 1931. See C. E. Cason, 'Additional lines to Bale's *Kynge Johan*', *Journal of English and Germanic Philology*, xxvii (1928). See also edition of *Three Laws* by A. Schröer, *Anglia*, v (1882).

an ingenious adaptation of the *Pammachius* of Naogeorgus, and therefore an Antichrist play, and therefore a lineal descendant of a mystery
play.[1] The Pope is frankly and shockingly identified with Antichrist
and is the leader of the earthly powers of sin and evil, and the play
accepts fully the always preposterous tradition that King John of
England was a Protestant hero, indeed, any kind of hero. King John
is there, as are his enemies—Pandulphus, Stephen Langton, and
Raymond of Toulouse, who are in turn obvious personifications of
Sedition, Worldly Wealth (in clerical hands), and Dissimulation.
Kynge Johan is not so far removed from the play of Antichrist that the
theme is not easily recognizable and, with *Pammachius* as an intermediary, the relation becomes obvious. Bale's play is divided into
two parts and is, in so far as it follows *Pammachius*, in the technique
of the Latin drama of the Continent.

Aside from the work of Bale there are a number of survivals of
mystery plays in transition. The most striking of these and one of the
most puzzling is the *Stonyhurst Pageants*.[2] The manuscript, which is in
the Library of Stonyhurst College in North Lancashire, was mentioned by Joseph Stevenson in 1872[3] and was edited in 1920 by
Carleton Brown, who gives full details of the cycle and the manuscript. The latter, which contains a very large fragment of a cycle
of Old Testament plays, is incomplete at beginning and end.
It lacks, as indicated by the numbering of the folios, fifty-five leaves
at the beginning, and one does not know how many at the end. Five
leaves that possibly contained a play of Ruth are missing after folio
153. In the margins at various places are scribbled names, some of
which may be those of former owners. They are identified as being
common in Lancashire. The handwriting, which is Italian, lapses
in a few places into secretarial forms. The text, although it has many
corrections in the hand of the scribe, is far from perfect. The language is
almost certainly that of Lancashire, and the metre, already archaic by
about 1585, is an unwieldy septenar line rhymed in couplets, the
rhymes being often mere assonances and in some cases missing.

---

[1] See the account of the relation between *Pammachius* and *Kynge Johan* by Herford, op. cit.,
135–8.
[2] Edited by Carleton Brown, *Hesperia*, Ergänzungsreihe 7 (Göttingen, 1920).
[3] Historical MSS. Commission, vol. iii, Appendix, p. 338a.

Everything seems to point to an amateur poet, and Brown, to whom we owe these particulars, concludes on very good grounds that the manuscript is not the work of a copyist, but is an author's original. The numbers of the pageants run up to eighteen, and the manuscript as it now stands begins with 106 lines forming the end of the sixth pageant of Jacob. Brown conjectures that the lost pageants at the beginning of the cycle dealt with the Creation, the Temptation and Fall of Man, Cain and Abel, Noah, and Abraham, and this would be true if the author, as seems probable, was engaged in composing a full cycle of Old Testament plays. Brown went farther and made a most interesting discovery, namely, that the author followed closely the Douay version of the Old Testament, whose publication in 1609 fixes the earliest date for the composition of the plays. The author not only used unmistakably the text of the Douay Old Testament but made frequent use of the copious annotations that appear in that text. On other grounds, mainly linguistic, Brown fixes on 1625 as the later limit of the dating. He suggests that the author was a priest and a student of the English College founded (1568) by Bishop (afterwards Cardinal) William Allen at Douay. However it may be, it is clear that the author had a serious religious purpose and refrained from both humour and religious controversy. In carrying on the action of the plays he makes extensive use of a figure called Chorus or Nun-tius, who, however, is not an importation from classical drama, but is merely the Doctor or Expositor of the medieval pageants, and it may be that, if Brown's conjectures as to the Lancashire origin of the plays are correct, the author knew something about the Corpus Christi play. The well-known statement of Weever in *Funeral Monuments*[1] that he had seen Corpus Christi plays acted in Lancashire as late as the beginning of the reign of James I is worth remembering in this connexion. Brown divides the cycle into three parts and suggests that pageants I–VII, all based on the book of Genesis, made up one part; pageants VIII–XII (Moses, Joshua, Gideon, Jephtha, and Samson), a second part; and pageants XII–XVIII (Ruth, Saul, David, Solomon, Elijah, and Naaman), a third part.

The editor observed that the pageant of Naaman differed from the others very greatly, being closely modelled after the style of Terence,

[1] See Chambers, op. cit. ii. 373.

and was indeed right as witnessed by the discovery by the present writer that the pageant of Naaman of the *Stonyhurst Pageants* is immediately translated from the play of Naaman in the *Terentius Christianus* of Cornelius Schonaeus.[1] None of the other pageants comes from Schonaeus, but the fact remains that what may be called the English traditional subjects from the Old Testament are abandoned after the play of Moses, and we get into the field of the Continental Latin drama of the Renaissance. The dependence on the Douay Old Testament is perceptible throughout, but seems a little relaxed in what Brown described as the third group of pageants. The Douay Old Testament is present even in the Naaman, but it is just possible that the author of the *Stonyhurst Pageants* followed unidentified Continental sources in other pageants besides the Naaman.

Another Tudor play with a biblical title is *John the Evangelist* of uncertain date and in spite of its name pretty obviously a morality.[2] Not so *Godly Queen Hester*, printed in 1561 and manifestly of Continental provenance,[3] which needs to be closely compared with various Continental versions of plays on this widespread and puzzling theme.[4] *King Darius*, which is described in the first printed edition (1565) as 'A pretie new Enterlude both pithie and pleasant—taken out of the third and forth Chapters of the third booke of Esdras', is also worth attention from the point of view of Continental Latin drama.[5] *Jacob and Esau* (1568), the best of these plays, is on an ancient theme of the mystery plays and was of continued popularity on the Continent in the sixteenth century.[6] These, with Arthur Golding's translation (1575) of Beza's *Abraham sacrifiant*, constitute the small and relatively insignificant remains of English drama on biblical subjects until we come to the occasional Old Testament plays in Elizabethan drama. But before we take these up it is desirable to call attention to two neoLatin dramatists of considerable importance.

---

[1] 'Terentius Christianus and the Stonyhurst Pageants', loc. cit., pp. 56–62, as above.

[2] C. F. Tucker Brooke, *The Tudor Drama* (Boston, 1911), pp. 104–6, 142; edition in Malone Society Reprints (1907); H. Bradley, 'Textual Notes on the "Enterlude of Johan the Evangelist"', *Modern Language Review*, ii (1907), 350–2; W. H. Williams, 'Irisdision in the Interlude of Johan the Euangelyst', *Modern Language Review*, iii (1908), 369–71.

[3] See Brooke, op. cit., pp. 131–2, 144. See edition by W. W. Greg, Bangs *Materiellen*, vol. v (1904).

[4] See Creizenach, op. cit. ii. 118–20 *et passim*.   [5] Ibid. ii. 452; iii. 557–8.

[6] Brooke, op. cit., pp. 133, 144; Creizenach, op. cit. iii. 557 ff., 571, *et passim*.

In two Latin plays by the Scottish humanist George Buchanan (1506–82), *Jephthes, sive Votum, Tragoedia* (Paris, 1554) and *Baptistes, sive Calumnia, Tragoedia* (Frankfurt, 1579), Great Britain, if not England, reached a high level in the new dramatic art and even exercised influence on the Latin drama of the Continent.[1] The former of these plays was written at Bordeaux (1540–3) while Buchanan was in exile after his escape from prison in St. Andrews, when he had incurred the wrath of Cardinal Beaton for satirizing the Franciscans. He was a teacher at Bordeaux and afterwards at Coimbra (until he was imprisoned by the Inquisition), so that he must have known something of the Latin drama, already an established institution on the continent. In *Jephthes* he deserted Terence in favour of Seneca, and his tragedy became very popular. There is no reason why it should not have been known to Sackville and Norton, the authors of *Gorboduc* (1561), or to Thomas Hughes and others, who wrote *The Misfortunes of Arthur* (1588). The *Baptistes*, written after Buchanan's return to Scotland, is the more mature performance of the two tragedies and is noted for its elegance in style, its dignity, and its sense of tragedy. It was long before Buchanan's plays were translated into English, and it is probable that their influence on English tragedy, such as it was, came mainly by way of the Continent.

The case of Nicholas Grimald (1519?–62?) is somewhat different from that of Buchanan, although he too has been regarded, on the basis of two Latin plays preserved, as a dramatist of superior merit. This idea has been strengthened by the fact that Grimald's English lyric poetry has been thought not unworthy of its inclusion with the poems of Wyatt and Surrey in *Tottel's Miscellany* (1557). Grimald migrated from Christ's College, Cambridge, to Oxford, where he became a don at Merton (1540) and later at Christ Church (1547). At some time before 1553 he became secretary to Bishop Ridley and was presumably occupied with clerical matters until his imprisonment in 1555, when he made peace with the new government by recantation. He wrote his Latin dramas presumably while

---

[1] Herford, op. cit., pp. 98–99 *et passim*; Creizenach, op. cit., ii. 426–32 *et passim*. See 'George Buchanan': *Glasgow Quater-centenary Studies* (Glasgow, 1907); *George Buchanan: A Memorial, 1506–1906* (St. Andrews, 1907); R. Lebègue, *George Buchanan: son influence en France et en Portugal* (Coimbra, 1931) and *La Tragédie religieuse en France: les débuts* (Paris, 1929).

he was at Oxford. Bale in his *Scriptores*[1] lists among Grimald's dramas *Archipropheta, Christus Nascens, Christus Redivivus, Athanasius seu Infamia,* and of these *Christus Redivivus* (Cologne, 1543) and *Archipropheta* (Cologne, 1548), the latter also in British Museum Royal MS. 12A. 46, survive. Certain questions arise in connexion with the dramatic work of Grimald. It is clear from two circumstances that he was a translator into Latin and something of a borrower. H. H. Hudson pointed out several passages in Grimald's works that were taken from Beza,[2] and G. C. Taylor showed that the episode of the Setting of the Watch and some other parts of *Christus Redivivus* were translated into Grimald's Latin from the Hegge Resurrection play.[3] It now appears from the unpublished researches of Mrs. Patricia Abel of the University of Missouri that the main body of *Christus Redivivus* was translated into Latin from the play of the Burial and Resurrection in Bodleian MS. e Museo, 160, f. 40.[4] The Bodley manuscript may have been available to Grimald in Oxford, but there is no answer to the puzzling question as to how Grimald got access to the Hegge manuscript. There is an obvious difference in dramatic technique, often noticed, between *Christus Redivivus*, which is in simple mystery-play form, and *Archipropheta*, which shows advanced classical technique and dramaturgy. Herford suggested that there is a resemblance between *Archipropheta* and *Johannes Decollatus vel Ectrachelistes* (1546) of Jakob Schoepper,[5] and P. Bahlmann regards Grimald's play as derived immediately from Schoepper's. In the light of the advanced technique of *Archipropheta* as compared to *Christus Redivivus* and of what is known about Grimald's habits of borrowing, one would be disposed to agree with Herford and Bahlmann. Grimald was of course a very good Latin scholar and would hardly translate too closely. Those who admire his Latinity are no doubt justified.[6]

---

[1] Chambers, op. cit. ii. 450–1; *Scriptores* (1557), i. 701.

[2] 'Grimald's Translations from Beza', *Modern Language Notes*, xxxix (1924), 388–94.

[3] 'The *Christus Redivivus* of Nicholas Grimald and the Hegge Resurrection Plays', *PMLA*, xli (1926), 840–59.

[4] The *Burial and Resurrection* is included in *The Digby Plays*, edited by F. J. Furnivall, E.E.T.S. (London, 1896).

[5] Herford, op. cit., pp. 114–19; Creizenach, op. cit. ii. 128–31; see also P. Bahlmann, *Die lateinischen Dramen* (Münster, 1893), p. 93.

[6] In any case, see the important monograph of L. R. Merrill, *The Life and Poems of Grimald*, Yale Studies in English (New Haven, 1925).

Not many plays on biblical subjects have survived in Elizabethan drama, but the record of lost plays yields a considerable harvest. There are in existence *David and Bethsabe* (1594) by George Peele, *Herod and Antipater* (1622) by Gervase Markham and William Sampson, *Absalon* possibly by Thomas Watson,[1] *The Most Virtuous and Godly Susanna* (1578) by Thomas Garter, and perhaps a few others. Of plays in manuscript there is a Latin text of *Judithae Constantia* by Cornelius Schonaeus with an incomplete English translation in the National Library of Wales;[2] also in a Cambridge University manu-script there is a play of *Herodes* dated in 1571; and in British Museum Additional MSS. 20061 there is *Sapientia Solomonis: Drama comico-tragicum* (1565-6), which is described by Chambers[3] as an expanded version of Sixt Birck's *Sapientia Solomonis* (1555).

Among titles of lost plays[4] of the Tudor period one notes *Abraham and Lot, Absalom, Adam's Tragedie* (?), *Esther and Haman, Ezechias, Hester and Ahasuerus, Jephtha* (Dekker), *Joseph's Affliction, Joshua, Judas* (2), *Jude* (?), *Nineveh's Repentance, Pontius Pilate, Queen of Ethiopia* (?), *Samson* (3), *Susanna,* and *Tobias.* Among the plays of the English comedians on the continent there is mention of *Abraham and Lot, Destruction of Sodom and Gomorrha, The Prodigal Son, Dives and Lazarus,* and *Esther and Haman.* There was also a lost play of *The Destruction of Jerusalem* by Dr. Thomas Legge.[5] All in all, one may say that the Tudor stage had some consciousness of the contemporary revival of religious drama on the Continent and some memory of the mystery plays.

Plays on the lives and martyrdoms of the saints went on, no doubt pretty much in their old forms, in France and other Catholic coun-tries long after the Reformation, but were suppressed and almost totally lost in England, and the Latin drama of the Renaissance passed them over for biblical subjects from the Old Testament. The

---

[1] E. K. Chambers, *The Elizabethan Stage* (4 v. Oxford, 1923), iii. 506.

[2] Ibid. iv. 44, 373-9, 404-6. See also G. A. Jones, 'A Play of Judith', *Modern Language Notes,* xxxii (1917).

[3] Chambers, *Elizabethan Stage,* loc. cit. iv. 378. See T. H. Vail Motter, *The School Drama in England* (London, 1929), pp. 93 n. 2, 152, 278, *et passim.*

[4] See Chambers, *Elizabethan Stage,* loc. cit. iv. 409-24 (Index of Plays); F. E. Schelling, *Elizabethan Drama* (2 v. Boston, 1908), ii. 538-624 (List of Plays); W. W. Greg, *Bibliography of English Printed Drama to the Restoration.* Bibliographical Society (2 v. Oxford, 1939, 1951).

[5] See Chambers, *Elizabethan Stage,* loc. cit. iii. 408-9.

legend of St. Dorothea, one of the oldest and most popular of all miracle plays, seems to have been an exception. We have seen that it was the subject of a 'comedia' by Chilianus Eques, *Dorothea* (1507). Christen Hansen translated this into Danish in 1531,[1] and in Den-mark it seems to have had great influence. This same great story appears in *The Virgin Martyr* (1622) by Dekker and Massinger. St. Catarina and other saints appear rather sparsely in the Jesuit drama. Almost the sole Tudor survival of the saints' play is *The Life and Repentance of Mary Magdalen* (1566) by Lewis Wager, and it is a very poor specimen of the kind. It is badly corrupted with ill-managed abstractions from the morality plays, and has lost faith in the inter-cessory powers of the holy saints. It lacks reverence and has no simple romantic wonder at miracles in distant lands and long ago. On the other hand, it does not take advantage, as the mystery plays often did, of the human features of the story derived from the New Testament. C. F. Tucker Brooke[2] thinks that Wager was influenced by Bale, and, although he acquits Wager of the 'fiery anti-Roman polemic' of Bale, regards Wager, as compared with the author of the *Three Laws*, as extremely flat. Brooke regards the play as late and as written after the bitterest of the Protestant–Catholic controversy was over, and not as an old play revamped.[3]

MORALITY PLAYS

The history of the morality play in the Renaissance and after the Reformation is very different from that of the miracle play and, indeed, from that of the mystery. The moral play was the latest comer in the field and from the beginning was closely associated with religion. The days of its piety, its religious service in bringing sinners to repent-ance, were passing (perhaps they never completely passed) at the time of the Reformation; but the allegorical drama proved to be an excel-lent weapon for religious controversy and for social criticism. The morality was, for example, invaluable for the teaching of moral lessons of industry and thrift to schoolboys and had many other social uses. The morality play of the sixteenth century was, however, a decadent form and attracted few authors of ability. Idea and form

---

[1] See Herford, op. cit., pp. 298 n., 403–4. [2] Op. cit., pp. 112–13.
[3] See, however, the valuable edition of the play by F. I. Carpenter (Chicago, 1902).

were beautifully united and combined in the early typical morality, and it is perhaps impossible that a broadly generalized and very perfect literary form should remain in that state, for the broader the generalization and the more adequate the form, the fewer the available topics. The English moral play in its first form took mankind as its hero, and when that one plot had been treated adequately by dividing mankind into its inevitable partitions, for example, into infancy, youth, manhood, and old age, and by the introduction of other universal features, the genre could go forward only by further sub-divisions at the expense of universality, such as man engaged in trades and occupations or individual men affected by environment, fortune, or creed. With the field thus particularized, there was plenty to be done and a strong demand for ingenuity. The result was that the English morality play almost, but not quite, lost its original distinctive feature of representing generalized humanity on the stage.

It retained the practice of introducing allegorical figures of virtues and vices on the stage, and this became its bane. These colourless abstractions became a *sine qua non* of the moral play and intruded themselves into other kinds of plays where they had no business to be. They were introduced without artistic propriety because they were expected to appear, so that they became mere symptoms of degenerate repetition. The Tudor moral interlude invented, or rather dissemin-ated, the Vice and brought it about that the Devil and the Vice often became the main attractions. The interpolation of humour and realism did much to break the continuity of the old drama. Universal signi-ficance, since it belongs to all great drama and great literature, had to take refuge in the stories of individual men and women whose motives and actions were those of all mankind. It is worth inquiring whether some such thing happened in sixteenth-century English drama and whether, when it happened, it was completely unrelated to the moral play.

In its original form what has been called the 'full-scope' morality lasted well and must have been widely familiar to English people, so that it is doubtful whether the general allegory was ever forgotten. Something has been said about *The Pride of Life*, the Macro morals, and *Everyman* as the oldest and most primitive of morality plays, but there is still the quite general theme to be found in others such as Medwall's *Nature*,

Rastell's *Nature of the Four Elements*, the Wit and Science group,[1] *Mundus et Infans* (1520), *The Interlude of Youth* (early in the reign of Henry VIII),[2] *Hickscorner* (1512?), *Like Will to Like* (1568) by Ulpian Fulwel, and in the lost *Cradle of Security*, reported with memorable picturesqueness by R. Willis in his seventy-fifth year in *Mount Tabor*, or *Private Exercises of a Penitent Sinner* (1639),[3] who records 'a stage-play which I saw when I was a child':

In the city of Gloucester the manner is, as I think it is in other like corporations, that, when the players of enterludes come to towne, they first attend the Mayor to enforme him what noble-mans servants they are, and so to get license for their publike playing; and if the Mayor like the actors, or would shew respect to their lord and master, he appoints them to play their first play before himselfe and the Aldermen and Common Counsell of the city; and that is called the Mayors play, where every one that will comes in without money, the Mayor giving the players a reward as hee thinks fit to shew respect unto them. At such a play my father tooke me with him, and made mee stand between his leggs as he sate upon one of the benches, where wee saw and heard very well. The play was called the Cradle of Security, wherin was personated a king or some great prince, with his courtiers of several kinds, amongst which three ladies were in speciall grace with him; and they, keeping him in delights and pleasures, drew him from his graver counsellors, hearing of sermons and listning to good coun-sell and admonitions, that, in the end, they got him to lye downe in a cradle upon the stage, where these three ladies, joyning in a sweet song, rocked him asleepe that he snorted againe: and in the meane time closely conveyed under the cloaths wherewithall he was covered a vizard, like a swine's snout, upon his face, with three wire chaines fastned thereunto, the other end whereof being holden severally by those three ladies who fall to singing againe, and then discovered his face that the spectators might see how they had transformed him, going on with their singing. Whilst all this was act-ing, there came forth of another doore at the farthest end of the stage two old men, the one in blew with a serjeant-at-armes his mace on his shoulder, the other in red with a drawn sword in his hand and leaning with the other hand upon the others shoulders; and so they two went along in a soft pace round about by the skirt of the stage, till at last they came to the cradle, when all the court was in greatest jollity; and then the foremost old man with his mace stroke a fearfull blow upon the cradle, whereat all the courtiers, with the three ladies and the vizard, all vanished; and the desolate prince

---

[1] See Tucker Brooke, op. cit., pp. 76–78. *Wit and Science* (1541–8?) by John Redford; reprinted in Manly, *Specimens*, loc. cit., vol. i; ed. A. Brown for the Malone Society (1951). *The Marriage of Wit and Science* (n.d.), facsimile by J. S. Farmer (1909); Hazlitt's Dodsley, ii (1874). *The Marriage of Wit and Wisdom* by Francis Merbury, in manuscript; edited by J. O. Halliwell for the Shakespeare Society (1846); facsimile by J. S. Farmer (1909). On the whole group of plays see J. Seifert, *Wit and Science—Moralitäten* (Prague, 1892).

[2] Ed. R. B. McKerrow and W. W. Greg in Bangs *Materiellen*, vol. xii (1905).

[3] J. O. Halliwell-Phillipps, *Outlines of the Life of Shakespeare*, 9th ed. (2 v. London, 1890), i. 41–43.

starting up bare-faced, and finding himselfe thus sent for to judgement, made a lamentable complaint of his miserable case, and so was carried away by wicked spirits. This prince did personate in the morrall the Wicked of the World; the three ladies, Pride, Covetousnesse and Luxury; the two old men, the End of the World and the Last Judgment. This sight tooke such impression in me that, when I came towards mans estate, it was as fresh in my memory as if I had seen it newly acted.

It is proper enough for Halliwell-Phillipps to call the *Cradle of Security* 'homely and rude', but 'simple, sincere, and affecting' would suit better the play in its time and place. The account suggests the strong appeal that the morality play, as long as it was simple and earnest, must have had to ordinary people, an appeal of a different sort from buffoonery and controversy and different, we may also believe, from school learning in any advanced form. A disproportionate number of sophisticated moral interludes have been preserved from the sixteenth century, but this does not mean that the old and genuine morality play may not have lived on with some vigour in the provinces.

There is, as suggested, no great narrowing of range in John Rastell's *Nature of the Four Elements* (1519) and his *Gentleness and Nobility*.[1] The former is a work rather overwhelming in its learning, one of its theses being 'Of the situation of the four elements, that is to say, the earth, the water, the air, the fire, and of their qualities and properties, and of the generation and corruption of things made of the commixtion of them'; and the latter (possibly by Heywood), a rather pretty moral interlude in the form of dialogues. Neither play may be described as religious.

The Vice was becoming an established institution for the sake of diversion and as an end in itself. Low comicality was perhaps the most active agency in the degeneration of the morality play, so that the more serious and intellectual purposes of the moral interludes suffered;[2] and yet, as we all know, the Elizabethan drama itself could stand an inordinate amount of buffoonery. The Renaissance had

[1] On Rastell's work and that of his group, see A. W. Reed, *Early Tudor Drama* (London, 1926), pp. 1–28 *et passim. Gentleness and Nobility* has been published by the Malone Society (1950).

[2] L. W. Cushman, *The Devil and the Vice in the English Dramatic Literature before Shakespeare* (Halle, 1900); R. Withington, *Excursions in English Drama* (New York, 1937), and articles in learned journals; E. Eckhardt, *Die lustige Person im älteren englischen Drama* (Berlin, 1902).

brought with it a new interest in the here and now and that in turn had replaced contemplation of the hereafter and the glorious history of the religious past. There was some change from the spiritual to the ethical, perhaps, and still more from the religious to the secular, but one must not urge on the sixteenth century too fast nor judge the people of the age solely by their most advanced thinkers. Controversy, political and religious, also diverted the morality from its main channel. Controversy is the mainspring of Skelton's splendidly executed *Magnificence* (1529–32).[1] But *A Satire of the Three Estates* (1540) by Sir David Lyndsay, in spite of its great variety of interests, is still a full-scope moral play that still devotes itself to the 'commendation of vertew and the vituperation of vyce'.

The morality *All for Money* (1578) by T. Lupton points a direction in which there was a good deal of perversion of the moral play, namely, secularization and social satire. Lupton's play is long and elaborate.[2] It combines scriptural characters with figures from religious and moral allegory. Its theme is the evil power of wealth, and its hero, All for Money, is a corrupt magistrate worse and more shameless than Sir Giles Overreach himself. One would not say that *All for Money*, in spite of its inordinate length, its mechanical plot, and its ponderous language, is without a certain merit in the fact that it strikes at something real. It is, for example, much better than *New Custom* (1578). Two plays, both very good of their kind, confront each other from opposite sides of the religious issue, *Lusty Juventus* (*c.* 1547–53) by R. Wever and *The Interlude of Youth* (of unknown date and authorship). Both follow in the wake of *Mundus et Infans* and have to do with the dangerous temptations of youth, and both vitiate their teachings by indulgence in religious controversy. *Lusty Juventus* (quite properly in the case of the hero) devotes much space to proving the falsity of the doctrine of salvation by works. *The Interlude of Youth*, closely related to *Hickscorner* (before 1534), is a less controversial and more intellectual play than is *Lusty Juventus*. A good many interludes, some of them of considerable merit, are tendentious and warped by controversy. There is a good deal to be said for W. Wager's *The Longer Thou Livest*,

---

[1] See edition of Skelton's *Magnificence* for E.E.T.S. by R. L. Ramsay (1904).

[2] Tucker Brooke, op. cit., pp. 17–19; facsimile by J. S. Farmer (1910); text edited by Ernst Vogel, *Shakespeare-Jahrbuch*, xl (1904).

the More Fool Thou Art, a play of uncertain date, which is a serious, though badly executed, attempt to write a play that would solve the problem of youth in the abstract. The *Trial of Treasure* (1567) presents side by side and in contrast a good and a bad way of living human life, and *Impatient Poverty* (1560) is a serious, almost tragic, morality of the way of the transgressor. Brooke[1] points to *The Conflict of Conscience* (1581) and *The Contention between Liberality and Prodigality* as the last, dullest, and most inept of Tudor moral interludes.

In his latest treatment of the Tudor moral interlude the late Professor C. F. Tucker Brooke, whose knowledge of the subject was extensive, gives an outline of the field[2] that, although slightly different in point of view from the preceding pages, is well worth considering. The first of his groups is made up of plays on the theme of the World and the Child. *Mundus* appears briefly in Medwall's *Nature* and prominently in *Mundus et Infans*;[3] also in *Hickscorner*,[4] in the *Interlude of Youth* (1557), and in *Lusty Juventus* (c. 1565). These plays all deal with the problem of youth, and with them are to be associated the somewhat merciless trio *Nice Wanton* (1560), *The Disobedient Child* (c. 1570) by Thomas Ingelend, and *The Glass of Government* (1575) by George Gascoigne. Also certain moral interludes, according to Brooke, developed in the direction of farce and comedy—Ulpian Fulwel's *Like Will to Like* (1568), George Wapull's *The Tide Tarrieth No Man* (1576), Thomas Lupton's *All for Money* (1578), and William Wager's *The Longer Thou Livest, the More Fool Thou Art* (c. 1568). One interlude, *The Conflict of Conscience* (1581), by Nathaniel Woodes, and perhaps others moralize actual events.

There is no doubt that Brooke is right in the matter of the great mixture of forms that appears in the Tudor interlude. What he calls 'stiffening for the wilted allegory' comes from the use of stories from the Bible, from classical literature, and even from medieval fiction. This makes it hard to determine whether in certain cases we have to do with the allegorization of events or with the dramatization of allegory. Brooke illustrates this by mention of the following plays: *Godly Queen Hester* (1561), *King Darius* (1565), *The Life and Repentance of*

---

[1] Op. cit., pp. 120–3. *The Conflict of Conscience* appears in Malone Society Reprints (1952).
[2] *A Literary History of England*, ed. A. C. Baugh (New York, 1948), pp. 358–66.
[3] Anonymous. Printed by Wynkyn de Worde in 1522.
[4] See W. W. Greg, 'Notes on Some Early Plays', *Library*, xi (1930–1), 44.

Mary Magdalene (1566), by Lewis Wager, *Cambises* (*c.* 1569), by Thomas Preston, *Orestes* (1567), by John Pickering, *Appius and Virginia* (1575), by R.B., *Patient Grissell* (*c.* 1566), by John Phillip, and *The Most Virtuous and Godly Susanna* (1578), by Thomas Garter. Some of these we have been disposed to regard as belated mystery plays into which the morality-play technique has entered deeply but without changing their dramatic kind; others as manifestations of the con- temporary Latin drama of the Continent. Indeed, the allegorizing style was very general in the age, and Brooke's own list of examples of plays with this feature contains *Jack Juggler* (1562), Robert Wilson's *The Three Ladies of London* (1584), *The Three Lords and Three Ladies of London* (1590), and *Cobbler's Prophecy* (attributed to Wilson); also the anonymous *Sir Clyomen and Sir Clamides* (1599), *Common Conditions* (1576), and *A Knack to Know a Knave* (1599). It is possible, however, in some of these cases that the general nature of the play is moralistic and that it may be said to be a dramatized allegory rather than an ordinary play to which allegorical features have been added. The line is hard to draw, but some of these plays in the two lists given seem to have quite general significance if not typification of all mankind by a single character. That feature we have taken as characteristic of the English morality, and the idea was certainly not lost. If it did not find expres- sion in the moral interlude, it certainly did find it in the presenta- tion of individual men whose dramatic situations were all-inclusive and whose actions were typical of human behaviour.

Our interest in tracing the later history of the morality may be restricted to two questions: Was there a formal as well as an actual likeness between the ethical appeal of the morality and the more sentimental appeal of Elizabethan tragedy; and, Did the universally representative character, the fundamental feature of English moralities, live on into Tudor and Stuart drama?

The pattern of crime in Elizabethan drama was obviously the same as that in the morality play: temptation, sin, discovery, repentance, punishment, and hope of salvation.[1] The solution presupposes a hero, and heroes undergo hardship, are liable to human error, and suffer

[1] Madeleine Doran, *Endeavours of Art: A Study of Form in Elizabethan Drama* (Madison, 1954), pp. 99, 103, 143, 160–5, 296, 349–53, *et passim*; H. H. Adams, *English Domestic Tragedy* (New York, 1943), pp. 168–9 *et passim*; A. Harbage, *Shakespeare's Audience* (New York, 1941), ch. iii.

persecution and sometimes martyrdom, but the rescue is no longer by supernatural intervention. Miss Doran's illustrations from the Italian comedies *Guglielma, Uliva, Stella,* and *Rosana* make the situation clear. The heroines of these plays are subject to deceit, slander, and persecution, but in the end are rescued by the Blessed Virgin Mary not that they may achieve eternal salvation but that they may secure proper husbands. Miss Doran also finds continuity of morality interest and universality in domestic tragedy. Certainly the apparatus of temptation and of warning against it is often set up with formal morality technique. *The Rare Triumphs of Love and Fortune* (1589) draws on pagan mythology in a way that suggests the morality. *The Three Ladies of London* (1584) and *The Three Lords and Three Ladies of London* (1590), both believed to be the work of the actor Robert Wilson, have, in spite of their drift towards mere comedy of London life, a good deal of the morality in the depiction of general human motives and habits. The same is true of a much better play, *A Knack to Know a Knave* (1594). We often find a simple morality technique, often in connexion with the Prodigal Son theme and set in the midst of city vice, presented by means of clearly conceived and consistent allegorical figures who participate in the action. The moral issues that underlie Patient Griselda, Susanna, and Virginia continually recur. The use of allegory in drama, and of course in masque, was long continued, on the whole skillfully employed, and certainly entered freely into later serious drama. Jonson, for example, reverts with perfect certainty of touch to the old form and the allegorical technique in *The Staple of News* (1625), as do Beaumont and Fletcher in 'The Triumph of Time' in *Four Plays or Moral Representations in One*. There are, besides, contemporary examples of completely allegorical plays, such as *The Contention between Liberality and Prodigality* (1601) and *Lingua* (1602–7?). Representation of internal conflict in an internal way characterizes *Doctor Faustus, Old Fortunatus,* and *A Looking-Glass for London and England,* and is perhaps not absent from *Othello* and *Macbeth*. The pattern of the Prodigal Son may be said to permeate Elizabethan drama, as witnessed by Heywood's *The Wise Woman of Hogsden,* Middleton's *Michaelmas Term, Eastward Ho!* and Shakespeare's Henry IV plays.[1] It is therefore reasonably certain that

[1] J. D. Wilson, *The Fortunes of Falstaff* (Cambridge, 1945), pp. 15–23 *et passim*.

the didactic intention of the morality play passes without interruption into Elizabethan drama.

The opinion was expressed at some length in the preceding chapter that the characteristic and apparently unique early morality play in England was an allegory of mankind and of the career of mankind in earthly life. Man as man was inescapably a sinner, so that he always lapsed from innocence into wickedness. Even his casual sincere reformations could not, except through the mercy of God in the sacrifice of Christ, save him from death and damnation. It was also suggested that moral plays of this universal type made their earliest appearance in England and did not, so far as one can tell, appear on the continent until much later, if, indeed, they ever appeared there in their typical form. It may be argued in very general terms that this play, the hero of which is Mankind, Everyman, or *Humanum Genus*, an essentially serious play, suited the English temperament. It would perhaps be acknowledged that the Englishman of the first three quarters of the sixteenth century was a serious character, and various more or less valid reasons for this seriousness, or, as it was called, 'sadness', would be forthcoming. Certainly the literature of this period points to such a state of mind and morals. England took the issues raised by the Reformation very hard and was not by any means of one mind about them. It is easy to distort the truth by calling the sixteenth-century English Protestants 'Puritans' and to take it for granted ignorantly that sixteenth-century Protestants were like seventeenth-century Puritans, or, rather, like the caricature that is accepted as a portrait of the followers of Cromwell and the settlers of Massachusetts. The anachronistic identification of the sixteenth-century Protestants with seventeenth-century Puritans is as misleading as it is false. English Protestants, and Catholics too, of the sixteenth century were men of many minds and made up of all classes in the community. They had not been divided into camps by political and social discrimination and unified or regimented into parties by years of prescription and discipline by nonconformity, papistry, or the Establishment. The medieval idea of the Field Full of Folk, or the brotherhood of man, was not dead in the sixteenth century, which knew that king and beggar, rich and poor were equal in the sight of God. All men had souls to save, and rank and class had not yet destroyed

c c

the idea that Death is a universal leveller and that what a man sows, that shall he also reap. The sophistications of the age of reason had not yet divided into compartments thought about men in relation to society and religion. Therefore the sixteenth-century Protestant, whether within or without the Establishment, was likely to be a man of reasoned religious and moral views like Spenser, Sidney, Hooker, Bacon, and Fulke Greville. Moreover, the question raised by the Reformation was one of the profoundest importance; nothing less, indeed, than the achievement of salvation. There was no general agreement among Englishmen as to how far the Reformation should go and as to whether there was need of reform, or, if it were needed, what should be reformed. The matter was serious and no doubt deepened the mind of the age, just as the mind of the age had given the English Reformation its original tone. To have achieved, after incredibly bitter and long-protracted controversy with the free use of cruelty and injustice, a settlement at all is an historical wonder, a thing that could not have been done if the race had not been deeply in earnest about the very question raised by the moral play. All the greater Elizabethans, including Bacon and Shakespeare, were deeply interested in human destiny. If this is true, can it be that the morality, in spite of its aberrations, carried on a trend of thought for a century and finally did something to restore the vision of Everyman to the world in the poems of Spenser and the plays of Shakespeare? If so, the moral play has great importance in the history of thought as well as the history of drama.

Most moral plays of the later Tudor period dealt, even when they proceeded according to the pattern of the morality play, with some special human situation already recorded in story or chronicle. A few of them did, however, present the idea of man as a representative of mankind. The conspicuous case is that of Marlowe's *Doctor Faustus*, which is a perfectly generalized morality, and, considering the way it is marked, it is absurd to think that Marlowe did not know exactly what he was doing when he wrote it. Faustus rejects, under the deceitful persuasions of the Devil, but not without a proneness to sin on his own part, all the good he had done in the past and all the good he might have done in the future in favour of a sinful life. He rounds out a career of twenty-four years of worldliness, characterized more by futility than by evil, and, at the end, stands as one condemned before the judgement of God and in the clutches of Satan and his rabble. There is in *Doctor Faustus* no implemented idea of divine intercession, but the idea of salvation through intercession is as passionately and intensely present as it is in any moral play. He says in his last great speech:

> See, see where Christ's blood streams in the firmament!
> One drop would save my soul—half a drop! ah, my Christ! . . .
> Mountain and hills, come, come and fall on me,
> And hide me from the heavy wrath of God! . . .
> Ah, Pythagoras' metempsychosis! were that true,
> This soul should fly from me, and I be chang'd
> Unto some brutish beast! All beasts are happy,
> For, when they die,
> Their souls are soon dissolv'd in elements;
> But mine must live, still to be plagu'd in hell.
> Curs'd be the parents that engend'red me! . . .
> O soul, be chang'd into little water-drops,
> And fall into the ocean—ne'er be found!—
> My God, my God, look not so fierce on me!

Faustus is still the same man, still a thinker, still a voyager, but he is ruined and condemned; but note that he has been stripped of his delusions and that there shines upon him the light of truth; and by virtue of this illumination it may be said that the noblest moment of his life is the last one. This brings his story into line with the moral play and into the realm of the purest tragedy, and, if he had been dehumanized, this could not be said. I wish to inquire if the same thing could be said of Macbeth.

Dekker's *Old Fortunatus* (1600) is quite as remarkable for its morality technique as is *Doctor Faustus*. In Dekker's hands the fairy tale that is his subject is made into a morality by the dominance of Virtue and Vice, by the moral responsibility of Fortunatus incurred by the folly of his choice, and by his sudden summons by death. Fortune tells the beggar to choose among wisdom, strength, health, beauty, long life, and riches. He chooses wealth, and gains the hat of the Sultan of Turkey, at once a wishing-cap and a magic carpet. At the height of his power Fortune puts an end to his life, and he leaves his quarrelsome sons to follow a course of disaster in perpetuity.

Shakespeare's transcendent merit is that he generalizes his heroes, so that most of them present not their own experiences only but the experience of all mankind. One sees this most obviously in such figures as King Richard II, Hotspur, King Henry V, Brutus, Mark Antony, Timon, and Coriolanus. But perhaps the perfect typicality of his heroes appears only in Hamlet and Macbeth.

Macbeth was essentially a good man, well regarded by his king and his compatriots. He was a professional soldier of great ability and matchless courage. He was tempted by the thin delusions of the devil, who had nothing to offer but flattery and temptation bolstered up by a slight and valueless framework of fact. He had the roots of sin in his heart, as all men have. Macbeth, like Faustus, Fortunatus, and Everyman, reaps a harvest of thorns, a devil's harvest without value or satisfaction. He has the realization of failure and futility, so that life is 'a tale told by an idiot'. When the diabolical assurances of the impregnability of his castle and of his own invulnerability break down before him, he arrives at a definition of evil perfectly in accord with what the morality play had to teach:

> And be these juggling fiends no more believ'd
> That palter with us in a double sense,
> And keep the word of promise to the ear,
> And break it to our hope.

What, then, is the final state of Macbeth and what will he do? He is still Macbeth, for souls as such might not undergo corruption. His state, like that of Everyman, is on the lowest level of actuality, and Macbeth dies with his sword in his hand.

There is only the faintest possibility that there was any tangible influence of the moral interlude on Shakespeare when he wrote *Macbeth*. Certainly there are no obvious traces of the form as there are in the cases of Marlowe's *Doctor Faustus*, Dekker's *Old Fortunatus*, *A Merry Knack to Know a Knave*, and other Elizabethan plays. One would not deny that Shakespeare knew morality plays and was familiar with their technique, for morality plays were still being written throughout his lifetime; but there is little evidence that they affected his own dramatic work except that they still expressed the moral sincerity of the Elizabethans. The case of Ben Jonson is different. There may be little reaching backwards by Jonson to earlier forms but there can be no doubt of his formalism. He was obviously interested in types of humanity and recurrent moral situations in human life. One can, for example, define the characters in *Volpone* in allegorical and moralistic terms. Indeed, Jonson obliges us by giving them names suggestive of generalized states. There is certainly some kinship between Jonson's comedies and the Tudor moral interludes, and, since his influence was long protracted, some very general features of the morality play may have lived on indefinitely.

Shakespeare's studies of human character in relation to human fate are but casually related to the medieval formalism that appears in the morality play, and yet there is a connexion between them. Macbeth reminds us of Everyman. We praise the Elizabethans for cleverness, energy, enterprise, and the vague thing we call genius. And yet in Shakespeare's King Richard II, Hamlet, Macbeth, and Prospero we are concerned with an Elizabethan trait possibly greater than any of these—the moral earnestness of the Elizabethans. As with Ascham, Spenser, and Hooker, it is difficult to see how this trait could be overlooked or subordinated. The quality of moral earnestness had been dominant in the race since before the days of Sir Thomas More, and it has been suggested above that the moral play was nurtured by this quality, indeed that the piety and sincerity of the fifteenth-century English brought this kind of drama into being. We could at least find no evidence that the broadest and finest kind of moral play had been imported from abroad. It is not therefore a matter of the formal and often thin thing called literary influence that makes Macbeth remind one of Everyman, but a community of race and purpose that found expression in the drama of two different though still closely connected ages.

Bibliography

Abraham und Isaac. Ed. L. T. Smith, *Anglia*, vii (1884), 316–37, and *A Commonplace Book of the Fifteenth Century*, 1886; R. Brotanek, *Anglia*, xxi (1898–99), 21–55.

Acta Sanctorum quotquot toto orbe quae collegit I. Bolandus. Operam continuavit G. Henschenius. Paris, 1734–1804.

ADAMS, H. H. *English Domestic Tragedy.* New York, 1943.

ADAMS, J. Q. *Chief Pre-Shakespearean Dramas.* Boston, 1924.

ALBRECHT, O. E. *Four Latin Plays of St. Nicholas from the Twelfth-Century Fleury Playbook.* Philadelphia, 1935.

ALLEN, P. S. *The Romanesque Lyric.* Chapel Hill, 1928.

Analecta Hymnica Medii Aevi. Ed. G. M. Dreves and C. Blume. Leipzig, 1886–1909 sqq.

The Ancient Cornish Drama. Ed. E. Norris. 2 v. Oxford, 1859.

Anecdota Literaria. Ed. T. Wright. 1844.

Anglo-Norman Resurrection, ed. T. A. Jenkins, J. M. Manly and M. K. Pope. Oxford, 1943; J. G.Wright. Paris, 1931.

Annales Ratisponensis. Ed. W. Wattenbach. M.G.H. Hannover, 1861.

ANZ, H. *Die lateinischen Magierspiele.* Leipzig, 1905.

APOLLONIO, MARIO. *Storia del teatro italiano.* 3 v. Florence, 1943–6.

ARNOULD, E. J. *Le Manuel des Péchés: Études de Littérature religieuse anglo-normande.* Paris, 1940.

The Assumption of the Virgin, A Miracle Play from the N-Town Cycle. Ed. W. W. Greg. Oxford, 1915.

BAHLMANN, P. 'Das Drama der Jesuiten', *Euphorion*, ii (1895), 271–94.

—— *Die Jesuiten Dramen der niederrheinischen Ordensprovinz.* Leipzig, 1896–7.

—— *Die lateinischen Dramen von Wimphelings Stylpho bis zur Mitte des sechzehnten Jahrhunderts, 1480–1550.* Münster, 1893.

BALE, JOHN. *A Comedy concerning Three Laws.* Ed. A. Schröer. *Anglia*, v (1882), 137–264.

—— *The Dramatic Writings of John Bale.* Ed. J. S. Farmer. Oxford, 1907.

—— *Index Britanniae Scriptorum.* Ed. R. L. Poole and M. Bateson. Oxford, 1902.

—— *Kynge Johan.* Ed. Manly, *Specimens*, vol. i (1897); Bangs *Materiellen*, vol. xxiv (1909); Malone Society (1931).

BASKERVILL, C. R. 'Mummers' Wooing Plays in England', *Modern Philology*, xxi (1924), 225–72.

BATIFFOL, B. *L'Histoire du bréviaire romain.* Paris, 1893; tr. A. M. Y. Bayley. 1912.

BAUGH, A. C. 'The Chester Plays and French Influence', *Schelling Anniversary Studies* (New York, 1923), pp. 35–65.

—— and others. *A Literary History of England.* New York, 1948.

BÄUMER, S. *Geschichte des Breviers.* Freiburg, 1895.

BLAIR, L. 'A Note on the Relation of the Corpus Christi Procession to the Corpus Christi Play', *Modern Language Notes*, lv (1940), 83–95.

BODEL, JEAN. *Le Jeu de S. Nicolas*, ed. E. Jeanroy (Paris, 1925); F. J. Warne (Oxford, 1931).

BONNELL, J. K. 'The Source in Art of the so-called Prophets' Play in the Hegge Collection', *PMLA*, xxix (1914), 327–40.

BOURNE, HENRY. *The History of Newcastle upon Tyne; or, the Ancient and Present State of that Town.* Newcastle-upon-Tyne, 1736.

BRADLEY, HENRY. 'Textual Notes on the Enterlude of Johan the Evangelist', *Modern Language Review*, ii (1907), 350–2.

BRAND, JOHN. *History and Antiquities of Newcastle upon Tyne.* 1789.

BRANDSTETTER, R. 'Die Technik der Luzerner Heiligenspiele', *Archiv für das Studium der neueren Sprachen und Literaturen*, lxxv (1886), 384–418.

BRINKMANN, H. 'Zum Ursprung des liturgischen Spieles', *Xenia Bonnensia* (Bonn, 1929).

BROOKE, C. F. Tucker. *The Tudor Drama.* Boston, 1911.

BROOKS, N. C. 'The Lamentations of Mary in the Frankfurt Group of Passion Plays', *Journal of English and Germanic Philology*, iii (1900–1), 415–30.

—— *The Sepulchre of Christ in Art and Liturgy.* Urbana, 1921.

BROWN, ARTHUR. 'The Tradition of the Chester Plays', *London Mediaeval Studies*, vol. ii, pt. 1 (1951), 68–72.

BROWN, CARLETON. 'An Early Mention of a St. Nicholas Play in England', *Studies in Philology*, xxviii (1931), 594–601.

[BUCHANAN, GEORGE.] *George Buchanan: Glasgow Quater-centenary Studies.* Glasgow, 1907; *George Buchanan: A Memorial, 1506–1906.* St. Andrews, 1907.

CABROL, F. *The Books of the Latin Liturgy.* 1932.

—— 'Breviary', *Catholic Encyclopaedia*; with bibliography.

—— *Les Origines liturgiques.* Paris, 1906.

CADY, F. W. 'The Liturgical Basis of the Towneley Mysteries', *PMLA*, xxiv (1909), 419–69.

—— 'The Passion Group in Towneley', *Modern Philology*, x (1913), 587–600.

Cambridge History of English Literature. 14 v. Cambridge, 1907–16.

Camden Miscellany. Vol. iii. Ed. J. P. Collier. 1859.

'Canterbury Text', *The Times*, 28 December 1937.

CAREY, MILLICENT. *The Wakefield Group in the Towneley Cycle.* Hesperia, vol. xi. Göttingen, 1929.

CARGILL, OSCAR. 'The Authorship of the *Secunda Pastorum*', *PMLA*, xli (1926), 810–31.

Carmina Burana. Ed. J. A. Schmeller. Breslau, 1894.

CASON, C. E. 'Additional Lines to Bale's *Kynge Johan*', *Journal of English and Germanic Philology*, xxvii (1928), 42–50.

CHAMBERS, E. K. *The Elizabethan Stage.* 4 v. Oxford, 1923.

—— *English Literature at the Close of the Middle Ages.* Oxford, 1945.

—— *The Mediaeval Stage.* 2 v. Oxford, 1903.

The Chester Plays. Ed. Thomas Wright. 2 v. Shakespeare Society, 1843, 1847; pt. 1, ed. H. Deimling; pt. 2, ed. G. W. Matthews. E.E.T.S. 1893, 1916.

CHEVALIER, U. *Ordinaires de l'Église cathédrale de Laon.* Paris, 1897.

CLARK, E. G. 'The York Plays and the Gospel of Nicodemus', *PMLA*, xliii (1928), 153–61.

CLOETTA, W. *Beiträge zur Literaturgeschichte des Mittelalters und der Renaissance.* 3 v. Munich, 1911–31.

COFFMAN, G. R. 'The Miracle play in England', *PMLA*, xxxi (1916), 448–65; *Studies in Philology*, xvi (1919), 57–66.

—— *A New Theory of the Origin of the Miracle Play.* Menasha, Wisconsin, 1911.

COHEN, G. *Le Théâtre en France au Moyen Âge.* 2 v. Paris, 1928–31.

COLLIER, J. P. *A History of English Dramatic Poetry.* 3 v. 1831.

COOK, A. S. *A Literary Middle English Reader.* Boston, 1915.

The Coventry Leet Book. Ed. Mary Dormer Harris. 4 v. E.E.T.S. 1907–33.

CRAIG, HARDIN. 'The Corpus Christi Procession and the Corpus Christi Play', *Journal of English and Germanic Philology*, xiii (1913), 589–602.

—— 'The Lincoln Cordwainers' Pageant', *PMLA*, xxxii (1917), 605–15.

—— Letter on the Pater Noster Play, *The Nation* (New York), 3 May 1917, 563–4.

—— 'The Origin of the Old Testament Plays', *Modern Philology*, x (1912–13), 473–87.

—— 'Terentius Christianus and the Stonyhurst Pageants', *Philological Quarterly*, ii (1923), 56–62.

CRAIGIE, Sir W. A. 'The Gospel of Nicodemus and the York Mystery Plays', *Furnivall Miscellany* (Oxford, 1901), pp. 56–61.

The Creation of the World. Ed. Whitley Stokes. Philological Society, 1859.

CREIZENACH, W. *Geschichte des neueren Dramas.* Vols. i–iii. Halle, 1893–1903.

—— 'Miracle Plays and Moralities', *Cambridge History of English Literature*, vol. v, pp. 26–39.

CROFT, J. *Excerpta Antiqua; or, a Collection of Original Manuscripts.* York, 1797.

Cursor Mundi. Ed. R. Morris. 6 pts. E.E.T.S. 1874–92.

CUSHMAN, L. W. *The Devil and the Vice in the English Dramatic Literature before Shakespeare.* Halle, 1900.

D'ANCONA, A. *Origini del teatro italiano.* 2 v. Turin, 1891.

—— *Sacre Rappresentazioni dei secoli xiv, xv e xvi.* 3 v. Florence, 1872.

DAVIDSON, CHARLES. *Studies in the English Mystery Plays.* Yale dissertation, 1892.

DAVIES, R. *Extracts from the Municipal Records of the City of York during the Reigns of Edward IV, Edward V, and Richard III.* 1843.

The Digby Mysteries. Ed. F. J. Furnivall. New Shakespeare Society; reprinted E.E.T.S. 1882.

DODDS, M. H. 'The Northern Stage', *Archaeologia Aeliana*, N.S. xi (1914), 36–47.

DORAN, MADELEINE. *Endeavors of Art: A Study of Form in Elizabethan Drama*. Madison, 1954.

Das Dorotheaspiel. Ed. H. Schachner. *Zeitschrift für deutsche Philologie*, xxxv (1903), 157–96.

DUCHESNE, L. *Christian Worship, its Origin and Evolution*. Tr. M. L. McClure. 1927.

DUGDALE, WILLIAM. *Antiquities of Warwickshire*. 2nd ed. revised by William Thomas. 2 v. 1730.

DU MÉRIL, E. *Origines latines du Théâtre moderne*. Paris, 1840, 1897.

ECKHARDT, E. *Die lustige Person im älteren englischen Drama*. Berlin, 1902.

EHRISMANN, G. *Geschichte der deutschen Literatur bis zum Ausgang des Mittelalters*. 2 v. Munich, 1935.

English Gilds: Original Ordinances of More than a Hundred Gilds. Ed. Toulmin Smith. E.E.T.S. 1870.

FOSTER, FRANCES A. 'Was Gilbert Pilkington Author of the *Secunda Pastorum*?' *PMLA*, xliii (1928), 124–36.

FRAMPTON, M. G. 'The Date of the "Wakefield Master"', *PMLA*, l (1935), 631–60.

—— 'Gilbert Pilkington Once More', *PMLA*, xlvii (1932), 622–35.

FRANK, GRACE. *The Medieval French Drama*. Oxford, 1954.

—— 'Genesis and Staging of the *Jeu d'Adam*', *PMLA*, lix (1944), 7–17.

—— 'Introduction to a Study of the Mediaeval French Drama', *Essays and Studies in Honor of Carleton Brown* (New York, 1940), pp. 62–78.

—— 'On the Relation of the York and Towneley Plays', *PMLA*, xliv (1929), 313–19.

FRERE, W. H. *The Principles of Religious Ceremonial*. 1906.

FRETTON, W. G. *Memorials of the Fullers' Guild*. Transactions of Birmingham and Midland Institute. 1877.

FRONING, R. *Das Drama des Mittelalters*. 3 pts. Stuttgart, 1891.

FRY, TIMOTHY, O.S.B. 'The Unity of the *Ludus Coventriae*', *Studies in Mediaeval Culture dedicated to George Raleigh Coffman*, *Studies in Philology*, xlviii (1951), 527–70.

FULLONIUS. *The Comedy of Acolastus*. Tr. from the Latin of Fullonius by John Palsgrave. Ed. P. L. Carver. E.E.T.S. 1937.

GARDINER, H. C., S.J. *Mysteries' End: An Investigation of the Last Days of the Mediaeval Religious Stage*. New Haven, 1946.

GAUTIER, L. *Histoire de la poésie liturgique au Moyen Âge: les Tropes*. Paris, 1886.

GAYLEY, C. M. *Plays of our Forefathers*. New York, 1907.

Gentleness and Nobility. Malone Society, 1950.

GERING, HUGO. *Islandische Legenden*. Halle, 1882–4.

Gesta Alberti Livoniensis Episcopi. Ed. J. B. Gruber. Leipzig, 1740.

Gesta Romanorum. Ed. S. J. H. Hertage. E.E.T.S. 1879.

Godly Queen Hester. Ed. W. W. Greg. Bangs Materiellen, vol. v (1904).

GREG, W. W. *Bibliographical and Textual Problems of the English Miracle Plays.* 1914.
—— *Bibliography of English Printed Drama to the Restoration.* 2 v. Oxford, 1939, 1951.
—— 'Notes on Some Early Plays', *Library*, xi (1930–1), 44–56.
GUÉRANGER, P. L. P. *The Liturgical Year.* Tr. L. Shepherd. 8 v. 1869–83; 4th ed., 15 v. Worcester, Mass., 1895–1903.

HALL, JOSEPH. *York Plays* (review). *Englische Studien*, ix (1886), 448–53.
HALLIWELL-PHILLIPPS, J. O. *Outlines of the Life of Shakespeare.* Brighton, 1881, 1882; other editions to the seventh (2 v. 1887).
HARDY, W. J. *A Calendar of the Records of the Borough of Doncaster.* 4 v. Doncaster, 1899–1903.
HARRIS, J. W. *John Bale: A Study of the Minor Literature of the Reformation.* Urbana, 1940.
HARRIS, MARY D. *Life in an Old English Town.* 1898.
HARROP, H. 'Particulars concerning Early Norwich Pageants', *Norfolk Archaeology*, iii. 3 ff.
HARTMAN, HERBERT. 'The Home of the *Ludus Coventriae*', *Modern Language Notes*, xli (1926), 530–1.
HARTSHORNE, C. H. *Ancient Metrical Tales.* 1929.
HASSELL, W. O. 'Plays at Clerkenwell', *Modern Language Review*, xxxiii (1938), 564–7.
HEMINGWAY, S. B. *English Nativity Plays.* New York, 1909.
Hereford Cathedral. *Extracts from the Cathedral Registers.* Tr. E. L. Dow. Hereford, 1932.
HERFORD, C. H. *Studies in the Literary Relations of England and Germany in the Sixteenth Century.* Cambridge, 1881.
HERTTRICH, O. *Studien zu den York Plays.* Breslau, 1886.
HEUSER, W. 'Dux Moraud, Einzelrolle aus einem verlorenen Drama des 14. Jahrhunderts', *Anglia*, xxx (1907), 180–208.
—— 'Das Interludium de Clerico et Puella und das Fabliau von Dame Siriz', *Anglia*, xxx (1907), 306–19.
Hilarii Versus et Ludi. Ed. J. B. Fuller. New York, 1929.
Himmelgarten Fragments. Ed. E. Sievers, *Zeitschrift für deutsche Philologie*, xxi (1889), 385–404.
Historia Monasterii Sancti Petri Gloucestriae. Rolls Series. *Chronicles and Memorials of Great Britain and Ireland during the Middle Ages*, ii. 44.
Historians and the Church of York. Rolls Series. 1879–94.
Historical Manuscripts Commission, Reports of. 1833– . Feast of Corpus Christi at Canterbury: Eighth Report, vii. 321; ix. 1, 245; St. Anne's Guild: Fourteenth Report, Appendix VIII; Inventory of stage properties for *Tobias*: Fourteenth Report, Appendix VIII; J. Stevenson, mention of the Stonyhurst Pageants: Third Report, Appendix, p. 338a; *A Calendar of the Manuscripts of the Dean and*

Chapter of Wells; Report on the Manuscripts of the Corporation of Beverley: Sixteenth Report. 1900.

HOHLFELD, A. R. 'Die englischen Kollektiv-Mysterien', *Anglia*, xi (1889), 219–310.

HOLSTEIN, H. *Die Reformation im Spiegelbilde der dramatischen Literatur des sechszehnten Jahrhunderts.* Halle, 1886.

HONE, W. *Ancient Mysteries Described.* 1823.

HUDSON, H. H. 'Grimald's Translations from Beza', *Modern Language Notes*, xxxix (1924), 388–94.

The Interlude of John the Evangelist. Ed. Malone Society, 1907; facsimile by J. S. Farmer, 1907.

The Interlude of Youth. Ed. R. B. McKerrow and W. W. Greg, Bangs *Materiellen*, vol. xii, 1905; Hazlitt's Dodsley, vol. vi; by J. S. Farmer, 1912.

JACOBSEN, J. P. *Essai sur les origines de la comédie en France au Moyen Âge.* Paris, 1910.

JEANROY, A. *Le Théâtre religieux en France du XIᵉ au XIIIᵉ siècles.* Paris, 1923.

JELLINGHAUS, H. 'Das Spiel vom Jüngsten Gericht', *Zeitschrift für deutsche Philologie*, xxiii (1891), 426–36.

JENNEY, ADELINA M. 'A Further Word as to the Origin of the Old Testament Plays', *Modern Philology*, xii (1915–16), 59–64.

JONES, G. A. 'A Play of Judith', *Modern Language Notes*, xxxii (1917), 1–6.

Le Jour du Jugement. Ed. É. Roy. Paris, 1902.

JUBINAL, A. *Mystères inédits du quinzième siècle.* 2 t. Paris, 1837.

KELLER, A. *Fastnachtspiele aus dem fünfzehnten Jahrhundert.* 3 v. Stuttgart, 1853.

KELLY, W. *Notices Illustrative of the Drama, and other Popular Amusements . . . of Leicester.* 1865.

KEMPE, MARGERY. *The Book of Margery Kempe.* Ed. Sanford Brown Meech and H. E. Allen. E.E.T.S. 1940

KER, W. P. *Mediaeval English Literature.* Oxford, 1912.

KRAMER, M. *Die Sprache und Heimat des sogenannten Ludus Coventriae.* Halle, 1892.

KRETZMANN, PAUL E. *Liturgical Elements in the Earliest Forms of the Mediaeval Drama.* Minneapolis, 1916.

Künzelsauer Frohnleichnamsspiel. Ed. H. Werner, *Germania*, iv. 38 ff.

KURTZ, L. P. *The Dance of Death.* New York, 1934.

LANGE, C. *Die lateinischen Osterfeiern.* Munich, 1887.

LEACH, A. F. 'Some English Plays and Players, 1220–1548', *Furnivall Miscellany* (Oxford, 1901), pp. 205–34.

LEBÈGUE, R. *George Buchanan: son influence en France et en Portugal.* Coimbra, 1931.

—— *Mystère des Actes des Apôtres.* Paris, 1929.

—— *La Tragédie religieuse en France: les débuts, 1514–1573.* Paris, 1929.

LEGGE, M. DOMINICA. *Anglo-Norman in the Cloisters.* Edinburgh, 1950.

Letters of the Kings of England. Ed. J. O. Halliwell. 2 v. 1846.

Lincoln Cathedral. *Statutes of Lincoln Cathedral.* Ed. C. Wordsworth. Cambridge, 1892.

LOOMIS, R. S. 'Lincoln as a Dramatic Centre', in *Mélanges d'histoire du Moyen Âge et de la Renaissance.* Paris, 1950.

Ludus Coventriae. A Collection of Mysteries, formerly represented at Coventry on the Feast of Corpus Christi. Ed. James Orchard Halliwell. Shakespeare Society, 1941; *Ludus Coventriae, or the Plaie called Corpus Christi.* Ed. K. H. Block. E.E.T.S. 1922.

LUKE, CORNELIUS. *The Rôle of the Virgin Mary in the Coventry, York, Chester, and Towneley Cycles.* Washington, D.C., 1933.

LUPTON, T. *All for Money.* Ed. J. O. Halliwell, 1851; E. Vogel, *Shakespeare Jahrbuch,* xl, 1904; facsimile by J. S. Farmer, 1910.

LYLE, MARIE C. *The Original Identity of the York and Towneley Cycles.* Minneapolis, 1919.

—— 'The Original Identity of the York and Towneley Cycles—A Rejoinder', *PMLA,* xliv (1929), 319-28.

LYNDSAY, SIR DAVID. *A Satire of the Three Estates.* Ed. T. Small and others. E.E.T.S. 1865-71; *The Works of Sir David Lindsay of the Mount.* Scottish Text Society, 1931-6.

MACKENZIE, W. R. *The English Moralities from the point of view of Allegory.* Boston, 1904.

MCKNIGHT, G. H. *Middle English Humorous Tales in Verse.* Boston, 1913.

The Macro Plays. Ed. F. J. Furnivall and Alfred W. Pollard. E.E.T.S. 1904.

MAETZNER, E. A. F. *Altenglische Sprachproben.* 2 v. Berlin, 1867-1900.

MANLY, J. M. '*Elckerlijk–Everyman:* The Question of Priority', *Modern Philology,* viii (1910-11), 269-77.

—— 'Literary Forms and the New Theory of the Origin of Species', *Modern Philology,* iv (1906-7), 577-95.

—— *Specimens of the Pre-Shaksperean Drama.* 2 v. Boston, 1897.

—— 'The Miracle Play in England', *Transactions of the Royal Society of Literature,* ser. 3, vol. vii (1927), 133-53.

MANNYNG, ROBERT, of Brunne. *Handlynge Synne.* Ed. F. J. Furnivall. 2 pts. E.E.T.S. 1901, 1903.

MARKLAND, J. H. *A Dissertation on the Chester Mysteries.* Roxburghe Club, 1818; *Shakespeare,* ed. Boswell–Malone (1821), ii. 525-49.

The Marriage of Wit and Science. Facsimile edition by J. S. Farmer. 1909; Hazlitt's Dodsley, ii, 1874.

MARRIOTT, W. A. *A Collection of Miracle Plays or Mysteries.* Basle, 1836.

MARSHALL, MARY H. 'Dramatic Tradition Established by the Liturgical Play', *PMLA,* lvi (1941), 962-91.

—— 'Theatre in the Middle Ages: Evidence from Dictionaries and Glosses', *Symposium,* iv (1950), 1-39, 366-89.

MASTERS, ROBERT. *History of Corpus Christi College.* Cambridge, 1753.

MATTHEW PARIS. *Gesta Abbatum S. Albani.* Ed. H. T. Riley. Rolls Series, i.

MAXWELL, A. *Old Dundee.* Dundee, 1891.

MEDWALL, HENRY. *Fulgens and Lucres.* Ed. F. S. Boas and A. W. Reed. Oxford, 1926.

MEPHAM, W. A. 'Village Plays at Dunmow and Heybridge in Essex', *Notes and Queries*, 19–20 May 1934, and 11 August 1934.

MERBURY, FRANCIS. *The Marriage of Wit and Wisdom.* Ed. J. O. Halliwell. Shakespeare Society, 1846; facsimile by J. S. Farmer, 1909.

MERRILL, L. R. *The Life and Poems of Nicholas Grimald.* New Haven, 1925.

MEYER, W. *Fragmenta Burana.* Berlin, 1901.

The Middle-English Harrowing of Hell and the Gospel of Nicodemus. Ed. W. H. Hulme. E.E.T.S. 1907.

MIGNE, J. P. *Patrologia Latina.* 221 v. Paris, 1844–64. *Liber Responsalis*, lxxviii. 725 *et seq.*; *Libellus de Antichristo*, ci. 1291 *et seq.*; *Liber de Antichristo*, xl. 1132; Gerhohus, *Comm. in Ps.* cxciv. 890; Comestor's *Historia Scholastica*, clviii. 39–44; Apostles' Creed, xxxix. 1034; Rufinus, xxi. 337; Letter to Optatus, xxxiii. 859.

MILCHSACK, G. *Die Oster- und Passionsspiele. i. Die lateinischen Osterfeiern.* Wolfenbüttel, 1880.

MILL, ANNA J. *Mediaeval Plays in Scotland.* Edinburgh, 1927.

—— 'The York Bakers' Play of the Last Supper', *Modern Language Review*, xxx (1935), 145–58.

—— 'York Plays of the Dying, Assumption, and Coronation of Our Lady', *PMLA*, lxv (1950), 866–76.

MILLER, E. S. 'The Antiphons in Bale's Cycle of Christ', *Studies in Mediaeval Culture dedicated to George Raleigh Coffman, Studies in Philology*, xlviii (1951), 629–38.

MILLER, FRANCES H. 'Metrical Affinities of the Shrewsbury *Officium Pastorum* and its York Correspondent', *Modern Language Notes*, xxxiii (1918), 91–95.

—— 'The Northern Passion and the Mysteries', *Modern Language Notes*, xxxiv (1919), 88–92.

Le Miracle de Théophile. Ed. Grace Frank. Paris, 1925.

Le Miracle de Théophile. Traduction nouvelle avec notes par A. Jeanroy. Paris, 1932.

Miracles de Nostre Dame par personnages, publiées par Gaston Paris et Ulysse Robert. Société des Anciens Textes. Paris, 1876–93.

Le Mistère du Viel Testament. Ed. J. Rothschild and E. Picot. Société des Anciens Textes. 6 t. Paris, 1878–91.

Mittelniederländisches Osterspiel. Ed. J. Zacher, *Zeitschrift für deutsches Altertum*, ii. 302–50.

MONE, F. J. *Altteutsche Schauspiele.* Leipzig, 1841.

—— *Schauspiele des Mittelalters.* 2 v. Karlsruhe, 1846.

MORF, H. 'Das liturgische Drama von den fünf klugen und den fünf thörichten Jungfrauen', *Zeitschrift für romanische Philologie*, xxii (1898), 385–91.

MORRIS, R. H. *Chester in Plantagenet and Tudor Reigns.* Chester, 1893.

MOTTER, T. H. VAIL. *The School Drama in England.* 1929.

Mystère de l'Incarnation et Nativité. Ed. Pierre Le Verdier. 3 t. Rouen, 1885–6.

Le Mystère de la Passion en France du xivᵉ au xviᵉ siècle. Ed. É. Roy. Dijon, 1903–4.

Mystères et Moralités du manuscrit 617 de Chantilly. Ed. Gustave Cohen. Paris, 1920.

Mystères Provençaux. Ed. A. Jeanroy et H. Teulie. Toulouse, 1893.

La Nativité et le Geu des Trois Roys, ed. Ruth Whittredge. Bryn Mawr dissertation, 1944.

NICOLL, ALLARDYCE. *Masks, Mimes and Miracles.* 1931.

Noah's Ship, or the Newcastle Play. Ed. F. Holthausen. *Göteborgs Högskolas Årsskrift,* iii (1897); ed. R. Brotanek, *Anglia,* xxi (1898–9), 165–200.

Non-Cycle Mystery Plays. Ed. Osborn Waterhouse. E.E.T.S. 1909.

Northern Legendary. Ed. W. M. Metcalfe. Scottish Text Society. 3 v. Edinburgh, 1896.

The Northern Passion. Ed. Frances A. Foster. 2 v. E.E.T.S. 1913, 1916.

OAKDEN, J. K. *Alliterative Poetry in Middle English.* 2 v. Manchester, 1930.

Oberhessisches Spiel von den zehn Jungfrauen. Ed. Max Rieger, *Germania,* x (1865), 311–37.

Ordo Representationis Adae. Ed. K. Gras (Halle, 1928); P. Studer (Manchester, 1928); trans. E. N. Stone (Seattle, 1926).

OWST, G. R. *Literature and Pulpit in Mediaeval England.* Cambridge, 1933.

PARKER, R. E. 'The Reputation of Herod in Early English Literature', *Speculum,* viii (1933), 59–67.

La Passion d'Autun. Ed. Grace Frank. Paris, 1934.

La Passion du Palatinus. Ed. Grace Frank. Paris, 1922.

La Passion de Semur. Ed. É. Roy. Paris and Dijon, 1903, 1904.

Paston Letters. Ed. J. Gairdner. 2nd ed. 4 v. 1900.

PEACOCK, M. H. 'The Wakefield Mysteries', *Anglia,* xxiv (1901), 509–24; see also letters, *The Times Literary Supplement,* 5 March and 7 June 1928.

PEARSON, KARL. *The Chances of Death and Other Studies in Evolution.* 2 v. Cambridge, 1897.

Petit de Julleville, L. *Les Mystères.* 2 v. Paris, 1880.

—— *Répertoire du Théâtre comique.* Paris, 1886.

PICOT, E. 'Fragments inédits de Mystères de la Passion', *Romania,* xix (1890), 260–82.

PIERSON, M. 'The Relation of the Corpus Christi Procession to the Corpus Christi Plays', *Transactions of the Wisconsin Academy of Sciences, Arts, and Letters,* xviii, pt. 1 (1915), 110–65.

The Play of Antichrist from the Chester Cycle. Ed. W. W. Greg. Oxford, 1935.

The Play of the Sacrament. Ed. Whitley Stokes. *Transactions of the Philological Society* (1861). Appendix.

PRACHTLER, G. M. *Ratio Studiorum et Institutiones scholasticae Societatis Jesu.* Berlin, 1887.

The Presentation in the Temple, as originally represented by the Corporation of Weavers in Coventry. Abbotsford Club, 1836.

RAUHUT, F. 'Der Sponsus,' *Romanische Forschungen*, l (1936), 21–50.

REDFORD, JOHN. *Wit and Science.* Ed. Manly, *Specimens*, 1897; ed. A. Brown. Malone Society, 1951.

REED, A. W. *Early Tudor Drama.* 1926.

REESE, J. B. 'Alliterative Verse in the York Cycle', *Studies in Mediaeval Culture dedicated to George Raleigh Coffman, Studies in Philology*, xlviii (1951), 639–68.

Register of the Gild of Corpus Christi. Ed. R. H. Skaife. Surtees Society, 1872.

Regularis Concordia. Ed. W. Logeman, *Anglia*, xiii (1891), 265–348; xv (1893), 20.

REICH, H. *Der Mimus.* Berlin, 1903.

Reliquiae Antiquae. Ed. T. Wright and J. O. Halliwell. 2 v. 1841–3.

The Resurrection of Our Lord. Malone Society, 1912.

Reuschel, K. *Die deutschen Weltgerichtspiele des Mittelalters und der Reformationszeit.* Leipzig, 1906.

ROBBINS, R. H. 'An English Mystery Play Fragment ante 1300', *Modern Language Notes*, lxv (1950), 30–35.

ROBERTSON, J. C. *Materials for the History of Becket.* 7 v. Rolls Series. 1875–85.

ROSSITER, A. P. *English Drama from Early Times to the Elizabethans.* 1950.

ROY, É. *Études sur le théâtre français du xive et xve siècle.* Paris, 1901.

SAINTSBURY, GEORGE. *A History of English Prosody.* 3 v. 1923.

SALTER, F. M. 'The Banns of the Chester Plays', *Review of English Studies*, xv (1939), 432–57; xvi (1940), 1–17, 137–48.

—— 'Old Testament Plays of *Ludus Coventriae*', *Philological Quarterly*, xii (1933), 406–9.

SCHELLING, F. E. *The Elizabethan Drama.* 2 v. Boston, 1908.

SCHIPPER, J. M. *Altenglische Metrik.* Bonn, 1881.

SCHMIDT, K. W. C. *Die Darstellung von Christi Höllenfahrt in den deutschen und den ihnen verwandten Spielen des Mittelalters.* Marburg, 1915.

—— *Die Digby Spiele.* Berlin, 1884; see also *Anglia*, viii (1885), 371–404.

SCOTT-ROBERTSON, W. A. 'The Passion Play and Interludes at New Romney', *Archaeologia Cantiana*, xiii. 216 ff.

SEELMAN, W. *Die Tötentanze des Mittelalters.* Verein für niederdeutsche Sprachforschung, *Jahrbuch*, Nr. 17 (1892).

SEIFERT, J. *Die Wit- und Science-Moralitäten des 16. Jahrhunderts.* Prague, 1892.

SEPET, M. 'Les Prophètes du Christ', *Bibliothèque de l'École des Chartes*, xxviii (1867), 1–27, 211–64; xxix (1868), 105–39, 261–93; xxxviii (1877), 397–443; also published separately, Paris, 1878.

SHARP, THOMAS. *Dissertation on the Pageants or Dramatic Mysteries, Anciently Performed at Coventry, by the Trading Companies of that City.* Coventry, 1825.

SHULL, V. 'Clerical Drama in Lincoln Cathedral, 1318–1561', *PMLA*, lii (1937), 946–66.

SKELTON, JOHN. *Magnificence.* Ed. R. L. Ramsay. E.E.T.S. 1904.

SMART, W. K. 'The Castle of Perseverance: Place, Date, and Source', *Manly Anniversary Studies* (Chicago, 1923), pp. 42–53.

—— '*Mankind* and the Mumming Plays', *Modern Language Notes*, xxxii (1917), 21–25.

—— *Some English and Latin Sources and Parallels for the Morality of Wisdom.* Menasha, Wis., 1912.

—— 'Some Notes on *Mankind*', *Modern Philology*, xiv (1916–17), 45–58, 293–313.

SPENCER, M. LYLE. *Corpus Christi Pageants in England.* New York, 1911.

STALEY, V. *The Liturgical Year.* 1907.

A Stanzaic Life of Christ, compiled from Higden's Polychronicon and the Legenda Aurea. Ed. Frances A. Foster. E.E.T.S. 1926.

STEVENS, J. Appendix to Dugdale's *Monasticon* (1722), vol. i.

The Stonyhurst Pageants. Ed. Carleton Brown. Göttingen, 1920.

STOW, JOHN. *A Survey of London.* Ed. C. L. Kingsford. 2 v. 1908.

STRUTT, JOSEPH. *Manners and Customs.* Edition of 1776, vol. iii.

The Summoning of Everyman. Ed. Hazlitt's Dodsley; by H. Logeman. Ghent, 1892; by A. W. Pollard. 1903; by J. S. Farmer. 1905–6; Bangs *Materiellen*, vol. iv, 1909.

SWENSON, ESTHER L. *An Inquiry into the Composition and Structure of Ludus Coventriae.* Minneapolis, 1914.

SYMMES, H. S. *Les Débuts de la critique dramatique en Angleterre.* Paris, 1903.

TAYLOR, G. C. 'The *Christus Redivivus* of Nicholas Grimald and the Hegge Resurrection Plays', *PMLA*, xli (1926), 840–59.

TEN BRINK, B. *History of English Literature.* English trans. 3 v. 1883–96.

THOMAS, A. 'Notice sur un recueil de mystères provençaux du quinzième siècle', *Annales du Midi*, ii (1890), 385–418.

THOMAS AQUINAS, St. *Summa Theologica.* Tr. by Fathers of the English Dominican Province. London and New York, 1912–25.

TIGG, E. R. 'Is *Elckerlijk* prior to *Everyman*?', *Journal of English and Germanic Philology*, xxxviii (1939), 568–76.

The Towneley Plays. Surtees Society. 1936; ed. G. England and A. W. Pollard. E.E.T.S. 1897.

TRAVER, HOPE. *The Four Daughters of God.* Bryn Mawr Monographs, No. 6. Philadelphia, 1907.

The Trial and Flagellation (ed. F. M. Salter) *with other Studies in the Chester Cycle* (by W. W. Greg). Malone Society, 1935.

Les Trois Maries. Ed. P. Meyer, *Romanische Forschungen*, xxxiii (1904), 239–45.

Two Coventry Corpus Christi Plays. Ed. Hardin Craig. E.E.T.S. 1902.

UNGEMACHT, H. *Die Quellen der fünf ersten Chester Plays.* Münchener Beiträge, 1. Munich, 1890.

VAN DER GRAAF, W. 'Miracles and Mysteries of S.E. Yorkshire', *Englische Studien,* xxvi (1906), 228–30.

WACKERNELL, J. E. *Altdeutsche Passionsspiele aus Tyrol.* Graz, 1897.

WAGER, LEWIS. *The Life and Repentance of Mary Magdalene.* Ed. F. I. Carpenter. Chicago, 1902.

WANN, LOUIS. 'A New Examination of the Manuscript of the Towneley Plays', *PMLA,* xliii (1928), 137–52.

WARD, A. W. *A History of English Dramatic Literature to the Death of Queen Anne.* 2 v., 1875; 3 v. 1899.

WARTON, THOMAS. *History of English Poetry, from the Twelfth to the Close of the Sixteenth Century.* Ed. W. C. Hazlitt. 4 v. 1871.

WELFORD, R. *History of Newcastle and Gateshead in the Sixteenth Century.* 2 v. 1885.

WELLS, J. E. *A Manual of the Writings in Middle English, 1050–1400.* New Haven, 1916; with nine supplements.

WILSON, J. D. *The Fortunes of Falstaff.* Cambridge, 1945.

The Winchester Troper. Ed. W. H. Frere. 1894.

WITHINGTON, R. *Excursions in English Drama.* New York, 1937.

WOODES, NATHANIEL. *The Conflict of Conscience.* Ed. Hazlitt's Dodsley, vol. vi; Malone Society, 1952.

WORDSWORTH, C. *Notes on Mediaeval Services in England, with an Index of Lincoln Ceremonies.* 1898.

—— and H. LITTLEHALES. *The Old Service Books of the English Church.* London, n.d.

WRIGHT, E. A. *The Dissemination of the Liturgical Drama in France.* Bryn Mawr dissertation, 1936.

WRIGHT, J. G. *Study of the Themes of the Resurrection in the Mediaeval French Drama.* Bryn Mawr dissertation, 1935.

WYCLIF, JOHN. *De Officio Pastorali.* In *English Works.* E.E.T.S. 1880.

The York Plays. The Plays performed by the Crafts or Mysteries of York on the Day of Corpus Christi in the 14th, 15th, and 16th Centuries. Ed. Lucy Toulmin Smith. Oxford, 1885.

Yorkshire Archaeological Society, *Publications,* Record Series, lxxiv (1925).

YOUNG, KARL. 'Concerning the Origin of the Miracle Play', *Manly Anniversary Studies* (Chicago, 1923), pp. 254–68.

—— *The Drama of the Medieval Church.* 2 v. Oxford, 1933.

—— 'Observations on the Origin of the Passion Play', *PMLA,* xxv (1910), 309–54.

—— *Ordo Rachelis.* Madison, 1919.

—— 'The Records of the York Play of the Pater Noster', *Speculum,* vii (1932), 540–6.

ZUPITZA, JULIUS. *Alt- und Mittelenglisches Übungsbuch.* Leipzig, 1915.

—— Discussion in Sitzungen der Berliner Gesellschaft, *Archiv für das Studium der neueren Sprachen und Literaturen,* lxxxii (1899), 204–7.

INDEX

Abel, Patricia, 375.

Aberdeen, Christmas and Easter groups separate at, 73; Passion play at, 142; Nativity play at, 143; St. George in procession at, 331.

Abraham and Isaac, play of, 65, 68, 69, 111, 138, 236, 291; Dublin play and Brome play of, 152; Chester, 185–6, 197, 306–7; Towneley, 206; York–Wakefield, 217, 221; *Gospel of Nicodemus*, 224, 237; Hegge, 247; Norwich, 300; Newcastle-upon-Tyne, 304; Brome Hall and Dublin MSS., 305–10; *Le Mistère du Viel Testament*, 307; *Le Sacrifice de Abraham à huit personnages*, 307, 309; nature of play, 308–9.

Abraham and Lot, play of, 69, 174, 185, 306, 376; lost play of, 376.

Abraham and Melchisedek, play of, 173, 185, 306.

Absalom, play of, *Absolon*, attrib. Thomas Watson, 376.

Acta Sanctorum, 94.

Acts of the Apostles, Book of, 30, 40.

Acts of the Apostles, play of, 108; *Les Actes des Apôtres*, French miracle cycle, 337.

Adam, play of the Death of, 69.

Adams, J. Q., translation of Orleans Resurrection, 37–38; staging of *Mary Magdalene*, 118–19.

Adeodatus, play of St. Nicholas, 84, 86 87.

Adso of Toul, *Libellus de Antichristo*, 75–76.

Advent, 21, 29, 62, 74–76, 90.

Ælfric, sermons, 67.

Agony and Betrayal, play of the, 42, 155; York–Wakefield, 216; York play in alliterative verse, 225, 226, 231; Hegge, 248.

Allen, William, cardinal, 372.

Alsfeld, Passion play from, 71, 106–7.

Amos, Book of, 207.

Analecta Hymnica, Ascension trope, 41.

Angers, Passion play from, 110.

Annanias, play of, 313; 16th-cent. Latin drama, 366.

Annunciation, play of the, 21, 30, 49, 61–62, 78, 80, 101, 105, 164, 186, 190, 236; York–Wakefield, 217, 222; *Gospel of Nicodemus*, 224, 237; in St. Anne's day play, 257; played in Lincoln cathedral, 268.

Antichristus, 29, 74–77, 90, 98, 101, 106, 116, 132, 138, 190; Chester, 167, 179–81, 193; York–Wakefield, 235.

Apparition of B.V. Mary to Thomas, play of, York play in alliterative verse, 225, 232–3.

Apocrypha (N.T.), used in revision, 155–8, 233; subordinate Apocrypha, 156–7; in St. Anne's day play, 257.

Apocrypha (O.T.), 157–8.

Archelaus, 57.

Aretino, Pietro, *Poliscene*, 367.

Arles, lectionary from, 58, 59.

Arneway, John, mayor of Chester, 168–9.

Arnold of Immessen, Passion play attrib. to, 107–8.

Arras, Passion play from, 109, 110, 175–6.

Arthur, Prince, 289.

Ascension, play of the, probably of liturgical origin, 37, 40–41 (trope of), 100–1, 106, 133, 138; in Chester cycle, 192, 196, 197; Towneley, 207; York–Wakefield, 222, 236; associated with Acts of the Apostles, 337.

Ashburnham, Lord, owner of York MS., 201.

Avignon, B.V. Mary plays at, 79.

Bahlmann, P., 375.

Balaam and Balak, play of, 60–61, 68, 174, 178, 181, 186, 190, 197 (Chester).

Bale, John, *Scriptores*, 369–70, 375; *Kynge Johan*, 368, 370–1; *God's Promises, John Baptist, Temptation, Three Laws*, 370; compared with Wager, 377.

Balticus, Martin, play of Joseph, 364.

Baptism, play of the, 236, 291; York–Wakefield, 216; Hegge, 243, 247, 262; Norwich, 300–1; Newcastle-upon-Tyne, 305; independent plays in Scotland, 333; 16th-cent. Latin drama, 366.

Barcelona, C.C. play at, 107.

Barking, convent at, *Visitatio*, 36.

Barlaam and Josaphat, legend, 347.

Barrenness of Anna, play of the, 79; Hegge, 249; in St. Anne's day play, 250–1.

Basingbourne, St. George play at, 331.

Bath, Resurrection play at, 143, 318.

REPRINTED LITHOGRAPHICALLY IN GREAT BRITAIN
AT THE UNIVERSITY PRESS, OXFORD
BY VIVIAN RIDLER
PRINTER TO THE UNIVERSITY